Margaret

Weight Watchers
INTERNATIONAL
COOKBOOK

Weight Watchers*
INTERNATIONAL
COOKBOOK

Introduction by
JEAN NIDETCH

NEW ENGLISH LIBRARY

Acknowledgements

The task of creating this book, selecting and testing the recipes, amassing and organising the information dealing with the foods of the various countries, and of preparing and supervising the colour photography was accomplished by many people who deserve special thanks. We gratefully express our appreciation to our dedicated staff, our publisher, and Nedda C. Anders and her staff for their tireless efforts in editing this cookbook.

Felice Lippert
Vice-President—
Food Research and Development
Weight Watchers International

For more information about this cookbook, its recipes and the Weight Watchers Classroom Programme contact:
Weight Watchers U.K.
635/637 Ajax Avenue
Slough
Berkshire

Copyright © 1977 by Weight Watchers International, Inc.
All rights reserved. Reprinted by arrangement with New English Library Ltd

Photoset in Great Britain by
Photobooks (Bristol) Limited
Printed and bound in Great Britain by
Hazell, Watson and Viney,
Aylesbury, Bucks.
ISBN: 0–450–04868–3

CONTENTS

*

INTRODUCTION

*

What a joy it is for me to introduce this book to you! In travelling around the world to Weight Watchers classes, I've often had the pleasure of tasting the food specialities of different countries, prepared for me by members and friends familiar with our Food Plan. And just as often, I've wished I could share those delicious dishes with our many other friends. Now my wish has come true.

Here is a gourmet taste-tour of the world's most scrumptious dishes, prepared our style. We've adapted the famous specialities of China, France, Italy, India, Mexico, Spain, and many other countries: 24 delicious cuisines! Enjoy savoury soups, piquant appetizers, exotic entrées, unusual vegetables and salads, an array of fabulous desserts, and a host of 'extras' you can snack on (in moderation!) without your waistline giving you away.

The dishes have come from a variety of sources. Nedda Anders and Felice Lippert have created and adapted many exciting recipes. Others were created or adapted by Weight Watchers chefs and home economists. Many other wonderful ideas came from our friends around the world. Whatever its source, almost every one of the the recipes has been tested in Weight Watchers kitchens. This means that *you* can duplicate each mouth-watering dish in *your* kitchen.

You should find our recipe directions easy to follow, even if you haven't spent much time cooking, or have never cooked in our special style. The inspiring colour photographs show that our foods look as delectable as they taste.

These splendid dishes from the world's great cuisines fit into our basic Food Plan. Therefore, the book may be used by Weight Watchers members. However, its value is not just for members, but for anyone who wishes to lose—or maintain—weight. In all cases, it is essential to realise that these exciting dishes are only part of an overall eating plan. They should be consumed with an awareness of the total amount of food appropriate for the day, and with a vigilant eye on portion control!

If you love good food . . . if you want to expand your culinary repertoire, without expanding your waistline . . . if you would like a collection of fabulous recipes done in our style . . . this is a book you should have.

And now, dear reader, I hope you will join us as we feast our way around the world.

Jean Nidetch

FOUNDER
WEIGHT WATCHERS INTERNATIONAL

GENERAL INFORMATION

*

1. In any recipe for more than one serving, it is important to mix the ingredients well and, when serving, *to divide the mixture evenly*, so that each portion is the same size.

2. For those following the Weight Watchers Food Programme, certain recipes will provide only part of a lunch or dinner. These recipes must be supplemented as required and have been marked with an asterisk.

3. Meat must be well trimmed, with all visible fat removed.

4. We use fruit fresh, frozen or canned with no sugar added. The canned fruit may be packed in its own juice or water or packed with artificial sweetener.

5. The herbs used in these recipes are dried unless otherwise indicated.

6. Nonstick pans make it possible for you to cook without fat. Use pans manufactured with a nonstick surface, or spray an ordinary pan with a nonstick cooking spray.

7. In any recipe calling for stock, you may use homemade chicken or homemade beef stock (see following recipes).

Homemade Chicken Stock

2 chicken carcasses
3 pints 10 fl oz (2 litres) water
1 oz (30 g) celery with leaves, sliced
1½ oz (45 g) carrot, sliced
6 peppercorns

3 parsley sprigs
1 garlic clove, crushed
1 bay leaf
¼ teaspoon thyme
Salt to taste

Combine all ingredients in a large saucepan. Bring to the boil; lower heat. Simmer for 1½ hours. Strain to remove solids. Chill in refrigerator. When fat congeals on surface, skim off and discard. Divide into 6 fl oz (180 ml) portions. Makes about 1 pint 10 fl oz (900 ml).

Homemade Beef Stock

3 lbs (1 kg 440 g) beef bones
2 oz (60 g) celery with leaves, cut up
4 oz (120 g) onion, quartered
3 oz (90 g) carrots, sliced
6 pints (3 litres 500 ml) water

6 oz (180 g) canned tomatoes,
  chopped
6 parsley stalks
10 peppercorns, crushed
2 cloves
1 bay leaf

Place bones on a rack in a roasting tin. Place celery, onion and carrots in another pan. Roast both bones and vegetables for 30 minutes or until browned, turning bones once. Place bones and vegetables in a large saucepan with remaining ingredients. Bring to the boil; lower heat. Simmer for 3 hours. Strain, discard solids. Chill in refrigerator. When fat congeals on surface, skim and discard. Divide into 6 fl oz (180 ml) portions. Makes about 3 pints (1 litre 750 ml).

In any recipe calling for Vegetable or Fish Stock, use the recipes below.

Vegetable Stock for Poaching Fish

Enough for about 2 lbs (960 g) of fish. If necessary, add more water to cover fish.

3 pints 10 fl oz (2 litres) water
4 oz (120 g) celery, diced
4 oz (120 g) carrots, sliced
¼ lemon, sliced
1 tablespoon chives
1 tablespoon lemon juice

2 teaspoons salt
4 parsley sprigs
3 peppercorns
2 cloves
1 garlic clove, crushed
1 bay leaf

Combine all ingredients in saucepan. Bring to the boil, simmer for 20 minutes. Drain and discard solids. Use vegetable stock as poaching liquid for fish.

Fish Stock or Fumet

This broth can be the beginning of a hearty soup. It costs nothing if you ask for the trimmings when you buy a filleted fish. Stock the trimmings in your freezer until you have enough to use, then just add vegetables and cook as below. You can vary seasonings: thyme and marjoram one time, a sprig of basil and oregano the next. The cooked, strained broth can be frozen too.

2 lbs (960 g) fish bones and heads, gills removed
2 pints (1 litre 200 ml) water
2 oz (60 g) carrots, sliced
2 oz (60 g) celery with leaves, chopped
2 oz (60 g) onion, sliced

1 tablespoon lemon juice
2 garlic cloves, crushed
2 parsley sprigs
1 bay leaf
5 peppercorns
Salt to taste

Rinse the fish bones and heads thoroughly under running water. Combine with remaining ingredients in large saucepan. Simmer for 30 to 40 minutes, skimming off scum. Strain, pressing out juices. Adjust seasonings, if desired. Use in recipes calling for Fish Stock.

In any recipe calling for Whipped Topping, use the recipe below.

Whipped Topping

2 fl oz (60 ml) water
1½ teaspoons unflavoured gelatine
Artificial sweetener to equal 1
  tablespoon sugar, or to taste

¼ teaspoon vanilla flavouring
½ oz (15 g) nonfat dry milk,
  reconstituted with 2½ fl oz
  (75 ml) water, chilled

Sprinkle gelatine over water in small pan. Heat slowly, stirring until gelatine dissolves. Pour into small mixing bowl; add artificial sweetener and vanilla; cool. Add chilled milk; beat at high speed until very thick. Cover and refrigerate. Makes 4 servings.

Your Microwave Oven

Many of our recipes may be used with your microwave oven. You will have to experiment with your unit and follow manufacturer's advice for timing, since there is no one standard that applies to all, but generally, you should allow about a quarter of the cooking time. That is, if our recipe suggests 16 minutes, allow 4 minutes in your microwave oven (or slightly less, since it's wiser to undercook than overcook). Please also note that our roasting procedures for beef, ham, lamb and pork require the use of a rack, so that fat will drain off into the pan. A rack is available for use in the microwave oven.

Our kitchen tested a number of basic foods and have the following timing tips for you:

Baked apple (1 medium): Set in small ovenproof bowl, cook 3 minutes; let stand several minutes. Makes 1 serving.

Baked fish fillets (12 oz (360 g)): Cook 7 minutes; let stand several minutes. Makes 2 servings.

Baked potato (1 × 3 oz (90 g)): Make crosswise cut, cook 4 minutes; let stand 2 to 3 minutes. Makes 1 serving.

Roast beef (12 oz (360 g) boneless): Cook 4 minutes on rack set in baking dish; turn, cook 4 minutes more; let stand 10 to 15 minutes. Makes 2 servings.

Hamburger patty (6 oz (180 g) 4-inch (10 cm) diameter): Coat with gravy browning. Place on rack set in baking dish. Cover with paper towel. Cook 2 minutes; turn patty, cook 1 minute. Makes 1 serving.

Roast chicken (3 lbs (1 kg 440 g)): Cook 7 minutes on rack set in baking dish, breast-side down; turn breast-side up, cook 7 minutes, turn dish, cook another 7 minutes. Let stand 10 to 15 minutes. Remove skin and bones. Weigh portions. Makes 4 servings.

Roast pork (12 oz (360 g) rolled): Cook 6 minutes on rack set in baking dish. Turn roast, cook 6 minutes more. Turn roast, cook 4 minutes. Let stand 10 to 15 minutes. Makes 2 servings.

Slow Cookers

If you enjoy using this appliance, there's no reason why you can't adapt many of our recipes to its use. We're giving you a headstart on your own experiments with the following guidelines from our kitchen. See index for the recipes:

Chicken Marengo: Cook chicken, stock, herbs and spices on low for

6 to 7 hours. Add vegetables and flavouring and cook, covered, on high for 30 to 40 minutes or until tomatoes are tender.

Chicken Cacciatore: After browning the chicken in frying pan, cook with remaining ingredients in slow cooker, covered, on low for 6 to 8 hours.

Haricot Bean Soup: Multiply to serve 4. Combine all ingredients and cook, covered, on low for 8 to 10 hours.

New England Baked Broad Beans: Divide recipe in half, to serve 4. Cook, covered, on low for 8 to 10 hours.

Devilled Chicken Legs: Follow recipe but cook in slow cooker, covered, on low for 8 hours.

Apricot Brown Betty: Multiply to serve 16 (smaller amounts impractical). Combine apricots and bread in slow cooker. Top with mixture of remaining ingredients. Toss, cover, cook on high for 2½ hours.

Homemade Chicken Stock: Combine all ingredients in slow cooker; cover and cook on low for 12 hours. Strain and proceed as in basic recipe.

Artificial Sweeteners

The use of artificial sweeteners on the Weight Watchers Food Programme has always been optional. Natural sweetness is available in the form of fruits which we do permit on our eating plan. Your use of artificial sweeteners is completely optional; and we believe that the decision about using them should be made by you. If you decide against these products, you will find many recipes in this book which are artificial sweetener-free.

AFRICA

*

Cyril Connolly, the famous critic and author, once punned that a midday meal in South Africa consists mainly of the 'cold table' which, he added, 'covers a multitude of tins'. The Dutch and British who settled here do indeed use lots of canned goods to provide a taste of homeland cooking but, in general, the food of this continent is far from dull. North African cuisine is pungent with peppers of every kind, from small red hot to large sweet green or red. Herbs and spices such as cinnamon, coriander, cumin, mint and thyme, a legacy of the Saracen invaders who swarmed across the deserts centuries ago from Syria and Arabia, are favourite seasonings. A typical tripe stew of Central Africa—made almost exactly the same way by the blacks of the West Indies—is hot and zesty with okra and thyme. So our African recipes are both savoury and spicy—a tasty start to your slim-gourmet's tour of the world of international cooking.

Minted Tuna Pâté

A North African appetizer, this could become a complete main course. For each serving, add 3 oz (90 g) cooked dried white beans seasoned with chilli pepper, and 3 oz (90 g) spinach (steamed in chicken or beef stock and well drained). Another variation: omit the bread and spoon the pâté into 'cups' of chicory leaves. Serve chilled.

8 oz (240 g) drained canned tuna or other cooked fish, flaked
4 teaspoons vegetable oil
1 $\frac{1}{2}$ teaspoons chopped fresh mint leaves

$\frac{1}{2}$ teaspoon nutmeg
$\frac{1}{2}$ teaspoon (or more to taste) Worcester sauce or lemon juice
4 slices white bread

15

Mash together all ingredients except bread to make a paste. Serve on bread. Makes 4 servings.

Congo Chicken and Okra (Fetri Detsi)

4 boned and skinned chicken
  breasts, 6 oz (180 g) each
4 oz (120 g) onion, chopped
1 teaspoon salt
6 oz (180 g) tomatoes, peeled
2 to 4 hot green chilli peppers,
  seeded, or ½ teaspoon crushed red
  pepper

2-inch (5 cm) slice fresh ginger root
1 pint 12 fl oz (960 ml) water
12 oz (360 g) fresh or frozen okra,
  sliced
4 tablespoons tomato purée
8 oz (240 g) cooked rice (optional)

Place chicken and onion in a heavy saucepan. Sprinkle with salt. Mince the tomatoes, chilli peppers and ginger finely, or chop very finely, by hand or in the blender. Add mixture to chicken. Pour in water and bring to the boil. Reduce heat and simmer, covered, for about 20 minutes or until chicken is barely tender. Add okra. Stir in tomato purée. Continue simmering, uncovered, until chicken and okra are tender. Place each breast on an individual dinner plate. Divide vegetables and liquid evenly and pour over chicken breast. Serve over 2 oz (60 g) rice if desired. Makes 4 servings.

Bobotie

8 oz (240 g) cooked minced beef
4 oz (120 g) onion, chopped
1 teaspoon curry powder
3 medium apricots, peeled, stoned
  and chopped
3 oz (90 g) tomato, peeled and
  chopped
2 slices white bread, made into
  crumbs
1 oz (30 g) nonfat dry milk,

reconstituted with 5 fl oz (150 ml)
  water
Salt and pepper to taste
1 bay leaf
8 teaspoons tomato purée
2 fl oz (60 ml) water
1 teaspoon beef stock powder
Gravy browning (optional)
1 teaspoon chopped fresh parsley

Place beef in a mixing bowl; lightly brown onions in a nonstick pan and add to beef with curry powder, apricots, tomato, bread and milk. Mix well. Season to taste. Shape into a loaf, place bay leaf on top and wrap in aluminium foil. Bake at 375°F (190°C), Gas Mark 5, for 35 minutes or until firm. Heat tomato purée with water, stock powder, and gravy browning as desired. Divide loaf equally and serve half the sauce over each portion. Sprinkle with parsley. Makes 2 servings.

Tripe Stew

12 oz (360 g) cooked beef cut in 1-inch (2.5 cm) squares could replace an equal amount of tripe. Then cook the beef and tripe together.

1 lb (480 g) precooked tripe, cut in 1-inch (2.5 cm) squares
Salt to taste
Water
8 oz (240 g) spinach, washed, stemmed and finely chopped
8 oz (240 g) onions

6 oz (180 g) tomatoes
2 hot green or red chilli peppers, stemmed and seeded
½ teaspoon nutmeg (optional)
3 oz (90 g) uncooked cornmeal, prepared according to package directions

Place tripe and salt in a large saucepan. Add enough water to cover. Bring to the boil; reduce heat to medium; cover and cook for 45 minutes or until tripe is very tender. Just before meat is ready, heat 10 fl oz (300 ml) salted water in a medium saucepan. Add spinach; cover and cook over medium heat about 5 minutes or until tender. Drain and discard liquid. Add spinach to tripe mixture. Chop onions, tomatoes and peppers very finely and combine in a large nonstick frying pan. Heat, stirring occasionally, until most of the liquid from the tomatoes has evaporated. Add to tripe mixture; stir to combine. Add nutmeg, if desired, and stir. Simmer for 1 hour uncovered. Drain and reserve liquid. Divide meat, vegetables and cornmeal into 4 equal portions. Measure liquid and pour a quarter of the liquid over each portion. Makes 4 servings.

Skewered Pork, Fruit and Vegetable (Sosaties)

An Arabic-style recipe adapted by the South African Dutch.

1 lb 2 oz (540 g) pork loin or fillet, cut in 1-inch (2.5 cm) pieces
9 oz (270 g) green peppers, cut in 1-inch (2.5 cm) pieces
4½ oz (135 g) tomatoes, cut in large wedges
¾ small pineapple, cut in 1-inch (2.5 cm) pieces
3 oz (90 g) onion, finely chopped
7 fl oz (210 ml) water

2 fl oz (60 ml) white vinegar
½ teaspoon salt
½ teaspoon curry powder
¼ teaspoon turmeric
¼ teaspoon paprika
¼ teaspoon pepper
4 tablespoons tomato purée
Gravy browning (optional)
6 oz (180 g) cooked rice
3 large skewers

Place pork, peppers, tomatoes, pineapple and onions in large mixing bowl. Add 4 fl oz (120 ml) water, vinegar, salt, curry, turmeric, paprika and pepper. Mix well and marinate for 4 hours. Divide first 4 ingredients into 3 equal portions and thread alternately on skewers. Grill on rack 4 inches (10 cm) from heat, 12 to 15 minutes, turning frequently until meat is cooked. Pour marinade in a saucepan; add tomato purée and remaining 3 fl oz (90 ml) water and cook until thick; add gravy browning as desired. Place each skewer on 2 oz (60 g) rice; divide sauce into 3 equal portions and serve over meat and rice. Makes 3 servings.

Rice Salad

Serve as a separate course. Cook the rice so that the grains are separate, not mushy. If necessary, fluff them with a fork or separate by rinsing quickly in colander.

8 oz (240 g) cold cooked brown rice
1 oz (30 g) chopped fresh parsley
8 oz (240 g) diced spring onions
4 to 8 tablespoons chopped fresh mint, or to taste
2 fl oz (60 ml) vegetable oil

2 fl oz (60 ml) lemon juice
Salt, pepper and cumin to taste
12 oz (360 g) tomatoes, chopped
8 radishes, sliced
1 head cos lettuce, quartered

In wooden salad bowl combine rice with parsley, spring onions, mint, oil, lemon juice and seasonings. Chill. Just before serving, toss well. Add tomatoes and radishes; serve over cos lettuce. Makes 4 servings.

Mango and Pineapple Salad

Two sweet peppers can replace the hot red peppers if you prefer a milder salad.

½ fresh small pineapple, peeled
2 small ripe mangoes, peeled and
   seeded
1 medium banana, peeled
2 fresh hot red peppers, or 2 × 6 oz
   (180 g) sweet peppers, seeds
   removed, finely diced

2 fl oz (60 ml) cider vinegar
⅛ teaspoon salt
Watercress sprigs

Cut pineapple, mangoes and bananas into ¾-inch (2 cm) pieces. Combine peppers, vinegar and salt in salad bowl. Add cut fruit, mixing well. Chill for 1 hour. Garnish with crisp watercress sprigs and serve as side dish for roast meat or poultry. Makes 8 servings.

AUSTRALIA AND NEW ZEALAND

*

Australia and New Zealand, its next-door neighbour, were colonized by the British, who also transplanted British customs and eating patterns. Morning and afternoon teatimes, double breakfasts, and after-dinner savouries, really meals in themselves, are habitual.

Yet for all its British roots, the food in these countries down under the equator has its own very distinctive quality. New recipes have developed from the tastes of Asian and non-British Europeans, and from the abundance of exotic fruits, vegetables, and Pacific Ocean fish and shellfish. In our selection, you'll find such authentic specialities as barbecued pork chops with a spiced fruit topping and such typical desserts as Pavlova. There are many other 'down under' treats you can enjoy at home while you get your weight down.

'Cream' of Chicken Soup*

2 tablespoons low fat spread
2 slices white bread, made into
  crumbs
1 pint 12 fl oz (960 ml) chicken
  stock, made with 2 stock cubes
1½ oz (45 g) nonfat dry milk,
reconstituted with 6 fl oz (180 ml)
  water
8 oz (240 g) cooked or drained
  canned chicken, shredded
Salt, pepper and chopped chives

Melt low fat spread in top of double boiler over water. Stir in breadcrumbs and stock; slowly add reconstituted milk; cook over boiling water until smooth and thickened. Add chicken; season to taste with salt and pepper. Serve topped with chives. Makes 4 servings.
CHICKEN CURRY SOUP: Add ½ teaspoon curry powder to melted low fat spread.

'Cream' of Lettuce Soup

1 pint 4 fl oz (720 ml) water
1 tablespoon dried onion flakes
1 teaspoon dried pepper flakes
1 teaspoon chopped fresh parsley

4 teaspoons beef stock powder
10 oz (300 g) shredded lettuce
10 fl oz (300 ml) skim milk

Heat water to boiling in saucepan; stir in onion, green pepper, parsley and beef stock powder. Add lettuce; simmer 15 minutes. Add milk; reheat. Makes 4 servings.

Pineapple French Toast

Fruit is plentiful in New Zealand, so this is a favourite dish.

1 egg
¼ teaspoon cinnamon

2 oz (60 g) canned crushed
   pineapple, no sugar added
1 slice currant bread

Beat the egg and ⅛ teaspoon cinnamon in a shallow dish. Drain juice from pineapple into egg mixture; beat again. Prick both sides of bread with a fork. Soak bread in egg mixture, turning several times until as much egg mixture as possible is absorbed. Carefully transfer to a nonstick baking sheet. Combine drained pineapple and remaining ⅛ teaspoon cinnamon with any leftover egg mixture. Spread on top of bread. Bake at 400°F (200°C), Gas Mark 6, for 20 minutes. Makes 1 serving.

Barbecue with Chuck Wagon Sauce

Australians like the free and easy informality of this kind of meal. It is easy on the hostess, too, because most of the work is done the day before.

2 lb 4 oz (1 kg 80 g) well-trimmed
   boneless beef roast (use top rump
   or similar cut), about 2½-inches

(6 cm) thick
Chuck Wagon Sauce
   (recipe follows)

Put beef on a rack in a roasting tin; cover top with foil and bake in slow oven, (300°F (150°C), Gas Mark 2) for 2 hours. Remove foil and continue baking until roast is done and brown. Let roast cool, then refrigerate overnight. The next day, combine the ingredients for the sauce and cook 20 to 30 minutes. Meanwhile, shred the beef roast into string-like pieces. Add to the sauce in pan and simmer gently for at least one hour. Watch pan and stir as necessary. For longer periods, set saucepan on asbestos pad over low heat. Can also be simmered in a casserole in the oven at 300°F (150°C), Gas Mark 2, or over a charcoal fire, placed to receive only moderate heat from bed of coals. And more water as necessary to keep sauce from drying out. Makes 6 servings.

Chuck Wagon Sauce

4 tablespoons tomato purée
9 fl oz (270 ml) water
1 tablespoon dried onion flakes
1 tablespoon Worcester sauce
2 fl oz (60 ml) vinegar

1 teaspoon paprika
1 garlic clove, crushed
2 teaspoons dry mustard
1 teaspoon chilli powder

Mix ingredients and simmer slowly together in covered saucepan on the stove or at side of the grill about 20 to 30 minutes. Makes 6 servings.

Billabong Beef Ring

6 oz (180 g) frozen peas
2 tablespoons unflavoured gelatine
10 fl oz (300 ml) cold water
6 slices canned pineapple, cut in
  half, with 6 tablespoons juice, no
  sugar added

1 lb (480 g) diced cooked beef
Lettuce leaves to garnish
12 radishes, cut into 'roses'

Cook peas in a minimum amount of salted water; drain; set aside to cool. In saucepan, sprinkle gelatine over water; add pineapple juice and heat over very low flame to dissolve gelatine. Coat a 1½ pint (900ml) ring mould (rinsed in water) with one-third of the gelatine and arrange 8 pineapple halves in mould. Refrigerate until gelatine becomes set. (Keep remaining gelatine in warm place.) Put cooled, drained peas on pineapple layer; spread evenly. Pour in one-third of the warm gelatine. Let set in refrigerator. When this layer is set, combine remaining warm gelatine with meat and spoon evenly into mould. Cover with 6 pineapple halves and let set. When ready, dip mould into hot water, put serving plate on top, reverse quickly. Serve with lettuce border and 2 remaining halves of pineapple. Fill centre with radishes. Makes 4 servings.

New Zealand Mutton Pie

6 oz (180 g) tomatoes, sliced
8 oz (240 g) cooked mutton (or
   lamb or beef), thinly sliced
6 oz (180 g) peeled, cooked potatoes,
   thinly sliced

Salt and pepper to taste
6 fl oz (180 ml) beef stock, made
   with ½ stock cube

Make a layer of sliced tomatoes in a pie dish, add a layer of cold mutton, and a layer of sliced potatoes. Repeat layers. Season each layer with salt and pepper. Pour in beef stock. Bake at 350°F (180°C), Gas Mark 4, about 30 minutes or until bubbly and hot. Serve immediately. Makes 2 servings.

Roast Baby Lamb with Mint Sauce

1 boned and trimmed leg of lamb,
   about 3 lbs (1 kg 440 g)
½ lemon
Salt and pepper to taste
4 fl oz (120 ml) chicken or beef

stock, made with ¼ stock cube
Mint Sauce (recipe follows)
Garnish: fresh mint sprigs and 3 oz
   (90 g) tomatoes, cut in wedges

Rub lamb with lemon and sprinkle with salt and pepper. Place lamb on a rack in roasting tin. Insert meat thermometer in centre. Roast in 300° to 325°F (150° to 160°C), Gas Mark 2 to 3, oven following the chart overleaf. Baste occasionally with stock. Remove from oven and let roast stand 15 minutes at room temperature to make carving easier. Serve 4 oz (120 g) portions, with Mint Sauce accompaniment and garnish. Makes about 8 servings.

	Meat Thermometer	Minutes per pound (480 g)
Rare	140°F (60°C)	25 to 30
Medium	160°F (70°C)	30 to 35
Well	170° to 180°F (75° to 85°C)	35 to 40

Mint Sauce

4 fl oz (120 ml) water
4 fl oz (120 ml) white vinegar
4 tablespoons chopped fresh mint

Artificial sweetener to taste
(optional)

Place water, vinegar, mint, and sweetener if desired, in saucepan; bring slowly to the boil. Remove from heat. Serve with Roast Lamb. Makes 8 servings.

Chicken Liver Rollups

12 oz (360 g) chicken livers, cut in thirds, rinsed quickly with boiling water and dried
1½ oz (45 g) sliced mushrooms

2 oz (60 g) sliced onion
¾ teaspoon salt
Pinch pepper
8 lettuce leaves

Cook chicken livers, mushrooms and onion in a nonstick covered pan until tender. Uncover and let juices reduce. Turn into bowl and chop finely. Add salt and pepper. Blend well; cool. Divide mixture into 8 lettuce leaves. Fold in sides and roll up leaves as in egg rolls. Serve with flaps underneath. Makes 2 servings.

Barbecued Pork Chops with Spiced Fruit Sauce

Meats are often cooked with fruit; hundreds of different varieties grow in a climate which includes a tropical north and a temperate south.

2 well-trimmed pork chops, 8 oz (240 g) each
Salt and pepper to taste

1 garlic clove, peeled and split
Spiced Fruit Sauce (recipe follows)

Lightly season chops and rub with garlic. Barbecue or grill on a rack, 4 inches (10 cm) from source of heat for 10 to 15 minutes or until pork is done with no trace of pink showing either in meat or juices when pork is cut; turn chops several times. Serve with sauce. Makes 2 servings.

Spiced Fruit Sauce

4 fl oz (120 ml) orange juice
4 teaspoons tomato purée
2 tablespoons water
1 teaspoon white wine vinegar

1 teaspoon dry mustard
Pinch cinnamon
Gravy browning (optional)

Combine all ingredients in saucepan. Place over heat and simmer 10 minutes to blend flavours. Divide evenly into two portions and serve hot with chops. Makes 2 servings.

Sardine Salad Wellington

1 lb 2 oz (540 g) peeled potatoes
12 oz (360 g) drained canned
  sardines
9 oz (270 g) cucumber, peeled and
  diced
6 oz (180 g) green pepper,
  seeded and chopped
6 oz (180 g) onion, chopped
3 tablespoons chopped fresh parsley
Lettuce leaves

2 fl oz (60 ml) vegetable oil
2 fl oz (60 ml) vinegar
½ teaspoon salt
⅛ teaspoon black pepper
3 eggs, hard-boiled and
  chopped
3 eggs, hard-boiled and
  halved
Capers, rinsed

Cut potatoes in halves, cover with salted boiling water and cook until potatoes are tender, about 30 minutes. Drain, cool, and cut in ½-inch (1 cm) dice. Lightly mash half the sardines and combine with potato, cucumber, pepper, onion and parsley. Line a salad bowl with lettuce leaves. Add sardine mixture. Mix oil, vinegar, salt, pepper and chopped hard boiled eggs. Sprinkle over sardines. Garnish with remaining whole sardines, hard-boiled egg halves and capers. Makes 6 servings.

Tomato Pie

4 slices white bread, made into soft
  crumbs
1 tablespoon chopped fresh parsley
1 teaspoon chopped fresh thyme
¼ teaspoon chopped fresh marjoram

4 oz (120 g) onion, chopped
Salt and pepper to taste
Juice of 1 lemon
12 oz (360 g) ripe medium tomatoes,
  peeled and cut in thick slices

Mix breadcrumbs, chopped herbs, onion, salt, pepper and lemon juice. Put a layer of tomato slices in an ovenproof pie dish; cover with a layer of seasoned breadcrumbs, then repeat tomato layer and finish with breadcrumbs. Bake covered in moderate oven, 350°F (180°C), Gas Mark 4, for 20 to 25 minutes. Makes 4 servings.

Sunshine Carrots

1 lb (480 g) carrots, sliced about
  1-inch (2.5 cm) thick
2 medium oranges, peeled and diced
  (reserve juice)

¼ teaspoon salt
¼ teaspoon ginger
4 teaspoons low fat spread

Cook carrots in boiling salted water until just tender, 15 to 20 minutes. Combine orange juice, salt and ginger in small saucepan. Boil 1 minute. Stir in orange dice. Pour over hot carrots, tossing to coat evenly. Remove from heat. Add 1 teaspoon low fat spread to each serving. Makes 4 servings.

Pineapple Surprise

Orange Sorbet (recipe follows)
1 ripe small pineapple
2 medium bananas

1 tablespoon brandy or rum
  flavouring

Prepare sorbet. Cut the pineapple in half lengthwise. Cut out all the pulp and dice it. Reserve the shell. Peel and slice the bananas. Combine diced pineapple and bananas with flavouring; stuff the shell with the fruit mixture. Serve at the table into fruit cups. Top each serving with a scoop of Orange Sorbet. Makes 8 servings.

Orange Sorbet

1 oz (30 g) nonfat dry milk   16 fl oz (480 ml) orange juice

Combine milk and orange juice in bowl. Mix thoroughly. Pour into ice-cube tray and put in freezer until slightly frozen. Transfer to a bowl and beat rapidly until smooth and creamy. Make 8 scoops. Return to tray and freeze slightly. Defrost slightly to serve. Makes 8 servings.

Pavlova*

4 eggs, separated
¼ teaspoon cream of tartar
Pinch salt
1 tablespoon vanilla flavouring
1 oz (30 g) nonfat dry milk,
    reconstituted with 5 fl oz (150 ml)
    water

Artificial sweetener to equal 3
    teaspoons sugar, or to taste
1 teaspoon unflavoured gelatine
2 fl oz (60 ml) cold water
1 medium papaya, peeled and sliced
5 oz (150 g) bilberries (optional)

Preheat oven to 200°F (100°C), Gas Mark ¼. Beat egg whites with cream of tartar and salt until stiff but still shiny. Fold in 2 teaspoons vanilla. Spoon out or pipe onto a nonstick baking sheet and shape into an 8-inch (20 cm) circular mound with an indentation 4-inches (10 cm) wide and 1-inch (2.5 cm) deep. Bake for 40 to 60 minutes. In top of double boiler combine egg yolks, milk, sweetener and remaining vanilla. Heat over simmering water, beating constantly with a wire whisk until mixture is a light lemony colour and slightly thickened. Soften gelatine in cold water. Add to egg yolk mixture; stir to dissolve thoroughly. Whip 2 to 3 minutes. Remove from heat. Chill until mixture thickens to pudding consistency. Pour into indentation in egg white mound, allowing the excess to run over sides, if desired. Surround with papaya slices, reserving 1 slice. Dice the slice and use to garnish pudding. Serve with bilberries if desired. Chill. Makes 4 servings.

Swede and Apple Pudding, Tasmania Style*

4 slices currant bread, made into
  crumbs
4 medium cooking apples, peeled and
  thinly sliced
8 oz (240 g) cooked swede, mashed
1 teaspoon cinnamon
Pinch salt

½ teaspoon mixed ground cloves,
  cinnamon and ginger
4 eggs
10 fl oz (300 ml) skim milk
1 teaspoon butter flavouring
¼ teaspoon vanilla flavouring

Combine breadcrumbs, apples, swede and salt in a mixing bowl. Add cinnamon and spices and mix lightly together. Beat eggs with milk; add butter and vanilla flavourings. Fold into the apple mixture. Pour into a 9 × 9-inch (23 × 23 cm) nonstick baking tin and bake at 350°F (180°C), Gas Mark 4, for 1 hour and 15 minutes, or until firm. Remove; cool. Makes 4 servings.

Apple Sundowner Cake*

4 oz (120 g) nonfat dry milk,
  reconstituted with 1 pint 12 fl oz
  (960 ml) water
Artificial sweetener to equal 6
  teaspoons sugar, or to taste
3 oz (90 g) uncooked cornmeal
4 eggs

1 teaspoon butter flavouring
½ teaspoon vanilla flavouring
½ teaspoon cinnamon
4 medium apples, peeled and thinly
  sliced
4 oz (120 g) mashed, cooked carrots

Combine milk and sweetener in a saucepan and place over low heat. When milk begins to simmer, sprinkle in cornmeal, stirring until mixture thickens. Cook for 1 minute and remove from heat; cool. Beat eggs and stir into mixture. Add butter and vanilla flavourings and cinnamon. Fold in apples and carrots. Pour into nonstick baking tin and bake in hot (400°F (200°C), Gas Mark 6) oven for 45 minutes. Remove from oven and cool. Remove cake from tin, place on rack and let stand for 4 hours before serving. Divide equally into 4 portions Makes 4 servings.

AUSTRIA AND HUNGARY

For some six hundred years before the First World War, Austria and Hungary were united as part of the Austro-Hungarian Hapsburg Empire, so a commingling of their recipes is in a long established tradition. Viennese pastry was part of that tradition, too. For obvious reasons, you won't find it here, but we have included a delicious Austrian-style cake—Tangerine Sponge Cake. Of course, we've included a *paprikash*. Would we dare not to, even in the knowledge that no Hungarian menu ever features more than one course flavoured with the native mild sweet paprika, and many Hungarian meals are prepared without it?

Other typical foods of this corner of Europe have been included. Enough, we hope, to give you a taste, however tiny, of the interesting cuisines which developed when Turkish, Slavic, Italian, French, Spanish and German food tastes met over the centuries in these two now-separate countries.

Cherry Soup (Cseresznyeleves)

4 oz (120 g) sweet cherries, with stones   1 slice white bread, toasted and
Water   diced
5 fl oz (150 ml) buttermilk

Cover cherries with water and cook until they are soft. Remove stones if desired, and put cherries back into pan. Add buttermilk and simmer but do not boil. Top with diced toast; serve hot. Makes 1 serving.

Emperor Soup (Kaisersuppe)

5 oz (150 g) shredded cabbage
2 oz (60 g) diced leek
5 oz (150 g) diced carrot
4 oz (120 g) diced cauliflower
2 oz (60 g) onion, diced

2 pints (1 litre 200 ml) chicken
   stock, made with 3 stock cubes
8 oz (240 g) cooked rice
Salt and freshly ground pepper to
   taste

Combine vegetables in large saucepan; add stock; cover and cook until vegetables are tender, 25 to 30 minutes. Add rice. Simmer 10 minutes more. Season with salt and freshly ground pepper. Serve hot. Makes 4 servings.

Tyrolean Liver Soup (Lebersuppe)

12 oz (360 g) liver (remove any
   membranes), sliced
16 fl oz (480 ml) chicken stock
   made with 1 stock cube, or
   homemade stock (see page 10)
5 oz (150 g) diced carrots
4 oz (120 g) diced turnips

4 oz (120 g) diced celery
2 oz (60 g) diced onion
1 bay leaf
Garnish: 1 tablespoon chopped fresh
   parsley, chives or watercress
Freshly ground pepper to taste

To wash the liver, put in strainer and pour boiling hot water through it. Drain, dry and transfer to preheated nonstick pan. Brown liver quickly on all sides, 3 to 4 minutes; dice finely. Add stock, vegetables and bay leaf; cover pan and cook about 20 minutes or until vegetables are tender. Discard bay leaf. Serve soup and liver in bowls with garnish sprinkled on top. Add freshly ground pepper to taste. Makes 2 servings.

Fisherman's Soup—Danube River (Halaszlé)

Danubian carp and white fish are famous throughout Hungary.

1 lb (480 g) carp (including bones and skin)	2 tablespoons lemon juice or mild vinegar
9 oz (270 g) diced celery	1 tablespoon mild paprika
5 oz (150 g) diced carrots	Bouquet garni (1 small garlic clove,
4 oz (120 g) diced string beans	bay leaf, 4 peppercorns, 1 sprig
4 oz (120 g) diced onion	thyme, 2 sprigs dill, 4 sprigs
4 oz (120 g) peas	parsley, tied in muslin)
4 oz (120 g) diced parsnips	12 oz (360 g) white fish and pike fillets, cut in 2-inch (5 cm) pieces

Put carp, celery, carrots, string beans, onion, peas, parsnips, lemon juice, paprika and bouquet garni in saucepan. Cover with water, bring to the boil, then simmer 45 minutes. Remove the carp to a strainer. Cut away flesh of carp and transfer 2 oz (60 g) to each of 4 soup bowls. With wooden spoon, press back into saucepan all liquid from carp bones in strainer. Add pieces of pike and white fish to pan and simmer gently for 6 to 7 minutes. Discard bouquet garni. Divide white fish, pike, vegetables and liquid into the 4 bowls holding the carp. Makes 4 servings.

Chicken Paprika

1 lb 8 oz (720 g) skinned and boned chicken	made with 1 stock cube
8 oz (240 g) onion, finely diced	1 tablespoon sweet Hungarian paprika
6 oz (180 g) green pepper, diced	10 fl oz (300 ml) buttermilk
16 fl oz (480 ml) chicken stock,	

Layer the chicken in an oven-to-table casserole. Brown onion and pepper in heated nonstick frying pan at moderately high heat for about 5 minutes, stirring to prevent scorching. Add chicken stock and paprika and bring to the boil; pour over chicken in casserole. Cover and bake at 375°F (190°C), Gas Mark 5, for 1 hour or until chicken is tender. Ten minutes before serving, add buttermilk to casserole. Mix well and bake 10 minutes more or until buttermilk is heated. Mix chicken well with the sauce before serving. Makes 4 servings.

Hungarian Veal Gulyas

Onions, peppers, tomatoes and sweet mild paprika are the basic ingredients of Hungarian gulyas. 3 oz (90 g) sliced mushrooms could be browned with the onions to make an even more substantial dish.

1 lb 8 oz (720 g) trimmed veal, cut in cubes
1 tablespoon mild Hungarian paprika
8 oz (240 g) chopped onion
6 oz (180 g) tomatoes, peeled and cut into 8 wedges

5 tablespoons tomato purée
4 fl oz (120 ml) water
12 oz (360 g) green peppers, cut in squares
1½ teaspoons salt
8 oz (240 g) hot cooked noodles

Dredge veal with paprika and brown on all sides in nonstick frying pan. Remove veal; wipe out pan. Return veal to pan. Add onion and brown lightly. Add tomatoes, tomato purée, water, green pepper and salt. Cover pan and simmer gently about 1 hour or until veal is tender. Serve with noodles. Makes 4 servings.

Viennese Gulyas

Using mortar and pestle, grind 1 garlic clove, 1 teaspoon caraway seeds and the rind of ½ lemon. Stir into veal about 10 minutes before it is done. Makes 4 servings.

Tokany Meat Loaf and Vegetable (Pörkölt)

1 lbs 8 oz (720 g) minced beef
2 fl oz (60 ml) water
1 teaspoon salt
¼ teaspoon rosemary or dill
⅛ teaspoon pepper
4 oz (120 g) carrots, scrubbed and
  sliced
4 oz (120 g) onion, sliced

4 oz (120 g) diced parsnips
2 oz (60 g) diced celery
1 large garlic clove, crushed
4 fl oz (120 ml) water
6 oz (180 g) tomatoes, diced
1 tablespoon mild paprika
4 oz (120 g) fresh or frozen young
  peas

Mix minced beef with water, salt, rosemary and pepper; shape into one long, large patty. Grill on rack about 4 inches (10 cm) from source of heat 15 minutes or until cooked throughout. Turn once during grilling. Meanwhile combine carrots, onion, parsnips, celery and garlic in pan with lid. Add water, tomatoes and paprika. Cover and simmer 15 minutes or until vegetables are almost tender and sauce reduced and quite thick. Add meat to pan. Top with peas. Simmer, covered, for 10 minutes or until beef is piping hot and peas are done. Serve immediately. Makes 4 servings.

Hungarian Wedding Rice

2 lbs 4 oz (1 kg 80 g) chicken livers,
  cut in halves
Salt and freshly ground pepper to
  taste
6 oz (180 g) sliced mushrooms,
  sprinkled with lemon juice
12 oz (360 g) cooked rice
9 oz (270 g) cooked tiny whole
  carrots

12 oz (360 g) cooked tiny white
  onions
2 fl oz (60 ml) chicken stock,
  made with ¼ stock cube
1 lb 2 oz (540 g) green peppers,
  roasted, peeled and cut into 12
  rings

Wipe chicken livers dry; sprinkle with salt and pepper and brown with mushrooms in a large preheated nonstick frying pan. Turn livers often to cook evenly on all sides. Do not overcook; liver should remain juicy. Remove from pan and place in the centre of a serving dish. In a large saucepan combine all remaining ingredients except green pepper, and heat through, stirring occasionally to prevent sticking. Spoon rice mixture round the chicken livers. Arrange green pepper slices, overlapping at the edges, over rice. Makes 6 servings.

Noodle-Cheese-Apple Pudding

4 oz (120 g) cooked noodles
5 oz (150 g) cottage cheese
2 medium Granny Smith apples,
  peeled, thinly sliced
¼ teaspoon cinnamon

5 fl oz (150 ml) skim milk
Artificial sweetener to equal 4
  teaspoons sugar, or to taste
2 eggs, well beaten
Nutmeg to garnish

Preheat oven to 350°F (180°C), Gas Mark 4. Combine noodles and cheese in a mixing bowl. Mix well. Lay half the mixture in a small baking dish; arrange the apples on top. Sprinkle with cinnamon. Cover with remaining noodle mixture. Add milk and sweetener to eggs. Pour over noodles and bake for 30 minutes. Remove and let stand for 30 minutes before serving (may also be served cold). Makes 2 servings.

Salzburg Noodles

Toast ½ teaspoon caraway or poppy seeds in nonstick frying pan, stirring constantly. In serving bowl, combine with 2 oz (60 g) freshly cooked wide noodles and 1 teaspoon margarine. Mix until margarine melts. Makes 1 serving.

Pearl Onions in Tomato Sauce

16 fl oz (480 ml) water
1 teaspoon salt
4 oz (120 g) pearl onions

4 teaspoons tomato purée
2 tablespoons water
1½ teaspoons vinegar

Bring water and salt to the boil in a medium saucepan. Add onions and cook until tender. In another saucepan combine tomato purée, water and vinegar. Place over low heat until heated through. Drain and rinse onions in a colander; add to tomato mixture and stir to coat. Heat for 2 to 3 minutes. Makes 1 serving.

Mushrooms in Caper Mayonnaise, Vienna Style

4 oz (120 g) mushrooms, cut in half
1 tablespoon lemon juice
4 fl oz (120 ml) water

⅛ teaspoon salt
Caper Mayonnaise (recipe follows)

Wipe mushrooms and sprinkle with lemon juice. In saucepan (not aluminium) bring water to the boil. Add salt and mushrooms; stir. Cover pan and cook quickly for 3 to 4 minutes. Drain mushrooms (save liquid and use in soup). Let mushrooms cool, stir in Caper Mayonnaise. Makes 2 servings.

Caper Mayonnaise

1½ oz (45 g) pickled cucumber, diced
3 capers, rinsed and halved
2 tablespoons mayonnaise

1 teaspoon chopped fresh parsley
1 teaspoon chopped fresh or frozen chives
2 teaspoons prepared mustard

Combine. Makes 2 servings.

Ham, Apple and Wilted Lettuce Salad (Häuptelsalat)

2 heads round or cos lettuce (remove larger outer leaves and use in mixed salad)
2 medium sharp flavoured apples, peeled, cored and sliced
1 tablespoon lemon juice

4 oz (120 g) diced celery
6 oz (180 g) sliced cooked ham
4 teaspoons vegetable oil
1 tablespoon vinegar
1 teaspoon chopped fresh chives
1 teaspoon chopped fresh parsley

Tear washed lettuce into pieces and arrange in 2 salad bowls. Brush apples with lemon juice. Divide evenly over lettuce. Add celery. Stack ham slices and cut into matchstick pieces. Divide evenly over apples. Combine remaining ingredients, mix well and serve evenly divided over each salad. Let stand about 15 minutes to wilt lettuce. Makes 2 servings.

Cucumber Pickle Slices

4 lbs 8 oz (2 kg 160 g) cucumbers, sliced
12 oz (360 g) onion, sliced
4 tablespoons salt
8 oz (240 g) celery, cut in matchstick pieces

12 fl oz (360 ml) wine vinegar
Artificial sweetener to equal 4 teaspoons sugar, or to taste
1 teaspoon celery seeds
1 teaspoon dry mustard
1 teaspoon cinnamon

Combine cucumbers and onion in medium bowl. Add salt, toss, and refrigerate overnight. Rinse and drain cucumbers and onions thoroughly. Place in saucepan with remaining ingredients. Cover, simmer 5 minutes, stirring occasionally. Serve chilled. Makes 12 servings.

Austrian Lentil (or Soybean) Salad (Linsensalat)

6 oz (180 g) cooked dried lentils or soybeans
2 oz (60 g) finely chopped spring onions

2 teaspoons vegetable oil
2 teaspoons vinegar
$\frac{1}{4}$ teaspoon savory
Salt and pepper to taste

Combine ingredients, mix well. Chill until ready to use. Makes 1 serving.

Spinach and Mushroom Salad with Poppy Seed Dressing

5 tablespoons tomato purée
4 fl oz (120 ml) water
1 teaspoon prepared horseradish
1 teaspoon poppy seeds
1 teaspoon lemon juice

¼ teaspoon salt
4 oz (120 g) mushrooms, sliced
8 oz (240 g) spinach leaves,
  thoroughly washed and dried

Combine tomato purée, water, horseradish, poppy seeds, lemon juice and salt in medium bowl; add mushrooms and marinate 1 hour. Place spinach leaves in large bowl and toss with poppy seed dressing. Makes 4 servings.

Tangerine Sponge Cake*

4 slices white bread, made into
  crumbs
4 oz (120 g) nonfat dry milk
Artificial sweetener to equal 4
  teaspoons sugar, or to taste
2 teaspoons baking powder
2 tablespoons low fat spread

4 eggs
¼ teaspoon orange flavouring
2 tablespoons water
4 fl oz (120 ml) orange juice
1 tablespoon unflavoured gelatine
4 small tangerines, peeled and
  sectioned

Preheat oven to 425°F (220°C), Gas Mark 7. Combine first 4 ingredients in a mixing bowl; blend in the low fat spread. Place eggs, flavouring and water in blender goblet. Blend 10 seconds and fold thoroughly into breadcrumb mixture. Pour into nonstick round shallow cake tin, 8½ × 1½-inches (22 × 4 cm), and bake 12 to 15 minutes or until golden brown. Cool. Place on wire rack. Pour orange juice in saucepan; add unflavoured gelatine. Place over low heat; stir until gelatine dissolves. Chill until gelatine mixture is slightly thickened. Arrange tangerine sections on top of cake; top with gelatine mixture. Chill several hours. Makes 4 servings.

Apple Pudding with Cherry Sauce

1 recipe Whipped Topping
  (see page 12)
12 oz (360 g) canned apple slices, no
  sugar added
⅛ teaspoon cinnamon

4 oz (120 g) stoned, canned sweet
  cherries, no sugar added
2 tablespoons water
1 teaspoon cornflour
½ teaspoon lemon juice

Prepare Whipped Topping. Cook apple slices gently until soft and mash. Cool and combine with cinnamon in bowl. Fold in Whipped Topping. Pour mixture into four small dessert dishes. Chill several hours or overnight. Drain liquid from cherries and heat with water, cornflour and lemon juice in small saucepan, stirring constantly until mixture comes to the boil, thickens and changes from cloudy to clear. Add cherries to thickened juice. Divide evenly and serve sauce with pudding. Makes 4 servings.

Apricot Bavarian*

1 egg
10 fl oz (300 ml) skim milk
Artificial sweetener to equal 4
  teaspoons sugar, or to taste
1 teaspoon freshly grated lemon rind
½ teaspoon sherry flavouring
¼ teaspoon lemon flavouring

1 tablespoon unflavoured gelatine
3 medium apricots, peeled, stoned
  and chopped
½ oz (15 g) nonfat dry milk,
  reconstituted with 2½ fl oz (75 ml)
  water and chilled

In a mixing bowl combine eggs, 10 fl oz (300 ml) skim milk, sweetener, lemon rind and flavourings. Mix well with beater. Sprinkle gelatine over mixture and let stand to soften. Pour mixture into saucepan. Place over low heat and stir until gelatine dissolves, and mixture begins to thicken. *Do not boil.* Remove and cool. Add apricots. Fold reconstituted dry milk into apricot mixture before it sets. Transfer to a small mould and chill for 2 hours before serving. Makes 1 serving.

BELGIUM
AND THE NETHERLANDS

*

Whether you visit the Netherlands in the Spring, in time for the tulips, or in the Summer when the annual flowers are in bloom, you'll find a country ablaze with colour, and friendly, rosy-cheeked people who could have stepped right out of a Frans Hals painting, except for a change to modern dress.

Of course, you'll also want to visit Belgium, the Netherland's neighbour on the North Sea. When you do, be sure to try the Waterzoi, famous meal-in-one-dish, which can be made with fish, as in our recipe, or with chicken, substituting chicken stock for the fish stock. Keeping in mind that a sweet tooth is the most international of all tastes, we end our gastronomic tour of Belgium and the Netherlands with two splendidly rich but 'legal' dessert treats.

Belgian Fish Soup (Waterzoi)

16 fl oz (480 ml) water
6 oz (180 g) peeled whole new
   potatoes
5 oz (150 g) diced celery
4 oz (120 g) sliced carrots
2 oz (60 g) onion, diced
2 tablespoons parsley sprigs
5 crushed peppercorns
½ bay leaf

¼ teaspoon thyme
4 fl oz (120 ml) fish stock
   (see page 11)
12 oz (360 g) assorted fillets of carp,
   perch or pike (at least two
   kinds), cut into 1½-inch (4 cm)
   pieces
1 teaspoon brandy or sherry
   flavouring

Combine water, potatoes, celery, carrots, onion and bouquet garni in a saucepan. (To make the bouquet put the parsley, peppercorns, bay leaf and thyme in muslin square and tie with string; or put into tea-infusion strainer.) Cook vigorously for about 20 minutes or until potatoes and vegetables are almost soft. Discard bouquet. Add Fish Stock, fish and flavouring. Cover pan lightly and simmer until fish is done, about 10 minutes. Divide into two soup bowls. Makes 2 servings.

Fish in Chicory Boats

6 oz (180 g) cod fillet	1 teaspoon margarine, melted
3 oz (90 g) peeled, cooked potato	1 teaspoon chopped fresh parsley
2 oz (60 g) large Belgian chicory	$\frac{1}{4}$ teaspoon chopped fresh chives
leaves, separated	$\frac{1}{4}$ teaspoon salt
1 teaspoon tomato purée	$\frac{1}{8}$ teaspoon chopped fresh dill
2 teaspoons water	Pinch onion powder

Put fish and potatoes through mincer. Fill individual chicory leaves with fish mixture. Arrange in a shallow ovenproof casserole. Combine remaining ingredients in a small bowl. Pour over fish boats. Bake in a moderate oven (350°F (180°C), Gas Mark 4) 15 to 20 minutes or until fish is done. Serve in casserole. Makes 1 serving.

Curried Shrimp Salad

Curry and ginger are widely used in Holland . . . seasonings and tastes acquired when the Dutch East Indies were colonized.

1 tablespoon vegetable oil	2 oz (60 g) cooked rice
1 teaspoon lemon juice	$1\frac{1}{2}$ oz (45 g) green pepper, diced
$\frac{3}{4}$ teaspoon curry powder	2 tablespoons chopped fresh parsley
$\frac{1}{2}$ teaspoon salt	Lettuce leaves
4 oz (120 g) cooked shrimps	Parsley sprigs for garnish

Combine first 4 ingredients in medium bowl. Mix in all remaining ingredients, except lettuce and parsley sprigs. Cover and chill. Serve on lettuce leaves and garnish with parsley sprigs. Makes 1 serving.

Kale and Pork

8 oz (240 g) trimmed and washed
  kale
Salted water

8 oz (240 g) roast pork
6 oz (180 g) peeled potato, diced

Cover kale with salted water (about 1 teaspoon salt) and cook until kale is tender. Drain kale (reserve liquid) and chop finely. Put kale back into saucepan with 4 fl oz (120 ml) liquid. Add roast pork, which has been put through mincer, and diced potato. Simmer for 30 minutes or until potatoes are tender. Makes 2 servings.

Golden Velvet Carrots

2 tablespoons low fat spread
12 oz (360 g) whole baby carrots
6 fl oz (180 ml) orange juice

¼ teaspoon vanilla flavouring
⅛ teaspoon cinnamon
Chopped fresh parsley to garnish

Melt low fat spread in top of double boiler over boiling water, then pour into blender goblet. Add 2 oz (60 g) carrots, all the orange juice, vanilla and cinnamon; blend at medium speed until smooth. Return low fat spread mixture to double boiler; add remaining carrots; heat. Garnish with chopped parsley. Makes 6 servings.

Cooked Batavian Endive

1 large head Batavian endive, about
  1 lb 8 oz (720 g)
16 fl oz (480 ml) water
½ teaspoon salt

2 teaspoons margarine
1 slice white bread, made into large
  crumbs
Pinch grated nutmeg

Cut Batavian endive in small pieces, using entire head except for the root end. Wash thoroughly. Cook rapidly in salted water until tender, 20 to 30 minutes. Drain; add the margarine, sprinkle with crumbs and season with nutmeg. Makes 2 servings.

'Creamed' Mushrooms

Herbed White Sauce (recipe follows)   1 tablespoon chopped fresh parsley
1 lb (480 g) raw mushrooms   1 tablespoon chopped chives
1 tablespoon lemon juice

Prepare Herbed White Sauce and keep hot in double boiler. Trim a
thin slice from ends of mushrooms (reserve ends and use in making
stock or soup); wipe the mushroom caps with damp towel. Cut in thin
slices through cap and stem. Cover with water, add lemon juice and
cook until done, about 10 minutes. Drain. Add to sauce and sprinkle
with parsley and chives. Serve hot. Makes 4 servings.

Herbed White Sauce

1 tablespoon margarine   Salt and freshly ground white pepper
1 tablespoon flour   to taste
10 fl oz (300 ml) skim milk   Thyme and marjoram to taste

Melt margarine in top of double boiler over boiling water. Stir flour
thoroughly into melted margarine until mixture is smooth. Slowly add
milk, stirring with wooden spoon. Add seasonings. Cook until mixture
is thick and smooth. Makes 4 servings.

Individual Onion Tart (Tarte à l'Oignon)*

Popular in Belgium as in neighbouring France.

8 oz (240 g) chopped onion   1 teaspoon salt
2 fl oz (60 ml) stock, made with $\frac{1}{4}$ teaspoon pepper
  $\frac{1}{4}$ stock cube   1 slice white bread, made into fine
2 eggs   breadcrumbs
1 oz (30 g) nonfat dry milk,
  reconstituted with 7 fl oz (210 ml)
  water

Preheat oven to 350°F (180°C), Gas Mark 4. Cook onions in 2 fl oz (60 ml) stock over low heat until onions are tender, about 15 minutes. Divide onion mixture evenly into two individual casseroles or baking dishes. Beat eggs, reconstituted milk, salt and pepper until light. Pour an equal amount into each casserole over onions. Sprinkle with breadcrumbs, evenly divided. Set casseroles in pan holding 1 inch (2.5 cm) of hot water. Bake about 25 to 30 minutes, or until set. Serve hot. Makes 2 servings.

Pineapple Dessert 'Cream'

Trade with their colonies brought pineapple to the Netherlands, along with coconut and curry.

1 tablespoon unflavoured gelatine
5 fl oz (150 ml) water
5 fl oz (150 ml) buttermilk
4 oz (120 g) canned crushed
   pineapple, no sugar added

½ teaspoon vanilla flavouring
¼ teaspoon pineapple flavouring
   (optional)
3 ice cubes

Sprinkle gelatine over water in small saucepan; heat slowly until gelatine dissolves. Pour dissolved gelatine into blender goblet; add all remaining ingredients except ice cubes; blend at medium speed until smooth. Turn blender to high speed; add ice cubes one at a time. Pour pineapple mixture into a medium bowl. Chill until set. Makes 1 serving.

Note: Some of the crushed pineapple may be reserved for garnish.

Strawberry Cheese Mousse

10 oz (300 g) cottage cheese
2 oz (60 g) nonfat dry milk
6 fl oz (180 ml) water
2 tablespoons lemon juice
½ teaspoon vanilla flavouring

½ teaspoon salt
Atificial sweetener to equal 3
   tablespoons sugar, or to taste
2 tablespoons unflavoured gelatine
10 oz (300 g) strawberries, sliced

In blender goblet, blend cheese, milk, 4 fl oz (120 ml) water, lemon juice, flavouring, salt and sweetener until smooth. Transfer to bowl. Pour remaining water into small saucepan. Sprinkle gelatine over it to soften. Place over low heat, stirring until dissolved. Pour into cheese mixture and mix well. Fold in strawberries. Pour into dessert mould and chill until set. Makes 2 servings.

THE BRITISH ISLES

*

There's a lot more to British food than roast beef, although this is still the dish which foreign visitors look for first! After that, of course, comes the famous British breakfast, and it's good to realise that you can still enjoy this while following the Programme.

In our round-up of 'home grown' recipes, we've included Cock-a-Leekie from Scotland, Welsh Cawl, and some light desserts using the best of our Summer fruits.

Scotch Broth

4 oz (120 g) cooked lamb, cut into
  small pieces
12 fl oz (360 ml) water
4 oz (120 g) diced celery
  (including leaves)
2 oz (60 g) diced carrots

2 oz (60 g) diced turnip
1 tablespoon dried onion flakes or
  1 oz (30 g) diced onion
Salt and pepper to taste
2 oz (60 g) cooked barley
2 tablespoons chopped fresh parsley

Place all ingredients except barley, salt, pepper and parsley in a saucepan. Bring to the boil. Reduce heat, add salt and pepper. Simmer covered, until vegetables are tender. Stir in barley; serve generously sprinkled with chopped parsley. Season to taste. Makes 1 serving.

Jellied Beef Stock

6 fl oz (180 ml) Homemade Beef
  Stock (see page 10), or beef
  stock, made with ½ stock cube
  or water with 1 teaspoon beef
  stock powder

1½ teaspoons unflavoured gelatine
Lemon wedge
Watercress or parsley

Pour Homemade Beef Stock or water and stock powder into small
saucepan; sprinkle with gelatine. Heat, stirring, until gelatine dissolves.
Pour into small bowl; cover and chill until almost set. Stir just before
serving. Serve with lemon wedge and watercress or parsley. Makes 1
serving.

Celery 'Cream' with Bread Squares

Cauliflower florets may be cooked this same way.

12 oz (360 g) diced celery (including
  leaves)
16 fl oz (480 ml) water
2 teaspoons chicken stock powder or
  1 stock cube
Nutmeg (freshly grated if possible)
  to taste

1 oz (30 g) nonfat dry milk,
  reconstituted with 7 fl oz (210 ml)
  water
1 slice white bread, toasted and cut
  into 8 pieces

Cover celery with boiling salted water and let stand for 2 minutes.
Drain and put into saucepan with 16 fl oz (480 ml) water. Cook for 20
minutes; add stock powder or crushed stock cube and nutmeg; cook
for 10 minutes longer. Place in blender goblet. Blend at medium speed
until smooth. Return to saucepan; stir in milk and water; heat without
boiling and spoon evenly into 2 bowls. Float 4 pieces of toast in each
bowl. Serve hot. Makes 2 servings.

Cock-a-Leekie

This Scottish soup is named for the chicken and leeks which compose it. Be sure the leeks are thoroughly washed. Remove some of green top and roots before weighing.

8 fl oz (240 ml) chicken stock,
  made with ½ stock cube
2 oz (60 g) leeks, diced
Bouquet garni (see page 113-114)

8 oz (240 g) cooked chicken,
  shredded
1 tablespoon chopped fresh parsley
Freshly ground pepper to taste

Combine stock, leeks and bouquet garni in small saucepan. Bring to the boil; simmer 20 minutes. Remove bouquet. Divide chicken evenly into 2 warm soup bowls. Pour soup over chicken. Garnish with parsley. Season at table with freshly ground pepper. Makes 2 servings.

    Note: 2 oz (60 g) cooked rice may be served with each portion of Cock-a-Leekie.

Carrot-Celery Soufflé*

5 fl oz (150 ml) skim milk
1 slice white bread, made into
  crumbs
1 egg, separated

3 oz (90 g) mashed cooked carrots
2 oz (60 g) finely chopped celery
Salt and pepper to taste

Combine milk, breadcrumbs and egg yolk in a small saucepan. Place over low heat. Heat, stirring, until thick. Remove from heat and add carrots and celery; season to taste. Beat egg white with rotary beater until stiff peaks form. Fold into mixture. Turn into a soufflé or other ovenproof dish. Bake at 400°F (200°C), Gas Mark 6, for 30 minutes. Makes 1 serving.

Buckingham Eggs

2 teaspoons margarine
2 slices white bread, toasted
2 eggs

¼ teaspoon Worcester sauce
2 × 1 oz (30 g) slices hard cheese

Spread margarine over the toast. Scramble eggs in preheated nonstick pan (slightly underdone). Sprinkle with Worcester sauce. Spread on toast and top with cheese. Bake in hot oven (450°F (230°C), Gas Mark 8) until cheese melts. Makes 2 servings.

Cod-Swede Bake, Dublin Style

12 oz (360 g) cod fillets
4 oz (120 g) onion, chopped
1 teaspoon lemon juice
2 teaspoons chicken stock powder
4 oz (120 g) cooked swede

6 oz (180 g) cooked potato
¼ teaspoon salt
2 teaspoons low fat spread
Paprika

In nonstick frying pan, cook cod, onion, lemon juice and stock powder, turning occasionally, until fish flakes. Mash the swede and potatoes together; stir in salt. Spread one quarter of the swede mixture on the bottom of each of 2 individual heatproof casseroles; top each evenly with fish mixture and remaining swede mixture. Dot each casserole with 1 teaspoon low fat spread; sprinkle with paprika. Bake at 350°F (180°C), Gas Mark 4 for 30 minutes. Makes 2 servings.

Finnan Haddock Stew

1 lb (480 g) cooked finnan haddock
1 pint 4 fl oz (720 ml) Homemade
   Chicken Stock (see page 10), or
   stock made with 1½ stock
   cubes
8 oz (240 g) cooked mushrooms,
   sliced through cap and stem
1 tablespoon chopped fresh chives

1½ teaspoons lemon juice
1 teaspoon fresh basil
¼ teaspoon onion powder
2 oz (60 g) nonfat dry milk,
   reconstituted with 10 fl oz
   (300 ml) water
Salt and pepper to taste
2 teaspoons chopped fresh parsley

Flake fish and place in saucepan. Add stock, mushrooms, chives, lemon juice, basil and onion powder. Simmer over low heat for 5 minutes; add milk. Reheat, *but do not boil*. Season. Sprinkle with parsley and serve. Makes 4 servings.

Baked Salmon with Caper Sauce

4 × 8 oz (240 g) salmon steaks (or
  bream, cod, flounder, haddock,
  mackerel, etc.)
12 oz (360 g) tomatoes, peeled and
  chopped
2 tablespoons chopped fresh chives

Salt and pepper to taste
Pinch grated nutmeg
4 fl oz (120 ml) water
Caper Sauce (recipe follows)
Lemon wedges and dill for garnish

Place steaks in baking dish. Top with tomatoes. Sprinkle with chives, salt, pepper and grated nutmeg. Add water. Bake at 350°F (180°C), Gas Mark 4, for 20 to 30 minutes, basting fish several times with liquid. Serve with Caper Sauce. Garnish with lemon wedges and dill. Makes 4 servings.

Caper Sauce

4 teaspoons margarine, melted
1 teaspoon capers, rinsed and cut in
  halves

$\frac{1}{4}$ teaspoon lemon juice or mild
  vinegar
$\frac{1}{2}$ teaspoon chopped fresh parsley
Salt and pepper to taste

Combine ingredients for sauce in small ovenproof bowl. Set bowl in hot water bath and let stand for 10 minutes while fish bakes. Stir occasionally. Makes 4 servings.

Jellied Whiting

1 lb (480 g) cleaned whole
  whiting (net weight after head, tail
  and fins are removed) or
  12 oz (360 g) fillets
3 fl oz (90 ml) cider vinegar
1 pint 10 fl oz (900 ml) water
$\frac{1}{2}$ teaspoon salt

1 bay leaf
2 teaspoons whole mixed pickling
  spice
$\frac{1}{2}$ teaspoon dried onion flakes
$\frac{1}{4}$ lemon, sliced
4 oz (120 g) onion, sliced

Cut fish into 1$\frac{1}{2}$-inch (4 cm) squares; refrigerate. Combine vinegar, water, salt, bay leaf, pickling spice and onion flakes in a saucepan; boil 15 minutes. Add lemon, cook 5 minutes more. Remove lemon. Add fish and simmer 10 minutes. Layer fish and sliced onions in a dish and add the liquid. Cool. Chill at least 1 hour before serving. Makes 2 servings.

Pressed Chicken

2 tablespoons unflavoured gelatine
12 fl oz (360 ml) chicken stock,
  made with 1 stock cube
2 tablespoons mayonnaise
8 oz (240 g) diced, cooked or
  drained canned boned chicken (no
  skin)

6 oz (180 g) cooked peas
3 oz (90 g) pickled cucumber,
  chopped
Lettuce

Soften gelatine in 2 fl oz (60 ml) stock in a saucepan; add remaining stock; place over low heat and stir occasionally until gelatine is dissolved, 3 to 4 minutes. Cool slightly. Add mayonnaise; stir to combine. Add chicken, peas and pickled cucumber; mix well. Pour into baking tin or mould; chill until firm. Slice into 2 equal portions and serve garnished with lettuce. Makes 2 servings.

Monday Hot Pot

A tasty way of using the meat left from Sunday's roast beef.

3 oz (90 g) peeled potato, diced
2 oz (60 g) diced onion
4 fl oz (120 ml) onion stock
  made with ¼ stock cube, or water
4 oz (120 g) cooked broccoli or
  cabbage, chopped

4 oz (120 g) cooked lean roast beef,
  cut in pieces
2 teaspoons vinegar (optional)
Salt and pepper to taste (optional)
Worcester sauce (optional)

Use a small flameproof cook-and-serve pan. Cover the potato and onion with onion stock or water and cook until liquid is almost evaporated and potato is tender. Mix in broccoli or cabbage, meat and vinegar (optional); heat thoroughly for 15 minutes, stirring occasionally. To keep hot, put pan on asbestos mat over low flame. If liquid evaporates, add more onion stock as necessary. Season to taste if desired. Makes 1 serving. Serve with pickled gherkins.

Shepherd's Pie

1 pint 12 fl oz (960 ml) water
12 oz (360 g) peeled potatoes, diced
12 oz (360 g) diced celery
2 tablespoons dried onion flakes
Salt and freshly ground pepper to
   taste
1 lb (480 g) cooked beef or
   lamb, cut into thin, even slices

6 oz (180 g) fresh sliced mushrooms
4 fl oz (120 ml) reserved potato
   liquid
1 teaspoon beef stock powder
1 tablespoon Worcester sauce

Combine water, potatoes, celery and onion flakes in a large saucepan. Cook over medium heat until potatoes are tender, about 15 minutes. Drain and reserve liquid. Place potato-celery mixture in the blender goblet and blend to form a purée. Season with salt and pepper. Line the bottom of a 9 × 5 × 3-inch (23 × 13 × 8 cm) baking tin with half the purée. In a large bowl combine beef, mushrooms, 4 fl oz (120 ml) reserved liquid, stock powder and Worcester sauce. Mix well. Transfer to baking tin. Top with remaining potato-celery mixture. Score top lengthwise and crosswise. Bake at 375°F (190°C), Gas Mark 5, for 30 minutes or until pie is heated through and top begins to brown. Makes 4 servings.

Sweetbread and Cucumber Salad

4 oz (120 g) cooked calf sweetbread,
   thinly sliced (see page 131 for
   directions for cooking
   sweetbreads)
2 oz (60 g) shredded lettuce
2 oz (60 g) cooked peas or diced
   artichoke hearts

1 tablespoon mayonnaise
$\frac{1}{2}$ teaspoon lemon juice
$1\frac{1}{2}$ teaspoons chopped fresh herbs
   (chives, tarragon, dill or parsley)
6 oz (180 g) cucumber, peeled and
   thinly sliced

Arrange the sweetbread on lettuce in a salad bowl. Sprinkle peas or artichoke hearts on top. Combine mayonnaise with lemon juice and herbs. Mix well and pile onto sweetbread. Make a border of cucumber slices. Chill before serving. Makes 1 serving.

Spiced Grilled Beef

4 fl oz (120 ml) cold water
1 small bay leaf, crumbled
¼ teaspoon grated lemon rind
¼ teaspoon allspice
¼ teaspoon ginger

⅛ teaspoon mace
⅛ teaspoon ground cloves
1 lb 8 oz (720 g) rump or top rump, in a
  piece

Combine water, bay leaf, lemon rind, allspice, ginger, mace and cloves in saucepan. Bring to the boil, then pour over steak. Marinate several hours or up to 2 days. Turn steak several times if it is not completely immersed in marinade. Drain before use; reserve marinade. Grill steak on a rack 5 minutes on each side, basting with marinade, either under a moderate grill or over charcoal that has turned ash-grey. Remove steak to carving board and cut thin slices diagonally across the grain. Makes 4 servings.

Jellied Beef Mould

6 oz (180 g) boneless lean shin beef
  (or chuck)
1½ oz (45 g) chopped celery
2 oz (60 g) onion, diced
3 oz (90 g) pickled cucumber, diced
1 teaspoon chopped fresh parsley
6 strips pimiento

1 tablespoon unflavoured gelatine
2 tablespoons water
12 fl oz (360 ml) beef stock, made
  with 1 stock cube
Salt and pepper to taste
Lettuce

Grill beef on rack 4 inches (10 cm) from source of heat. Put through mincer (coarse blade); set aside. Cook celery and onion in water until tender but firm; drain, add to meat with pickled cucumber and chopped parsley. Arrange pimiento strips on the bottom of a small baking tin. Spoon in beef mixture. Sprinkle gelatine over water in small saucepan to soften. Add stock; place over low heat (2 to 3 minutes). Stir until dissolved. Remove; season if necessary. Pour over beef; chill for 2 to 3 hours. Turn out on lettuce and serve. Makes 1 serving.

'Sherried' Kidneys and Mushrooms

6 oz (180 g) veal kidney, cut in
  ½-inch (1 cm) cubes
2 oz (60 g) chopped onion
1½ oz (45 g) mushrooms, quartered
1½ oz (45 g) green pepper, finely
  chopped
4 teaspoons tomato purée

2 tablespoons water
½ teaspoon sherry flavouring
Gravy browning (optional)
Salt and pepper to taste
8 fl oz (240 ml) beef stock, made
  with ½ stock cube
1 teaspoon chopped fresh parsley

Grill kidney on rack, 4 inches (10 cm) from source of heat, until done, about 5 minutes. Turn once. Combine in pan with onions, mushrooms, pepper and stock. Simmer until pepper is tender. Add tomato purée, water, flavouring and gravy browning, if desired. Simmer an additional 10 minutes or until mixture thickens slightly. Season to taste with salt and pepper. Serve garnished with chopped parsley. Makes 1 serving.

Welsh Cawl

6 oz (180 g) lean boneless lamb
  (shoulder, chop, etc.) or 4 oz
  (120 g) roast lamb
3 oz (90 g) peeled potato, diced
1 oz (30 g) onion, chopped
1 oz (30 g) celery, chopped
2 oz (60 g) carrot or 2 oz (60 g)
  parsnip, cut in 2 pieces
⅛ teaspoon thyme

⅛ teaspoon rosemary
16 fl oz (480 ml) water
Salt and pepper to taste
1 oz (30 g) cooked peas or diced
  artichoke hearts
6 oz (180 g) cooked asparagus,
  cauliflower, green beans, etc.,
  cut up
1 teaspoon chopped fresh parsley

If using uncooked lamb, grill on rack 4 inches (10 cm) from heat, about 5 minutes on each side. Remove; cool and cut into 1-inch (2.5 cm) pieces. If using roast lamb, cut into 1-inch (2.5 cm) pieces. Combine lamb with potato, onion, celery, carrot (or parsnips), thyme and rosemary in a saucepan. Pour in water; bring to the boil, season to taste. Simmer, uncovered, 25 minutes or until sauce is thick and lamb tender. Add peas or artichoke hearts and asparagus, etc. Reheat. Sprinkle with parsley and serve. The meat is served in the middle of the plate, surrounded by the vegetables. The pan liquid can be combined with beef stock and used as a separate course or served over the meat and vegetables. Makes 1 serving.

Lamb Brochette with Rice

12 oz (360 g) boned leg of lamb, cut
   in 1-inch (2.5 cm) pieces
6 oz (180 g) green pepper, cut in
   1-inch (2.5 cm) pieces
3 oz (90 g) tomatoes, cut in wedges
½ small pineapple, cut in 1-inch
   (2.5 cm) pieces
2 oz (60 g) onion, finely chopped
4 fl oz (120 ml) water
2 fl oz (60 ml) white vinegar

1 teaspoon curry powder
½ teaspoon salt
¼ teaspoon turmeric
¼ teaspoon paprika
¼ teaspoon pepper
8 teaspoons tomato purée mixed with
   2 fl oz (60 ml) water
Gravy browning (optional)
4 oz (120 g) cooked rice

Combine lamb, green pepper, tomatoes, pineapple and onion in large mixing bowl. Add water, vinegar, curry powder, salt, turmeric, paprika and pepper. Mix well and marinate for 4 hours. Drain off liquid and reserve. Thread even amounts of lamb, pepper, tomato and pineapple alternately on each of two skewers. Grill on a rack 4 inches (10 cm) from heat, 12 to 15 minutes, turning frequently until meat is cooked. Add marinade liquid to tomato purée mixed with water and cook over low heat until thick; then add gravy browning as desired. Place each skewer on 2 oz (60 g) rice. Divide sauce evenly and serve. Makes 2 servings.

Boiled Brussels Sprouts with Lemon Balls

Lemon Balls (recipe follows)
1 lb (480 g) Brussels sprouts

½ teaspoon salt

Prepare Lemon Balls and refrigerate. Cut a cross at the base of each sprout to speed cooking. Cover sprouts with boiling water and add salt. Bring to the boil. Cook until tender, 10 to 14 minutes. Drain and keep hot for a few minutes until ready to serve. Serve with a separate lemon ball for each portion, to be stirred into the vegetable at the table. Makes 4 servings.

Lemon Balls

8 teaspoons low fat spread
2 teaspoons grated lemon rind

2 teaspoons chopped fresh parsley

Cream ingredients together. Shape into 4 equal balls and refrigerate until ready to use. Makes 4 servings.

Vegetable Hotch Potch

1 pint 4 fl oz (720 ml) water
1 tablespoon beef stock powder or
  1½ beef stock cubes
3 tablespoons dried onion flakes or
  3 oz (90 g) diced onion
3 oz (90 g) finely chopped carrot
2 oz (60 g) diced turnip

3 oz (90 g) cauliflower florets
4 oz (120 g) drained, canned cut
  green beans
2 oz (60 g) diced celery
1 bouquet garni (see page 113)
1 oz (30 g) shredded lettuce
1 tablespoon chopped fresh parsley

Combine water, stock powder, onion flakes, carrot, turnip, cauliflower, beans, celery and bouquet garni in saucepan. Simmer, covered, 20 minutes. Add lettuce and simmer 10 minutes. Remove bouquet and serve hot with parsley garnish. Makes 2 servings.

Spinach and Egg Salad*

1 oz (30 g) young spinach leaves
1 cut garlic clove
2 oz (60 g) diced spring onions
2 teaspoons vinegar or lemon juice

1 tablespoon vegetable oil
Salt and pepper
1 egg, hard-boiled and
  quartered

Wash the spinach until free from grit, dry thoroughly. Rub salad bowl with cut clove of garlic. Add spinach and spring onions. Add vinegar to oil; season with salt and pepper, pour over the spinach and mix well. Border with sections of egg and serve. Makes 1 serving.

Peach Rice Custard*

2 oz (60 g) cooked rice
4 oz (120 g) canned sliced peaches,
no sugar added, drained (reserve
juice)

1 egg
10 fl oz (300 ml) skim milk
¼ teaspoon lemon juice
Pinch nutmeg

Combine rice and peaches in casserole. Beat egg with milk and juices in small bowl. Stir into rice; sprinkle with nutmeg. Place casserole in pan containing approximately 1 inch (2.5 cm) of water. Bake at 350°F (180°C), Gas Mark 4, for 25 minutes or until set. Serve hot or cold. Makes 1 serving.

Strawberry Fool

1 lb 4 oz (600 g) ripe whole
strawberries
Artificial sweetener to taste

1 teaspoon lemon juice or sherry
flavouring (optional)
Whipped Topping
(see page 12)

Slice all but 4 strawberries. If they are sweet and ripe, added sweetener may not be necessary. Otherwise sprinkle it and juice or flavouring on fruit as desired. Let stand a few minutes while you prepare Whipped Topping. Fold sliced fruit into topping; divide evenly into 4 glass dessert dishes. Top each with 1 reserved strawberry. Chill until ready to serve. This can be prepared just before dinner. Makes 4 servings.

Rhubarb Fool

Whipped Topping
(see page 12)
1 lb 2 oz (540 g) cooked rhubarb
Artificial sweetener to taste

2 slices dried white bread (remove
and reserve crusts)
1 teaspoon vanilla flavouring
Cinnamon and artificial sweetener
(optional)

Prepare Whipped Topping. Purée the rhubarb in blender goblet. Add sweetener. Transfer to bowl. Cut trimmed bread into 16 pieces and mix with rhubarb and vanilla flavouring. Fold in Whipped Topping and spoon evenly into 4 tall glasses. Refrigerate. Make crumbs of bread crusts and mix with cinnamon and artificial sweetener, if desired. Sprinkle over parfaits before serving. Makes 4 servings.

A Cup of Tea

Tea is still undoubtedly our national drink, although coffee runs it a close second these days. Try the many different types of tea, and also herb teas which are becoming popular.

Weak tea without milk is very refreshing, and may be flavoured with lemon juice, orange peel, or even spices such as ginger and cinnamon.

If you have fresh herbs in the garden, try making your own herb teas, using about 1 tablespoon of the crushed leaves for each serving. Cover with boiling water, leave for 10 to 15 minutes and strain.

CANADA

*

The Canadian cuisine is hard to classify. Like a stew in which none of the ingredients lose their distinct form, Canada is a mixture of English, French, Indian and other separate national groups, each living in its own geographical pocket and each, therefore, preserving its own food customs.

But throughout Canada, everybody enjoys the fish which comes from its abundant lakes and streams and the syrup tapped from its towering maples. Canadian fish include bass, pike, salmon, trout and whitefish, much of it frozen and exported to the United States.

Pea Soup Quebec Style

Potage St. Germain in France. It is best with fresh peas but frozen may be used. 3 oz (90 g) combined vegetable trimmings (lettuce, celery leaves, parsley, watercress, etc.) may be shredded and cooked with the peas. Curry powder is a popular seasoning for this soup, or use hot pepper sauce or Worcester sauce for a 'hotter' flavour.

16 fl oz (480 ml) water (see note)
1 teaspoon chicken stock powder
6 oz (180 g) fresh or frozen green
  peas

1 oz (30 g) diced onion
Salt and pepper to taste
Green food colouring, if desired
2 sprigs fresh mint

Combine water, stock powder, peas and onion in saucepan. Simmer, covered, for 30 minutes. Put through food mill or strainer, or blend in blender until smooth. Add seasoning and colouring, if desired. Serve hot, garnished with mint. Makes 2 servings.

Note: Or replace 16 fl oz (480 ml) water and stock powder with 12 fl oz (360 ml) Homemade Chicken Stock (see page 10 for recipe) and 4 fl oz (120 ml) water.

'Cream' of Pea Soup

Heat ½ oz (15 g) nonfat dry milk reconstituted with 2½ fl oz (75 ml) water in double boiler. Add Pea Soup Quebec and heat thoroughly. Season to taste with nutmeg or hot pepper sauce or Worcester sauce. Makes 2 servings.

Pumpkin Stuffed with Frankfurters

1 × 12 oz (360 g) pumpkin, yields
  8 oz (240 g)
½ teaspoon maple flavouring

6 oz (180 g) cocktail frankfurters
2 teaspoons margarine
Pinch cinnamon

Wash and cut pumpkin in half. Remove seeds. Bake pumpkin cut side down on foil-lined shallow baking tin at 375°F (190°C), Gas Mark 5 for 40 minutes. Remove from oven. Stir ¼ teaspoon maple flavouring into each half. Place 4 oz (120 g) cocktail frankfurters in each pumpkin half. Return to baking tin. Reduce oven to 350°F (180°C), Gas Mark 4, and bake 30 minutes. Dot each half with one teaspoon margarine and pinch of cinnamon and return to oven for a minute. Makes 2 servings.

Scotia Stew

Just one of the many ways in which Canadians serve the products of their lakes and rivers. If frozen fillets are used, defrost first. 3 oz (90 g) green beans or asparagus could be cooked with the carrots.

6 fl oz (180 ml) water
3 oz (90 g) peeled potato, diced
3 oz (90 g) diced carrots
1 oz (30 g) diced onion or 1
  tablespoon dried onion flakes
Salt and pepper to taste
8 oz (240 g) fish fillets, cut in
  chunks

1 oz (30 g) nonfat dry milk,
  reconstituted with 5 fl oz (150 ml)
  water
1 tablespoon low fat spread
Freshly ground pepper
Chopped fresh parsley

Heat water to boiling in medium saucepan. Add potato, carrots, onion and salt. Cover and simmer until potato and carrots are tender; 25 to 30 minutes. Add fish, simmer, covered, 10 additional minutes or until fish flakes when tested with fork. Stir in milk. Heat through; *do not boil*. Remove from heat. Stir in low fat spread. Sprinkle fresh pepper and parsley on top. Makes 1 serving.

Ham and Macaroni Salad

3 oz (90 g) boiled ham, cut into
  ¼-inch (5 mm) strips
2 oz (60 g) cooked elbow macaroni
1 tablespoon mayonnaise
½ oz (15 g) diced pimiento
2 teaspoons white vinegar

1 teaspoon chopped fresh parsley
1 oz (30 g) diced onion or
  ½ teaspoon dried onion flakes
Salt and pepper to taste
Lettuce

Combine all ingredients except lettuce in mixing bowl. Allow to chill at least one hour. Serve on a bed of lettuce. Makes 1 serving.

'Creamy' Carrot Pudding

4 eggs
10 oz (300 g) cottage cheese
4 oz (120 g) finely shredded carrots

½ teaspoon vanilla flavouring
¼ teaspoon salt

Beat eggs in medium bowl. Stir in remaining ingredients. Pour into four individual ovenproof dishes. Bake at 325°F (160°C), Gas Mark 3, for about 1 hour. Makes 4 servings.

Cauliflower and Cheese Puff

3 oz (90 g) cauliflower florets
2 oz (60 g) Cheddar cheese, grated
1 slice white bread
2 teaspoons prepared mustard
2 teaspoons mayonnaise

2 eggs
10 fl oz (300 ml) skim milk
½ teaspoon paprika
Pinch salt and pepper

Cook cauliflower florets in boiling water to barely cover; drain and transfer to 9 × 5 × 3-inch (23 × 13 × 8 cm) nonstick baking tin. Top with grated cheese. Slice bread horizontally to make two slices. Spread one side of each slice with 1 teaspoon mustard and the other side with 1 teaspoon mayonnaise. Place bread, mustard side up, on cheese. Beat remaining ingredients in small bowl; pour over bread. Bake at 400°F (200°C), Gas Mark 6, 35 to 40 minutes. Remove from oven. Heat the grill. Place loaf under grill, 4 inches (10 cm) from source of heat until top is golden brown. Makes 2 servings.

Spinach-Cheese Ring

1 tablespoon unflavoured gelatine
2 fl oz (60 ml) cold water
4 fl oz (120 ml) boiling water
5 oz (150 g) cottage cheese
2 oz (60 g) blue cheese
1 teaspoon beef stock powder
1 tablespoon chopped fresh chives

4 oz (120 g) chopped spinach
1 oz (30 g) finely chopped celery
Shredded lettuce
3 oz (90 g) small tomatoes
Spinach leaves
Radish roses

In blender goblet, sprinkle gelatine over cold water to soften. Pour in boiling water. Blend at low speed until gelatine is dissolved. Add cottage cheese, blue cheese, stock powder and chives; blend at medium speed until smooth. Chill until the consistency of unbeaten egg whites. Fold in spinach and celery. Pour into a ring mould. Chill until firm. Turn out. Fill centre with small tomatoes. Garnish with spinach leaves and radish roses. Makes 2 servings.

Bilberry Tartlets

1 slice currant bread, cut in quarters   5 oz (150 g) bilberries
2 teaspoons unflavoured gelatine   ¼ teaspoon lemon juice
2 fl oz (60 ml) water

Roll bread with a rolling pin, until quite thin. Press 2 pieces of bread in each of 2 patty tins, keeping the crust round the top edges. Sprinkle with water, if necessary to make it pliable. Bake at 300°F (150°C), Gas Mark 2, for 10 minutes or until firm. Remove from tins; set aside and cool. In a saucepan sprinkle gelatine over water and add bilberries and lemon juice. Place over low heat and stir until gelatine dissolves. Remove from heat. Strain, reserving liquid, and cool. Divide berries evenly into each tartlet. Chill liquid until it becomes syrupy. Spoon evenly divided into tartlets and chill. Makes 2 servings.

Three-Layer Moulded Apple Custard*

12 fl oz (360 ml) water
3 tablespoons unflavoured gelatine
Artificial sweetener to equal 5
   teaspoons sugar, or to taste
1 medium apple, peeled, diced and
   sprinkled with 1 teaspoon lemon
   juice
3 drops red food colouring

2 eggs, slightly beaten
10 fl oz (300 ml) skim milk
1 oz (30 g) nonfat dry milk,
   reconstituted with 5 fl oz (150 ml)
   water
1 teaspoon freshly grated lemon rind
3 drops green food colouring
Mint sprigs for garnish

Pour 8 fl oz (240 ml) water into saucepan. Sprinkle 1 tablespoon gelatine over water to soften. Add sweetener to equal 3 teaspoons sugar. Place over low heat and stir until gelatine is dissolved. Remove from heat. Add apple and red food colouring. Mix to combine. Pour into a medium mould and chill until firm. Sprinkle 1 tablespoon gelatine over 2 fl oz (60 ml) water; set aside. In top of double boiler, combine eggs, skim milk and sweetener to equal 1 teaspoon sugar and heat over boiling water, stirring until mixture is slightly thickened. Add softened gelatine, stirring until dissolved, and pour over apple mixture. Chill until firm. Sprinkle remaining 1 tablespoon gelatine over 2 fl oz (60 ml) water in small saucepan to soften. Place over low heat and stir until gelatine dissolves. Remove from heat. In a large mixing bowl combine reconstituted milk, lemon rind, remaining sweetener to equal 1 teaspoon sugar, dissolved gelatine and green food colouring. Beat with rotary beater until peaks form. Spread evenly over egg layer in mould. Chill until set. Turn out and garnish with mint. Makes 2 servings.

Rhubarb and Strawberry Mould with Lemon 'Cream' Topping

1 lb 2 oz (540 g) fresh rhubarb, sliced
16 fl oz (480 ml) water
Artificial sweetener to equal 6 teaspoons sugar, or to taste
2 tablespoons unflavoured gelatine

$\frac{1}{2}$ teaspoon strawberry flavouring
Red food colouring
10 oz (300 g) strawberries, sliced
Lemon wedges to garnish
Lemon 'Cream' (recipe follows)

Combine rhubarb and 12 fl oz (360 ml) water in a saucepan. Add sweetener; simmer over low heat until rhubarb is tender but firm. Sprinkle gelatine over remaining water and let stand to soften. Add to rhubarb, stirring gently until gelatine dissolves. Remove from heat. Add flavouring and colour as desired. Let cool slightly. Fold in strawberries. Pour into medium mould rinsed in cold water and refrigerate until set. Turn out. Garnish with lemon wedges. Serve with Lemon 'Cream'. Makes 4 servings.

Lemon 'Cream' Topping

1 tablespoon unflavoured gelatine
2 fl oz (60 ml) cold water
4 fl oz (120 ml) boiling water
2 oz (60 g) nonfat dry milk

1 teaspoon freshly grated lemon rind
1 teaspoon lemon juice
6 to 8 ice cubes
Lemon slices

Soften gelatine in cold water in blender goblet. Add boiling water; blend until smooth. Add all remaining ingredients except ice cubes and lemon slices. Blend. Add ice cubes one at a time, blending after each addition. Pour into serving dish. Garnish with lemon slices. Serve immediately. Makes 4 servings.

CARIBBEAN AND WEST INDIES

*

Very few of us are lucky enough to visit the enchanting islands of the West Indies, but we can all enjoy recipes inspired by their native foods. The foods of the West Indies are exceedingly varied, since the islands are inhabited by many different kinds of people including African, British, Chinese, Dutch, French, Indian, Scandinavian, Spanish and North American groups, all with culinary traditions and preferences of their own. But overall there is a lively West Indian cuisine which accents native fish and shellfish, tropical fruits and vegetables and some typical spices. All are sampled in recipe form in the next pages.

Pumpkin Soup (Sopa de Zapallo)

8 oz (240 g) cooked pumpkin purée, fresh or canned
16 fl oz (480 ml) tomato juice
8 fl oz (240 ml) chicken stock, made with ½ stock cube
6 oz (180 g) green pepper, diced
1 tablespoon dried onion flakes

Pinch of cayenne pepper
½ bay leaf
1 oz (30 g) nonfat dry milk, reconstituted with 5 fl oz (150 ml) water
Salt and pepper to taste
1 tablespoon chopped fresh parsley

Combine pumpkin, tomato juice, stock, green pepper and onion flakes in a saucepan. Bring to the boil; add cayenne and bay leaf. Simmer until green pepper is tender. Add milk; season to taste. Reheat, but *do not boil*. Sprinkle with parsley. Makes 4 servings.

Calaloo Soup-Stew

A caribbean favourite, originally made with crab.

8 oz (240 g) spinach or turnip tops,
  coarsely chopped
12 oz (360 g) drained okra, fresh,
  frozen or canned
2 oz (60 g) finely chopped celery
1 pint 4 fl oz (720 ml) water
4 tablespoons tomato purée mixed with
  3 fl oz (90 ml) water

¼ teaspoon thyme
½ bay leaf
Salt and pepper to taste
½ small hot red pepper (optional)
1 lb 8 oz (720 g) fish fillets, cut in
  1-inch (2.5 cm) pieces

In saucepan combine spinach or turnip tops, slices of fresh or frozen okra and celery with water; bring to the boil and cook for 6 minutes. Add tomato purée mixed with water, thyme, bay leaf, salt, pepper and hot red pepper if desired. (If you are using canned okra, add it now.) Place the fish pieces on top; bring to the boil and lower heat to simmering temperature. Let simmer until fish flakes, about 10 minutes, basting several times with liquid from pan. Makes 4 servings.

Baked Lemon-Lime Bass or Trout

6 oz (180 g) trout or bass fillets
Salt and pepper (or hot pepper
  sauce) to taste
2 fl oz (60 ml) chicken stock
  made with ¼ stock cube
1 oz (30 g) chopped celery
1 tablespoon fresh lime or lemon
  juice

4 to 5 parsley sprigs
1 slice fresh white bread, made into
  crumbs
1 teaspoon chopped fresh parsley
1 teaspoon low fat spread
1 lemon wedge, peeled and finely
  chopped

Season fish with salt and pepper. Place in baking dish. Add stock, celery, lime juice and parsley sprigs. Bake in hot oven (400°F (200°C), Gas Mark 6) for 20 minutes or until easily flaked with fork, basting frequently. Place fish on a flameproof dish. Mix together breadcrumbs, parsley, low fat spread and lemon. Sprinkle on fish. Reheat in oven or under grill for about one minute, and serve. Makes 1 serving.

Shrimps Haiti

2 oz (60 g) finely chopped onion
4 fl oz (120 ml) chicken stock,
   made with ¼ stock cube
4 teaspoons tomato purée
2 tablespoons water
½ garlic clove, crushed
3 oz (90 g) tomato, peeled and
   chopped

1½ oz (45 g) green pepper, blanched
   and diced
Salt and pepper to taste
4 oz (120 g) cooked shrimps
2 oz (60 g) cooked white rice
2 teaspoons chopped fresh parsley

Lightly brown onion in nonstick frying pan. Add stock, purée, water, garlic, tomato and green pepper. Simmer 5 minutes or until pepper is tender; season to taste. Add shrimps, rice and parsley. Heat and serve. Makes 1 serving.

Chicken Curry Trinidad

Curries are popular in Trinidad where so many Indians have settled and where they continue to make their own curry powder, in the old tradition, and as you can do, following our recipe. As a general rule allow 1 tablespoon curry powder for every 2 lbs (960 g) of meat and poultry; a lesser amount for fish, shellfish and vegetables—and for people with timid palates. Hot curries are usually served over rice.

6 oz (180 g) onion, finely chopped
16 fl oz (480 ml) chicken stock,
   made with 1 stock cube
2 garlic cloves, crushed
1 or 2 tablespoons Caribbean Curry
   Powder (recipe follows)
1 lb 8 oz (720 g) diced cooked
   chicken or turkey
6 oz (180 g) peeled and sliced
   courgettes or marrow

9 oz (270 g) peeled and diced
   aubergine
12 oz (360 g) peeled and sliced
   christophene (chayote)
1 or more fresh hot chillies, seeded
   and chopped
1 teaspoon fresh lime or lemon juice
Salt to taste

Cook onions in large pan in small amount of stock until golden; add garlic and curry powder and cook, stirring, for 3 to 4 minutes. Add all remaining ingredients except lime juice and salt. Cover and simmer gently until vegetables are cooked. Stir in lime juice and add salt to taste. Makes 6 servings.

Caribbean Curry Powder

2 tablespoons cumin seeds
1 tablespoon coriander seeds
1 tablespoon mustard seeds, preferably brown
1 tablespoon whole cloves

1 tablespoon peppercorns
2 tablespoons ground turmeric
1 tablespoon ground ginger, preferably Jamaican

Toast the cumin, coriander and mustard seeds in a heavy iron frying pan until the mustard seeds begin to jump about. Add cloves and pepper; grind in a mortar or in an electric blender; then mix with the turmeric and ginger. Put through a fine sieve and store in a glass jar. Makes about 3 oz (90 g).

Baked Ham with Piquant Orange-Flavoured Sauce (Jambon à la Bigarade)

3 lb (1 kg 440 g) cooked smoked ham
Whole cloves
Artificial sweetener to taste
6 fl oz (180 ml) frozen orange juice concentrate
6 oz (180 g) sliced onion or 2 tablespoons dried onion flakes reconstituted in water

2 tablespoons water
2 garlic cloves, crushed
2 teaspoons beef stock powder
1 pint 4 fl oz (720 ml) water
4 tablespoons tomato purée
2 teaspoons prepared mustard
1 teaspoon dried orange peel

Place ham on a rack in roasting tin. Score it with a knife; stud with cloves; sprinkle with sweetener. Bake at 325°F (160°C), Gas Mark 3, 15 to 18 minutes per pound or 45 to 55 minutes. Baste with orange juice. When done, reserve any pan juices that may accumulate. In large nonstick frying pan heat onion, garlic and stock powder until slightly browned. Add water, tomato purée and pan juices; cook until sauce is reduced by one-third or to desired consistency. Stir in mustard and orange peel. Serve weighed portions of ham with equal portions of sauce. Makes 16 servings.

Puerto Rican Moulded Ham Salad (Jamon en Gelatina)

3 oz (90 g) cooked ham, finely
  chopped
1 oz (30 g) finely diced celery
½ oz (15 g) chopped pimiento
2 teaspoons chopped fresh parsley
½ teaspoon mustard
Pinch pepper
2 teaspoons unflavoured gelatine

2 tablespoons water
1 oz (30 g) nonfat dry milk,
  reconstituted with 3 fl oz (90 ml)
  water
Lettuce
1½ oz (45 g) tomato, sliced
Parsley sprigs

Combine ham, celery, pimiento, parsley and mustard in small mixing bowl. Season with pepper. Sprinkle gelatine over water in small saucepan to soften. Dissolve over low heat. Remove. Add milk and beat with hand whisk until 3 times its volume (soft peaks). Fold into ham mixture; transfer to a mould and refrigerate 2 hours, or until firm, before serving. Turn out on lettuce and garnish with tomato and parsley. Makes 1 serving.

Coconut Rice and Beans Ochos Rios

As a variation, decrease cooked dried kidney beans to 6 oz (180 g) and add 4 oz (120 g) cooked pork. Makes 2 servings.

4 oz (120 g) diced onion
6 fl oz (180 ml) chicken stock,
  made with ½ stock cube
½ hot red chilli pepper
⅛ teaspoon thyme
Salt to taste
4 oz (120 g) cooked rice

12 oz (360 g) cooked dried kidney
  beans
4 teaspoons nonfat dry milk,
  reconsitituted with 2 tablespoons
  water
½ teaspoon coconut flavouring

Brown onion over high heat in saucepan, stirring to prevent scorching. Add chicken stock, chilli pepper, thyme and salt if desired. Bring to the boil. Stir in rice and beans; reduce heat and simmer uncovered for 20 minutes or until beans and rice have absorbed flavours and liquid. Stir in milk and coconut flavouring; heat gently and serve hot. Makes 2 servings.

Caribbean Fruit and Cheese Salad Ring*

1 medium orange, peeled and
  sectioned
1 medium banana, diced
4 oz (120 g) canned pineapple
  chunks, no sugar added
2 tablespoons unflavoured gelatine
16 fl oz (480 ml) water

2 teaspoons orange flavouring
1 teaspoon coconut flavouring
2 to 3 drops yellow food colouring
Lettuce
10 oz (300 g) cottage cheese
Sprigs of mint

Combine orange sections, banana and pineapple and arrange in a ring mould. In a saucepan, sprinkle gelatine over 8 fl oz (240 ml) water to soften. Place over low heat and stir until gelatine is dissolved. Remove from heat; stir in remaining water, flavourings and colour as desired. Pour over fruit in mould and chill. Turn out on bed of lettuce. Fill centre of ring with cottage cheese and garnish with sprigs of mint. Makes 4 servings.

Bananas Antillean with Lime-Whipped Topping

Lime-Whipped Topping
  (recipe follows)
2 medium bananas
8 fl oz (240 ml) water
10 oz (300 g) canned crushed
  pineapple, no sugar added

2 tablespoons fresh lime or lemon
  juice
1 teaspoon grated lime or lemon rind
½ teaspoon rum flavouring
4 teaspoons margarine

Prepare Topping. Peel and cut bananas in half lengthwise. Heat water, pineapple and lime juice to boiling in a large pan; reduce heat and stir in lime rind and rum flavouring. Add bananas; heat. Remove pan from heat. Place each banana half on an individual serving dish. Stir margarine into pineapple mixture until margarine melts; divide evenly and pour over bananas. Serve with Topping. Makes 4 servings.

Lime-Whipped Topping

1½ teaspoons unflavoured gelatine
2 fl oz (60 ml) water
4 fl oz (240 ml) boiling water
1 teaspoon vanilla flavouring

2 oz (60 g) nonfat dry milk
Artificial sweetener to equal
  2 teaspoons sugar, or to taste
1 teaspoon lime or lemon rind
8 ice cubes

Pour water into blender goblet; sprinkle gelatine over water to soften. Add boiling water and blend at low speed until gelatine dissolves. Add vanilla, dry milk, sweetener and lime rind. Add ice cubes, one at a time, and blend at high speed. Pour topping into a small bowl; chill. Stir topping just before serving and divide evenly. Makes 4 servings.

Pineapple Rice Pudding (Arroz con Leche y Piña)*

4 oz (120 g) cooked white rice
2 oz (60 g) nonfat dry milk,
  reconstituted with 12 fl oz
  (360 ml) water
¼ teaspoon almond flavouring

4 oz (120 g) canned crushed
  pineapple, no sugar added
2 eggs
¼ teaspoon cinnamon
¼ teaspoon nutmeg

Combine rice and milk in top of double boiler. Add flavouring. Cook 30 minutes over boiling water or until mixture thickens. Drain pineapple and reserve juice. Add pineapple, simmer for 10 minutes. Remove. Place eggs and reserved pineapple juice in blender goblet. Blend until smooth. Stir into rice; reheat, do not boil. Pour into two dishes. Sprinkle with cinnamon and nutmeg; cool. Chill 2 to 3 hours in refrigerator before serving. Makes 2 servings.

Kingston Tonic

4 fl oz (120 ml) iced tea
3 to 4 ice cubes
Artificial sweetener to equal
  1 teaspoon sugar, or to taste

4 fl oz (120 ml) low calorie tonic
  water
1 slice lemon

Place tea in a tall glass; add ice cubes, sweetener and tonic water. Stir
and serve with lemon. Makes 1 serving.

Coconut Tropical

4 fl oz (120 ml) low calorie tonic
  water
4 fl oz (120 ml) soda water
1 teaspoon lemon juice
$\frac{1}{2}$ teaspoon coconut flavouring

$\frac{1}{4}$ teaspoon fruit flavouring
Artificial sweetener to equal
  1 teaspoon sugar, or to taste
2 oz (60 g) shaved ice

Combine all ingredients in a tall glass and serve over ice. Garnish with
a flower blossom. Makes 1 serving.

Caribbean Ginger Punch

6 fl oz (180 ml) low calorie ginger
  ale
$2\frac{1}{2}$ fl oz (75 ml) fresh lime or lemon
  juice

2 teaspoons rum flavouring
4 to 5 ice cubes, crushed
Artificial sweetener to taste

Combine in blender goblet. Blend until smooth. Serve in tall glasses.
Makes 2 servings.

Rum Milk

5 fl oz (150 ml) buttermilk   ½ teaspoon rum flavouring
½ teaspoon coconut flavouring   3 ice cubes

Place all ingredients in blender goblet. Blend at high speed until all traces of ice disappear. Serve in tall glass. Makes 1 serving.

Grapefruit Juice Mint Cocktail

4 fl oz (120 ml) grapefruit juice   1 sprig of fresh mint
1 small piece lemon rind

Using well-chilled stemmed glass, pour in juice. Twist lemon rind to release its oils and add to juice. Top with mint sprig. Makes 1 serving.

Café Puerto Rico

8 fl oz (240 ml) cold strong coffee   10 fl oz (300 ml) skim milk
1 lb (480 g) canned crushed
  pineapple, no sugar added

Combine all ingredients in blender goblet in two batches. Blend until smooth. Chill. Stir before serving. Makes 4 servings.

CHINA

*

The wisdom of Confucius has been famous for more than 2,500 years, but did you know that he was also an epicure, as were many Chinese sages? Is it any wonder, then, that the Chinese—with a national proclivity for excellence in food and with thousands of years of practice—have created a cuisine which ranks among the two or three best in the world? It is a perfect cuisine for the weight-conscious.

Chinese table etiquette follows a strict pattern. Although a dozen or more dishes are served at important meals, the diners, who are taught restraint from childhood, help themselves to only small portions from each central dish. Meal customs in general slow down the whole act of eating. Ingredients are cut into small pieces in the kitchen, sizes just large enough to be managed with chopsticks. As you know if you've used them, it's hard to gulp greedy mouthfuls with chopsticks as the sole implements, especially since table manners dictate that the chopsticks be put down at frequent intervals during the meal. So, in effect, the Chinese practise the kind of disciplined eating which we advocate.

An ancient Chinese proverb, this one not attributed to Confucius, says, 'Good food brings happiness.' We hope our recipes will make you happy, too.

Clear Soup

8 fl oz (240 ml) chicken stock
   made with ½ stock cube
½ teaspoon finely chopped fresh
   ginger

½ teaspoon sherry flavouring
Soy sauce to taste
Chopped fresh parsley or shredded
   spinach to garnish

Combine stock and ginger in small saucepan. Heat to boiling. Stir in sherry flavouring and serve at once with soy sauce (to be added at the table). Garnish with parsley or spinach. Makes 1 serving.

Egg Drop Soup*

8 fl oz (240 ml) chicken stock
  made with ½ stock cube
1 teaspoon cornflour, dissolved in
  1 tablespoon cold water

1 egg, beaten
1 small slice ginger root, diced
1 oz (30 g) spring onions, including
  part of green top, finely chopped

Bring chicken stock to the boil; stir in cornflour mixture. Remove from heat. With a chopstick in one hand stir the soup. With your other hand, slowly pour the beaten egg into soup, stirring to create egg shreds. Remove from heat. Put ginger in soup bowl and add soup. Top with spring onions. Serve at once. Makes 1 serving.

Sizzling Mushroom Soup

3 Chinese dried mushrooms, 1½ oz
  (45 g) reconstituted
8 fl oz (240 ml) beef stock, made
  with ½ stock cube

1 oz (30 g) chopped fresh or frozen
  spinach
1 tablespoon chopped fresh parsley
  or chives
½ teaspoon sherry flavouring

Clean mushrooms by rinsing in cold water. Combine stock and dried mushrooms in saucepan. Let stand 15 minutes or until softened. Lift out mushrooms, cut away stems, and slice mushrooms. Bring stock to the boil, add mushroom slices. Simmer, covered, for 20 minutes. Stir in spinach and cook 2 minutes more. Stir in parsley and sherry flavouring. Serve hot. Makes 1 serving.

Oyster Soup

8 fl oz (240 ml) beef stock, made
   with ½ stock cube (or use part
   mushroom liquid)
1½ oz (45 g) sliced fresh mushrooms
   or 3 dried reconstituted in hot
   water and sliced
2 oz (60 g) diced celery
1 oz (30 g) sliced bamboo shoots or
   carrots

1 small slice ginger root, diced
4 oz (120 g) drained canned oysters,
   sliced, or 2 oz (60 g) oysters and
   2 oz (60 g) shredded roast pork
2 oz (60 g) mange tout peas
2 oz (60 g) spring onions, including
   green tops
½ teaspoon sherry flavouring
   (optional)

Combine stock, mushrooms, celery, bamboo shoots and ginger
root in saucepan. Bring to the boil; cover and simmer 10 to 15 minutes
or until vegetables are tender. Add oysters (or oysters and pork) and
peas; heat gently 2 to 3 minutes. Turn off heat, add spring onions
and sherry flavouring if desired. Serve at once. Makes 1 serving.

Hot and Sour Chicken Soup with Bok Choy Shreds

To serve this as a complete meal, add 3 oz (90 g) tofu (soybean curd) cut
into slivers and heated with the shredded vegetables.

1 oz (30 g) Chinese cabbage, Swiss
   chard or watercress with stems
   removed
8 fl oz (240 ml) chicken stock,
   made with ½ stock cube

2 oz (60 g) cooked chicken, sliced in
   matchstick strips
1 small piece lemon rind, shredded

To prepare cabbage, cut it in half lengthwise, then slice into thin
diagonals. Shred Swiss chard or watercress if used. Bring stock to
the boil in a small saucepan, add shredded vegetables, and cook until
cabbage is wilted, but still crunchy, about 3 minutes. Pour over chicken
in soup bowl. Garnish with lemon rind. Makes 1 serving.

Chinese Egg Roll

Wrappers

1 egg   **Filling (recipes follow)**
1 tablespoon water

Combine egg and water in blender goblet. Blend for 10 seconds. Pour mixture into a cup with a spout, such as a measuring jug, and let it stand until bubbles subside, at least 15 minutes. Heat a 7-inch (18 cm) nonstick frying pan. Pour half the egg mixture into pan, tilting pan until the entire bottom is covered with a thin sheet of egg. Cook until egg is firm enough to turn, but not yet crispy. Turn; cook on second side for 10 to 15 seconds or until just solid. Remove from pan. Repeat procedure with remaining egg mixture. Prepare one of the fillings. Place half the filling in the centre and roll wrapper round filling, first folding in the sides. Place seam-side down on a nonstick baking sheet. Bake at 350°F (180°C), Gas Mark 4, for 15 minutes or until wrapper becomes crisp and filling is thoroughly heated. Makes 1 serving of 2 egg rolls.

Shrimp Egg Roll Filling

2 oz (60 g) cooked shrimps, finely   1 teaspoon finely chopped celery
  diced   1 oz (30 g) green pepper, finely
1 oz (30 g) finely chopped, cooked   chopped
  mange tout peas   1 teaspoon soy sauce
$\frac{1}{2}$ oz (15 g) finely chopped, cooked $\frac{1}{2}$ teaspoon sherry flavouring
  bean sprouts   Salt to taste
$\frac{1}{2}$ oz (15 g) finely chopped cooked
  mushrooms

Combine all ingredients in a small mixing bowl. Filling for 2 egg rolls.

Chicken Egg Roll Filling

In this recipe, 1 oz (30 g) grated cabbage, crisp-cooked, may be used instead of the spinach-mushroom-bean sprouts mixture.

2 oz (60 g) cooked chicken, finely diced
1 oz (30 g) finely chopped, cooked spinach
½ oz (15 g) finely chopped, cooked mushrooms

½ oz (15 g) finely chopped, cooked bean sprouts
1 tablespoon soy sauce
Pinch salt (optional)

Combine all ingredients in a small mixing bowl. Filling for 2 egg rolls

Bass or Perch Szechuan

12 oz (360 g) fillets of bass or perch, cut in 1-inch (2.5 cm) pieces
2 oz (60 g) spring onions, including green tops, cut in ¼-inch (5 mm) slices
2 garlic cloves, crushed
8 fl oz (240 ml) beef stock, made with ½ stock cube

2 to 3 tablespoons soy sauce
2 teaspoons cider or rice vinegar
1 teaspoon finely chopped ginger root
1 teaspoon sherry flavouring
¼ teaspoon crushed red pepper flakes or Szechuan pepper or hot pepper sauce to taste

In preheated nonstick frying pan or wok with lid, combine fish, spring onions and garlic. Brown fish on both sides over moderate heat. Add stock, soy sauce, vinegar, ginger, sherry flavouring and pepper. Cook, covered, over low heat 20 minutes or until fish flakes easily, basting it several times. Makes 2 servings.

Sliced Flounder with Garlic, Ginger and Spinach

12 oz (360 g) flounder fillets
Salt and pepper to taste
Boiling water
2 oz (60 g) fresh spinach; trim off
tough stems
3 oz (90 g) tomato, sliced

2 tablespoons beef stock, made
with stock cube according to
package directions
½ teaspoon finely chopped ginger
root
1 garlic clove, crushed

Slice fish into 2 × 3-inch (5×8 cm) pieces. Sprinkle with salt and pepper. Pour boiling water over spinach and let stand, covered, for 3 minutes. Drain well, pressing out moisture. Shred or chop finely. Divide spinach evenly and top each piece of fish with a spoonful. Roll up fish from short end to enclose stuffing and fasten with toothpick. Place fish rolls in a heatproof serving dish or small shallow casserole. Add sliced tomato. Combine stock, ginger and garlic; spread on fish. Place dish in a Chinese steamer or on a rack in a large saucepan containing water at least 1 inch (2.5 cm) below the bottom of the dish. Place greaseproof paper over dish to keep excess moisture out. Cover steamer or saucepan loosely so steam does not build up. Heat to steam-cook fish for 15 to 20 minutes or until fish flakes with a fork. Replenish hot water in steamer or saucepan if necessary. Make 2 servings.

Red-Simmered Fish with mixed Vegetables

This dish is called 'red' because it's cooked with soy sauce.

12 fl oz (360 ml) water
2 tablespoons lemon juice
2 teaspoons soy sauce
1 slice fresh ginger root, finely
chopped
1 teaspoon dried onion flakes
Salt and pepper to taste
Pinch of cinnamon

2 × 8 oz (240 g) fish steaks
2 oz (60 g) cauliflower, broken into
florets
2 oz (60 g) asparagus, cut in 1-inch
(2.5 cm) pieces
4 oz (120 g) peas
2 oz (60 g) diced celery
1½ oz (45 g) sliced mushrooms

Combine water, lemon juice, soy sauce, ginger, onion flakes, salt, pepper and cinnamon in wide saucepan. Add fish. Bring to fast boil; surround fish with cauliflower, asparagus, shelled peas, celery and mushrooms. Return to the boil. Cover pan and cook gently until fish and vegetables are done, about 20 minutes. Makes 2 servings.

Sweet-Sour Fish with Pineapple

1 lb 8 oz (720 g) fish fillets
1 lb (480 g) canned pineapple
 chunks, no sugar added
6 fl oz (180 ml) water
2 fl oz (60 ml) cider vinegar
1 tablespoon soy sauce
1 garlic clove, crushed
1½ teaspoons salt

8 oz (240 g) canned bamboo shoots, rinsed
6 oz (180 g) green pepper, cut in 1-inch (2.5 cm) squares
3 oz (90 g) tomato, cut in thin wedges
8 oz (240 g) hot, cooked fluffy rice

Cut fish into 1-inch (2.5 cm) pieces. Drain pineapple chunks; reserve liquid. Combine pineapple juice, water, vinegar, soy sauce, garlic and salt in saucepan; blend well. Bring to the boil. Add fish; cook over low-medium heat until fish flakes when tested with fork. Add bamboo shoots, green pepper and tomato and cook 1 minute longer. Serve over rice, divided onto 4 serving plates. Makes 4 servings.

Steamed Eggs with Vegetables

You can vary this custard in many ways. Change the vegetables, use beef stock powder, liquid left from cooking vegetables, tomato juice, or water. However, be sure to boil whatever liquid you use because it forces out the air bubbles and gives the dish its typically creamy texture.

1 tablespoon chicken stock powder, dissolved in 12 fl oz (360 ml) hot water

3 oz (90 g) green beans or mushrooms or 2 oz (60 g) spinach, in thin diagonal slices

4 oz (120 g) spring onions, including green tops, in thin diagonal slices

½ teaspoon sherry flavouring

½ teaspoon salt

4 eggs, lightly beaten

Boiling water

2 teaspoons soy sauce (optional)

You will need a large deep pot or saucepan for steaming. Pour stock into a small flameproof dish and bring to the boil. Turn off heat. Stir in green beans (spinach or mushrooms), spring onions, sherry flavouring and salt. Gently mix in eggs. Place dish on a rack set in the large pot on the stove or, instead of a rack, use 2 small ovenproof dishes, side by side, and balance dish on them. Pour boiling water into the pot to reach 1 inch (2.5 cm) below the level of the rack. Place a piece of greaseproof paper over egg mixture to prevent steam from dripping into eggs and cover the pot, enclosing the entire mixture in this 'steamer'. Simmer 20 to 30 minutes or until a skewer inserted in the centre of egg mixture comes out clean. Add boiling water to pot as it evaporates. Top each portion with 1 teaspoon soy sauce, if desired. Makes 2 servings.

Steamed Eggs with Fish

Follow preceding recipe but add 12 oz (360 g) finely cut raw fish fillets, stirring them into the stock with the vegetables just before adding the eggs. Steam as directed above for 30 to 40 minutes. Makes 4 servings.

Crab Foo Yung

Ingredients like bamboo shoots are popular in Chinese dishes, because, while lacking flavour, their texture and ability to absorb and reflect seasonings is essential to the cuisine. If bamboo shoots are not available, crisp vegetables—parboiled cabbage, bean sprouts, broccoli, cucumbers, carrots, green beans or green peppers—may be substituted. For crabmeat, substitute cooked shredded chicken, pork, shrimps or 3 oz (90 g) cooked ham.

2 eggs
Pinch salt and pepper
4 oz (120 g) cooked crabmeat,
  flaked
2 oz (60 g) celery, finely diced

1½ oz (45 g) canned bamboo shoots,
  rinsed and finely diced
1 oz (30 g) canned mushrooms,
  finely diced
1 teaspoon soy sauce

Beat eggs in bowl. Sprinkle with salt and pepper. Add crab, celery, bamboo shoots, mushrooms and soy sauce. Mix well. Divide into two equal portions. Pour one of the portions into a preheated nonstick frying pan. Cook at moderately high heat. When bottom is lightly golden, turn with spatula to brown the other side. Remove omelette and keep warm. Repeat for second omelette. Makes 2 servings.

Steamed Fish with Ginger Topping

8 oz (240 g) fish fillet (see note)
1 oz (30 g) spring onions, including
  crisp green tops, cut in ½-inch
  (1 cm) pieces
1 tablespoon chicken stock, made
  with stock cube according to
  package directions
1 tablespoon soy sauce
1 tablespoon chopped fresh parsley

1 teaspoon finely chopped ginger
  root
1 garlic clove, finely chopped,
  (optional)
Artificial sweetener to equal ½
  teaspoon sugar, or to taste
  (optional)
Salt and pepper to taste

Rinse fish and wipe dry. Transfer it to a shallow heatproof individual serving plate. Combine remaining ingredients and spread over fish. Put the plate on a steaming rack (or cake rack on top of a coffee tin). Set rack in pan holding boiling water. Water should be at least 1 inch (2.5 cm) below the level of the fish. Bring water to the boil, loosely cover the pot so steam doesn't build up too heavily and steam fish for 15 to 20 minutes or until fish flakes when tested with a fork, and is white and opaque. Add boiling water as necessary to maintain the water level. Serve fish at once in the plate in which it was cooked. Makes 1 serving.

Note: Use bass, carp, mullet, perch, pike, shad and whitefish etc.

Lobster Cantonese

For an inexpensive substitute, replace the lobster with cod or hake. A small piece of ginger root may be cooked in the saucepan to release its essence in the chicken stock. Add the ginger just before serving if you want only a trace of it in the sauce. Light soy sauce is preferred in Cantonese cooking.

6 oz (180 g) shelled lobster, cut into
   bite-size pieces
1 garlic clove, cut in half
6 fl oz (180 ml) chicken stock
   made with ½ stock cube
2 teaspoons cornflour

2 teaspoons soy sauce
2 eggs, beaten
2 oz (60 g) spring onions, chopped
⅛ teaspoon salt
Freshly ground pepper
4 oz (120 g) hot cooked rice

Rub lobster pieces with cut clove of garlic. Put in saucepan with chicken stock. Simmer, covered, for 5 minutes. Mix cornflour with soy sauce and add to lobster, stirring constantly until sauce thickens. Stir in beaten eggs and spring onions and cook until eggs coagulate; break them into small pieces with stirring spoon. Season with salt and pepper, and serve each portion over 3 oz (90 g) rice. Makes 2 servings.

White-Cooked Chicken

5 pints (2 litres 850 ml) water
1 oz (30 g) chopped chives
3 slices ginger root, grated
8 teaspoons chicken stock powder

1 chicken, 3 lbs (1 kg 440 g),
   skinned and trussed*
Fresh Ginger Sauce (see page 94)

Combine first 4 ingredients in a large saucepan. Place over high heat and bring to the boil. Immerse chicken, breast-side down into boiling mixture. Return to the boil. Reduce heat, cover, and simmer 20 to 25 minutes. Turn breast-side up and simmer an additional 20 minutes or until done. Remove chicken and cool. Discard truss, drain well and chill. Reserve stock (see note). Just before serving, chop chicken into bite-sized pieces; this keeps it moist and juices stay in the meat. Serve cold with Fresh Ginger Sauce. Makes 4 servings.

Note: Stock may be chilled in refrigerator, then skimmed to remove congealed fat. Measure 6 fl oz (180 ml) portions and freeze. Use in recipes calling for stock.

*A 3 lb (1 kg 440 g) chicken will yield about 1 lb (480 g) cooked meat.

White-Cooked Chicken with Mushrooms and Peas

2 fl oz (60 ml) chicken stock,
made with ¼ stock cube
14 oz (420 g) fresh mushrooms,
halved
8 oz (240 g) celery, sliced on the
diagonal

8 oz (240 g) peas
1 lb (480 g) White-Cooked Chicken
(see recipe above), cut in 1-inch
(2.5 cm) squares
1 tablespoon soy sauce

Place stock in a medium saucepan and heat. Add mushrooms, celery and peas; cook, stirring, for 4 minutes or until tender but crisp. Drain. Add chicken and soy sauce; heat through thoroughly. Makes 4 servings.

Lemon Pineapple Chicken, Peking Style

2 × 6 oz (180 g) boned, skinless
chicken breasts
2 tablespoons chicken stock, made
with stock cube according to
package directions
1 tablespoon soy sauce
1 garlic clove, crushed
¾ teaspoon salt
2 teaspoons cornflour
2 tablespoons lemon juice

4 fl oz (120 ml) water
2½ fl oz (75 ml) cider or rice
vinegar
8 oz (240 g) canned pineapple
chunks, no sugar added
2 oz (60 g) grated carrot
6 oz (180 g) green pepper, cut into
1½-inch (4 cm) squares
1 teaspoon grated lemon rind
2 oz (60 g) shredded lettuce

Preheat grill. Wash chicken and wipe dry. Combine next 4 ingredients in a shallow dish. Place chicken in marinade and spread out well. Let stand 15 minutes, turning occasionally so that entire surface of chicken gets coated. Grill on rack 4 inches (10 cm) from heat, turning once, until done on both sides. While chicken is cooking, prepare the sauce: stir cornflour into lemon juice; combine with water and vinegar in a saucepan. Add pineapple, carrot, green pepper and lemon rind. Bring to the boil. Lower heat and simmer until thickened. When chicken is cooked, place on two individual serving plates. Pour Lemon-Pineapple Sauce over chicken. Serve immediately with a border of shredded lettuce. Makes 2 servings.

Note: In a variation of this recipe, 8 teaspoons tomato purée, 2 fl oz (60 ml) water and 3 oz (90 g) diced onion or spring onions, or 2 tablespoons dried onion flakes, are stirred into the Lemon-Pineapple mixture before it is brought to the boil. Pour this Lemon-Pineapple-Tomato Sauce over grilled chicken breasts in a shallow baking tin and bake at 350°F (180°C), Gas Mark 4, for 15 to 20 minutes.

Five-Fragrant Beef

A Shanghai stew. Nice with a bean sprout salad or, if stew is to be served hot, with potatoes. Add 12 oz (360 g) of peeled new potatoes cut in even dice to the boiling beef stock. Cook until potatoes are tender, about 20 minutes, before reheating the beef in the hot liquid.

1 lb 8 oz (720 g) well-trimmed stewing steak, (chuck or other inexpensive cut)
2 small pieces ginger root, crushed
2 small garlic cloves, crushed
1 sprig Chinese parsley (coriander) see note
1 teaspoon five-spice powder
2 tablespoons white vinegar
¾ teaspoon salt or to taste

Cut meat into 1½-inch (3 cm) cubes, cover with boiling water in saucepan and bring to the boil. Cook 1 hour or until beef is tender. Drain off liquid, refrigerate it to congeal the fat. Discard the congealed fat. Reheat the beef stock, bring to the boil with remaining ingredients, and cook 10 minutes. Pour over the beef. Beef may be served hot, cold or at room temperature. To serve it hot, let the beef simmer (not boil or it will toughen) 15 minutes in the stock. To serve it cold, marinate the beef in the hot stock until cooled, then refrigerate overnight, turning beef several times. Or serve at room temperature. Makes 4 servings.

Note: Or omit coriander and substitute 4 oz (120 g) whole spring onions. Flatten onions with cleaver, tie in bundles using pieces of the green tops, and serve with stew.

Chicken with Vegetables and Mushrooms (Moo Goo Gai Pan)

2 oz (60 g) Chinese cabbage, cut in thin diagonal slices (or use 4 oz (120 g) broccoli florets)
2 oz (60 g) celery, cut in thin diagonal slices
1½ oz (45 g) mushrooms, sliced
1 oz (30 g) drained canned bamboo shoots, cut in thin slices
8 fl oz (240 ml) chicken stock, made with ½ stock cube

8 oz (240 g) cooked chicken, cut in thin pieces
6 oz (180 g) fresh or frozen mange tout peas
2 teaspoons soy sauce
1 teaspoon sherry flavouring (optional)
1 teaspoon finely chopped ginger root
Salt and pepper to taste

In a preheated wok or a nonstick frying pan with lid, stir-cook cabbage, celery, mushrooms and bamboo shoots until heated through, but crisp to the bite. Add stock and bring to the boil. Reduce to simmering and add remaining ingredients. Cover the pan tightly and simmer for 5 minutes. Makes 2 servings.

Chicken Dynasty

12 oz (360 g) chicken cutlets,
  (boneless, skinless chicken
  breasts), cut in strips
4 oz (120 g) onions, chopped
8 fl oz (240 ml) chicken stock,
  made with ½ stock cube
2 oz (60 g) shredded Chinese
  cabbage
4 oz (120 g) diced celery

4 oz (120 g) sliced bamboo shoots
1½ oz (45 g) sliced mushrooms
2 oz (60 g) bean sprouts
2 fl oz (60 ml) soy sauce
½ teaspoon garlic powder
½ teaspoon ginger
¼ teaspoon dry mustard
2 oz (60 g) mange tout peas
4 oz (120 g) cooked white rice

Cook chicken and onions in heated nonstick frying pan or wok until chicken is tender, turning often. Stir in all remaining ingredients, except mange tout peas and rice. Cover and simmer 8 minutes. Add mange tout peas. Cook 2 minutes more. Divide chicken mixture evenly and serve each portion over 2 oz (60 g) hot cooked rice. Makes 2 servings.

Red-Cooked Chicken

1 roasting chicken, 3 lbs
  (1 kg 440 g)*
8 fl oz (240 ml) soy sauce (dark
  preferred)
Water to cover

1 tablespoon chives
1 slice fresh ginger root
1 star anise
½ teaspoon sherry flavouring

Place chicken in a heavy pan with soy sauce and cold water. Bring to the boil over medium heat; add remaining ingredients, then simmer, covered, until done (30 to 40 minutes). Turn once or twice for even colouring. Let cool slightly, remove skin, cut chicken into 2-inch (5 cm) sections. Makes 4 servings.

*A 3 lb (1 kg 440 g) chicken will yield about 1 lb (480 g) cooked meat.

Lo Mein

8 fl oz (240 ml) chicken stock
made with ½ stock cube
2 oz (60 g) sliced celery
2 oz (60 g) cooked or canned bean
sprouts (see note) or 4 oz (120 g)
cooked green beans or broccoli
2 oz (60 g) diced spring onions,
including green tops, or ½ oz
(15 g) shredded lettuce

1 teaspoon chopped ginger root or
pinch of ginger
1 teaspoon dried onion flakes
Salt and freshly ground pepper to
taste
4 oz (120 g) cooked minced chicken,
turkey, pork or veal
2 oz (60 g) cooked noodles
Mustard-Soy Sauce (recipe follows)

In small flameproof serving casserole, combine chicken stock, celery, bean sprouts, or green beans or broccoli, spring onions or lettuce, ginger root, onion flakes, salt and pepper; bring to the boil. Stir in chicken and noodles. Heat and serve with Mustard-Soy Sauce. Makes 1 serving.

Note: To cook fresh sprouts, cover them with boiling water in saucepan; simmer for 3 minutes. Drain. To use canned bean sprouts, rinse first under running water.

Mustard-Soy Sauce

1 tablespoon dry mustard

1½ teaspoons soy sauce

Combine ingredients to make a paste. Use with Lo Mein.

Beef with Peppers and Tomatoes

1 lb 8 oz (720 g) tender boneless steak
(flank, top sirloin or fillet)
2 fl oz (60 ml) soy sauce
1 tablespoon water
2 garlic cloves, finely chopped
1 teaspoon sherry flavouring
(optional)
1 teaspoon salt

½ teaspoon pepper
1 lb 2 oz (540 g) green peppers, cut
into 1½-inch (4 cm) squares
9 oz (270 g) tomatoes, cut into 18
wedges
8 oz (240 g) cooked or canned bean
sprouts (see note page 93)

Grill meat on preheated rack in grill pan, 4 inches (10 cm) from heat, until brown on all sides, 10 to 12 minutes; turn steak once. Cut into thin slices and put on dish. Combine soy sauce, water, garlic, sherry flavouring, salt and pepper. Pour over steak slices. Lightly brown green peppers in nonstick pan. Tilt dish holding beef and marinade over pan so marinade liquid flows into it. Bring to the boil and let cook 15 minutes. Add tomatoes and cook a minute or two—until tomatoes are soft but not mushy; do not overcook them. Remove pan from heat, add beef slices, and stir them into vegetable mixture. Serve on warmed serving plates, over lightly cooked bean sprouts. Makes 4 servings.

Soy Sauce Anise Beef

1 lb 8 oz (720 g) lean beef top rump
4 slices ginger root, chopped
2 fl oz (60 ml) soy sauce
2 tablespoons chopped chives
1 tablespoon sherry flavouring
1 teaspoon salt
8 fl oz (240 ml) cold water
1 star anise

Place meat on rack in open shallow roasting pan. Roast at 350°F (180°C), Gas Mark 4, until cooked to taste. Remove and let stand 15 minutes. Cut in 1-inch (2.5 cm) cubes. Heat medium saucepan and add meat and ginger. Cook, stirring constantly, until meat is browned on all sides. Add soy sauce, chives, flavouring and salt. Mix; add water and bring to the boil. Cover and cook over medium heat 30 minutes, stirring occasionally. Add star anise, cover and cook another 30 minutes. There should only be 4 fl oz (120 ml) liquid left. If more, uncover and continue cooking to reduce. Makes 4 servings.

Charcoal-Grilled Steak Szechuan

1 lb 8 oz (720 g) skirt steak
Cut garlic clove
3 tablespoons lemon juice
1 tablespoon soy sauce
1½ teaspoons salt
⅛ teaspoon crushed Szechuan pepper
Hot Pepper Dip (recipe follows)

With tines of fork, pierce steak on both sides and rub with cut clove of garlic. Combine lemon juice, soy sauce, salt and crushed pepper. Pour over steak and let marinate 4 hours, turning several times. Grill in hinged rack over hot coals until done on both sides. Slice on wooden steak board and serve with a bowl of Hot Pepper Dip set in the centre of the table. You could also grill this, guests participating, on individual hibachis. Just slice the marinated steak in serving portions, ready for the flame. Makes 4 servings.

Hot Pepper Dip

4 fl oz (120 ml) soy sauce
1 tablespoon hot pepper sauce (or to taste)

2 garlic cloves, crushed
Pinch dry mustard

Combine ingredients in serving bowl. Serve immediately. Makes 4 servings.

Ginger Beef

1 oz (30 g) finely chopped onion
8 fl oz (240 ml) beef stock, made with ½ stock cube
4 teaspoons tomato purée
2 tablespoons water
½ teaspoon ginger
¼ teaspoon chilli powder
¼ garlic clove, crushed
¼ teaspoon turmeric

3 oz (90 g) tomato, peeled and chopped
4 oz (120 g) grilled skirt steak, cut diagonally across grain into thin slices
Salt and pepper to taste
1 teaspoon chopped fresh parsley
2 oz (60 g) cooked noodles

Lightly brown onion in nonstick pan. Add stock, tomato purée, water, ginger, chilli powder, garlic, turmeric and tomato; simmer 5 minutes. Arrange the beef slices in sauce, reheat; season to taste. Sprinkle with parsley and serve over noodles. Makes 1 serving.

Barbecued Pork

1 lb 8 oz (720 g) lean boneless pork (or pork fillet)
4 fl oz (120 ml) soy sauce
3 tablespoons vinegar or lemon juice
1 tablespoon Worcester sauce
Artificial sweetener to equal 3 teaspoons sugar, or to taste

2 teaspoons tomato purée
4 teaspoons water
1 teaspoon sherry flavouring
1 teaspoon red food colouring
1 teaspoon salt
1 teaspoon chopped fresh ginger root
Pinch pepper

Slice pork along the grain into pieces 1½-inches (3 cm) thick, 1½-inches (3 cm) wide and 4-inches (10 cm) long. With a fork, pierce the pieces on all sides. Combine remaining ingredients and pour over the pork. Refrigerate and let stand overnight, turning pork several times. Remove from marinade reserving liquid. In preheated oven, 350°F (180°C), Gas Mark 4, roast pork on rack in aluminium foil-lined roasting pan for 40 to 45 minutes. Cut pork against the grain into slices ½-inch (1 cm) thick and serve hot or cold. Heat marinade and serve with pork. Makes 4 servings.

Ginger Pork

To avoid peeling garlic, wrap the clove between two folds of grease-proof paper, smack it with the flat part of a chopper, or with a rolling pin; remove peel and drop clove from paper into pan.

4 fl oz (120 ml) chicken stock made with ¼ stock cube
2 oz (60 g) spring onions, chopped
2 tablespoons soy sauce
1 teaspoon sherry flavouring
1 small garlic clove, crushed
Artificial sweetener to equal ½ teaspoon sugar, or to taste

½ teaspoon ginger
Pinch pepper
8 oz (240 g) cooked pork, cut in 1-inch (2.5 cm) cubes
2 oz (60 g) hot cooked rice

Combine chicken stock, spring onions, soy sauce, sherry flavouring, garlic, sweetener, ginger and pepper in saucepan. Stir in pork. Simmer, covered, for 15 minutes. Serve over rice. Makes 2 servings.

Stir-Cooked Pork with Chinese Vegetables

12 oz (360 g) boneless tender pork, trimmed of all visible fat and cut into thin strips
4 fl oz (120 ml) soy sauce
1 oz (30 g) onion, finely chopped
2 garlic cloves, crushed
2 teaspoons grated fresh ginger root or $\frac{1}{2}$ teaspoon ground ginger

8 oz (240 g) diagonally sliced celery
4 oz (120 g) green beans, diagonally cut into 1-inch (2.5 cm) pieces
3 oz (90 g) thinly sliced bamboo shoots
4 oz (120 g) cooked rice
1 oz (30 g) spring onions, finely chopped

Place pork in bowl with soy sauce, onion, garlic and ginger. Stir to mix well; cover and let marinate 1 hour. Preheat grill. Remove meat from marinade, reserving liquid. Place pork on rack and grill about 15 minutes, turning meat once, until pork is thoroughly cooked. Place pork and marinade in a wok or medium saucepan. Add celery, green beans and bamboo shoots. Stir-cook 5 minutes or until vegetables are tender-crisp. Serve each portion over 2 oz (60 g) rice. Garnish each serving with $\frac{1}{2}$ oz (15 g) spring onions. Makes 2 servings.

Meat Shreds with Green Beans

1 lb (480 g) cooked pork or beef, sliced
1 lb (480 g) fresh green beans
2 garlic cloves, crushed
8 fl oz (240 ml) chicken stock, made with $\frac{1}{2}$ stock cube

1 tablespoon light soy sauce
1 tablespoon cornflour, dissolved in 1 tablespoon water
$\frac{1}{4}$ teaspoon sherry flavouring

Stack slices of pork or beef. Cut through stacks to make fine shreds. Set meat aside or refrigerate until ready to use. Cut off tips of green beans, wash, dry and cut into 2-inch (5 cm) diagonal pieces. Boil water in large saucepan and drop beans into strainer. Immerse strainer in boiling water and cook until beans are tender but still crisp and bright green. Cool in strainer under cold running water (to set bright colour). Drain; refrigerate until ready to use. At serving time, heat wok or frying pan. Stir-cook garlic with blanched beans just long enough to spread garlic essence through the vegetable. Add shredded meat and stir together to combine (all this takes about 3 minutes). Add stock, soy sauce, cornflour and sherry flavouring. Heat thoroughly. Serve in individual china bowls. Makes 4 servings.

Stir-Cooked Chicken Livers with Bamboo Shoots and Water Chestnuts

12 oz (360 g) chicken livers (partially frozen to make slicing easier)
5 teaspoons water
1 teaspoon sherry flavouring
2 fl oz (60 ml) chicken stock, made with ¼ stock cube
1 tablespoon soy sauce

3 oz (90 g) bamboo shoots, sliced thinly, then in ½-inch (1 cm) strips
4 oz (120 g) drained canned water chestnuts, sliced
Salt to taste
1 tablespoon chopped fresh chives

Cut chicken livers in ½-inch (1 cm) slices; add water and sherry flavouring and toss gently. Let stand 5 minutes. Heat stock in saucepan or wok. Add livers and stir-cook until they change colour. Add soy sauce; stir to blend. Stir in bamboo shoots and water chestnuts, then add salt and chives and mix well. Serve at once. Makes 2 servings.

Five-Spice Powder

You can buy this sweet and pungent spice mixture by weight, in Chinese stores, or make your own using a mortar and pestle or blender to crush the following ingredients into a powder: 50 peppercorns; 4 star anise; 2 teaspoons fennel seeds; 3 one-inch (2.5 cm) pieces of stick cinnamon; 10 whole cloves. Wrap the powder tightly in plastic bag and store in screwtop jar. It will stay fresh for several months. Allspice, or a mixture of powdered cinnamon, cloves, ginger and nutmeg, is sometimes substituted for five-spice powder.

Sprouting Beans

The idea for sprouting beans originated in China. Sprouts are nutritious and easy and economical to grow, 1 lb (480 g) of dried beans making 4 or 5 lbs (1 kg 920 g or 2 kg 400 g) of fresh vegetables. Here are the simple instructions: Line a colander with two layers of muslin. Soak 4 tablespoons of mung beans in lukewarm water for 1 hour. Arrange beans in colander, one layer deep. Cover top with paper towel. Put colander into basin to catch dripping water. Rinse three times daily to prevent mould. In 4 to 5 days you will have fresh sprouts, all ready to use. Rinse the sprouts a few times so that the dark skins come off (they will usually float to the surface), then drain. Refrigerate unused sprouts for up to three to four days only. For longer storage blanch them as directed below.

Bean Sprout Salad (Dow Ngah)

4 oz (120 g) fresh bean sprouts
1 oz (30 g) grated carrot
1 oz (30 g) chopped spring onions,
** including firm green tops**

1 tablespoon soy sauce
1½ teaspoons vegetable oil
1½ teaspoons sesame oil

Blanch fresh sprouts by pouring boiling water over them in saucepan, let stand 2 minutes. Then drain, rinse in cold water and drain again. (To freshen canned bean sprouts, drain and rinse in colander under cold running water.) Refrigerate until ready to use. Combine remaining ingredients, pour over beans; mix well and serve. Makes 2 servings.

Plum Sauce

To serve over steamed fish, grilled chicken and roast or barbecued meat. For a hotter flavour, add a few drops garlic juice (made by crushing clove of garlic) or a few drops hot pepper sauce. Other seasoning possibilities include ⅛ teaspoon allspice, ½ teaspoon dry mustard, ¾ teaspoon gravy browning.

10 fl oz (300 ml) chicken stock,
  made with ½ stock cube
2 medium plums, peeled, stoned and
  diced
4 fl oz (120 ml) cider vinegar
Artificial sweetener to equal 2
  tablespoons sugar, or to taste

1 tablespoon dried onion flakes
1 teaspoon finely chopped ginger
  root
Salt to taste
2 drops red food colouring (optional)

Combine all ingredients (except food colouring) in saucepan. Bring to the boil, cook over moderate heat, uncovered, until sauce is thick, stirring frequently. Add food colouring, if desired. Makes 2 servings.

Fresh Ginger Sauce

Make this recipe only if the ginger is very young and tender and free of fibres.

2 fl oz (60 ml) vegetable oil
2 tablespoons peeled and finely
  chopped fresh ginger root

1 tablespoon dried onion flakes,
  reconstituted
1 teaspoon salt

Place all ingredients in a jar with lid. Shake to combine, and let stand. Pour into 4 small individual dishes and use with cold chicken. Makes 4 servings.

Bok Choy with Mushrooms and Bean Sprouts

6 oz (180 g) Chinese cabbage, cut in
  1-inch (2.5 cm) pieces
4 oz (120 g) soaked dried black
  mushrooms, cut in 1-inch (2.5 cm)
  pieces (discard tough stems)
  Measure 2 fl oz (60 ml) liquid

Salt to taste
8 oz (240 g) rinsed canned bean
  sprouts
1 tablespoon cornflour

In a wok or nonstick frying pan with lid, stir-cook cabbage in mushroom liquid over medium heat, about 2 minutes. Add salt, bean sprouts and mushrooms; mix. Stir cornflour into 1 tablespoon water and add. Cover, turn heat down to simmer and cook about 5 minutes, to thicken sauce. Cabbage and sprouts should be crisp. Makes 4 servings.

Steamed Cucumbers

12 oz (360 g) cucumbers
½ teaspoon salt

Lemon Sauce (recipe follows)

Peel cucumbers, cut in half lengthwise and remove seeds. Slice lengthwise into wedges about ½-inch (1 cm) wide and cut into pieces 2½-inches (6 cm) long. Place on individual flameproof serving dish, place on a rack in a large saucepan holding boiling water (at least 1-inch (2.5 cm) below level of serving dish). Cover dish with greaseproof paper and fit a cover loosely over pan. Steam about 25 minutes or until tender. Serve with Lemon Sauce. Makes 2 servings.

Lemon Sauce

1 tablespoon prepared mustard
2 teaspoons lemon juice

2 teaspoons soy sauce

Combine. Mix until smooth. Serve with Steamed Cucumbers. Makes 2 servings.

Stuffed Cucumbers

Filling (recipe follows)
1 lb 8 oz (720 g) cucumbers
6 fl oz (180 ml) chicken stock,
  made with ½ stock cube

1 teaspoon soy sauce
½ teaspoon sherry flavouring

Prepare and reserve filling. Peel cucumbers and cut cross-wise into 2-inch (5 cm) thick slices. Scoop out seeds from one side of each section, not right through, creating a cup shape to hold filling. Stuff the centre of each section with filling, packing it in tightly and rounding out the edges. Place cucumbers in pan; pour next 3 ingredients over and bring to the boil. Then cover and simmer 5 minutes or until cucumbers are tender. Makes 4 servings.

Filling for Cucumbers*

8 oz (240 g) cooked minced pork or beef, crumbled
2 slices fresh ginger root, chopped

1 tablespoon soy sauce
$\frac{1}{4}$ teaspoon sherry flavouring
Salt to taste

Combine all ingredients in a medium bowl. With a large mixing spoon, spoon mixture into cucumber shells. Makes 4 servings.

Chinese Cucumber Salad

12 oz (360 g) cucumbers, peeled
$\frac{1}{2}$ teaspoon salt
1 tablespoon soy sauce
1 tablespoon rice vinegar or wine vinegar

Artificial sweetener to equal $1\frac{1}{2}$ teaspoons sugar, or to taste
2 teaspoons sesame oil

Cut cucumbers in half lengthwise. Scoop out seeds and slice thinly. Sprinkle with salt and let stand about 30 minutes in a colander or strainer, allowing liquid to run off. Place in bowl and toss cucumber slices with remaining ingredients. Allow to stand 5 minutes before serving. Makes 2 servings.

Steamed Aubergine

Tearing the cooked aubergine in this recipe gives it a more interesting texture than chopping. For luncheon, arrange aubergine shreds on a serving dish radiating out like flower petals. Leave space in centre and fill this with 4 scrambled eggs, cooked and broken into pieces. Makes 2 servings.

1 × 8 oz (240 g) aubergine
1 tablespoon soy sauce

1 teaspoon vegetable oil (optional)
½ teaspoon salt

Wash aubergine. Cut skin with a few lengthwise slashes, about ½-inch (1 cm) deep. Place on heatproof dish. Steam until soft (15 to 20 minutes). Let cool slightly, then strip off skin and discard it. Tear aubergine into lengthwise shreds, discarding seeds. Measure 4 oz (120 g) aubergine. Place in small bowl. Stir in soy sauce, oil and salt. Serve hot or cold. Makes 2 servings.

Variation: Add 1 or 2 slices chopped fresh ginger root and ½ crushed garlic clove to soy sauce.

Stir-Cooked Vegetables

4 fl oz (120 ml) water
1 teaspoon chicken stock powder
2 slices fresh ginger root, chopped
2 oz (60 g) cauliflower, broken into small florets
2 oz (60 g) asparagus, cut in 1-inch (2.5 cm) pieces
2 oz (60 g) diced celery

4 oz (120 g) peas
1½ oz (45 g) Chinese cabbage, chopped
1½ oz (45 g) diced mushrooms
2½ oz (75 g) diced bamboo shoots, rinsed
1 tablespoon soy sauce

Heat water and stock powder in a heated wok or large saucepan; add ginger root, cauliflower, asparagus, celery and peas; stir-cook 2 minutes; add cabbage, mushrooms and bamboo shoots, stir; add soy sauce and stir to blend in. Simmer over low heat about 2 minutes. Do not overcook—vegetables should be tender-crisp. Makes 4 servings.

Simmered Stuffed Green Pepper

Stuffing (recipes follows)
2 × 6 oz (180 g) green peppers
6 fl oz (180 ml) chicken stock, made with ½ stock cube

1 tablespoon soy sauce
Pinch pepper

Prepare one of the stuffings. With a sharp knife, cut the tops off peppers, then scoop out the seeds. Stuff peppers with one of the mixtures; replace the tops as lids. Stand stuffed peppers upright in a shallow pan; pour in stock and soy sauce; sprinkle with pepper. Bring stock to the boil; lower heat and simmer, covered, 40 minutes. Serve with liquid as a sauce, poured over peppers. Makes 2 servings.

Vegetable Stuffing

4 oz (120 g) shredded carrots
4 oz (120 g) cooked bean sprouts (if canned, rinse first)
4 oz (120 g) onions, diced
8 teaspoons tomato purée

2 fl oz (60 ml) water
1 teaspoon rice vinegar or pinch each onion and garlic powder
1 teaspoon salt
$\frac{1}{8}$ teaspoon pepper

Combine ingredients. Fills 2 × 6 oz (180 g) peppers. Makes 2 servings.

Fish Stuffing

8 oz (240 g) cooked haddock or halibut, flaked, or cooked diced shrimps
1 slice fresh ginger root, chopped

1 teaspoon dried onion flakes, reconstituted
$\frac{1}{2}$ teaspoon salt
Pinch pepper

Blend all ingredients. Fills 2 × 6 oz (180 g) peppers. Makes 2 servings.

Chinese Noodles

2 oz (60 g) cooked thin noodles   1 teaspoon soy sauce

Combine noodles and soy sauce. Thinly spread on shallow nonstick tin, 10 × 15-inches (25 × 38 cm), and bake at 350°F (180°C), Gas Mark 4, until crisp and brown. Remove from oven and break noodles apart if necessary. Makes 1 serving.

Spinach with Peppery Sauce, Peking Style

4 oz (120 g) Chinese cabbage, cut in 2-inch (5 cm) pieces, could replace the spinach.

Boiling water
4 oz (120 g) cleaned spinach, stems
    removed
4 oz (120 g) shredded carrots
1 tablespoon sesame oil
1 tablespoon lemon juice

1 teaspoon chopped fresh ginger root
$\frac{1}{4}$ teaspoon crushed red pepper or
    hot pepper sauce
1 teaspoon salt

Place spinach in a colander. Pour boiling water over it to blanch. Drain well. Chop and transfer to serving bowl or dish. Top with carrots. Combine remaining ingredients and pour over vegetables. Makes 1 serving.

'Fried' Rice*

For variation add 2 oz (60 g) cooked shrimps or chicken or roasted pork, diced or cut in thin strips.

1 egg, slightly beaten
2 oz (60 g) onion, diced
2 oz (60 g) diced celery

1 oz (30 g) shredded carrots
2 oz (60 g) cold cooked rice
2 tablespoons soy sauce

Scramble egg in a heated wok, or a hot nonstick pan. Remove scrambled egg from pan and cut up into tiny pieces. Set aside. Stir-cook onion, celery and carrot in the same pan until slightly softened. Stir in rice; add soy sauce. Cook at high heat for 3 minutes, stirring constantly. Stir in scrambled egg, remove from heat and serve immediately. Makes 1 serving.

Individual Grain Rice

Here is a good way to prepare cooked rice so that the grains remain separate every time. (You can estimate that 1 part raw rice equals about 3 parts cooked.) Extra rice may be frozen and used at another time.

14 fl oz (420 ml) cold water   **6 oz (180 g) uncooked rice**

Combine water and rice in medium saucepan with lid. Bring to the boil, lower heat and continue cooking on lowest heat 20 minutes. Turn flame off; let rice 'relax' for 20 or more minutes before opening lid. Stir to break up rice. Makes 8 servings.

Almond Cookies*

For anise cookies use fennel seeds instead of almond flavouring in the following recipe.

2 eggs
2 oz (60 g) nonfat dry milk
1 slice white bread, made into crumbs
Artificial sweetener to equal 7 teaspoons sugar, or to taste

1 teaspoon butter flavouring
Pinch salt
1 teaspoon unflavoured gelatine
$\frac{1}{4}$ teaspoon almond flavouring
$\frac{1}{2}$ teaspoon water

Preheat oven to 325°F (160°C), Gas Mark 3. Combine eggs, milk, breadcrumbs and sweetener to equal 6 teaspoons sugar, butter flavouring and salt. Beat with electric mixer until well blended. Sprinkle in gelatine. Mix 1 minute on medium-high speed. Drop by spoonfuls 1½-inches (4 cm) apart on nonstick baking sheet. Bake for 15 minutes or until a golden ring appears round the edges of each cookie. Remove from sheet with spatula. Combine almond flavouring with water and remaining sweetener. Spread on cookies with a pastry brush to form a glaze. Makes 2 servings (about 20 cookies).

Variation: Add 1 teaspoon fennel seeds with first 6 ingredients.

Pulverize seeds with a mortar and pestle or in blender goblet before mixing. Omit glaze.

Fruit with Sesame Dressing

2 small tangerines or 1 medium
  orange
¼ small pineapple
2 medium bananas
1 medium cantaloupe melon
8 large lettuce leaves
2 tablespoons lemon juice

4 teaspoons vegetable oil
4 teaspoons sesame oil
1 teaspoon dried onion flakes
⅛ teaspoon Worcester sauce
Pinch each dry mustard, salt and
  paprika
Dash hot pepper sauce

Peel the fruit over a large bowl to catch juices. Discard skins and rinds and reserve liquid. Cut fruit into uniform bite-size pieces. Place in a medium bowl and toss lightly to combine. Place each portion on a lettuce leaf in individual salad bowls. Combine remaining ingredients in jar with tight lid, (including juices from fruit), and shake well. Pour over fruit in the lettuce leaves. Makes 8 servings.

Banana-Pineapple Jelly

1 pint 12 fl oz (960 ml) water
2½ tablespoons unflavoured gelatine
2 oz (60 g) nonfat dry milk,
  reconstituted with 10 fl oz
  (300 ml) water

Artificial sweetener to equal 5
  teaspoons sugar, or to taste
2 teaspoons banana flavouring
1 teaspoon pineapple flavouring
Few drops yellow food colouring

Sprinkle gelatine over 5 fl oz (150 ml) water in saucepan and let stand to soften. Add remaining water and sweetener and cook over low heat, stirring, until gelatine dissolves. Stir in milk, sweetener, flavourings and colouring. Pour mixture into 10 × 15-inch (25 × 38 cm) tin (or ice cube trays). Refrigerate until set. Dice and serve in dessert dishes. Makes 8 servings.

Steamed Sponge Cake

6 eggs, separated
Artificial sweetener to equal
  2 tablespoons sugar, or to taste
2½ tablespoons water
3 slices white bread, made into
  crumbs

½ teaspoon black pepper
½ teaspoon vanilla flavouring
½ teaspoon almond flavouring

Beat yolks in a large bowl until light lemony colour, about 5 minutes. Add sweetener and water; beat until fluffy. Combine breadcrumbs and black pepper and blend into egg yolks, then add flavourings and mix well. Beat whites until they form peaks and are stiff, but not dry. Fold into batter. Line an 8 × 8 × 3-inch (20 × 20 × 8 cm) square cake tin with greaseproof paper. Pour batter into pan. Rap pan sharply on table several times to remove air bubbles. Cover top with greaseproof paper. Steam until done, 20 to 25 minutes. Makes 3 servings.

Almond Jelly

1 tablespoon unflavoured gelatine
16 fl oz (480 ml) water
2 oz (60 g) nonfat dry milk

Artificial sweetener to equal
  4 teaspoons sugar, or to taste
1 tablespoon almond flavouring

Sprinkle gelatine over 4 fl oz (120 ml) water in small saucepan; heat, stirring, until gelatine dissolves; pour into medium bowl. Add remaining water, dry milk, artificial sweetener and almond flavouring; mix thoroughly. Pour into four individual dishes. Chill. Makes 4 servings.

FRANCE

*

It is said that one-third of the world prefers Italian food, one-third Chinese, and one hundred percent favour *la bonne cuisine* of France. French culinary genius is reflected in an infinite capacity for taking pains, with housewives often marketing at least once a day to buy ingredients at the peak of quality. And what a wealth of ingredients is available! More than 400 distinct varieties of cheese alone are produced, each region of France having its own specialities made according to centuries-old recipes.

France, like so many sophisticated countries, is very weight-conscious, and this has encouraged her famous chefs to recreate slimmed-down versions of classic dishes, a practice we applaud and have followed for more than a decade. The French recipes in this chapter are adaptations of classic ones, but they give you the characteristic flavour while eliminating heavy creams and unnecessary fats.

Since soup is a daily—sometimes twice daily—tradition in France, we begin with a mouth-watering collection of soup recipes from hearty vegetable purées to sparkling 'consommés'.

Quick Carrot Bisque (Purée de Carottes à la Crème)

A rich 'cream' soup thickened with puréed vegetables.

8 fl oz (240 ml) Homemade Chicken Stock (see page 10) or 8 fl oz (240 ml) water and 1 teaspoon chicken stock powder, or ½ chicken stock cube
6 oz (180 g) sliced carrots
1½ oz (45 g) sliced celery
1 oz (30 g) diced onion or 2

teaspoons dried onion flakes
1 oz (30 g) nonfat dry milk, reconstituted with 5 fl oz (150 ml) water
2 fl oz (60 ml) water
1 sprig parsley or thyme, chopped, or ⅛ teaspoon dried
Freshly ground black pepper

103

Heat stock (or water and stock powder, or stock cube), carrots, celery and onions to boiling in a medium saucepan. Reduce heat; cover and simmer until carrots are tender. Place in blender goblet and blend at medium speed until smooth. Return to saucepan; stir in milk and water; heat. Sprinkle top with parsley and freshly ground pepper. Makes 2 servings.

Celery 'Consommé' (Consommé de Celeri or Consommé au Fumet de Celeri)

1 pint 12 fl oz (960 ml) beef stock, made with 2 stock cubes

8 oz (240 g) sliced celery including tops
Black pepper to taste

Combine stock and celery in saucepan; cover and cook for 10 minutes. Remove several slices of celery and reserve for garnish. Continue cooking celery for 35 minutes. Put through food mill or strainer, pressing out as much liquid as possible from the cooked celery. Or blend in blender at medium speed until smooth (however, this will not remove the fibres). Serve hot with celery slices garnishing each serving. Add freshly ground black pepper to taste. Makes 4 servings.

'Consommé Chiffonnade'

Blanch 1 oz (30 g) shredded green lettuce leaves in boiling salted water to cover. Let stand 5 minutes. Drain. Serve in bowl with 8 fl oz (240 ml) hot chicken stock, made with $\frac{1}{2}$ stock cube. Season with salt and pepper and garlic (optional). Makes 1 serving.

Potato and Radish Purée

2 oz (60 g) peeled potato, sliced
3 oz (90 g) radishes, trimmed and
  sliced

1 teaspoon margarine, melted
2 fl oz (60 ml) skim milk
Salt and pepper to taste

Cover potato with boiling salted water in small saucepan and bring to
the boil. Cover and simmer until potato is tender. Cook radishes in a
separate pan, in boiling water until tender. Drain potato and radishes.
Add remaining ingredients. Purée, using food mill or blender. Serve
hot. Makes 1 serving.

Spinach 'Consommé' (Consommé d'Epinards)

Cut 2 oz (60 g) young spinach leaves (washed and well-dried) into very
thin strips or shreds. Sprinkle into saucepan holding 1 pint 12 fl oz
(960 ml) boiling chicken stock made with 2 stock cubes. Cook 3 to 5
minutes or until spinach is wilted, then serve hot with a thin slice of
lemon and grated nutmeg added to each serving. Makes 4 servings.

Jellied 'Wine Consommé'

1 pint 12 fl oz (960 ml) chicken
  stock, made with 2 stock cubes
6 oz (180 g) green pepper, finely
  chopped
2 tablespoons each chopped fresh
  parsley and chives
1 tablespoon dried onion flakes
1 tablespoon chopped fresh chervil,
  if available, or 1 teaspoon dried

1 tablespoon unflavoured gelatine
2 tablespoons cold water or stock
  made from stock cube according
  to package directions
1 tablespoon sherry flavouring
1 teaspoon hot pepper sauce, or to
  taste
4 slices lime or lemon, dusted with
  paprika

Heat stock, green pepper, parsley, chives, onion flakes and chervil,
if available, to simmering. Soften gelatine in cold water or stock,
then add to hot stock, and stir until gelatine is dissolved. Add sherry
flavouring and hot pepper sauce. Divide the 'consommé' evenly into 4

mugs or soup cups and chill. When jelled, beat with fork to make coarse pieces. Top each mug with a thin slice of lime or lemon sprinkled with paprika. Makes 4 servings.

'Consommé' Suzette

12 fl oz (360 ml) chicken stock, made with 1 stock cube
4 fl oz (120 ml) tomato juice
4 oz (120 g) carrots, cut in thin matchstick strips
2 oz (60 g) celery, cut in thin strips

1½ oz (45 g) mushrooms, cut in thin slices
½ teaspoon chopped fresh herbs, or ¼ teaspoon dried (parsley, dill, chives and chervil)

Bring stock, tomato juice, carrots and celery to the boil in a saucepan; cook 5 to 8 minutes (vegetables will be almost done but still quite crisp). Add mushrooms; cook another 2 to 3 minutes; serve, sprinkling each portion with chopped herbs. Makes 2 servings.

'Consommé' à l'Indienne

To 8 fl oz (240 ml) hot chicken stock, made with ½ stock cube, add ¼ teaspoon coconut flavouring and a pinch (or more to taste) curry powder. Pour over 2 oz (60 g) cooked rice. Makes 1 serving.

'Consommé' Portugaise

Combine 5 fl oz (150 ml) beef stock, made with ½ stock cube, with 3 fl oz (90 ml) tomato juice. Sprinkle with cayenne pepper and salt, and serve chilled in cups. Makes 1 serving.

Watercress Soup (Potage au Cresson)

Select rich green crisp watercress. Rinse very well under cold running water in colander, dry thoroughly, keep refrigerated until ready to use. Cut away tough ends before use.

2 oz (60 g) white part of leeks, spring onions, shallots or onions, diced

12 oz (360 g) courgettes, diced

1 pint 12 fl oz (960 ml) chicken stock, made with 2 stock cubes

1 large bunch or 2 small bunches watercress, washed (only use leaves)

2 slices bread, cut into 32 small cubes

Combine leeks, courgettes and chicken stock in saucepan. Simmer, uncovered, until courgettes are very soft, 20 to 25 minutes. Add watercress and bring soup to the boil. Blend in blender goblet, a small amount at a time (or hot mixture may overflow), until smooth. Serve hot in bowls. Garnish each serving with 8 cubes of bread. Makes 4 servings.

'Crème' Cressonniere

Follow directions above, but after soup is blended, add $1\frac{1}{2}$ oz (45 g) nonfat dry milk, reconstituted with 6 fl oz (180 ml) water, and pinch of nutmeg. Reheat but do not boil. Stir well and serve at once. Makes 4 servings.

Spring Vegetable Soup (Consommé Printanier)

Springtime—printemps—is the right time for this soup made from all the earliest vegetables. Be thrifty and use the green trimmings from the salad bowl and the tops of leeks and spring onions.

1 pint 12 fl oz (960 ml) beef stock, made with 2 stock cubes or 4 teaspoons stock powder

2 oz (60 g) shredded lettuce or watercress

4 oz (120 g) young sliced green beans (mixed with mushroom stalks, if available)

1 oz (30 g) shredded spinach leaves

2½ oz (75 g) sliced asparagus tips and ends, or ends only

3 oz (90 g) green peas

2 oz (60 g) sliced carrot

2 oz (60 g) sliced leeks or spring onions

1 garlic clove, crushed

4 teaspoons low fat spread (optional)

4 sprigs fresh parsley or ½ teaspoon dried parsley, chives or chervil (for garnish)

Salt and pepper to taste (optional)

Combine stock, vegetables and garlic in a large saucepan. Bring to the boil; cover pan and simmer 35 to 45 minutes. Stir gently, then divide into 4 soup bowls. Stir a teaspoon of low fat spread into each bowl if desired and float a parsley sprig or few flakes of herbs over each serving. Add salt and pepper if necessary. Makes 4 servings.

Bread Soup (Panade)*

4 oz (120 g) finely diced celery including leaves

2 oz (60 g) shredded spinach

12 fl oz (360 ml) hot water

2 slices stale white bread, diced

2 oz (60 g) nonfat dry milk, reconstituted with 10 fl oz (300 ml) water

2 eggs

½ teaspoon salt

Freshly ground pepper to taste

Freshly grated nutmeg

Combine celery and spinach in saucepan; add water; bring to the boil, cover and cook for 20 minutes. Add bread, bring to the boil then simmer for 10 minutes more. Cool slightly and transfer to blender goblet. Blend and return soup to saucepan. In small mixing bowl, beat milk and eggs together with salt and pepper. Stir into the soup, and let it heat but not boil. Serve in mugs with grated nutmeg. Makes 2 servings.

Eggs Basque Style (Pipérade)*

For a change, 2 oz (60 g) pimiento may be substituted for the 12 oz (360 g) peppers.

6 oz (180 g) tomatoes, diced
12 oz (360 g) green peppers, seeded
  and diced (remove white pulp)
2 slices white bread, made into
  crumbs in blender

5 fl oz (150 ml) skim milk
4 eggs, beaten
Salt and pepper to taste

In upper part of covered double boiler placed over direct heat, steam tomatoes and green peppers, until peppers are soft, about 10 minutes. Cover crumbs with 3 tablespoons milk. Add to tomato-green pepper mixture with all remaining ingredients. Stir well. Pour hot water into bottom part of double boiler, insert top and cook covered about 20 minutes, until eggs are done to taste, stirring frequently. Serve on hot plates. Makes 4 servings.

Poached Eggs with Lettuce (Oeufs à la Maraîchère)*

4 oz (120 g) shredded lettuce,
  washed
2 eggs

Salt and pepper to taste
1 teaspoon chopped fresh chives

Steam lettuce until wilted (3 to 5 minutes) in steamer or strainer placed over hot water. Line 2 cocottes or small ovenproof dishes with wilted lettuce. Break an egg over each bed of lettuce, season with salt and pepper, and garnish top with chopped chives. Place dishes in shallow pan holding hot water and let cook gently on top of the stove 8 to 10 minutes, or until eggs are done to taste. Serve in the dishes. Makes 2 servings.

Eggs Florentine (Oeufs à la Florentine)

10 oz (300 g) frozen chopped
  spinach, thawed
1 teaspoon salt
⅛ teaspoon pepper

3 eggs
3 oz (90 g) freshly grated cheese
  (Parmesan or Swiss)

Drain spinach well and squeeze it dry. Season with salt and pepper.
Divide evenly between 3 individual pie dishes. Break an egg over each
bed of spinach; sprinkle each with an ounce (30 g) of grated cheese.
Bake in moderate oven (350°F, (180°C) Gas Mark 4) until egg whites
are firm, about 15 minutes. Serve immediately. Makes 3 servings.

Oeufs à l'Arlésienne

Replace spinach with Ratatouille (see recipe, page 140) allowing 4 oz
(120 g) for each serving. Follow directions given above. Makes 3
servings.

Omelette with Bread and Cheese (Omelette Grand'mère)

1 slice fresh white bread, made into
  crumbs
4 fl oz (120 ml) warm skim milk
2 eggs, lightly beaten

2 oz (60 g) grated Swiss cheese
Freshly grated nutmeg
Salt and pepper to taste

Combine all ingredients in a mixing bowl and stir well. Heat
nonstick frying pan. Pour in egg mixture, let it set for several seconds,
and stir it with fork, lifting the edges and tilting the pan to let the
uncooked mixture flow underneath. Cook the omelette until it is set
and the underside is browned; loosen it from the pan with a spatula,
and invert it onto a heated plate. Makes 2 servings.

Mushroom-Asparagus Open Omelette*

One or two-egg omelettes should be made in small frying pans (5 to 8-inch (13 to 20 cm) bottom diameter). Use a nonstick pan or heavy ironware, and heat it. You can make an open omelette of 8 to 10 eggs in a 10 or 12-inch (25 or 30 cm) pan and serve it in wedges for even division.

2 eggs	¼ teaspoon salt
1½ oz (45 g) cooked asparagus tips, drained and chopped	Freshly ground pepper to taste
1 oz (30 g) cooked mushrooms, drained and chopped	1 teaspoon water or liquid left from cooking vegetables

Place eggs in a bowl and beat until frothy. Stir in remaining ingredients. Pour into heated nonstick frying pan. Cook over moderate heat. As mixture sets, lift up edges with fork, tilting pan so that uncooked portions flow evenly to bottom. When underside is set, turn it with spatula (or flip it from pan to plate, then slide back into pan so that the top of the omelette is now on the bottom). Cook until the bottom is set and golden brown. Divide in half and serve immediately. Makes 2 servings.

Lobster Omelette with Tomato Sauce

For a satisfying and colourful luncheon dish, serve with 5 oz (150 g) cooked courgette strips.

3 oz (90 g) tomato, sliced	2 oz (60 g) cooked lobster meat or boneless halibut, or a combination, diced
2 teaspoons tomato purée	
1 tablespoon water	
1 teaspoon chicken stock powder	1 egg, lightly beaten with ½ teaspoon water
½ teaspoon mixed dried or fresh herbs to taste (chives, parsley, tarragon or basil)	Salt and freshly ground pepper to taste

Cook tomato, tomato purée, water, stock powder and herbs in small saucepan until tomato is soft. Blend in blender goblet and pour back into saucepan. Add fish and keep saucepan over low heat, so contents stay hot without boiling. Pour egg into small heated nonstick frying pan, and cook over moderate heat, lifting edges on all sides and tilting pan so that uncooked portions flow evenly to bottom. When omelette is set, place some of the tomato-fish mixture across the centre, fold it in half, and slide it onto a warmed serving plate. Top with remaining tomato-fish mixture. Makes 1 serving.

Scrambled Egg with Diced Bread (Oeufs Brouillés aux Croûtons)

1 egg
Salt and pepper to taste
1 tablespoon water
1 slice white bread, toasted (dried in oven or toaster), made into croûtons

¼ teaspoon chopped fresh herbs (parsley, chives, rosemary), or pinch of dried herbs to taste

Break egg into a bowl; add salt, pepper and water. Beat thoroughly. Pour into small heated nonstick or heavy iron pan. Cook over moderate heat, stirring gently. When egg is almost done, sprinkle with croûtons and herbs. Scramble and serve. Makes 1 serving.

Codfish with Herbs and Tomatoes (Cabillaud à la Provençale)

1 pint 4 fl oz (720 ml) water
1½ oz (45 g) sliced celery
1 teaspoon chicken stock powder
½ lemon
2 tablespoons dried onion flakes
1 teaspoon chopped fresh parsley
½ bay leaf

⅛ teaspoon ground cloves
⅛ teaspoon thyme
4 boned and skinned cod steaks, 6 oz (180 g) each
6 oz (180 g) tomatoes, cut in halves
12 oz (360 g) green peppers, seeded and cut in halves

In a 12-inch (30 cm) pan, combine water, celery, stock powder, lemon, onion flakes, parsley, bay leaf, cloves and thyme. Bring to the boil, then reduce heat to a simmer. Add fish and poach 5 to 7 minutes. Add tomato and green pepper halves, and finish cooking until fish flakes easily. Remove fish and vegetables, keep hot. Cook liquid until reduced by half. Remove lemon and bay leaf. Place liquid and half the cooked tomato and peppers in a blender goblet. Purée until smooth. Slowly reheat in saucepan. Pour over fish and remaining tomato and peppers. Makes 4 servings.

Fish Stew Brittany Style (Cotriade)

1 lb 8 oz (720 g) assorted fish fillets, frozen
12 oz (360 g) peeled potato, diced
8 oz (240 g) diced turnips
7 oz (210 g) diced carrots
2 tablespoons dried onion flakes
1 tablespoon chopped fresh herbs (marjoram, tarragon, savory, chervil and thyme) or 1½ teaspoons dried
1 garlic clove
2 pints 10 fl oz (1 litre 500 ml) water
Salt and pepper to taste
4 teaspoons chopped fresh parsley

While the fish is still frozen, cut into small even pieces and set aside. Combine potato, turnips, carrots, onion flakes, herbs and garlic in saucepan. Cover with water. Bring to the boil, cover and simmer until vegetables are tender but not mushy. Add the fish to the liquid and simmer until fish is cooked, about 5 to 8 minutes. Do not overcook. Season with salt and pepper. Divide into 4 serving bowls; sprinkle each portion with parsley. Makes 4 servings.

Bouquet Garni

4 sprigs parsley or 1 teaspoon dried parsley
½ crushed bay leaf
2 sprigs fresh thyme, or tarragon, or marjoram
2 cloves, crushed
2 teaspoons chopped celery leaves or chives

Many different herbs can be used in making a bouquet garni. Gather the herbs in 4-inch (10 cm) squares of muslin and tie with white thread, or put them into metal tea-infusion spoons. Add the bouquet garni during the last half hour of cooking, or as the recipe indicates.

Rolled Fillets of Fish with Carrots (Paupiettes de Poisson aux Carottes)

Use any skinless fillet: flounder, sole, whiting, etc. Cooked puréed sorrel is a favourite vegetable in France, often served with fish.

2 × 6 oz (180 g) fish fillets, fresh or frozen
Salt and pepper to taste
2 carrots, 1½ oz (45 g) each cooked firm
Paprika
2 slices lemon
1 medium orange, unpeeled and sliced thinly over bowl to save juices
Parsley sprigs or watercress
2 oz (60 g) cooked peas (optional)

Thaw fish if frozen. Season with salt and pepper. Roll each fillet round a carrot. Trim length of carrot, if necessary. Place in baking tin with the join underneath. Sprinkle with paprika, top with lemon slices, and any juice from orange. Cover with foil and bake at 350°F (180°C) Gas Mark 4, for 15 to 20 minutes or until fish flakes easily with a fork. Remove foil and transfer to serving dish. Cut orange slices into half circles and, dividing evenly, arrange half the orange slices round each fillet with cut edge against fish. In between orange slices arrange clumps of parsley or watercress. Sprinkle 1 oz (30 g) of peas over each fillet, if desired. Makes 2 servings.

Baked Stuffed Sole

1 oz (30 g) diced celery
1 oz (30 g) onion, diced
4 fl oz (120 ml) chicken stock, made with ¼ stock cube
1 oz (30 g) peas and carrots, cooked
1 tablespoon mayonnaise
¼ teaspoon Worcester sauce
¼ teaspoon lemon juice
Few drops hot pepper sauce
Salt and pepper to taste
1 × 6 oz (180 g) fillet of sole
Paprika
Lemon slices (optional)

Cook celery, onion and stock in a saucepan until celery is tender. Remove from heat. Drain well; add peas and carrots, mayonnaise, Worcester sauce, lemon juice, hot pepper sauce, salt and pepper. Mix thoroughly. Lay fish fillet on a flat surface; spread stuffing mixture over sole and roll securely. Place in an individual baking tin. Sprinkle with paprika and garnish with lemon slices. Cover with foil. Bake at 350°F (180°C), Gas Mark 4, for about 15 to 20 minutes or until fish flakes easily with a fork. Makes 1 serving.

Sole Argenteuil

6 oz (180 g) fillet of sole
6 oz (180 g) cooked or canned white
  asparagus
1½ oz (45 g) tomato, chopped
½ oz (15 g) nonfat dry milk,

reconstituted with 2½ fl oz
(75 ml) water
½ oz (15 g) diced pimiento
¼ teaspoon dried onion flakes
Salt and pepper to taste

Place fish in a small nonstick baking tin. Bake at 400°F (200°C), Gas Mark 6, for 15 to 20 minutes, or until fish flakes easily with a fork. Blend half the asparagus, the tomato, milk, pimiento, onion flakes, salt and pepper in blender goblet until smooth. Pour into a small saucepan and heat slowly. *Do not boil.* When cooked, remove fish to serving dish; pour heated sauce over and arrange the remaining asparagus on top. Makes 1 serving.

Grilled Fish Steaks with Grapefruit (Poisson aux Pamplemousses)

4 × 6 oz (180 g) boned fish steaks
  (cod, halibut, turbot, pollock)
1½ teaspoons salt
¾ teaspoon pepper
Paprika
4 oz (120 g) grapefruit sections, no

sugar added, drain and reserve
juice
2 tablespoons chicken stock, made
  from stock cube according to
  package directions
Chopped fresh parsley

Sprinkle fish with salt, pepper and paprika, and place in grill pan. Combine grapefruit juice and chicken stock. Spoon half the mixture over fish. Grill about 4 inches (10 cm) from source of heat for 5 to 6 minutes. Turn fish; spoon remaining grapefruit juice mixture on each fish steak. Continue grilling until fish flakes easily with fork, 4 to 6 minutes. Serve with pan juices, sprinkle with parsley and top with grapefruit sections. Makes 4 servings.

Mackerel Stew Brittany Style (Maquereau à la Bretonne)

½ bay leaf
¼ teaspoon thyme or 2 sprigs fresh
1 tablespoon dried onion flakes
1 small garlic clove
Salt and pepper to taste

1 lb 8 oz (720 g) mackerel fillets, cut into large pieces
4 × 3 oz (90 g) cooked potatoes
1 tablespoon chopped fresh parsley or chives

Cover the bottom of a shallow saucepan with an inch (2.5 cm) of water. Add bay leaf, thyme, dried onion flakes, garlic, salt and pepper. Simmer gently 3 to 5 minutes. Add mackerel pieces, cover saucepan and let simmer gently for 15 minutes. Add potatoes; cover and cook 10 minutes. Transfer fish and potatoes to serving dish and keep hot. Quickly boil down sauce until reduced by half. Strain sauce over fish. Sprinkle with parsley or chives. Serve hot. Makes 4 servings.

Carp with Parsley

Follow preceding recipe but substitute chunks of carp for mackerel. Omit potatoes. Serve cold with horseradish and plenty of chopped parsley. Makes 4 servings.

Crabmeat Mousse

6 oz (180 g) cooked crabmeat
8 fl oz (240 ml) tomato juice
1 tablespoon mayonnaise
½ oz (15 g) chopped pimientos
1 teaspoon lemon juice
1 teaspoon chopped fresh chives
1 teaspoon chopped fresh parsley

2 fl oz (60 ml) water
1 tablespoon unflavoured gelatine
Salt and pepper to taste
½ oz (15 g) nonfat dry milk,
  reconstituted with 2½ fl oz
  (75 ml) water

Flake crabmeat in small bowl; add 1 tablespoon tomato juice and next 5 ingredients and mix well. Pour water into a small saucepan, sprinkle gelatine on top and heat until gelatine is dissolved. Stir into crab mixture. Season with salt and pepper. Fold milk into crabmeat. Place in small mould. Chill until ready to serve. Turn out. Serve with remaining tomato juice. Makes 1 serving.

Cold Lobster Cardinale

4 oz (120 g) cooked lobster, diced
2 fl oz (60 ml) tomato juice
1 oz (30 g) diced celery
1 tablespoon mayonnaise
1 teaspoon lemon juice
1 teaspoon brandy flavouring
1 teaspoon chopped fresh chives

1 teaspoon chopped fresh parsley
1 tablespoon unflavoured gelatine
2 fl oz (60 ml) water
Salt and pepper to taste
½ oz (15 g) nonfat dry milk,
  reconstituted with 2½ fl oz
  (75 ml) water

Combine lobster and next 7 ingredients in a mixing bowl. Mix thoroughly. Sprinkle gelatine over water in saucepan. Place over low heat and stir until gelatine is dissolved. Add lobster mixture. Season with salt and pepper. Fold milk into lobster mixture. Pour into small mould. Chill until set. Turn out. Makes 1 serving.

Scallops in Shell (Coquilles St. Jacques)

12 oz (360 g) fresh scallops
Boiling water with ¾ teaspoon salt
2 fl oz (60 ml) scallop liquid
3 oz (90 g) mushrooms, sliced thinly
1 oz (30 g) diced onion or
   1 teaspoon dried onion flakes
4 fl oz (120 ml) chicken stock,
   made with ¼ stock cube
2 slices white bread, made into fine
   crumbs

Salt and pepper to taste
Pinch grated lemon rind
1 oz (30 g) nonfat dry milk,
   reconstituted with 5 fl oz (150 ml)
   water
¼ teaspoon lemon juice
4 teaspoons margarine
Garnish: 2 lemon wedges and sprigs
   of parsley

Wash and dry scallops. Cut large scallops into 3 or 4 pieces, cover with boiling water, and parboil for 3 minutes. Remove from heat; drain (reserving 2 fl oz (60 ml) liquid), cover and set aside. In nonstick frying pan, brown mushrooms and onions; add chicken stock, all but 4 tablespoons of the breadcrumbs, salt, pepper and lemon rind. Cover and let simmer over low heat for 5 minutes. Add milk and continue cooking over low heat until sauce is thick. Stir in lemon juice, salt and pepper. Remove from heat; stir in scallops and reserved liquid and transfer to 2 large shells or ramekins. Mix margarine with remaining crumbs and sprinkle on top of scallops. Put under grill just long enough to brown crumbs (less than 1 minute). Serve piping hot. Garnish with lemon wedges and parsley. Makes 2 servings.

Shrimp Salad (Salade de Crevettes)

1 lb (480 g) cleaned, cooked shrimps
6 oz (180 g) cucumber, peeled,
   seeded and diced
2 oz (60 g) diced celery
1 tablespoon capers
1 tablespoon chopped fresh chives or
   parsley

4 tablespoons mayonnaise
½ teaspoon salt
Pinch pepper
Cupped lettuce leaves
3 oz (90 g) tomatoes, cut in wedges

Combine shrimps, cucumber, celery, capers and parsley in mixing bowl. Add mayonnaise, salt and pepper. Toss lightly. Chill. Serve in lettuce cups. Garnish with tomato wedges. Makes 4 servings.

Lobster Divan

2 frozen lobster tails, about 8 oz (240 g)
6 oz (180 g) frozen broccoli spears
1 slice white bread made into crumbs
2 oz (60 g) nonfat dry milk, reconstituted with 10 fl oz (300 ml) water
2 oz (60 g) diced Cheddar cheese
Salt and pepper
½ teaspoon sherry flavouring
2 slices lemon

Drop lobster tails into boiling salted water. Bring water to boil again; cook for 5 minutes, drain immediately, cool under cold water, and drain again. Cut away underside membrane and remove meat from shells in one piece. Weigh 4 oz (120 g). Keep warm. Cook broccoli according to package directions. Drain. Line 2 small shallow casseroles evenly with broccoli, and place 2 oz (60 g) of lobster tail on top. Combine bread, cheese and milk in blender goblet; blend until smooth; place in saucepan, heat to just below boiling; simmer 3 minutes. Season with salt, pepper and sherry flavouring. Pour over casseroles. Serve at once or brown lightly under the grill before serving. Garnish with lemon slices. Makes 2 servings.

Chicken in Vinaigrette (Poulet au Vinaigre)

The vinegar is often boiled for a few minutes with an equal amount of chicken stock and other seasonings listed below. We've eliminated this step in our simplified procedure and increased the marinating time.

2 garlic cloves
1 chicken, 3 lbs (1 kg 440 g), skinned and quartered*
12 fl oz (360 ml) wine vinegar
Pinch each of any of the following
ground seasonings or to taste:
cloves, salt, black pepper, poultry seasoning, juniper berries, tarragon, chicken stock powder

Push garlic through garlic press onto folds of greaseproof paper. Rub paper over chicken. Stack chicken quarters in mixing bowl. Combine vinegar with any desired seasoning, and pour over chicken in bowl. Let marinate, covered, in refrigerator overnight. Drain; reserve marinade. Grill chicken 4 inches (10 cm) from source of heat (or over hot charcoal) until done, 15 to 20 minutes on each side, basting several times with reserved marinade. Serve hot or cold. Makes 4 servings.

*A 3 lb (1 kg 440 g) chicken will yield about 1 lb (480 g) cooked meat.

Chicken with Grapes (Poulet Véronique)

1 chicken, 3 lbs (1 kg 440 g)*
Salt, pepper and poultry seasoning
　to taste
8 fl oz (240 ml) orange juice

1 teaspoon chicken stock powder
1 tablespoon chopped fresh parsley
2 tablespoons grated orange rind
6 oz (180 g) seedless grapes

Sprinkle chicken with salt, pepper and poultry seasoning, inside and out. Place chicken on a rack and roast at 375°F (190°C), Gas Mark 5, for 50 minutes or until chicken is done. Meanwhile, prepare the sauce. In saucepan, bring orange juice, stock powder and parsley to the boil, lower heat and simmer for 30 minutes, stirring occasionally. Add orange rind and cook 10 minutes longer or until rind is tender. Transfer chicken to serving dish, remove skin; cut into serving pieces. Add grapes to sauce; stir well to combine. Pour over chicken. Serve at once. Makes 4 servings.

*See note on Chicken in Vinaigrette recipe.

Chicken Marengo

Napoleon's French chef was supposed to have invented this dish, using ingredients available in the war-torn countryside. In the original version, crayfish and eggs were included, but today's recipe writers omit them. So we have a delicious chicken-tomato-mushroom-onion mixture in the French-Italian family of continental recipes. Cooked rice or noodles are the usual accompaniment.

1 lb 8 oz (720 g) boned and skinned
chicken breasts, cut in 1½-inch
(4 cm) pieces
1 crushed garlic clove
16 fl oz (480 ml) Homemade
Chicken Stock (see page 10)
12 oz (360 g) tomatoes, peeled and
chopped
2 oz (60 g) diced celery
½ bay leaf

1 tablespoon chopped fresh parsley
½ teaspoon mixed herbs (thyme,
basil, tarragon) or 1½ teaspoons
chopped fresh
Salt and pepper to taste
2 teaspoons sherry flavouring
6 oz (180 g) mushrooms, sliced
4 oz (120 g) drained cooked or
canned pearl onions

Brown chicken and garlic on all sides in a nonstick saucepan. Remove
chicken. Add stock, tomatoes, celery and bay leaf. Bring to the boil.
Simmer 30 minutes. Add parsley, mixed herbs, sherry flavouring, salt
and pepper and cook for 5 minutes. Put sauce in blender goblet and
blend. If sauce is too thick, add more stock. Stir in mushrooms and
onions. Simmer for 10 minutes. Pour over chicken and serve hot. (Or
pour sauce into a casserole, top with chicken and add mushrooms and
onions.) Refrigerate until ready to use, cook 30 minutes at 350°F
(180°C), Gas Mark 4. Makes 4 servings.

Veal Marengo

Thyme, a native herb of the Mediterranean, is traditional both in the
Chicken and Veal Marengo. More may be added if to your taste.
Replace chicken with 1 lb 8 oz (720 g) thin sliced veal cut from leg (veal
escalopes). Pound thinly and cut in 2-inch (5 cm) squares. Then follow
preceding recipe. Makes 4 servings.

'Brandied' Chicken (Poulet Alsacien)

Add a green salad to complete this one-dish meal.

4 skinned and boned chicken breasts
  or cutlets, 6 oz (180 g) each
4 teaspoons flour
Salt and pepper to taste
6 oz (180 g) carrots, cut in thick
  slices
2 oz (60 g) shallots or spring onions,
  finely chopped
6 oz (180 g) tiny white onions,
  peeled and blanched

4 tablespoons chopped fresh parsley
1 teaspoon salt
$\frac{1}{2}$ teaspoon pepper
1 garlic clove
8 fl oz (240 ml) chicken stock,
  made with $\frac{1}{2}$ stock cube
6 oz (180 g) small mushroom caps
$\frac{1}{2}$ teaspoon brandy (or sherry)
  flavouring

Sprinkle chicken with flour, salt and pepper. Brown in nonstick pan over moderately high heat, turning frequently. Transfer chicken pieces to dish. Lightly brown carrots and shallots or spring onions in same pan. Return chicken pieces to pan. Add blanched onions, parsley, salt, pepper and garlic. Pour in chicken stock and simmer, covered for 20 minutes. Add mushrooms and brandy flavouring and continue simmering until chicken is tender and mushrooms are done, about 10 minutes more. Makes 4 servings.

Chicken with Apples (Poulet Normand)

In Normandy, small white onions would be the usual accompaniment.

1 chicken, 3 lbs (1 kg 440 g), cut in
  quarters, skin removed*
$\frac{3}{4}$ teaspoon poultry seasoning
8 to 12 fl oz (240 to 360 ml) chicken
  stock made with $\frac{1}{2}$ to 1 stock
  cube
3 oz (90 g) sliced celery
1 medium apple, peeled, cored and
  sliced
2 tablespoons dried onion flakes

1 tablespoon mixed chopped fresh
  herbs or 1 teaspoon dried (parsley
  tarragon, basil and perhaps a little
  sage)
1$\frac{1}{2}$ oz (45 g) nonfat dry milk,
  reconstituted with 7$\frac{1}{2}$ fl oz
  (225 ml) water
$\frac{1}{2}$ teaspoon sherry flavouring
Salt and pepper to taste

Season chicken with poultry seasoning and set aside. Cook stock, celery, apple and onion flakes in saucepan for about 20 minutes over low heat. Add herbs for the last few minutes. Meanwhile, grill chicken on rack 4 inches (10 cm) from source of heat, 12 to 15 minutes or until firm to touch, turning to cook both sides. When celery and apple mixture is soft, blend and put back into saucepan. Mixture should now have consistency of a thick sauce. If not, reduce it by quick boiling. Let cool slightly; add milk and sherry flavouring. Heat gently (mixture must not boil). Turn off heat. Add hot chicken, season with salt and pepper and serve promptly (or cover and keep hot). Makes 4 servings.

*A 3 lb (1 kg 440 g) chicken will yield about 1 lb (480 g) cooked meat.

Tarragon Roast Chicken (Poulet Rôti à l'Estragon)

1 chicken, 3 lbs (1 kg 440 g)
1 garlic clove, cut in half
Salt and pepper to taste
½ teaspoon tarragon or 2 large
  sprigs of fresh tarragon chopped

4 fl oz (120 ml) chicken stock,
  made with ¼ stock cube
Tarragon Sauce (recipe follows)

Rub chicken on all sides with cut garlic clove. Season with salt and pepper, inside and out. Sprinkle cavity with tarragon. Truss chicken with string or skewers. Using brush or fingers, moisten all sides of chicken with stock. Place on rack in roasting tin and bake until chicken is done, 50 to 60 minutes, turning every 15 minutes so back, breast and sides are equally browned and all parts of the bird are juicy and succulent. Remove skin and bones. Weigh portions (4 oz (120 g) per portion) and serve with Tarragon Sauce. Makes 4 servings.

Tarragon Sauce

4 teaspoons margarine
4 teaspoons flour
6 fl oz (180 ml) Homemade Chicken
  Stock (see page 10) or stock
  made with ½ stock cube
½ oz (15 g) nonfat dry milk,

reconstituted with 2½ fl oz
  (75 ml) water
½ teaspoon tarragon or 2 large
  sprigs fresh tarragon, chopped
Salt and pepper to taste

Melt margarine in top of double boiler. Stir flour into melted margarine until mixture is smooth. Slowly add stock stirring with a wooden spoon until smooth. Continue to cook until thickened. Add milk and tarragon. Adjust seasonings. Divide evenly and serve over chicken. Makes 4 servings.

Chicken with Aubergine (Coq Basque)

1 chicken 3 lbs (1 kg 440 g), skinned*
Marinate as in Chicken in Vinaigrette (see page 119–120) if desired
1 garlic clove
6 oz (180 g) peeled aubergine, cut into 3-inch (8 cm) lengths
6 oz (180 g) diced mushrooms
6 oz (180 g) tomatoes, quartered
12 oz (360 g) green peppers, cut into squares (remove seeds and white pulp)
8 oz (240 g) small onions, parboiled in water to cover for 10 minutes
6 fl oz (180 ml) chicken stock, made with ½ stock cube
1 bay leaf
1 teaspoon mixed dried herbs, including basil and thyme
1 sliced truffle (optional)

Whether or not you marinate the chicken, be sure to rub it with garlic before cooking. Put chicken in a casserole. Combine vegetables and remaining ingredients and spread over chicken. Cover and bake in moderate oven (375°F (190°C), Gas Mark 5), for 40 to 50 minutes or until chicken is tender. If necessary, to evaporate excess liquid, continue baking without lid. Mix well before serving. Makes 4 servings.

*A 3 lb (1 kg 440 g) chicken will yield about 1 lb (480 g) cooked meat.

Devilled Chicken Mousse

4 oz (120 g) cooked chicken, finely chopped
1½ oz (45 g) finely chopped celery
1½ oz (45 g) green pepper, diced
1 oz (30 g) onion, finely chopped
1 tablespoon chopped fresh parsley
½ oz (15 g) chopped pimiento
1 teaspoon mayonnaise
1 teaspoon Worcester sauce
½ teaspoon dry English mustard
½ teaspoon chicken stock powder
6 fl oz (180 ml) cold water
2 teaspoons unflavoured gelatine
Salt to taste
Lettuce
Watercress

Combine chicken, celery, green pepper, onion, parsley and pimiento in a mixing bowl; add mayonnaise, Worcester sauce and mustard; mix well. Add stock powder; stir to combine. Pour water into a saucepan. Sprinkle gelatine over it to soften. Place over low heat and stir until gelatine dissolves. Add to chicken mixture and blend thoroughly. Add salt and continue to blend. Turn into a small mould and chill until set, about 3 hours. Turn out and serve on a bed of lettuce and watercress. Makes 1 serving.

Marinated Roast Veal

In spring serve this with cooked fresh asparagus tips, 5 oz (150 g) per serving.

4 lbs (1 kg 920 g) veal roast	1 teaspoon celery seed
1 pint 4 fl oz (720 ml) white vinegar	½ bay leaf
1 teaspoon peppercorns, crushed	Salt and pepper to taste
2 garlic cloves, crushed	2 lemons, cut in quarters
2 sprigs parsley	Sprigs of watercress, fresh parsley
1 sprig thyme or tarragon	or celery leaves

Cover veal roast in large bowl with a mixture of all remaining ingredients (except lemon and watercress). Refrigerate for 24 hours, turning frequently so all sides of meat are immersed. Remove meat to baking tin, reserving marinade. Roast in slow oven—slow roasting is the secret of this recipe—at 325°F (160°C), Gas Mark 3, for 2½ hours, basting frequently with reserved marinade until veal is thoroughly cooked. (Internal temperature on meat thermometer will be 170°F (75°C). Let roast cool for 10 to 15 minutes to gather juices, then slice and serve with garnish: quarters of lemon and sprigs of watercress, or other leaves. Makes 8 servings.

Veal Chops in Foil (Côtes de Veau en Papillote)

4 white veal chops, 10 oz (300 g)
each
4 sheets aluminium foil, each 12 ×
16-inches (30 × 40 cm)
2 × 3 oz (90 g) tomatoes, cut in
halves

8 oz (240 g) drained tiny canned or
cooked white onions
4 teaspoons chopped mixed fresh
herbs (parsley, chives, tarragon,
thyme) or 2 teaspoons dried
Salt and pepper to taste

Brown chops in heated nonstick frying pan over moderate heat,
turning once, until done on both sides, about 15 minutes. Put one chop
in the centre of each sheet of foil. Top each with a tomato half and a
quarter of the onions. Sprinkle each with a mixture of herbs, salt and
pepper. Wrap, double-folding the edges to make a tightly sealed
package. Bake on baking sheet at 400°F (200°C), Gas Mark 6, for 20
minutes, or longer at lower temperature if dinner must wait. Serve the
foil packages, to be opened at the table. Makes 4 servings.

Veal Chops with Orange (Côtes de Veau à l'Orange)

4 × 8 oz (240 g) rib veal chops
1 garlic clove, cut
Salt and pepper to taste
4 teaspoons margarine
4 teaspoons chopped fresh basil or
tarragon or 2 teaspoons dried

8 oz (240 g) hot cooked rice
4 medium oranges, peeled, cut in
slices (reserve rind for garnish, see
note)

Buy the whitest chops you can find. Preheat grill. Wipe chops dry. Rub
them on all sides with garlic. Grill 4 inches (10 cm) from source of heat
until completely cooked through, turning once. Season with salt and
pepper. Meanwhile cream margarine with basil to make a smooth
paste. Transfer chops to individual serving plates, each holding 2 oz
(60 g) rice in centre, with a border or orange slices. Spread margarine
mixture over each chop and serve at once. Makes 4 servings.

Note: For garnish—cut matchstick pieces of orange rind. Place in
water until soft and pile in centre of veal before serving.

Veal in Aspic

A perfect summer lunch dish.

1 tablespoon unflavoured gelatine
6 fl oz (180 ml) cold chicken
    stock, made with ½ stock cube
2 oz (60 g) grated onion
2 tablespoons mayonnaise
2 tablespoons lemon juice
1 teaspoon Worcester sauce
½ teaspoon dry mustard

¼ teaspoon salt or to taste
⅛ teaspoon hot pepper sauce
8 oz (240 g) roast veal, diced
3 oz (90 g) diced celery
1 oz (30 g) diced pimiento
Garnish: lettuce leaves and 2
    pimiento strips

Sprinkle gelatine over cold stock in small saucepan. Place over low heat; stir constantly until gelatine dissolves, about 3 minutes. Remove from heat. Combine onion, mayonnaise, lemon juice, Worcester sauce, dry mustard, salt and hot pepper sauce; mix thoroughly with gelatine mixture. Chill, stirring occasionally until mixture thickens to the consistency of unbeaten egg whites. Combine roast veal, celery and pimiento. Stir into thickened gelatine mixture. Transfer to medium mould. Chill until set. Turn out on a bed of lettuce leaves. Crisscross bright red pimiento strips across the top before serving. Makes 2 servings.

Beef with Parsley (Persillade de Boeuf)

8 oz (240 g) cooked beef, thinly
    sliced
16 fl oz (480 ml) beef stock, made
    with 1 stock cube
4 tablespoons chopped fresh parsley

1 tablespoon dried onion flakes
1 tablespoon lemon juice
Salt and pepper to taste
4 oz (120 g) cooked rice (see note)

Cut stacked slices of beef into strips with a sharp knife and set aside. In saucepan, bring stock to the boil; add beef, parsley and onion flakes. Reduce heat, cover pan and let simmer 15 minutes. Stir in lemon juice and simmer for 10 minutes more. Season with salt and pepper. Put 2 oz (60 g) rice into each of two serving bowls and top with beef mixture. Makes 2 servings.

Note: To reheat or plump up cold rice, place in strainer and pour hot water over it. If rice is lumpy, gently press out lumps between fingers.

Beef and Celery Ragout

1 lb 8 oz (720 g) boneless lean beef (cut from less tender cuts: rump, top rump, chuck etc.)
1 garlic clove, cut
12 oz (360 g) sliced celery
16 fl oz (480 ml) beef stock, made with 1 stock cube
6 oz (180 g) mushrooms, sliced through cap and stem

8 oz (240 g) tiny white onions, peeled
½ oz (15 g) chopped fresh parsley
3 cloves, slightly crushed
1 teaspoon thyme
1 teaspoon salt
8 peppercorns, slightly crushed

Preheat grill and rack. Rub beef with cut garlic clove and cut into 1-inch (2.5 cm) cubes. Transfer to rack in grill pan. Brown all sides 4 inches (10 cm) from source of heat for 15 to 20 minutes. Transfer meat to large saucepan with tight lid. Add remaining ingredients. Bring to the boil, reduce heat, cover pan and simmer gently for 1 to 1½ hours or until beef is very tender. Serve hot. Makes 4 servings.

Meat Patties (Hamburgers and Vealburgers, Chickenburgers, Lamburgers, Liverburgers)

As well as beef, we've listed some of the other minced meats commonly served. Seasonings and fillers are varied to taste or omitted, since good meat has its own distinctive flavour when cooked simply. We think salt should be added only after cooking because it seems to draw juices from grilled meat . . . and on our Food Programme we leave behind in the pan the fluids and fats rendered in the first grilling. The following recipe for 1 serving is easily multiplied for a family.

AFRICA: Tripe Stew (page 17); Rice Salad (page 18)

AUSTRALIA AND NEW ZEALAND: Pavlova (page 27); Roast Baby Lamb (page 23)

AUSTRIA AND HUNGARY: Cherry Soup (Cseresznyelves) (page 29); Tyrolean Liver Soup (Lebersuppe) (page 30); Hungarian Fisherman's Soup (Halászlé) (page 31)

BELGIUM AND THE NETHERLANDS: Golden Velvet Carrots (page 41); Belgian Fish Soup (Waterzoi) (page 39)

THE BRITISH ISLES: Baked Salmon with Caper Sauce (page 49); Strawberry Fool (page 56)

CANADA: Three-Layer Moulded Apple Custard (page 62);
Rhubarb and Strawberry Mould with Lemon 'Cream' Topping (page 63); Spinach-Cheese Ring (page 61)

CARIBBEAN AND WEST INDIES: Pineapple Rice Pudding (Arroz con Leche y Piña) (page 70); Pumpkin Soup (Sopa de Zapallo) (page 64)

CHINA: Chinese Eggroll with Shrimp Filling (page 76); Chicken with Vegetables and Mushrooms (Moo Goo Gai Pan) (page 85); Clear Soup (page 73)

FRANCE: Rolled Fillets of Fish with Carrots (page 114); Watercress Soup (Potage au Cresson) (page 107); Poached Whole Pears (page 147)

GERMANY: Delicatessan (page 155); Potato Salad (page 157); Sweet and Sour Cole Slaw (page 158)

GREECE AND THE OTHER BALKAN STATES: Albanian Lamb Stew with Okra (page 166)

INDIA: Easy Chicken Curry with Tomatoes (Murghi Kari) (page 174); Vegetable Chutney (page 176); Apple Chutney (page 176); Condiments (sliced bananas, diced oranges, sliced spring onions, cantaloupe melon balls)

6 oz (180 g) liver, skinned and boned
chicken, or boneless veal, lamb, or
beef
1 tablespoon dried onion flakes,
reconstituted in 2 tablespoons
water or stock made from stock
cube according to package
directions

1½ teaspoons dried celery flakes,
reconstituted
½ teaspoon dried herbs or to taste:
rosemary, thyme, basil, sage or
dill or 1 teaspoon chopped fresh
Salt and pepper to taste

Put meat through fine blade of mincer with onion flakes and celery flakes. Add herbs and mix well with fork. Shape into 1 large or 2 small flat compact patty(ies). Cook as below. Season at table with salt and pepper. Makes 1 serving.

(a) Grill on rack in pan, 4 inches (10 cm) from source of heat, about 5 to 8 minutes on each side or until done to taste.

(b) Bake on rack in pan set in preheated moderate oven (375°F (190°C), Gas Mark 5), until well-browned, about 20 minutes.

(c) Only for veal, chicken or liver patties: Brown in heated nonstick frying pan until done to taste, turning once.

Beef in a Pot (Pot-au-feu)

1 lb 8 oz (720 g) lean stewing beef, cut
in 3-inch (8 cm) pieces
8 oz (240 g) sliced celery and leaves
5 oz (150 g) shredded cabbage
10 oz (300 g) diced carrots
4 oz (120 g) diced turnips

8 oz (240 g) well cleaned leeks,
white part only, sliced
2 garlic cloves
½ bay leaf
1 clove
Salt and pepper to taste
8 oz (240 g) frozen broad beans

Cover meat with water, bring to the boil and cook 1 hour. Remove beef, refrigerate stock, to congeal the fat. Skim to remove fat and bring 1 pint 4 fl oz (720 ml) stock to the boil; add the beef with remaining ingredients, except beans, and enough water to cover. Cook 30 minutes longer or until vegetables are tender. Add broad beans and cook until beans are done. Serve soup as first course, meat, vegetables and beans as second course. Makes 4 servings.

Steak with Peppercorns (Bifteck au Poivre)

1½ teaspoons peppercorns
2 boneless steaks, 6 oz (180 g) each,
    trimmed of all visible fat

Piquant Sauce, optional
    (recipe follows)
Salt (optional)

With rolling pin, crush peppercorns on a towel until they are flattened (the pepper mill grinds too finely). Using palm of hand or side of cleaver, push pepper as deeply as possible into both sides of steaks. Let stand 30 minutes. Preheat grill pan and rack. Grill steaks on rack at high heat about 3 inches (8 cm) from source of heat for 8 to 16 minutes or until done to taste, turning once. Serve on heated plates with optional Piquant Sauce or salt for added seasoning. Makes 2 servings.

Piquant Sauce

2 tablespoons margarine
1 teaspoon Worcester sauce

2 teaspoons wine vinegar

Make the sauce in two small individual ovenproof dishes. To 1 tablespoon melted margarine (melted over pilot light or in warming drawer) add ½ teaspoon Worcester sauce and 1 teaspoon wine vinegar. Serve in tiny dishes with steak. Repeat for each serving. Makes 2 servings.

Sausage with Potato Salad (Saucisson à la Lyonnaise)

12 oz (360 g) spicy all-beef sausage,
    knackwurst or frankfurters,
    pierced with fork
12 oz (360 g) cooked and peeled
    potatoes
2 fl oz (60 ml) vegetable oil

2 tablespoons dried onion flakes in
    2 fl oz (60 ml) vinegar
1 teaspoon Dijon-style mustard
2 oz (60 g) shredded round or cos
    lettuce
Chopped fresh parsley

Cook sausage in a large saucepan in plenty of boiling water to cover. Cut potatoes into a bowl, in ¼-inch (5 mm) slices. While they are still warm, combine oil, vinegar, onion flakes and mustard, and gently toss with potatoes. Drain the sausage and cut into slices ½-inch (1 cm) thick. (Remove skin covering if necessary.) Serve sausage slices, potato salad and shredded lettuce evenly divided on dinner plates. Garnish with parsley and serve with additional Dijon-style mustard. Makes 4 servings.

Sweetbreads with Melted 'Butter'

4 oz (120 g) cooked tiny peas
  (optional)
2 tablespoons low fat spread
2 teaspoons chopped fresh parsley
1 teaspoon lemon juice

Salt and pepper to taste
8 oz (240 g) cooked trimmed
  sweetbreads, cut into bite-size
  pieces (see note)

In each of 2 individual casseroles, place half the peas, if desired, and half the low fat spread, parsley, lemon juice, salt and pepper. Divide sweetbreads evenly into casseroles. At the table, gently turn sweetbreads with a fork to absorb all the sauce. Makes 2 servings.

Note: To prepare sweetbreads, soak in salted water to cover for 1 hour. Drain. Transfer to a saucepan, cover with cold water and add 1 tablespoon white vinegar. Bring to the boil. Let simmer for 15 minutes. Drain, dip them quickly into cold water and discard tough parts and membrane. Weigh cooked and trimmed sweetbreads for recipe.

Ham with Grapes (Jambon aux Raisins)

May be served with cooked rice and braised celery.

6 oz (180 g) seedless grapes
8 fl oz (240 ml) boiling water
1 teaspoon unflavoured gelatine
1 teaspoon lemon juice

Pinch cinnamon and nutmeg
4 baked ham slices, 3 oz (90 g)
  each

Simmer the grapes in water for 20 minutes. Add gelatine, lemon juice and spices. Serve hot on slices of ham (or roast pork). Makes 4 servings.

Roast Lamb with Beans (Gigot Rôti aux Haricots)

Lamb is a young animal and its tender meat is ideal for roasting or grilling, but by French standards cooks in other countries overcook it. Try it this way, roasted in a hot oven to a medium-rare stage. You'll find it juicy and pink inside rather than the dried, well-done lamb you may be accustomed to.

1 leg of lamb, 5 lbs (2 kg 400 g)	Salt and pepper to taste
Cut garlic clove	Broad Beans I or II (recipes follow)

Season lamb on all sides by rubbing it with a cut garlic clove. Sprinkle with salt and pepper. Insert meat thermometer; avoid bone. Roast on rack for 12 to 15 minutes per pound or until thermometer reaches 150°F to 160°F (65° to 70°C). Let lamb stand 15 minutes before carving (so juices gather). Carve and serve weighed portions (4 oz (120 g) each) with broad beans. Makes 6 servings.

Broad Beans I

1 oz (30 g) sliced mushrooms	3 oz (90 g) cooked fresh broad beans
1 tablespoon dried onion flakes, reconstituted	Pinch marjoram and parsley
3 oz (90 g) tomato, peeled and diced	Salt and freshly ground pepper to taste

Brown mushrooms and onion flakes in a medium nonstick frying pan. Add tomato and heat until most of the liquid has evaporated. Stir in broad beans, marjoram, parsley, salt and pepper. Cook until heated through. Serve with slices of lamb. Makes 1 serving.

Broad Beans II

3 oz (90 g) sliced carrots
2 oz (60 g) onions, sliced
Water
Pinch thyme
Pinch ground cloves
Salt and pepper to taste

½ oz (15 g) nonfat dry milk,
  reconstituted with 2 tablespoons
  water
2 oz (60 g) cooked fresh broad beans
1 teaspoon margarine

Cook carrots and onions in a saucepan in enough water to cover, with thyme, cloves, salt and pepper added. Cook until carrots are tender and water almost evaporated. Stir in milk and broad beans. Reheat at low temperature; do not boil. Remove from heat and add margarine. Serve with sliced lamb. Makes 1 serving.

Lamb Stew (Navarin d'Agneau)

Prepare as many individual casseroles as there are members of your family for an easy one-course meal. Lamb left from a roast can be substituted for the first ingredient, and the first step omitted.

6 oz (180 g) boneless well-trimmed
  lamb steak, or shoulder of lamb
  with gristle and fat removed
8 fl oz (240 ml) beef stock, made
  with ½ stock cube
3 oz (90 g) tomato, diced
2 oz (60 g) sliced green beans

3 oz (90 g) peeled potato, sliced
2 oz (60 g) sliced turnips
1½ oz (45 g) diced carrots
1 teaspoon dried onion flakes
½ garlic clove
Pinch each of thyme and parsley
Salt and pepper to taste

Grill lamb steak on a rack 5 minutes on each side. Cut into 1-inch (2.5 cm) pieces and place in flameproof casserole. Add remaining ingredients. Cover (use aluminium foil if casserole has no lid) and simmer slowly on top of stove for 35 minutes or bake at 350°F (180°C), Gas Mark 4, for 50 minutes or until potato is tender. Add hot water or stock if stew shows signs of dryness. Makes 1 serving.

Lamb Steaks with Orange and Grapefruit

Serve this over cooked rice.

2 boneless lean lamb steaks, 6 oz
   (180 g) each
1 lemon, cut
1 garlic clove, cut
Pinch thyme

1 medium orange
½ medium grapefruit
Salt and pepper to taste
2 sprigs of mint for garnish

Order steaks about ¾-inch (2 cm) thick. Wipe them with cut lemon and refrigerate until needed. Before using, rub both sides of chops with cut garlic clove and press thyme into them. Peel orange and grapefruit and cut into sections over a small grill pan to catch juices. (To do this, just cut down along each section, and lift out the pieces of fruit discarding the membranes which separate the segments.) Place fruit in pan with juice. Put the lamb on another grilling rack and grill 4 inches (10 cm) from source of heat for 10 to 14 minutes, or until lamb is done to your taste, turning the chops once. Grill fruit for last 5 minutes of grilling time. Serve fruit with lamb, and provide salt and pepper mill for added seasoning at the table. Artificial sweetener for the fruit may also be provided at the table, but this is really not needed as grilling the fruit releases its juices and flavour. If fresh mint sprigs are available, use as garnish. Makes 2 servings.

Roast Pork (Rôti de Porc)

1 lb 8 oz (720 g) boneless pork roast
   (trimmed of fat)
Salt and pepper to taste

1 teaspoon thyme
Fresh sage leaves if available or
   1 teaspoon powdered sage

Have butcher bone a pork loin or shoulder and tie it well. Season with salt, pepper and crushed thyme. If fresh sage leaves are available insert them in slits cut into the pork, or use powdered sage with the other seasonings. Place pork on rack in roasting tin. Insert meat thermometer so bulb is in thickest part of roast. Bake at 375°F (190°C), Gas Mark 5, uncovered for 1¼ hours, allowing 35 minutes per pound or until internal temperature reaches 170°F to 185°F (75° to 85°C).

Note: For health reasons, pork must be well cooked with no trace of pink showing either in the juices or in the meat—prick the roast with a fork to test. If pink shows, return to oven and continue cooking. Remove pork to serving dish, slice and serve plain or in any of the following styles. Makes 4 servings.

Roast Pork with Cherries (Rôti de Porc Montmorency)

Drain and reserve liquid from 1 lb (480 g) stoned, canned sweet cherries, no sugar added. Blend 4 oz (120 g) in blender goblet until smooth. Combine all whole and puréed cherries in small saucepan with cherry liquid. Simmer for 20 to 30 minutes or until cherries are soft. Add salt and pepper to taste. Pour evenly around 4 oz (120 g) servings of roasted pork. Garnish each serving with 3 oz (90 g) thinly sliced pickled cucumber. Makes 4 servings.

Roast Pork with Sauerkraut (Rôti de Porc avec Choucroute)

2 lbs (960 g) sauerkraut, washed and
   drained
4 medium cooking apples, peeled,
   cored and sliced
1 teaspoon cinnamon

Pinch each of ground cloves, nutmeg
   and ginger
6 fl oz (180 ml) beef stock, made
   with ½ stock cube
1 teaspoon lemon juice

Arrange a layer of half the sauerkraut and sliced apples in baking dish. Sprinkle with spices. Repeat layers. Pour in stock and lemon juice. Cover and bake at 375°F (190°C), Gas Mark 5, for 40 minutes. Serve hot with Dijon-style mustard and Roast Pork (see page 134–135). Makes 4 servings.

Pork Chops with Bananas (Côtelettes de Porc aux Bananes)

Decorate the chops with paper cutlet frills, if available.

4 thick well-trimmed pork chops, 8 oz (240 g) each	4 ripe medium bananas
Salt, pepper and rosemary to taste	1 tablespoon lemon juice
2 × 6 oz (180 g) green peppers	Nutmeg to taste
	4 teaspoons margarine, melted

Season chops with salt, pepper and rosemary. Grill on preheated rack in pan 4 inches (10 cm) from source of heat until thoroughly cooked, turning once. Test by piercing thickest part of chop with a fork to be certain no trace of pink shows either in the juice or in the meat. While chops are cooking, cut peppers in half horizontally (through stem). Remove seeds and white pulp from insides. Cover peppers with boiling water in saucepan and cook over medium heat for 5 minutes. Remove from water, plunge quickly into cold water and drain dry. Mash the bananas, sprinkle with lemon juice and nutmeg. Fill pepper cases with bananas and put under grill with pork chops for last 5 minutes. Remove from heat. Dot 1 teaspoon margarine over banana mixture. Serve hot. Makes 4 servings.

Chicken Livers Chasseur (Foies de Volaille Chasseur)

6 oz (180 g) chicken livers	4 fl oz (120 ml) tomato juice
4 oz (120 g) onion, sliced	Pinch each garlic powder, rosemary
3 oz (90 g) tomato, diced	and thyme
1½ oz (45 g) sliced mushrooms	Salt and pepper to taste
4 fl oz (120 ml) chicken stock, made with ¼ stock cube	2 oz (60 g) cooked rice
	½ teaspoon chopped fresh parsley

Cook livers and onion in heated nonstick pan turning often with a spatula until lightly browned, about 5 minutes. Add tomato, mushrooms, stock, tomato juice and a pinch each of garlic powder, rosemary and thyme. Cook over low heat for 10 minutes or until mixture thickens. Season with salt and pepper. Serve over rice. Sprinkle with parsley. Makes 1 serving.

Chicken Livers in Aspic (Foies de Volaille en Gelée)

4½ teaspoons unflavoured gelatine
8 fl oz (240 g) chicken stock, made with ½ stock cube
4 oz (120 g) finely chopped shallots, onions or spring onions
12 oz (360 g) chicken livers, cut in half

Pinch each of allspice and thyme
Salt and pepper to taste
4 slices truffle (optional)
Lettuce leaves

Sprinkle gelatine over 3 tablespoons cold stock in saucepan. Add remaining stock and heat, stirring to dissolve. Prepare two small moulds. Pour a ¼-inch (5 mm) layer of gelatine into bottom of each mould and chill until set. Place onions in preheated nonstick frying pan. Top with livers. Cover pan and cook over moderately high heat, turning as necessary to prevent scorching (onions should be soft and liver cooked but still juicy inside). Remove from pan. Sprinkle allspice, thyme, salt and pepper into pan, mix well and bring to the boil. Remove from heat and stir into cooked livers. Add 2 slices of truffle to chilled gelatine in each mould, if desired. Divide liver evenly into the moulds. Add remaining gelatine mixture. Refrigerate until set. When ready to serve, turn out onto lettuce leaves. Makes 2 servings.

Calf's Liver with Apples (Foie de Veau aux Pommes)

2 slices trimmed calf's liver, 6 oz (180 g) each
Salt and pepper to taste
2 medium cooking apples
2 tablespoons chicken stock, made with stock cube according to package directions

1 tablespoon lemon juice
½ teaspoon brandy flavouring
2 lemon slices
1 teaspoon chopped fresh parsley

Sprinkle liver with salt and pepper. Peel, core and cut apples into thin slices. Cook covered in small saucepan at very low heat; they should soften but not turn into sauce. Using a small heated nonstick frying pan, brown the liver on both sides, turning once (about 8 minutes in all). Remove it to 2 individual heated plates. Stir stock, lemon juice and brandy flavouring into pan to mix with juices, heat; divide evenly and pour over liver. Surround each slice of liver with half the apple slices. Serve with lemon slice and chopped parsley. Makes 2 servings.

Liver Pâté Salad (Salade de Foies de Volaille)

1 lb 8 oz (720 g) chicken livers
1 oz (30 g) diced celery
4 oz (120 g) onion, diced
6 oz (180 g) mushrooms, sliced
1 pint 4 fl oz (720 ml) chicken
  stock, made with 2 stock cubes
¾ teaspoon nutmeg

2 teaspoons sherry or brandy
  flavouring
12 oz (360 g) firm-cooked green
  asparagus
10 oz (300 g) firm-cooked green
  beans
4 lettuce leaves
Vinaigrette Dressing (recipe follows)

Brown livers quickly in heated nonstick frying pan (about 2 minutes); remove liver and add celery, onion and mushrooms; cook until lightly browned. Add stock and simmer until celery is tender. Return liver to pan and simmer for 2 minutes. Cool. Place in blender goblet a little at a time; add nutmeg and flavouring and purée for 30 seconds. Chill in 4 individual moulds (or coffee cups) for 1 hour or more before serving. Turn out into centre of large lettuce leaf on each of 4 chilled individual salad plates. Surround with asparagus and green beans. Makes 4 servings.

Vinaigrette Dressing

2 fl oz (60 ml) vegetable oil
¼ teaspoon lemon juice

1 teaspoon Dijon-style mustard
Salt and pepper to taste

Prepare the vinaigrette dressing by combining the oil, lemon juice, mustard, salt and pepper in jar. Shake well. Spoon over the salads (about 1 tablespoon per serving). Makes 4 servings.

Celery Victor

2 celery hearts
8 fl oz (240 ml) chicken stock,
   made with ½ stock cube
2 fl oz (60 ml) vegetable oil
2 fl oz (60 ml) white vinegar
¼ teaspoon salt

⅛ teaspoon pepper
Shredded lettuce
4 capers
3 oz (90 g) tomato, cut in 4 wedges
Chopped fresh parsley or celery
   leaves

You can sometimes find hearts of celery in the shops or use the tender inside sticks only. Split celery hearts lengthwise and put in saucepan with chicken stock. Bring to boil and simmer 15 to 20 minutes, or until tender-crisp. Drain and cool. Mix oil, white vinegar, salt and pepper. Add cooled celery hearts. Marinate in refrigerator at least 2 hours. Drain and reserve dressing. On each of 4 salad plates, arrange celery on a bed of shredded lettuce. Place a caper on each portion. Garnish with tomato wedge and sprinkle with chopped parsley or celery leaves. Serve with reserved dressing, evenly divided. Makes 4 servings.

Alsatian Sauerkraut (Choucroute Alsacienne)

Fully cooked frankfurters or ham (3 oz (90 g) for each dinner serving) may be reheated by placing them on top of sauerkraut for last half hour.

8 oz (240 g) sauerkraut
8 fl oz (240 ml) water
1 garlic clove

1 tablespoon white wine vinegar
6 juniper berries, cracked
6 peppercorns, cracked

Wash sauerkraut and drain it, pressing out excess liquid. Put it in a heavy saucepan with water and seasonings. Cover and cook slowly for 1½ hours. Serves 4.

Ratatouille

There are a number of variations on the theme of ratatouille, or ratatouia—as it is occasionally spelled. In some regions cooked dried white beans are added. In Provence, there's almost as much garlic as aubergine, or so it seems. Herbs vary too. Serve it as an appetizer; with melted cheese for luncheon; as a base for scrambled or poached eggs; or as a dinner vegetable. When cold it may be mixed with a little wine vinegar and served as a relish or salad.

6 oz (180 g) sliced aubergine
10 oz (300 g) sliced courgettes
12 oz (360 g) green peppers
6 oz (180 g) tomatoes
16 fl oz (480 ml) tomato juice
4 tablespoons chopped fresh parsley

2 tablespoons dried onion flakes
1 teaspoon marjoram or oregano
2 garlic cloves, lightly crushed
1 teaspoon salt
Pepper to taste

Cut the washed but unpeeled aubergine, well-scrubbed courgettes, green peppers and tomatoes into pieces of about the same size, roughly 1-inch (2.5 cm) squares. Combine in saucepan with remaining ingredients, heat to boiling point, then lower heat, cover and cook until vegetables are tender, stirring gently to prevent scorching, about 30 minutes (more for very soft vegetable mixture). If there is too much liquid, uncover and continue cooking until the sauce thickens. Serve hot or cold. Makes 4 servings.

Courgette Quiche (Quiche aux Courgettes)

2 slices white bread, made into
  crumbs
3 tablespoons water
10 oz (300 g) courgettes
1 teaspoon salt
2 eggs
1 oz (30 g) nonfat dry milk,
  reconstituted with 4 fl oz (120 ml)
  water

5 fl oz (150 ml) skim milk
2 oz (60 g) freshly grated Gruyère
  or Parmesan cheese
Salt and pepper to taste

Combine crumbs and water, mix to a paste and press into bottom of a 9-inch (23 cm) pie plate or quiche dish. Bake at 400°F (200°C), Gas

Mark 6, for 10 minutes. Set crust aside to cool. This can be done ahead of time. Wash courgettes, peel and grate them against the coarse blade of grater and place in strainer over bowl. Toss with salt. Let stand 20 to 30 minutes. Drain, pressing out as much liquid as possible. If courgettes are too salty for your taste, wash them. Dry very well. Beat eggs; add to courgettes with milk, cheese, salt and pepper. Mix well. Pour into prepared pie shell and bake at 400°F (200°C), Gas Mark 6, for 35 to 40 minutes. Makes 2 servings.

Courgette and Tomato Quiche

Scald 6 oz (180 g) tomatoes in boiling water for a few minutes; pull off skin and discard; cut open and remove seeds. Cut pulp into pieces and let drain in strainer. Reduce amount of courgettes in preceding recipe by about a quarter. Add drained tomato pulp to eggs (and add to courgettes) as in preceding recipe. Fill pie shell and bake as above. Makes 2 servings.

Macedoine of Vegetables

3 oz (90 g) potato, diced
2 oz (60 g) frozen peas
1 oz (30 g) sliced onion
1 oz (30 g) sliced carrot
1½ oz (45 g) sliced celery

2 oz (60 g) frozen cut green beans
6 fl oz (180 ml) water
1 teaspoon beef stock powder
½ teaspoon dill weed
1 garlic clove, crushed

Place vegetables in a medium casserole. Heat water, stock powder, dill and garlic in small saucepan; pour over vegetables. Cover casserole and bake at 350°F (180°C), Gas Mark 4, for 45 minutes. Makes 1 serving.

Vegetables a la Grecque

Another classic way with vegetables, but we change the procedure, adding oil to individual servings.

Court Bouillon (recipe follows)   beans (ends trimmed) or celeriac
9 oz (270 g) whole small mushrooms   3 tablespoons vegetable oil
  or 11 oz (330 g) young green

Prepare Court Bouillon and add vegetables, bring to the boil, then
reduce heat and simmer until vegetables are done but crisp. (They
continue to cook in their own steam.) Lift vegetables from liquid with
slotted spoon and arrange in serving dish. Using high heat, boil the
Court Bouillon down until it has reduced by about half. Remove from
heat and stir in oil. Pour over vegetables and refrigerate until well
chilled. Serve cold as an hors d'oeuvre. Makes 6 servings.

Court Bouillon

1 pt 4 fl oz (720 ml) water   3 sprigs parsley
1 lemon, sliced $\frac{1}{2}$ bay leaf
2 oz (60 g) diced celery and leaves   1 garlic clove, crushed
1 tablespoon dried onion flakes $\frac{1}{2}$ teaspoon salt
6 peppercorns, crushed $\frac{1}{8}$ teaspoon thyme or 1 sprig fresh
2 cloves

In saucepan, bring all ingredients to the boil; let simmer 5 minutes.
Strain before adding vegetables. Makes 1 pint 4 fl oz (720 ml).

Château Potatoes

1 lb 2 oz (540 g) cooked peeled $\frac{1}{2}$ teaspoon butter flavouring
  potatoes   Salt to taste
8 fl oz (240 ml) chicken stock,
  made with $\frac{1}{2}$ stock cube

Place potatoes in small ovenproof dish; add stock and butter
flavouring and sprinkle with salt. Bake at 400°F (200°C), Gas Mark 6,
basting occasionally with stock until brown on top. Makes 6 servings.

Peas with Lettuce (Petits Pois à la Française)

2 oz (60 g) shredded lettuce, (round,
cos or iceberg)—do not dry after
washing
3 oz (90 g) tiny peas, fresh or frozen
1 tablespoon dried onion flakes
Pinch each of salt and pepper

$\frac{1}{4}$ teaspoon each thyme and savory
3 tablespoons water or chicken
stock, made from stock cube
according to package directions
1 teaspoon vegetable oil
$\frac{1}{2}$ teaspoon chopped fresh parsley

In small heavy saucepan, with tight-fitting lid, make a layer of lettuce, add peas and another layer of lettuce. Sprinkle with onion flakes, salt, pepper, thyme and savory. Add water or stock. Cover pan and cook over moderate heat until peas are tender, 25 to 30 minutes (5 to 10 minutes if you are using frozen peas which are already blanched.) Remove peas from heat while they are still a fresh green colour and slightly underdone. Bring them to the table where they will continue to steam in their own juices. Just before serving, stir in oil and parsley. Makes 1 serving.

Note: It is usual in France to sweeten this dish. If you wish, sprinkle the peas with artificial sweetener to equal $\frac{1}{2}$ teaspoon sugar, or to taste.

Tomato Mousse

1 tablespoon unflavoured gelatine
2 fl oz (60 ml) cold water
1 oz (30 g) nonfat dry milk,
reconstituted with 5 fl oz (150 ml)
water
12 oz (360 g) tomatoes, peeled,
seeded and chopped

5 tablespoons tomato purée
4 fl oz (120 ml) water
2 teaspoons lemon juice
Salt and cayenne pepper to taste
Bed of lettuce (optional)

Sprinkle gelatine over water in blender goblet to soften. Scald milk in a small saucepan. Pour into blender. Blend. Cook tomato in purée and water until soft. Season with lemon juice, salt and cayenne pepper. Let cool. Add to blender and blend. Divide into 4 individual moulds and chill for 2 hours or until set. Turn out and serve on a bed of lettuce leaves, if desired. For creamier mousse, whip again immediately before serving and pour into individual dishes. Makes 4 servings.

Rice and Radish Salad Vinaigrette

Vinaigrette Sauce (recipe follows)
4 oz (120 g) sliced radishes
5 oz (150 g) cooked green beans,
  sliced

4 oz (120 g) cooked rice
Lettuce leaves
Chopped fresh parsley

Prepare Vinaigrette Sauce; pour over radishes and beans; toss. Refrigerate 2 hours. Remove vegetables from sauce and arrange on lettuce leaves in two chilled salad bowls; mix remaining sauce with rice; arrange on vegetables and serve. Sprinkle with parsley. Makes 2 servings.

Vinaigrette Sauce

4 teaspoons vegetable oil
2 teaspoons wine vinegar
Pinch dry mustard

Salt and pepper to taste
1 teaspoon chopped fresh parsley

Combine ingredients. Makes 2 servings.

Raw Mushroom Salad

Serve as a separate course after the main dish.

6 oz (180 g) sliced raw mushrooms
2 tablespoons vegetable oil
2 tablespoons lemon juice or wine
  vinegar

¼ teaspoon dry mustard
1 small head round or cos lettuce,
  washed and torn

Wipe the mushrooms, cut off the tips and slice vertically (through cap and stem) into pieces about ⅛ inch (3 mm) thick. Combin oil, lemon juice and mustard and pour over mushrooms. Let marinate for 30 minutes. Serve over lettuce. Makes 2 servings.

Japanese-Style Salad (Salade Japonaise)

2 oz (60 g) shredded lettuce
¼ small pineapple
2 teaspoons lemon juice
1 medium orange, peeled and
  sectioned

6 oz (180 g) tomatoes, sliced
2½ fl oz (75 ml) natural
  unsweetened yogurt

Make a bed of greens on each of two chilled salad plates. Cut pineapple quarter away from skin, remove core and slice fruit into small triangular segments. Sprinkle with lemon juice. Arrange half the pineapple, orange sections and the tomato slices in a circle on the lettuce with half the yogurt in the middle. Repeat. Makes 2 servings.

Blue Cheese Dressing*

For a mixed green salad rub your wooden bowl with garlic. Add crisp dry salad greens—one kind or a mixture (Batavian endive, round or cos lettuce and chicory). Toss with watercress or parsley. Serve with this dressing.

5 fl oz (150 ml) buttermilk or
  natural unsweetened yogurt
2 oz (60 g) grated Danish blue
  cheese

1 tablespoon lemon juice
¼ garlic clove, crushed
⅛ teaspoon salt

Combine ingredients, mix well and serve over green salad. Makes 2 servings.

Lemon Fresh Dressing (Sauce Piquante)

A tangy French dressing for the days when you've consumed your allotment of fat. Use it on freshly cooked vegetables (asparagus, broccoli, string beans, etc.) and serve at room temperature, not chilled. Good for salads, too.

1 tablespoon cold water
1 teaspoon unflavoured gelatine
2 fl oz (60 ml) boiling water or
    stock, made from stock cube
    according to package directions
4 fl oz (120 ml) fresh lemon juice

¼ teaspoon Worcester sauce
1 teaspoon grated lemon rind
1 garlic clove
½ teaspoon salt
¼ teaspoon dry mustard
Pinch ground pepper

Sprinkle gelatine over cold water in container or jar with lid; then pour in boiling water or stock. Screw lid on jar and shake to dissolve gelatine. Open jar and add remaining ingredients; cover and shake well. Serve at room temperature. If made ahead and refrigerated, this will set. Put the jar into a saucepan holding hot water until dressing is liquified. Makes 4 servings.

'Melba' Style Peaches

4 medium peaches, blanched and
    peeled
1 teaspoon vanilla flavouring
5 oz (150 g) raspberries, or ¾
    teaspoon raspberry flavouring

Artificial sweetener to equal
    1 tablespoon sugar or to taste
Whipped Topping (see page 12)

Cut peaches in half and remove stones. Place on individual dessert dishes. Sprinkle vanilla over peaches to coat. Mash berries with sweetener in a small bowl. Divide evenly and spoon over peach halves (or mix raspberry flavouring with sweetener and sprinkle over peach halves). Refrigerate while preparing Whipped Topping. Spoon topping over peaches. Serve immediately or chill 1 hour. Makes 4 servings.

Note: To blanch, immerse peaches in boiling water for a minute or two, cool slightly; peel while still warm.

Peach Pie

Pie Crust

5 fl oz (150 ml) skim milk
1 teaspoon peach, raspberry or other
    fruit flavouring
1 teaspoon vanilla flavouring

Artificial sweetener to equal 4
    tablespoons sugar, or to taste
8 slices white bread, toasted and
    made into crumbs

Combine skim milk, flavourings and sweetener in mixing bowl. Add breadcrumbs and stir with fork until crumbs are evenly moistened. Press into bottom and sides of a 9-inch (23 cm) pie plate. Bake at 400°F (200°C), Gas Mark 6, 10 to 12 minutes. Cool.

Pie Filling

8 medium peaches, peeled and sliced
8 fl oz (240 ml) water
Artificial sweetener to equal 4
   tablespoons sugar, or to taste

2 fl oz (60 ml) cold water
1 ½ tablespoons unflavoured gelatine
Whipped Topping (see page 12)

Place peaches in saucepan with water and sweetener. Bring to the boil; reduce heat, simmer 5 minutes. Place water in a small bowl. Sprinkle gelatine over water to soften. Stir into peach mixture; stir until gelatine dissolves. Refrigerate until syrupy. Pour mixture into crumb shell; refrigerate until set. Serve with Whipped Topping. Makes 8 servings.

Poached Whole Pears

4 medium ripe pears
8 fl oz (240 ml) low-calorie
   carbonated lemon or orange drink
1 piece lemon rind

1 small piece cinnamon stick
Artificial sweetener to equal 3
   teaspoons sugar, or to taste

Remove skin from top half of pears. Combine fruit with all remaining ingredients except sweetener in saucepan and simmer until soft. Remove fruit to serving dish. Cook liquid quickly until reduced by half; stir in sweetener and pour sauce over fruit. Serve hot or chilled. Makes 4 servings.

'Brandied' Peaches

Poach peaches as above. Add 1 tablespoon brandy flavouring to liquid, mix and pour over fruit. Makes 4 servings.

Cherries Jubilee

This is an adaptation of a favourite dessert, but it cannot be 'flamed' when using brandy flavouring.

½ recipe Whipped Topping
  (see page 12)
Cherry juice plus water to equal
  6 fl oz (180 ml) liquid

1 lb (480 g) stoned canned sweet
  cherries, no sugar added
1 teaspoon brandy flavouring
½ teaspoon cherry flavouring

Just before dinner prepare the Whipped Topping and spoon it into 4 dessert dishes. Freeze. Bring the liquid to the boil in a saucepan, add cherries and cook briefly until cherries are just tender, turning them in the liquid so they cook evenly and quickly. This will take just a few minutes, don't overcook. Cool. Stir in flavourings. Remove dessert dishes from freezer. Spoon on the fruit sauce and serve immediately. Makes 4 servings.

Cheese Fruit Bombe*

5 oz (150 g) cottage cheese
5 oz (150 g) strawberries, sliced
2½ fl oz (75 ml) skim milk
1 teaspoon strawberry flavouring
1 medium apple, cored and diced
2 fl oz (60 ml) water

2 tablespoons unflavoured gelatine
1 oz (30 g) nonfat dry milk,
  reconstituted with 3 fl oz (90 ml)
  water
1 teaspoon grated lemon rind

Place cottage cheese, 2½ oz (75 g) strawberries, skim milk and flavouring in blender goblet. Blend until smooth. Pour into bowl; add apple and remaining strawberries; mix well. Set aside. Pour water into a small saucepan; sprinkle gelatine over it to soften. Place over low heat and stir until gelatine is dissolved; cool. Combine reconstituted milk and lemon rind. Pour gelatine slowly into milk and continue beating; fold into fruit mixture. Pour into medium-size mould and chill 1 hour. Turn out. Makes 2 servings.

Strawberry Omelette (Omelette aux Fraises)*

2½ oz (75 g) strawberries   2 eggs
½ teaspoon vanilla flavouring   Pinch of salt

Hull the strawberries and cut them in half into small bowl. Sprinkle them with half the vanilla. Beat the eggs until blended; add salt and remaining vanilla. Pour into heated 6-inch (15 cm) nonstick frying pan. As mixture sets, lift up the edges so uncooked portions flow to the bottom edges. When eggs are set, place berries on one half of the omelette and with a spatula fold the other half over fruit. Roll out of pan onto a warmed plate; serve immediately. Makes 2 servings.

Grape Omelette (Omelette aux Raisins)

Follow the preceding recipe, but substitute 6 oz (180 g) grapes for the strawberries, and rum flavouring for the vanilla. Makes 2 servings.

Hot Fruit Soufflé*

2 medium apples, or peaches, or   2 tablespoons water
   2 medium pears, peeled and cored   2 eggs, separated
   or stoned   Dash lemon juice

Combine fruit with water in small saucepan, cover and cook until fruit is very soft. Put fruit and liquid in blender goblet and blend; transfer to small bowl. Beat yolks lightly and add to fruit in bowl with lemon juice. Beat whites until stiff and fold them into the first mixture. Transfer to 2 individual soufflé dishes and bake at 350°F (180°C), Gas Mark 4, until tops are brown, about 20 minutes. Serve at once. Makes 2 servings.

Hot Fruit Compote (Compote Composée)

16 fl oz (480 ml) boiling water
6 medium apricots, halved and
stoned
4 medium plums, halved and stoned
2 medium peaches, halved and
stoned

6 oz (180 g) seedless grapes
1 x 2-inch (5 cm) piece of vanilla bean
or 2 teaspoons vanilla flavouring
1 lemon slice
Artificial sweetener to equal 4
tablespoons sugar, or to taste

Pour boiling water over apricots, plums and peaches in large saucepan.
Simmer for 12 minutes or until fruit is almost tender. Add grapes and
vanilla bean (or flavouring) and lemon slice. Cook a minute or two
longer. Stir in sweetener. Serve hot or chilled. Makes 8 servings.

Plum Mousse

1½ teaspoons unflavoured gelatine
4 fl oz (120 ml) water
2 medium plums, peeled and stoned
1 oz (30 g) nonfat dry milk

⅛ teaspoon vanilla flavouring
Artificial sweetener to equal 1
teaspoon sugar, or to taste
2 to 3 ice cubes

Sprinkle gelatine over water in small saucepan. Heat, stirring, until
gelatine dissolves. Pour into blender goblet. Add plums, milk, flavouring, and sweetener; cover and blend at low speed until smooth. Add ice
cubes, one at a time, blending at high speed until all traces of ice
disappear. Pour into dessert dish; chill 5 minutes, or until set. Makes 1
serving.

Macedoine of Fruit

1 medium orange, peeled and
  sectioned, or ½ ripe medium
  cantaloupe melon (remove rind)
3 ripe medium apricots or 6 canned
  apricot halves, no sugar added,
  and 2 tablespoons juice
1 ripe medium peach or 4 oz (120 g)
  canned peach slices, no sugar
  added

3 oz (90 g) seedless grapes
Artificial sweetener to taste
1 tablespoon lemon juice (optional)
1 tablespoon brandy or rum
  flavouring

Cut the fruits into even pieces. Sprinkle lightly with artificial sweetener.
Add lemon juice if mixture seems dry, and stir in brandy or rum
flavouring. Makes 4 servings.

GERMANY

As you can see from the pages which follow, German fare isn't all sauerbraten and sausage, popular as they are. You can enjoy Pfannkuchen (pancakes) for breakfast, Frischkäse (cottage cheese, even better with a sprinkling of caraway seed and chopped chives) at Mittags, and Kalbsbraten or Kalbsleber (roast veal or calf's liver) and other meats and fish for dinner. And as Germans are as fond of sweets as the rest of us, we have included a few hearty dessert specialities, too.

If you are searching for some foolproof German recipes done the new way but with old-fashioned charm, recipes in the spirit of German Gemütlichkeit or conviviality, here they are. Gesegnete Mahlzeit!

Lentil Soup*

As a 'rule of thumb', 4 oz (120 g) of uncooked dried lentils will yield 12 oz (360 g) when cooked.

1 pint (600 ml) water	1 garlic clove, crushed
5 oz (150 g) freshly chopped celery	½ bay leaf
2 oz (60 g) freshly chopped onion	¼ teaspoon thyme or 1 sprig fresh
1 teaspoon beef stock powder	12 oz (360 g) cooked dried lentils

Bring water to the boil in a large saucepan. Add all remaining ingredients except lentils; simmer until vegetables are tender. Add lentils; cook 20 minutes longer. Serve hot. (For a smoother soup, blend in a blender.) If soup is too thick, add hot water and reheat; stir to prevent burning. Makes 4 servings.

Farmhouse Omelette

2 oz (60 g) onion, finely chopped
3 oz (90 g) cooked potato, diced
2 eggs, beaten

1 teaspoon freshly chopped chives
1 tablespoon water
Salt and pepper to taste

Brown onion lightly in nonstick omelette pan. Add potato and heat for one minute. Combine eggs, chives, water, salt and pepper, and add to omelette pan. As mixture sets at edges, draw edges toward centre with a spatula so that uncooked portions flow to bottom of pan. Tilt pan. Using a spatula, carefully roll or fold omelette in half and transfer to serving dish. Makes 1 serving.

Country Lunch

5 oz (150 g) cottage cheese
1 teaspoon caraway seeds
1 tablespoon chopped fresh chives
3 oz (90 g) cooked potato, sliced

Few small red radishes
1½ oz (45 g) tomato, sliced
Salt and pepper to taste
5 fl oz (150 ml) chilled buttermilk

Sprinkle cottage cheese with caraway and chives, and put in centre of a chilled plate. Surround with mounds of potato slices, radishes and tomato slices. Add salt and pepper to taste. At table, pour some of your buttermilk on top of the salad, and drink the rest of it. Makes 1 serving.

Marjoram Veal Chops

4 × 8 oz (240 g) veal chops
6 oz (180 g) mushrooms
1 oz (30 g) nonfat dry milk,
   reconstituted with 5 fl oz (150 ml)
   water
4 fl oz (120 ml) chicken stock,
   made with ¼ stock cube

1 teaspoon marjoram
½ teaspoon paprika
1½ teaspoons salt
1 teaspoon sherry flavouring
   (optional)

Pound veal chops until thin. Brown on both sides over moderate heat in nonstick frying pan. Remove chops and wipe out pan. Brown mushrooms in same pan and stir in milk, stock, marjoram, paprika, salt and sherry flavouring. Do not boil. Transfer to baking tin or shallow serving casserole and bake in moderate oven 350°F (180°C), Gas Mark 4, until chops are tender. Makes 4 servings.

Sauerbraten

Sour roast, traditionally served with braised red cabbage, and often with prepared horseradish.

2 lbs 4 oz (1 kg 80 g) well-trimmed beef,
   rolled sirloin or other tender roast
8 fl oz (240 ml) beef stock, made
   with ½ stock cube
4 fl oz (120 ml) wine vinegar
1 teaspoon salt

¼ teaspoon pepper
5 cloves, crushed
2 bay leaves, crumbled
1 tablespoon burgundy or sherry
   flavouring

Place meat in shallow heatproof casserole. Combine remaining ingredients and pour over meat. Refrigerate 2 to 3 days, turning frequently. When ready to cook, drain meat (reserve marinade). Bake on rack in roasting tin at 325°F (160°C), Gas Mark 3, for 2 hours or until meat is very tender, basting frequently with part of the reserved marinade. Slice meat diagonally across the grain and serve hot. Makes 6 servings.

Delicatessen

1 lb (480 g) cold, cooked pork
1 tablespoon chopped fresh parsley
1 small garlic clove (optional)
$\frac{1}{2}$ teaspoon grated lemon rind
$\frac{1}{4}$ teaspoon sage or marjoram
$\frac{1}{4}$ teaspoon grated nutmeg
Sprinkling of black pepper

2 tablespoons unflavoured gelatine
8 fl oz (240 ml) beef stock, made
  with $\frac{1}{2}$ stock cube
3 pimiento strips
$2\frac{1}{2}$ oz (75 g) pickled cucumber, cut
  in 3 strips

Put pork, parsley, garlic if desired, lemon rind, sage, nutmeg and pepper through mincer with medium blade. In small saucepan, sprinkle gelatine over 2 fl oz (60 ml) cold beef stock to soften. Stir in remaining stock and heat over low heat until gelatine is dissolved. Stir into pork mixture; mix well. Press one third of the mixture tightly into a small loaf tin or mould. Arrange 2 pimiento strips and 1 pickled cucumber strip on top. Press half remaining pork mixture over strips. Arrange remaining strips over mixture. Top with remaining pork mixture, pressed down. Bake 1 hour at 325°F (160°C), Gas Mark 3. Refrigerate. Slice evenly and serve cold. Makes 4 servings.

Knackwurst Sauce for Cooked Kale

Serve over cooked kale or shredded cabbage.

6 oz (180 g) knackwurst
2 oz (60 g) diced onion
4 oz (120 g) sliced celery
1 teaspoon chopped fresh parsley

4 tablespoons tomato purée
3 fl oz (90 ml) water
1 bay leaf
$\frac{1}{8}$ teaspoon crushed red pepper

Pierce knackwurst with fork and put in saucepan with water to cover. Bring to the boil and cook until heated. Pour off water and dry knackwurst by shaking pan over moderate heat. Remove from pan; slice. Return to pan; add onion and celery and brown on all sides, turning as necessary. Add all remaining ingredients, cover pan and cook until sauce is thick, about 1 hour. (If necessary, keep warm on an asbestos mat.) Makes 2 servings.

Ham with Green Beans

1 lb 14 oz (900 g) boneless ham joint
Water
1 lb (480 g) fresh green beans

1 lb 2 oz (540 g) potatoes, peeled
and quartered
Salt and pepper to taste

Cover the ham with water and simmer slowly for three hours. Add water from time to time during cooking, so that ham is covered at all times. After 3 hours, drain the ham and add 2 pints (1 litre 200 ml) water. Break the beans into small pieces and add to the ham. Bring back to the boil and continue cooking for about 25 minutes. Add potatoes to beans and ham, and cook until potatoes are tender. A few minutes before serving, stir in salt and pepper. Serve hot, with vinegar, mustard and horseradish on the table. Makes 6 servings.

Liver Dumplings with Tomato Sauce

6 oz (180 g) beef liver, coarsely
minced
1 slice white bread, made into
crumbs
1 tablespoon skim milk
1 teaspoon chopped fresh parsley

1 teaspoon dried onion flakes
Salt and pepper to taste
16 fl oz (480 ml) water
1 teaspoon beef stock powder
Tomato Sauce (recipe follows)

Combine minced liver, breadcrumbs, milk, parsley, onion flakes, salt and pepper in medium bowl; form into small balls. Heat water to boiling in medium saucepan, add stock powder. Drop dumplings into boiling beef stock; cook until each dumpling rises to the surface; remove dumplings, serve with Tomato Sauce. Makes 1 serving.

Note: Sauce may be eliminated if desired and liver may be served in stock.

Tomato Sauce

8 fl oz (240 ml) tomato juice
1 teaspoon beef stock powder

1 tablespoon green pepper, chopped
½ teaspoon hot pepper sauce

Combine all ingredients in small saucepan; cook until pepper is tender and mixture thickens to sauce consistency. Makes 1 serving.

'Creamed' Liver Rhine Valley

12 oz (360 g) calf liver
10 fl oz (300 ml) buttermilk
4 or 5 capers, rinsed and chopped

1 teaspoon grated lemon rind
Salt and pepper to taste
4 oz (120 g) cooked noodles

Wipe liver clean and brown quickly on both sides in heated nonstick frying pan. Do not overcook (it should remain juicy). Slice. Combine with all remaining ingredients except noodles. Cover and heat without boiling. Serve with hot noodles. Makes 2 servings.

German Potato Salad (Kartoffelsalat)

1 lb 2 oz (540 g) cooked potatoes, peeled and sliced thinly
Salt and pepper to taste
1 teaspoon chopped fresh parsley
$\frac{1}{2}$ teaspoon chopped fresh chives
2 fl oz (60 ml) strong chicken stock (dissolve $\frac{1}{2}$ teaspoon

chicken stock powder in 2 fl oz (60 ml) boiling water
2 tablespoons vegetable oil
1 tablespoon wine vinegar
1 lb 2 oz (540 g) cucumbers, sliced
6 oz (180 g) sliced cooked beetroot

Layer potato slices in a salad bowl. Season each layer with salt, pepper, parsley and chives. Combine stock, oil and vinegar and pour over salad. Mix lightly; serve warm, accompanied with slices of cucumber and beetroot. Makes 6 servings. For carrying to a picnic, pack cucumbers and beetroot separately.

Sweet and Sour Cole Slaw

3 fl oz (90 ml) vinegar
2 fl oz (60 ml) vegetable oil
Artificial sweetener to equal 2
  teaspoons sugar, or to taste
1 teaspoon dried onion flakes
1 teaspoon celery salt

$\frac{1}{2}$ teaspoon dry mustard
$\frac{1}{2}$ teaspoon salt
$\frac{1}{4}$ teaspoon pepper
2 tablespoons chopped pimiento
10 oz (300 g) shredded cabbage

Combine all ingredients except pimiento and cabbage in a large mixing bowl. Add pimiento and cabbage; toss. Cover and chill. Makes 6 servings.

Potatoes with Cheese (Kartoffeln mit Käse)

1 egg
5 fl oz (150 ml) skim milk
3 oz (90 g) cooked potato, diced
1 oz (30 g) diced Cheddar cheese

4 oz (120 g) diced cooked
  cauliflower
Salt and pepper to taste
Prepared mustard

For each serving use a good-sized individual casserole. Beat the egg; stir in the milk, potato, cheese and cauliflower. Season with salt and pepper. Bake at 350°F (180°C), Gas Mark 4, for 20 minutes or so. Serve hot with prepared mustard. Makes 1 serving.

Mixed Vegetable Hotpot (Allerlei)

4 oz (120 g) string beans
3 oz (90 g) shredded cabbage or
  cauliflower florets
3 oz (90 g) mushrooms sliced
2 oz (60 g) carrot
4 oz (120 g) onion
6 oz (180 g) tomatoes, sliced
4 to 6 fl oz (120 to 180 ml) water or
  chicken stock, made with $\frac{1}{4}$ to
  $\frac{1}{2}$ stock cube

1 garlic clove
$\frac{1}{2}$ oz (15 g) nonfat dry milk,
  reconstituted with $2\frac{1}{2}$ fl oz
  (75 ml) water
2 teaspoons margarine
1 tablespoon chopped fresh parsley
Salt (optional)

Cut string beans, cabbage or cauliflower, mushrooms, carrot, onion and tomatoes into approximately even dice. Combine in saucepan and add water and garlic; cover pan and cook until vegetables are tender. Carefully remove vegetables with slotted spoon so they do not break up. Remove and discard garlic clove; boil down liquid in pan, reduce heat and stir in milk. Heat but do not boil. Remove from heat. Stir margarine into sauce and pour over vegetables. Sprinkle with parsley. Makes 2 servings.

Pears and Beans (Birnen und Bohnen)

4 medium pears, peeled and cored, cut in quarters
6 fl oz (180 ml) boiling water
1 small piece lemon rind

1 lb (480 g) frozen cut green beans
2 teaspoons lemon juice
Pepper to taste

Cover pears with boiling water in saucepan; add lemon rind and cook for 15 minutes. Add beans and continue cooking for 20 mintues, or until most of liquid has evaporated. If necessary remove lid for the last few minutes and cook rapidly to reduce liquid. Stir in lemon juice and pepper. Serve hot as meat side dish. Makes 4 servings.

German Apple Pancake (Pfannkuchen)*

1 egg
2 tablespoons skim milk
Artificial sweetener to equal 1 teaspoon sugar, or to taste

¼ teaspoon cinnamon
1 slice white bread made into crumbs
1 medium apple, peeled and grated

Combine egg, milk, sweetener and cinnamon in mixing bowl. Add breadcrumbs and beat for one minute with whisk or fork. Pour into heated nonstick omelette pan that has a heatproof or removable handle. Arrange apple on top. Bake in hot oven 400°F (200°C), Gas Mark 6, for 3 to 4 minutes until set. Remove; fold in half and serve. Makes 1 serving.

Apple Butter

4 medium apples, cored, peeled, cut
  in eighths
4 fl oz (120 ml) water
Artificial sweetener to equal 2
  tablespoons sugar, or to taste

½ teaspoon cinnamon
⅛ teaspoon each cloves and
  allspice

Place apples and water in medium saucepan; cover; cook slowly until apples are soft but not mushy. Pour mixture into blender goblet; add remaining ingredients; blend at medium speed just until apples are puréed. Pour into medium bowl; chill. Makes 8 servings.

German Apple Custard*

4 eggs, slightly beaten
1 oz (30 g) nonfat dry milk,
  reconstituted with 5 fl oz (150 ml)
  water
4 teaspoons margarine, melted, or
  vegetable oil

Artificial sweetener to equal 1
  tablespoon sugar, or to taste
1 teaspoon grated lemon rind
1 teaspoon almond flavouring
4 medium apples, peeled, cored and
  sliced

In bowl, combine eggs, milk, melted margarine or oil, sweetener, lemon rind and almond flavouring. Mix well together. Arrange sliced apples in a medium casserole. Pour egg mixture over apples. Place casserole in a pan containing 1 inch (2.5 cm) water. Bake in moderate oven, 350°F (180°C), Gas Mark 4, 35 to 45 minutes or until eggs are set. Makes 4 servings.

GREECE AND THE OTHER BALKAN STATES

*

Travellers love Greece and its fabled islands. All the ancient Hellenic legends come alive for you as you cruise to Crete or Skiathos, relax on the sun-dappled beaches, and swim in the sparkling blue Aegean water. But the next best thing to being there is to cook the Greek way.

Although ethnic hostilities have ravaged the Balkans for many centuries, in the pages of our cookbook Albania, Bulgaria, Rumania, Yugoslavia and Greece live a peaceful coexistence. You'll enjoy our sampling of dishes from the countries that share the mountains with Greece.

Bulgarian Vegetable Soup

12 fl oz (360 ml) water
1 oz (30 g) carrot, diced
1 oz (30 g) parsnip, sliced
1½ oz (45 g) cauliflower florets

2½ oz (75 g) asparagus pieces
½ teaspoon chopped fresh dill
1 teaspoon chicken stock powder
Salt and pepper to taste

Combine water, carrot, parsnip, cauliflower florets, asparagus and dill in saucepan. Cook until vegetables are tender. Stir in chicken stock powder and seasonings to taste. Makes 1 serving.

Egg and Lemon Soup (Avgolemono)*

Lemon juice flavours almost every course in Greek menus, beginning with a favourite soup, Avgolemono.

1 pint 12 fl oz (960 ml) chicken
stock, made with 2 stock cubes
4 eggs, well beaten
8 oz (240 g) cooked rice

Juice of 1 lemon
3 tablespoons chopped fresh dill or
parsley
Salt and white pepper to taste

Bring stock to the boil. Remove from heat. Slowly pour about 8 fl oz (240 ml) of hot soup into eggs, beating constantly. Pour egg mixture back into remaining hot soup, continuing to beat. Heat but do not boil. Stir in rice and lemon juice, add dill or parsley, and season with salt and pepper to taste. Makes 4 servings.

Rumanian Fish Soup

1 pint 12 fl oz (960 ml) water
5 teaspoons chicken stock powder
1 lb 8 oz (720 g) bass or carp fillets, cut
into 4 equal pieces
1 small head round lettuce, cut into
pieces

4 oz (120 g) spring onions, cut into
1-inch (2.5 cm) pieces
1 bay leaf
4 peppercorns
Salt to taste

Pour water into a large saucepan. Bring to the boil; add stock powder. Lower heat; simmer for 2 to 3 minutes or until powder is completely dissolved. Add fish, lettuce, spring onions and seasonings; return to the boil; lower heat and simmer, covered, 10 minutes. Remove bay leaf. Divide mixture evenly into 4 soup bowls. Makes 4 servings.

Lentil Soup (Faki)

This lentil soup, sharpened with vinegar, can be made ahead of time and refrigerated for several days as it improves with keeping. It also freezes well.

1 pint 12 fl oz (960 ml) beef
stock, made with 2 stock cubes
1 lb 2 oz (540 g) cooked dried lentils
Salt and pepper to taste
2 tablespoons tomato purée
1½ fl oz (45 ml) water

3 oz (90 g) onion, finely chopped
1 oz (30 g) finely chopped carrot
½ oz (15 g) celery, finely chopped
½ garlic clove, chopped or crushed
1 tablespoon vinegar or lemon juice

Combine stock, lentils, salt and pepper in a large saucepan. Bring to the boil. Add all remaining ingredients except vinegar. Return mixture to the boil; reduce heat and simmer for at least 30 minutes, or until vegetables are tender. Divide evenly into 3 soup bowls. Stir 1 teaspoon vinegar or lemon juice into each bowl of soup as it is served. Makes 3 servings.

Rumanian Cheese Balls

5 oz (150 g) dry cottage cheese
2 eggs, beaten
¼ teaspoon salt
Pinch of pepper

6 oz (180 g) cooked mashed potatoes
1 pint 4 fl oz (720 ml) chicken
stock, made with 2 stock cubes

Mash cottage cheese through sieve. Add eggs and seasonings; add potatoes and mix well. Drop by spoonfuls into simmering stock. Let simmer gently 8 to 10 minutes. Divide evenly into 2 servings.

Spinach Cheese Pie (Spanakopita)

1 teaspoon dried onion flakes
1½ teaspoons water
2 eggs
5 oz (150 g) cottage cheese

6 oz (180 g) drained, cooked,
chopped spinach
4 tablespoons chopped parsley leaves
1 teaspoon salt
½ teaspoon dill weed

Soak onion flakes in water. Beat eggs in medium bowl. Beat in cottage cheese, spinach, parsley, salt, dill and soaked onions. Pour into 2 shallow nonstick individual casseroles. Place casseroles in a larger baking tin. Pour boiling water into baking tin until until it reaches halfway up sides of casseroles. Bake at 350°F (180°C), Gas Mark 4, for 30 minutes. Makes 2 servings.

Mussel Pilaff

4 oz (120 g) onion, finely chopped	6 oz (180 g) canned tomatoes,
2 fl oz (60 ml) chicken stock,	chopped
made with ¼ stock cube	¾ teaspoon oregano
8 oz (240 g) drained canned	Salt and pepper to taste
mussels	4 oz (120 g) cooked rice

Cook onion in stock in a medium saucepan until tender. Add all remaining ingredients except rice, and simmer, covered, until hot. Divide on to two plates, each holding 2 oz (60 g) rice. Makes 2 servings.

Stuffed Mussels

6 oz (180 g) mussels (20 mussels in shell)	2 teaspoons chopped fresh basil or 1 teaspoon dried
2 oz (60 g) grated Cheddar cheese	1 teaspoon oregano
1 slice white bread, made into crumbs	1 garlic clove, crushed
4 tablespoons chopped fresh parsley	1 tablespoon water

Using a sharp knife, open mussel shells, running the knife horizontally to separate shells. Remove mussels and discard half the shell; reserve the other half of each shell. Weigh 6 oz (180 g) of the raw mussels and divide equally into the half-shells. Place on a nonstick baking sheet, and set aside. In a small mixing bowl, combine cheese, bread, parsley, basil, oregano and garlic. Sprinkle water over mixture and stir to moisten. Divide mixture evenly into the same number of portions as there are mussel shells. Spoon each portion over mussels and mound slightly. Bake at 500°F (260°C), Gas Mark 10, for 5 minutes or until mussels are cooked and cheese is melted. Serve hot. Makes 2 servings.

Scallops with Rice

8 oz (240 g) onion, finely chopped
2 fl oz (60 ml) stock, made with
 ¼ stock cube
1 lb 8 oz (720 g) scallops, washed

Salt to taste
8 oz (240 g) cooked rice
Chopped parsley (optional)

In a large saucepan, cook onions in stock until tender. Add scallops; bring mixture to the boil (liquid will accumulate as mixture cooks). Lower heat and simmer for 10 minutes. Divide evenly into 4 portions and serve each portion in an individual bowl over 2 oz (60 g) rice. Garnish with chopped parsley if desired. Makes 4 servings.

Shrimp Scorpio

2 fl oz (60 ml) chicken stock,
 made with ¼ stock cube
4 oz (120 g) finely chopped onion
4 tablespoons finely chopped fresh
 parsley
1 tablespoon finely chopped fresh
 dill
1 garlic clove, crushed
⅛ teaspoon dry mustard

12 oz (360 g) tomatoes, blanched,
 peeled and chopped
8 teaspoons tomato purée
2 fl oz (60 ml) water
⅛ teaspoon thyme
12 oz (360 g) peeled and deveined
 shrimps
4 oz (120 g) feta cheese, crumbled

Heat stock in a saucepan; add onion. Cook, stirring, until onion starts to brown. Add parsley, dill and garlic. Stir in the mustard. Do not add salt at any time. Add tomatoes, tomato purée, water and thyme and simmer 30 minutes. Rinse cleaned shrimps, drain and add to the sauce, cook covered 3 to 5 minutes. Pour the mixture into a medium casserole and sprinkle evenly with cheese. Bake at 425°F (220°C), Gas Mark 7, 10 to 15 minutes, or until the cheese is melted. Serve immediately. Makes 4 servings.

Variation: Grated mozzarella cheese may be substituted for the feta cheese. If so, season the tomato sauce with salt to taste before adding the shrimps.

Yugoslav Beef Rolls (Čevapčići)

In Yugoslavian restaurants, this is accompanied by a spicy coleslaw.

6 oz (180 g) minced beef
½ teaspoon Worcester sauce

Salt, pepper and garlic powder to
taste

Preheat grill. Season beef with Worcester sauce, salt, pepper and garlic powder. Form into 2-inch (5 cm) long sausage-shapes; place on a rack 4 inches (10 cm) from source of heat. Grill until well browned, turning once. Makes 1 serving.

Baked Lamb Chops

4 × 6 oz (180 g) loin lamb chops,
  grilled
Salt and pepper to taste
16 teaspoons tomato purée

4 fl oz (120 ml) water
1 tablespoon Worcester sauce
½ teaspoon oregano
¼ teaspoon garlic salt

Sprinkle salt and pepper on both sides of lamb chops and place in a shallow casserole. Combine remaining ingredients in a small bowl and pour over meat. Cover and bake in moderate oven 350°F (180°C), Gas Mark 4, for 1 hour. Makes 4 servings.

Albanian Lamb Stew with Okra

12 oz (360 g) fresh or frozen okra
12 oz (360 g) green peppers, diced
4 oz (120 g) celery, diced
4 oz (120 g) onion, diced
4 garlic cloves, crushed
Salt and pepper to taste

4 fl oz (120 ml) water
1 lb (480 g) roasted lamb, cut into
  bite-sized pieces
¼ teaspoon thyme
Paprika
Strips of lemon rind for garnish

Cook okra in a frying pan, stirring occasionally, for about 5 minutes or until liquid evaporates. Add green peppers, celery, onions, garlic, salt and pepper and cook for 10 minutes longer, stirring to keep vegetables from sticking to the bottom of the pan. Add water, lamb and thyme, and let simmer, covered, on a low heat for 20 to 25 minutes or until meat is thoroughly heated through and vegetables are tender. Sprinkle with paprika and garnish with lemon rind. Makes 4 servings.

Balkan One-Pot Liver and Vegetable Dinner

2 fl oz (60 ml) beef stock, made with ¼ stock cube
6 oz (180 g) green pepper, thinly sliced
2 oz (60 g) onion, chopped
1 small piece cinnamon stick (about 1 inch (2.5 cm))
1 tablespoon tomato purée

1 tablespoon water
6 oz (180 g) calf liver, cut into 1-inch (2.5 cm) squares
1½ oz (45 g) mushrooms, sliced
2 oz (60 g) cooked rice
Salt and pepper to taste
1 teaspoon chopped fresh parsley

Heat stock in a saucepan. Add green pepper, onion and cinnamon stick. Cook until vegetables are tender. Stir in tomato purée and water, mix well, and add liver and mushrooms. Continue to cook, stirring constantly, until liver is done to taste. Remove cinnamon stick. Stir in rice, season with salt and pepper and heat through. Sprinkle with parsley to garnish. Makes 1 serving.

Mixed Vegetable Salad

Tavernas in Greece serve the famous salads made of heaps of fresh raw vegetables and large bowls of assorted salad greens dressed with oil and lemon juice—sprinkled over at the table.

Coarse salt to taste
1 garlic clove, peeled and split
8 oz (240 g) salad greens (endive, Batavian endive or cos lettuce or other greens) torn into bite-sized pieces
1½ oz (45 g) radishes, cut into 'roses'

4 oz (120 g) red onion, cut into rings
6 oz (180 g) green pepper, seeded and cut into thin rings or strips
3 oz (90 g) tomatoes, sliced
Freshly ground pepper to taste
2 tablespoons lemon juice or vinegar
2 fl oz (60 ml) vegetable oil

Pour a little coarse salt into a salad bowl; rub the salt with the garlic clove round the surface of the bowl. Add the salad greens and raw vegetables. Sprinkle with pepper and lemon juice or vinegar and toss lightly. Add oil and toss again. Serve immediately. Makes 4 servings.

Aubergine Salad (Melitzanes Salata)

1 × 1 lb (480 g) aubergine
4 oz (120 g) onion, grated
6 oz (180 g) tomatoes, peeled,
  chopped
1 garlic clove, crushed
2 tablespoons chopped fresh parsley
2 tablespoons vegetable oil

2 tablespoons red wine vinegar
½ teaspoon marjoram
½ teaspoon salt
Pepper to taste
Lettuce leaves
Chopped fresh parsley for garnish

Bake whole aubergine in shallow tin in moderate oven, 350°F (180°C), Gas Mark 4, for 1 hour. Dip in cold water; peel off skin. Dice aubergine and weigh 8 oz (240 g); put in large bowl. Add onion, tomato, garlic, parsley, vegetable oil, vinegar, marjoram, salt and pepper. Mix well. Serve on lettuce; sprinkle with parsley. Serve at luncheon or dinner. Makes 4 servings.

Cucumbers Greek Style

10 fl oz (300 ml) buttermilk
12 oz (360 g) cucumber, peeled,
  seeded and diced
6 oz (180 g) tomatoes, cut into
  wedges
4 teaspoons vegetable oil
2 teaspoons lemon juice

1 garlic clove, finely chopped
1 teaspoon oregano
½ teaspoon mint leaves
Salt and freshly ground black pepper
  to taste
Chilled celery strips

Pour buttermilk into a mixing bowl; add all remaining ingredients except celery strips. Let stand 1 hour in refrigerator until ready to serve. Mix well before serving. Serve with chilled celery strips as an appetizer. Makes 4 servings.

Artichoke Hearts

1 lb (480 g) frozen artichoke hearts, thawed
4 fl oz (120 ml) water
1 tablespoon lemon juice

$\frac{1}{2}$ teaspoon salt
1 teaspoon chopped fresh dill
4 teaspoons vegetable oil

Combine artichokes, water, lemon juice and salt in medium saucepan. Cover; bring to a full boil over high heat, separating artichokes with fork. Reduce heat; simmer covered 5 to 8 minutes until tender. Drain and sprinkle with chopped dill. Mix to combine. Divide evenly onto 4 dishes. Add 1 teaspoon oil to each serving and mix well. Makes 4 servings. Serve with luncheon or dinner.

Stuffed Grape Leaves (Dolmadakia)

4 oz (120 g) onion, finely chopped
1 oz (30 g) finely chopped celery
8 fl oz (240 ml) beef stock, made with $\frac{1}{2}$ stock cube
8 oz (240 g) cooked minced beef
8 oz (240 g) cooked minced lamb
8 oz (240 g) cooked rice
4 tablespoons finely chopped fresh parsley

1 tablespoon finely chopped fresh mint or 1 teaspoon dried mint
Salt and freshly ground pepper to taste
3 oz (90 g) grape leaves
2 fl oz (60 ml) wine vinegar
2 tablespoons lemon juice

Cook onions and celery in 2 fl oz (60 ml) stock until tender. Place meat in a bowl and add the onion and celery. Add rice, parsley, mint, salt and pepper. Blend well. Gently turn the grape leaves into a colander and rinse them under cold running water, separating the leaves. Dry gently and place one at a time on a flat surface, shiny side down. Place an even amount of filling in the centre of each leaf and roll each tightly from the stem end towards the point of the leaf. Arrange the leaves in layers in a heavy saucepan. Add the remaining stock, vinegar and lemon juice and cover with a heavy plate to prevent the leaves from opening. Cook, tightly covered, for 30 minutes over low heat. Makes 4 servings.

Rumanian Rice Pudding with Apples

4 medium apples
Water
1 teaspoon lemon juice

2 tablespoons margarine, softened
8 oz (240 g) cooked rice (see note)
Cinnamon

Core, peel and slice apples (see note below for using the peel). Place in medium saucepan with water to cover and add lemon juice. Simmer until apple slices are soft but still hold their shape. Remove from heat. Drain and discard liquid. Stir in margarine. Let stand while preparing rice. Place one third of the rice and half the apple mixture in a medium nonstick oven-to-table dish. Sprinkle with cinnamon. Layer another one-third rice, remaining apple mixture and a sprinkling of cinnamon and top with remaining rice. Bake in moderate oven 350°F (180°C), Gas Mark 4, until edges turn brown, 35 to 45 minutes. Makes 4 servings.

Note: Boil the peel in water to cover for 30 minutes. Drain, press out juice. Use this liquid plus additional water as necessary to cook the rice, following package directions.

Mocha Frappé

8 fl oz (240 ml) strong black coffee
2 oz (60 g) nonfat dry milk

Artificial sweetener to equal 2
   teaspoons sugar, or to taste
2 to 3 ice cubes

Pour coffee, milk and sweetener into blender goblet; cover and blend at low speed to combine. Add ice cubes; cover and blend at high speed until all traces of ice disappear. Pour into two glasses. Makes 2 servings.

INDIA

*

India is spice merchant to the world, so naturally its foods are pungent with appetizing seasonings of all kinds. If you are a curry buff, this may be your favourite section, but would it surprise you to know that in its own country there is no one spice called curry? Curry powder is a blend of many different condiments. One old recipe calls for 8 oz of turmeric, 6 oz coriander, 3 oz each of cardamom, cumin and fenugreek, 1 oz each of cloves and peppercorns and ¼ oz cayenne pepper, all reduced to a powder. However, we assume you'll buy the curry blend in your supermarket or oriental grocery shop. Since the strength of the curry powder is variable, add it to taste. Start with the minimum suggested amount and then increase as desired.

Curries are not inevitable at an Indian meal, but spicy foods are popular, as is natural in a tropical country, and drinks are an important part of the menu. We don't mean alcoholic beverages—in fact, few Indians drink spirits with their meals. We do mean refreshing cool drinks such as freshly squeezed limes or lemons with ice water, or iced tea . . . Darjeeling and Assam are two very fine teas grown in India. Add a colourful pinch of saffron, a few crushed cardamom seeds or a sprig of mint to tea and you'll give it an authentic Indian touch.

Our chapter concludes with authentic buttermilk and yogurt drinks to help cool you down after a hot curry.

Mulligatawny

1 oz (30 g) diced celery
3 oz (90 g) green pepper, chopped
½ teaspoon dried onion flakes
8 fl oz (240 ml) chicken or onion stock, made with ½ stock cube

½ to 1 teaspoon curry powder or to taste
3 oz (90 g) tomato, cut in thin wedges
⅛ teaspoon ground cardamom

In saucepan cook celery, pepper and onion in 2 fl oz (60 ml) chicken or onion stock over low heat until tender, about 5 minutes. Stir in curry. Add tomatoes, cardamom and remaining stock. Cook 15 minutes. Serve hot. Makes 1 serving.

Chicken Soup with Lemon and Mint

8 oz (240 g) cooked chicken, cut into
  ⅛-inch (3 mm) strips
16 fl oz (480 ml) onion stock,
  made with 1 stock cube

4 oz (120 g) cooked rice
1 tablespoon fresh lemon juice
Salt and pepper to taste
2 tablespoons chopped fresh mint

Combine all ingredients, except mint, in medium saucepan. Simmer long enough to heat chicken. Place 1 tablespoon mint in each of 2 bowls. Ladle soup over mint and serve at once. Makes 2 servings.

Split Pea Soup (Dal)*

This can be cooked down to become a stew.

12 oz (360 g) well-drained cooked
  dried yellow split peas (reserve
  liquid), see note
1 pint 12 fl oz (960 ml) liquid (water
  plus reserved liquid)
4 oz (120 g) diced celery
1 tablespoon curry powder

1 tablespoon dried onion flakes
1 teaspoon salt or to taste
2 hot green chilli peppers, finely
  chopped
1 bay leaf
Garnish: chopped fresh parsley

Combine all ingredients in saucepan (except garnish) and bring to the boil. Reduce heat and simmer 45 minutes. Purée in blender and serve in bowls with garnish. Makes 4 servings.

Cooking Note: As a 'rule of thumb', 4 oz (120 g) uncooked dried yellow split peas will yield 12 oz (360 g) when cooked.

Curry of Eggs*

You can omit the eggs and use the curry sauce over cooked vegetables such as cauliflower or broccoli, cooked dried beans; or over cooked chicken, fish, meat or shell fish. Curries are usually served over cooked rice, but you may substitute cooked bean sprouts. Try stirring saffron or turmeric powder into bean sprouts to add colour.

8 oz (240 g) sliced onion
2 small garlic cloves, crushed
12 oz (360 g) tomatoes, chopped
2 green medium apples, sliced
4 oz (120 g) chopped celery
1 tablespoon curry powder, or to taste
1 teaspoon diced fresh ginger root

16 fl oz (480 ml) chicken stock, made with 1 stock cube
1½ teaspoons salt
1 teaspoon coconut flavouring
¼ teaspoon pepper
8 eggs, hard boiled, cut in halves
1 lb (480 g) cooked rice

Brown onion and garlic in nonstick pan. Add tomatoes, apples, celery, curry powder and ginger. Simmer for 5 minutes. Stir in all remaining ingredients except eggs and rice. Place eggs and rice in casserole and pour mixture over. Serve very hot. Provide seasoning at table . . . salt, pepper and more curry powder. Makes 8 servings.

Chicken Tandoori

Tandoor is an Indian clay oven, but the term now applies to the spiced chicken dish which was originally made in it.

3 lbs (1 kg 440 g) chicken, skinned*
2 garlic cloves, crushed
1 teaspoon allspice
½ teaspoon grated fresh ginger root or ¼ teaspoon ground ginger

¼ teaspoon crushed red pepper
Lemon juice to moisten
8 fl oz (240 ml) buttermilk

Pierce chicken with fork. Make a paste of seasonings and lemon juice and rub into chicken. Bake chicken on rack in moderate oven 350°F (180°C), Gas Mark 4, for 45 minutes, or until done to taste (or barbecue over hot coals turning frequently). Serve with 2 fl oz (60 ml) buttermilk poured over each portion. Makes 4 servings.

* A 3 lb (1 kg 440 g) chicken will yield about 1 lb (480 g) cooked meat.

Easy Chicken Curry with Tomatoes (Murghi Kari)

1 lb (480 g) onion, diced
8 fl oz (240 ml) chicken stock,
　made with ½ stock cube
2 tablespoons curry powder (more or
　less to taste)
16 teaspoons tomato purée

4 fl oz (120 ml) water
Salt to taste
1 lb 8 oz (720 g) boned and skinned
　chicken breasts, diced
6 fl oz (180 ml) hot water
8 oz (240 g) cooked rice

Place onion, stock and curry powder in a casserole or large frying pan with lid and cook, covered, over low heat for 10 to 15 minutes. Add tomato purée, water and salt. Stir to combine. Place chicken in sauce; stir sauce over chicken; cook, covered, over medium heat, turning occasionally until chicken is done, about 15 minutes. Add water; stir to combine; replace lid and cook over low heat for 5 minutes. Serve with rice. Makes 4 servings.

Veal Loaf Madhya

For a fiery loaf, you can add lots more ginger, paprika and cayenne.

12 oz (360 g) minced veal
1 tablespoon tomato purée
1 tablespoon water
1½ teaspoons prepared mustard
½ teaspoon paprika

¼ teaspoon grated fresh ginger root
　or pinch ground ginger
¼ teaspoon cayenne pepper or
　crushed red pepper
⅛ teaspoon ground cardamom

Combine all ingredients. Shape into loaf and place on a nonstick baking sheet. Bake at 350°F (180°C), Gas Mark 4, for 35 minutes or until cooked right through. Makes 2 servings.

Chopped Meat with Peas (Keema Matar)

1 lb 2 oz (540 g) minced lamb or
  beef
4 fl oz (120 ml) beef stock, made
  with ¼ stock cube
2 tablespoons curry powder
1 teaspoon garlic powder

1 cinnamon stick
1 teaspoon chopped fresh ginger root
  or ½ teaspoon ground ginger
1 teaspoon salt
9 oz (270 g) frozen green peas,
  thawed

Grill meat or bake at 350°F (180°C), Gas Mark 4, on rack in oven. Remove and break into small pieces. Place in a large nonstick pan. Add next 6 ingredients; cook, stirring constantly, to keep meat crumbly not caked, for about 5 minutes or until flavours blend and mixture is hot. Stir in peas, remove cinnamon stick; serve hot. Makes 3 servings.

Cooked Cucumber with Buttermilk

12 oz (360 g) cucumber, peeled
5 fl oz (150 ml) buttermilk
1 tablespoon chopped fresh coriander
  or parsley

½ teaspoon chopped fresh ginger
  root or pinch ground ginger
Salt and pepper to taste
Cayenne pepper to taste

Cut the cucumber in half and remove the seeds if they are large. Slice. Cover cucumber with boiling water and simmer until tender. Drain. Add remaining ingredients and heat but do not boil. Makes 2 servings.

Rayta Salad

In recipe above, add 3 oz (90 g) diced tomato, 1 seeded diced green chilli pepper, and slivers of lemon rind to the cooked cucumber. Chill. Serve on shredded lettuce with lemon or lime wedges. Makes 2 servings.

Spiced Salsify Salad

12 oz (360 g) salsify
16 fl oz (480 ml) water
1½ teaspoons vinegar
¼ teaspoon each sage and dried mint
2 fl oz (60 ml) vegetable oil

2 teaspoons chopped fresh parsley
1½ teaspoons lemon juice
½ teaspoon chilli pepper
¼ teaspoon thyme

Cut cleaned salsify into long thin strips. Combine salsify, water and vinegar in saucepan. Let stand 10 minutes. Add sage and mint, and cook until salsify is tender; drain well. (If using canned salsify, continue from here.) Combine oil, parsley, lemon juice, chilli pepper and thyme in a jar with tight-fitting lid. Shake well and pour over salsify. Makes 4 servings.

Apple Chutney

6 oz (180 g) green pepper
1 tart medium apple
1½ tablespoons lemon juice

¾ teaspoon paprika
¼ teaspoon cayenne pepper
¼ teaspoon salt

Peel and seed pepper; peel and core apple; grate both very finely, mashing or chopping thoroughly (or blend until finely chopped). Add lemon juice, paprika, cayenne pepper and salt. Makes 4 servings.

Vegetable Chutney

6 oz (180 g) cucumber
1 teaspoon salt
6 oz (180 g) green pepper, seeded
2 tablespoons chopped celery

2 tablespoons lemon juice
1 teaspoon paprika
½ small garlic clove, crushed
¼ teaspoon pepper

Peel cucumber; cut in quarters and remove seeds, then slice. Sprinkle with salt. Let stand 1 hour; drain and rinse. Blanch green pepper in boiling water. Combine all ingredients; chop finely until mixture is well-blended (or combine all ingredients in blender goblet until mixture is finely chopped). Makes 4 servings.

Lentil and Tomato Stew*

4 oz (120 g) sliced onion
1 garlic clove, crushed
1 lb (480 g) cooked dried lentils
6 oz (180 g) tomatoes, peeled and
  chopped

¾ teaspoon crushed mustard seed
½ teaspoon salt
¼ teaspoon dried crushed red chilli
  pepper

Cook onion and garlic in nonstick pan, stirring often until soft. Add all remaining ingredients and simmer 10 to 15 minutes. Makes 4 servings.

Curried Potatoes with String Beans

9 oz (270 g) peeled potatoes, sliced
12 oz (360 g) frozen young string
  beans, thawed
2 fl oz (60 ml) chicken stock,
  made with ¼ stock cube

1 teaspoon curry powder
1 teaspoon salt
1 tablespoon lemon juice

Cook potatoes in saucepan in water to cover until barely tender; drain. Add string beans, chicken stock, curry powder and salt, and cook over very low heat until string beans are done. Stir in lemon juice and serve. Makes 3 servings.

Spicy Banana Sauce

As accompaniment for a poached fish or roast or grilled chicken, lamb or beef.

2 medium bananas, firm but ripe
10 fl oz (300 ml) buttermilk
1 teaspoon ground cumin

½ teaspoon dry mustard
¼ teaspoon salt

Mash bananas with fork. With egg beater, gradually beat in buttermilk and seasonings. Beat steadily for several minutes until thick. Makes 4 servings.

Minty Apricot Whip

6 very ripe medium apricots, stoned
1¼ oz (40 g) nonfat dry milk,
 reconstituted with 5 fl oz (150 ml)
 water
Artificial sweetener to equal 1
 tablespoon sugar, or to taste

¼ teaspoon lemon flavouring
1 tablespoon unflavoured gelatine
2 fl oz (60 ml) water
Mint leaves

Place half the fruit in blender goblet. Add milk, sweetener and flavouring. Sprinkle gelatine over water in small saucepan and let stand to soften. Place over low heat; stir until gelatine is dissolved. Add to apricot mixture. Blend until smooth. Lift off blender goblet and chill for a few minutes in refrigerator. Replace goblet and blend again until mixture becomes thick. Dice remainder of fruit and fold into gelatine mixture. Divide evenly into two tall dessert glasses. Chill at least 30 minutes before serving. Garnish with fresh mint leaves. Makes 2 servings.

Orange Shake (Lassi)

4 ice cubes, crushed
4 fl oz (120 ml) orange juice

5 fl oz (150 ml) natural unsweetened
 yogurt

Put crushed ice in blender goblet and add remaining ingredients. Blend and serve at once. Makes 2 servings.

Borani

This refreshing Kashmir drink is a summertime favourite.

10 fl oz (300 ml) buttermilk
8 ice cubes, crushed
Lemon rind, 1 strip
1 tablespoon each chopped fresh
  mint or basil or ¼ teaspoon dried

Pinch chilli powder
Salt and freshly ground black pepper
  to taste
Garnish: Mint or basil leaves

Combine buttermilk and ice in blender goblet. Add lemon rind, chopped mint or basil, chilli powder, salt and pepper. Blend at high speed. Serve in tall dessert glasses with garnish of mint or basil leaves. Makes 4 servings.

ISRAEL

*

Like the Jewish people, the recipes in this section have wandered from one country to another for hundreds and even thousands of years. This medley of food ideas picked up in scattered countries would be a gastronomical hotchpotch but for the blending and unification which took place as the dishes were modified in obedience to Kashruth. Under this ancient rabbinic law, orthodox Jews were required to use only sanctioned foods certified as ritually clean. Shellfish and pork were prohibited. Milk products could not be served with meats. So, adapted to fit these requirements, the old recipes, whatever their origins, acquired a common character and became Jewish. Our recipes from the re-established Jewish homeland are very old, very new (potato latkes without guilt) and very delicious. Naturally, we begin with the famous soup . . .

Chicken Noodle Soup

8 fl oz (240 ml) chicken stock, made with ½ stock cube
4 tablespoons diced celery leaves

4 tablespoons shredded watercress or parsley
2 oz (60 g) cooked noodles

Bring chicken stock, celery leaves and watercress or parsley to the boil in small saucepan. Strain and serve hot over noodles in small bowl. Makes 1 serving.

Chicken Noodle Soup with Chicken

1 skinned grilling or roasting chicken
   3 lbs (1 kg 440 g)
1 pint 12 fl oz (960 ml) water
2 oz (60 g) celery and leaves, diced
2 teaspoons dried onion flakes

2 teaspoons salt
3 peppercorns
8 oz (240 g) cooked noodles
3 tablespoons chopped fresh parsley

Cut chicken into 8 pieces and grill on all sides, turning as necessary. Allow about 20 minutes. Transfer browned chicken to large saucepan, cover with water, and add diced celery and leaves, onion flakes, salt and peppercorns. Cook 1½ hours. Serve soup hot in soup bowls each containing 2 oz (60 g) noodles. Garnish with parsley. Chicken should be weighed and served (4 oz (120 g) servings when cooked and boned) either in the bowls (for chicken in the pot) or as a separate course. Makes 4 servings.

Gefilte Fish with Horseradish

12 oz (360 g) whiting fillets, cut in
   small pieces
12 oz (360 g) pike fillets, cut in small
   pieces
1 oz (30 g) celery, sliced
2 tablespoons dried onion flakes
1 teaspoon garlic powder

Salt and pepper to taste
4½ teaspoons unflavoured gelatine
6 fl oz (180 ml) cold water
4 lettuce leaves
3 oz (90 g) cooked, sliced carrots
Grated fresh horseradish

Put fish and celery through mincer three times. Add onion flakes, garlic powder, salt and pepper; mix well. Sprinkle gelatine over mixture. Add cold water, about 2 fl oz (60 ml) at a time, mixing constantly until absorbed. Divide evenly into 4 oval loaves. Bake at 350°F (180°C), Gas Mark 4, in 15½ × 10½ × 1-inch (40 × 27 × 2.5 cm) baking tin for about 25 minutes or until cooked through; serve on lettuce leaves. Garnish with carrot slices. Serve with horseradish. Makes 4 servings.

Potato Pancake Puffs (Latkes)*

For applesauce to go with potato pancakes: bring 3 tablespoons water and ½ teaspoon lemon juice to the boil in a saucepan with 1 medium apple, peeled and diced. Add a pinch of cinnamon and artificial sweetener to equal 1½ teaspoons sugar, or to taste. Cook 2 to 3 minutes. Makes 1 serving.

3 oz (90 g) freshly cooked potato, mashed	½ teaspoon salt
	Pinch of pepper
1 egg	½ slice white bread, made into fine
1 oz (30 g) grated onion	crumbs
¼ teaspoon chopped fresh parsley	½ teaspoon baking powder

Combine potato, egg, onion, parsley, salt, pepper, breadcrumbs and baking powder in a bowl. Mix well. Drop by spoonfuls onto heated nonstick frying pan or griddle and brown until golden on both sides. Makes eight pancakes. Makes 1 serving.

Spinach Pancakes*

In recipe above, substitute 3 oz (90 g) well-drained chopped cooked spinach for the potato, add a pinch of nutmeg and brown as above. Makes 1 serving.

Chilled Fish and Vegetables (Yakne)

8 oz (240 g) onion, sliced thinly	Freshly ground pepper to taste
6 sprigs fresh parsley, cut coarsely	2 tablespoons water
4 oz (120 g) celery with leaves, diced	1 lb 8 oz (720 g) fish fillets, fresh
12 oz (360 g) tomatoes, peeled, cut in pieces	(or frozen and partly thawed), sliced
¾ teaspoon salt	

Brown onion slices in heated nonstick pan. Add parsley, celery and tomatoes; sprinkle with salt and pepper and stir in the water. Cover and simmer over low flame for 20 to 30 minutes until vegetables are tender. Place fish slices on top and cover. Simmer until much of the liquid is reduced and the fish flakes with a fork, about 15 minutes. Refrigerate. Yakne tastes best cold, but may also be served hot. Makes 4 servings.

Cholent

12 oz (360 g) boneless beef chuck
   shoulder steak
4 oz (120 g) onion, sliced
8 fl oz (240 ml) beef stock, made
   with ½ stock cube
½ garlic clove

16 fl oz (480 ml) tomato juice
½ bay leaf
Pinch paprika
Salt and pepper to taste
4 oz (120 g) cooked broad beans
1 teaspoon chopped fresh parsley

Grill steak 3 inches (8 cm) from source of heat 5 minutes on each side or until brown. Remove and cool. Cut into large pieces. Brown onions in nonstick frying pan. Add stock and garlic; bring to the boil. Pour into saucepan. Add steak, tomato juice, bay leaf and paprika. Season with salt and pepper to taste. Simmer 1½ hours or until meat is tender and sauce thickens. Add broad beans; reheat. Remove bay leaf. Divide into 2 equal portions. Sprinkle with parsley. Makes 2 servings.

Beetroot in Piquant Sauce

3 tablespoons lemon juice or vinegar
1 tablespoon dried onion flakes
1 tablespoon frozen orange juice
   concentrate
½ teaspoon salt

⅛ teaspoon whole cloves
1 small piece grated orange rind
6 oz (180 g) cooked beetroot, diced or
   sliced

Heat lemon juice, onion flakes, orange juice and other seasonings in saucepan. Add beetroot, stir gently and serve hot or cold. Makes 2 servings.

Red Sea Cabbage and Apple Slaw

½ teaspoon salt
1 lb (480 g) shredded red cabbage
12 fl oz (360 ml) boiling water
2 teaspoons lemon juice

2 tablespoons vegetable oil
Pinch pepper
2 medium apples, peeled and diced
2 oz (60 g) onion, finely diced

Sprinkle salt over shredded cabbage; add boiling water. Let stand 10 minutes; drain. Combine lemon juice, oil and pepper. Add to cabbage with the diced apple and onion. Mix well. Chill at least 30 minutes before serving. Makes 4 servings.

Marrow Tsimiss

8 oz (240 g) cooked marrow
4 oz (120 g) canned pineapple
  chunks, no sugar added, drained,
  reserve juice
2 teaspoons cinnamon

1 teaspoon nutmeg
¼ teaspoon ginger
1 medium apple, cored, peeled, diced
1 tablespoon margarine

Combine marrow, pineapple juice, cinnamon, nutmeg and ginger in medium bowl. Layer half marrow mixture in an 8-inch (20 cm) baking dish. Arrange apple and pineapple over marrow layer; top with remaining marrow. Dot with margarine. Cover. Bake at 325°F (160°C), Gas Mark 3, for 30 minutes. Makes 2 servings.

Chick Pea Croquettes (Falafel)

12 oz (360 g) canned, cooked, dried
  chick peas
½ teaspoon salt
¼ teaspoon each basil, marjoram
  and thyme

¼ teaspoon hot pepper sauce
1 garlic clove, crushed
1 slice white bread, toasted and
  made into crumbs

Put chick peas through mincer. Combine chick peas, salt, herbs, hot pepper sauce, garlic and toasted crumbs in medium bowl. Form into balls, 1 inch (2.5 cm) in diameter. Place on nonstick shallow pan. Bake 20 minutes at 350°F (180°C), Gas Mark 4. Makes 2 servings.

Pineapple Charlotte

8 oz (240 g) canned crushed
  pineapple, no sugar added,
  drained, reserve liquid

1 tablespoon unflavoured gelatine
$1\frac{1}{2}$ teaspoons lemon juice
Whipped Topping (see page 12)

Place pineapple juice in small saucepan. Sprinkle gelatine over liquid and place over low heat, stirring with a wooden spoon until gelatine is dissolved. Add pineapple and lemon juice. Stir. Chill until mixture begins to thicken. Fold in Whipped Topping. Transfer to medium mould and chill until set, about $1\frac{1}{2}$ hours, or overnight. Makes 2 servings.

Fluffy Lemon Pie*

3 eggs, separated
Artificial sweetener to equal 7
  teaspoons sugar, or to taste

2 tablespoons cold water
Juice and grated rind of 1 lemon
Few grains salt

Beat egg yolks thoroughly with artificial sweetener to equal 4 teaspoons sugar. Stir in water and lemon. Cook in double boiler until thick. Remove from heat. Add salt and remaining sweetener to equal 3 teaspoons sugar to egg whites and beat until stiff. Fold into hot egg yolk mixture. Fill 8-inch (20 cm) nonstick pie plate. Bake in moderate oven 350°F (180°C), Gas Mark 4, until top is lightly browned. Makes 3 servings.

Strawberry 'Jam'

2 teaspoons unflavoured gelatine   ½ teaspoon vanilla flavouring
6 fl oz (180 ml) water   Artificial sweetener to equal 2
5 oz (150 g) strawberries, crushed   teaspoons sugar, or to taste

Sprinkle gelatine over water in small saucepan. Heat, stirring, until
gelatine dissolves. Add remaining ingredients. Pour into small dish.
Chill. Makes 4 servings.

ITALY

 *

La cucina Italiana! Magnifica! It offers something for everyone. Hearty Sicilian specialities redolent with garlic, soups that are meals in themselves and the more subtly flavoured dishes of Northern Italy. In fact, recipes from Italy have such distinct characteristics that we might more accurately refer not to one Italian cuisine but to the two dozen or more regional cuisines of Italy.

The roots of these regional specialities can be found in the history, geography and agriculture of the country. In Sicily, the Arab conquest is apparent in the use of spices and such savoury vegetable stews as Caponata. Artichokes, aubergine and broad green beans are grown and favoured in the South; potatoes and polenta in the North. In the Italian Alps, the cuisine shows Germanic influence from its Tyrol neighbours.

Pasta, however, is more or less common throughout Italy, although its shape varies from one place to another. In modern Italy, particularly in cities around Milan and Rome where Weight Watchers classes exist, restaurateurs often give you a choice of delectably cooked vegetables—contorni—rather than pasta or soup. We've done as well for you. Try fingers of courgettes with garlic; pickled artichoke hearts; crisp bright green flowers of broccoli; crunchy whole green beans al dente; mustard-spiced spinach and mushroom salads; and our other wonderfully Italian foods.

Cold Antipasto (As Appetizer)

In Italy, antipasto (literally, before the pasta) is generally served only at elaborate meals. But as it is a popular first course on Italian style restaurant menus, we've indicated a few methods of serving it to fit the

187

Food Programme. Antipasto is as variable as the seasons and regions in which it is eaten. It can include many different foods, or two or three, or even just one. Whatever you choose, serve each food so it is separated from the others on the antipasto plate, arranging forms, colours and sizes with an eye to contrast and eye appeal.

1. *Vegetables and garnishes*: Select in reasonable amounts. Raw (only if garden fresh), blanched or cooked al dente broccoli or cauliflower florets, whole green beans, courgette spears. Raw carrot curls, cucumbers scored with a fork and cut in slices; radishes; tomato wedges or tiny whole tomatoes; sliced green pepper; fennel. Roasted pimientos or peppers, sliced or shredded. Whole button mushrooms; crisp salad greens, endive, sprigs of parsley and watercress, all washed and thoroughly dried.

2. *Limited vegetables*: Select up to 3 oz (90 g) servings—beetroot, parsnips, peas, broad beans.

3. *Fruits*: Select 1 of the following, if desired. Serve whole, halved or quartered, as appropriate. 3 medium apricots; 5 oz (150 g) melon balls; 4 oz (120 g) cherries; 1 large fig; 1 medium fresh pear with lemon juice; 2 medium fresh plums.

4. *Salad dressing*: Select 1 per serving (recipes on page 189).

Antipasto (As Main Dish)

Select vegetables, limited vegetables, or salad greens, and a dressing, from the preceding recipe. Add the following:
(Choose 2 per serving)

1 hard boiled egg, halved, quartered or sliced

1 oz (30 g) hard cheese, mozzarella, Swiss, Romano or fresh Parmesan (Parmesan is often sliced and eaten as a delicious table cheese in Italy)

2 oz (60 g) ricotta cheese, in a ball

2 oz (60 g) drained tuna, in one piece

2 oz (60 g) slivered roast beef or evenly diced cooked veal or chicken

1½ oz (45 g) cooked ham, rolled round a gherkin

½ recipe Lentil Salad (see page 36)

Pasta, Bread or Potato (Choose 1 per serving, if desired).

2 oz (60 g) cooked macaroni, chilled
1 recipe Garlic Bread, Herb Fingers
  or Salty Sticks (see page 225)
3 oz (90 g) boiled new potato, whole,
  halved, sliced; or dice and

combine with dice of 2 fresh
medium plums or 1 small fresh
pear sprinkled with lemon juice to
preserve colour

Dressings for Antipasto or Salads

Garlic Dressing: Combine 1 tablespoon vegetable oil, 1 tablespoon vinegar or lemon juice, $\frac{1}{2}$ garlic clove, crushed, salt, freshly ground black pepper and a pinch each of oregano and basil. Makes 1 serving.

Lemony Vinaigrette Dressing: Combine 2 tablespoons white vinegar, 1 tablespoon lemon juice, $\frac{1}{2}$ small garlic clove, crushed, $\frac{1}{2}$ teaspoon Worcester sauce and Dijon-style mustard in mixing bowl; mix all ingredients well with fork or wire whisk; add 2 fl oz (60 ml) vegetable oil, a spoonful at a time, stirring constantly. Add 2 teaspoons chopped parsley, 1 teaspoon chives, $\frac{1}{8}$ teaspoon salt and freshly ground pepper. Makes 4 servings.

Red Vinegar Dressing (No oil): Combine 2 tablespoons red wine vinegar, 1 tablespoon tomato purée, 1 tablespoon water, $\frac{1}{4}$ teaspoon salad seasoning mix, or to taste, $\frac{1}{2}$ teaspoon Worcester sauce and a pinch each of cinnamon and dry mustard. Makes 1 serving.

Mayonnaise: Combine 1 tablespoon mayonnaise with chopped washed capers, parsley, dry mustard and chives. Thin with lemon juice or thicken with measured amount of tomato purée or chopped vegetables such as cucumber, green pepper, spinach, etc. Good over fish. Makes 1 serving.

Fish Soup (Brodetto)

Brodetto is Italy's answer to France's bouillabaisse. Or, maybe France copied from Italy when Catherine de Medici married Henry II, and brought, with her dowry, to France, a staff of Italian cooks and their fine Italian recipes. On the other hand, whenever fishermen's wives—whatever their port—are given a plentiful supply of fish, you can be certain the fish will end up as a soup or a stew.

In Italy, the local fish used for Brodetto might include (but not all at the same time): anguilla (eel); cefalo and triglie (types of mullet); carpa;

luccio (pike); cernia (bass); sgombro (mackerel); and vongole (small clams). However, there are almost as many recipes for Brodetto as there are fishermen's wives, but saffron and tomatoes seem to be the two necessities. (Turmeric may be used instead of saffron.)

2 lbs (960 g) (if with bones and skin) assorted fish cut in slices, or 1 lb 8 oz (720 g) skinned and boned fillets including shellfish if desired
4 oz (120 g) onion, sliced
3 oz (90 g) sliced carrot
1 garlic clove
12 oz (360 g) tomatoes, or 16 teaspoons tomato purée, mixed with 4 fl oz (120 ml) water

4 oz (120 g) diced celery
1 tablespoon chopped fresh parsley
16 fl oz (480 ml) water
16 fl oz (480 ml) Fish Stock (see page 11)
1 teaspoon wine flavouring
½ teaspoon salt
½ teaspoon saffron or turmeric
½ bay leaf
¼ teaspoon pepper
¼ teaspoon fennel seeds (optional)

Fish with bones should be cut into slices; fillets into 2-inch (5 cm) pieces; refrigerate until ready to use. Brown onions, carrots and garlic in heated nonstick saucepan for 5 minutes, turning so they do not scorch. Press garlic clove with fork to extract juices, then discard it. Add tomatoes, celery, parsley and all remaining ingredients except fish and bring to the boil. Cook for 20 minutes. Reduce heat to simmering temperature; add the fish; cover pan and cook 15 to 20 minutes longer. Serve the soup and fish separately—but at the same meal. Makes 4 servings.

Chicken Soup (Zuppa di Pollo)

A hearty meal-in-one-bowl

1 lb 8 oz (720 g) skinned and boned chicken, in pieces
10 oz (300 g) cleaned asparagus pieces
1 oz (30 g) celery, diced
2 teaspoons chopped fresh parsley

1 teaspoon dried onion flakes
½ garlic clove
3 peppercorns, crushed
2 pints 8 fl oz (1 litre 440 ml) water
8 oz (240 g) cooked rice

Brown chicken under grill, turning as necessary, 15 to 20 minutes. Transfer to large saucepan. Add asparagus, celery, parsley, onion flakes, garlic, peppercorns and water. Bring to the boil, cover saucepan and cook for 1 hour. Remove chicken. Continue simmering soup. Cut chicken into dice and divide pieces evenly into 4 large soup bowls. Put 2 oz (60 g) rice in each bowl. Pour soup into bowls. Makes 4 servings.

'Cream' of Cauliflower Soup (Crema di Cavolfiori)

16 fl oz (480 ml) water
2 teaspoons chicken stock powder
4 oz (120 g) chopped celery
1 tablespoon dried onion flakes
½ teaspoon salt and pinch of white pepper

13 oz (390 g) cooked chopped cauliflower
3 oz (90 g) nonfat dry milk reconstituted with 15 fl oz (450 ml) water
Garnish: chopped watercress or pinch of paprika

Heat water to boiling in saucepan; add stock powder, celery, onion flakes, salt and pepper; cover and cook until celery is tender. Pour celery mixture into blender goblet; blend at medium speed until smooth. Gradually add cauliflower, blending after each addition until smooth. Pour into saucepan; stir in milk; heat. Garnish. Makes 6 servings.

Endive and Chicken Soup (Zuppa di Pollo con Escarole)

You can save the white inside leaves for a salad.

8 oz (240 g) Batavian endive, well washed
16 fl oz (480 ml) chicken stock, made with 1 stock cube

¼ teaspoon chopped fresh ginger root
¼ teaspoon sherry flavouring
Salt and pepper to taste

Shred leaves. Transfer to saucepan containing boiling chicken stock and ginger. Cover and simmer 30 minutes. Season with sherry flavouring, salt and pepper. Serve hot. Makes 2 servings.

Lentil Soup (Zuppa di Lenticchie)

6 oz (180 g) cooked dried lentils
3 oz (90 g) tomato, peeled and
chopped
8 fl oz (240 ml) chicken stock,
made with ½ stock cube
1 teaspoon dried onion flakes

1 garlic clove
Salt and pepper to taste
2 teaspoons chopped fresh herbs:
½ teaspoon each of basil, parsley,
chives, and mint, or to taste

Combine cooked lentils, tomato, chicken stock, onion flakes, garlic, salt and pepper in saucepan. Bring to the boil, stir well. Cover pan and simmer 15 minutes. Stir in herbs and serve hot. Makes 1 serving.

Pasta and Potato Soup (Zuppa di Pasta e Patate)

3 oz (90 g) potato, peeled and diced
3 oz (90 g) tomato, diced
12 fl oz (360 ml) chicken stock,
made with 1 stock cube
1 tablespoon chopped chives or 1
teaspoon dried onion flakes

2 teaspoons chopped fresh basil or ¼
teaspoon dried
Salt and pepper to taste
2 oz (60 g) hot cooked elbow
macaroni

Combine potato, tomato, chicken stock, chives and basil in small saucepan. Bring to the boil; reduce to simmer, cover pan and cook 30 to 40 minutes, stirring several times. Season with salt and pepper and serve, divided into two bowls, each holding 1 oz (30 g) elbow macaroni. Makes 2 servings.

Egg and Cheese Broth (Stracciatelle)

Add a pinch of cinnamon, as the Romans frequently do.

8 fl oz (240 ml) beef stock, made
  with ½ stock cube
1 egg
1 oz (30 g) Parmesan cheese, freshly
  grated

Salt and freshly ground black pepper
  to taste
1 teaspoon finely chopped fresh
  parsley and marjoram
Twist of lemon rind or grated lemon
  rind

Bring stock to the boil in the medium saucepan. Beat egg with cheese in a small mixing bowl. Pour into stock, stirring vigorously with fork or wooden spoon until egg is set. Bring to boiling point; serve hot with salt and pepper to taste. Garnish top with parsley, marjoram and lemon rind. Makes 1 serving.

Egg, Cheese and Spinach Soup (Stracciatelle con Spinaci)

Follow preceding recipe, but add 6 oz (180 g) well-drained, cooked, frozen chopped spinach to the stock before bringing it to the boil. Continue as above. Makes 1 serving.

Minestrone alla Genovese

3 pints 4 fl oz (1 litre 920 ml) beef
  stock, made with 4 stock cubes
4 oz (120 g) chopped leeks or onion
3 oz (90 g) diced carrots
2 oz (60 g) diced celery
4 tablespoons chopped fresh parsley
4 tablespoons tomato purée
3 fl oz (90 ml) water
1 small garlic clove, crushed

5 oz (150 g) shredded cabbage
5 oz (150 g) sliced courgettes
2 oz (60 g) shredded spinach
4 oz (120 g) sliced green beans, or
  peeled diced aubergine
8 oz (240 g) cooked fresh broad
  beans
Salt and pepper to taste
Chopped basil or parsley to garnish

Combine beef stock with leeks, carrots, celery, parsley and basil in saucepan and bring to the boil. Add tomato purée, water and garlic; simmer for 30 minutes. Stir in cabbage, courgettes, shredded spinach and green beans (or aubergine). Cook for 30 minutes. Add broad beans and salt and pepper to taste. Serve piping hot in deep bowls, sprinkled with more chopped fresh basil or parsley. Makes 4 servings.

Soup with Bread and Cheese, Roman Style* (Zuppa con Crostini alla Romana)

1 slice white bread, toasted
1 oz (30 g) grated Parmesan cheese
1 teaspoon dried onion flakes
  reconstituted
⅛ teaspoon garlic powder
8 fl oz (240 ml) hot stock, made
  with ½ stock cube

Place toast in a small individual earthenware casserole. Combine cheese, onion flakes and garlic. Sprinkle over toast; brown top lightly under the grill. Pour in stock and serve hot (or keep hot in oven until ready to serve). Makes 1 serving.

Vermicelli and Courgette Soup (Zuppa di Vermicelli e Zucchini)

4 oz (120 g) onion, diced
6 oz (180 g) tomatoes, peeled, diced
1 pint 12 fl oz (960 ml) beef stock,
  made with 2 stock cubes
12 oz (360 g) diced courgettes
1½ tablespoons chopped fresh basil
  or ¾ teaspoon dried
8 oz (240 g) cooked vermicelli (thin
  spaghetti) cut into 1-inch (2.5 cm)
  lengths

Simmer onion and tomatoes in saucepan for 5 minutes. Pour in stock and bring to the boil. Add courgettes and basil. Cook 30 minutes, or until courgettes are very soft, Divide evenly into 4 soup bowls, each containing 2 oz (60 g) cooked vermicelli. Pass salt and pepper mill at the table. Makes 4 servings.

Broccoli Omelette (Frittata di Broccoli)

2 fl oz (60 ml) water
1 teaspoon chicken stock powder
½ teaspoon salt
⅛ teaspoon thyme
2 oz (60 g) onion, chopped

1 garlic clove, crushed
3 oz (90 g) tomato, chopped
4 oz (120 g) cooked chopped
  broccoli
4 eggs

Heat water, stock powder, salt and thyme to boiling in large nonstick pan. Add onion and garlic; cook until onion is tender. Add tomato; cook only until tomato is soft. Remove from heat; stir in broccoli. Beat eggs in medium bowl. Add broccoli mixture. Return pan to heat; pour in broccoli-egg mixture. Cook until lightly browned on the bottom. Immediately place pan under grill (cover handle with foil); cook until eggs are just set. Makes 2 servings.

Eggs Florentine (Uova alla Fiorentina)

4 oz (120 g) frozen chopped spinach
4 oz (120 g) grated mozzarella
  cheese (reserve 2 tablespoons)
1 oz (30 g) nonfat dry milk,
  reconstituted with 5 fl oz (150 ml)
  water
2 slices white bread, made into
  crumbs

¾ teaspoon salt
¼ teaspoon basil or 1 teaspoon
  chopped fresh
¼ teaspoon nutmeg
¼ teaspoon pepper
4 eggs

Cook spinach according to package directions. Drain. Dry out by cooking in saucepan over moderate heat. Add cheese (all but 2 tablespoons), milk, breadcrumbs (reserve 2 tablespoons), salt, basil, nutmeg and pepper. Heat, mixing thoroughly. Divide mixture evenly into 4 ramekins or shallow individual oven-to-table baking dishes. Poach 4 eggs in boiling salted water until just set. Remove from water to spinach mixture in ramekins. Combine 2 tablespoons reserved cheese and 2 tablespoons reserved crumbs. Sprinkle 1½ teaspoons over each egg. Bake at 375°F (190°C), Gas Mark 5, until top is browned and mixture is piping hot. Makes 4 servings.

Tuna-Spinach Omelette (Frittata con Tonno e Spinaci)

An excellent lunch for two.

2 eggs	Dash hot pepper sauce
2 tablespoons skim milk	6 oz (180 g) drained, cooked
1 tablespoon mayonnaise	chopped spinach
1 tablespoon fresh lime or lemon	4 oz (120 g) drained canned tuna,
juice	flaked
1 teaspoon dill	2 slices white bread, cut in ½-inch
1 teaspoon dried onion flakes	(1 cm) cubes
¼ teaspoon salt	

In medium bowl, beat together the eggs, milk, mayonnaise, lime juice, dill, onion flakes, salt and hot pepper sauce. Combine with spinach and tuna; fold in bread cubes. Pour mixture into an 8-inch (20 cm) nonstick tin. Bake at 375°F (190°C), Gas Mark 5, for 10 to 12 minutes, or until mixture is set on the bottom. Transfer pan to grill; grill about 4 inches (10 cm) from source of heat for about 1 minute until light gold on top. Makes 2 servings.

Cheese Omelette (Frittata al Formaggio)

4 eggs, separated	½ oz (15 g) nonfat dry milk,
4 oz (120 g) grated Swiss or	reconstituted with 2½ fl oz
mozzarella cheese	(75 ml) water
	½ teaspoon salt

Beat egg whites until stiff. Combine egg yolks, cheese, milk and salt. Fold into the beaten whites. Pour mixture into 9 or 10-inch (23 or 25 cm) heated nonstick frying pan and cook over low heat, lifting edges of egg as they set so uncooked part flows to bottom. Turn to brown second side. Serve in wedges. Makes 4 servings.

Baked Vegetable Pudding (with Eggs and Cheese) (Sformato di Legumi)

Sformato is served usually as a side dish or meat accompaniment. However, we present it as a luncheon main dish. For an optional sauce, heat 4 tablespoons tomato purée with 3 fl oz (90 ml) water.

16 fl oz (480 ml) skim milk	2 sprigs tarragon or parsley,
2 slices white bread, made into	chopped
crumbs	4 eggs
8 oz (240 g) cooked cauliflower	4 oz (120 g) grated Parmesan cheese
10 oz (300 g) cooked green beans	Salt and freshly ground pepper to
1 tablespoon dried onion flakes	taste

Heat milk in saucepan until bubbles form round the side but do not let it boil. Add crumbs. Simmer 5 minutes. Remove from heat. Stir in cauliflower, green beans, onion flakes and tarragon. Transfer to blender goblet and blend until smooth (in two batches, so hot mixture does not overflow). Pour into large mixing bowl. Stir in eggs, cheese, salt and pepper. Transfer to 8 or 9-inch (20 or 23 cm) square baking tin; cover with foil and bake at 350°F (180°C), Gas Mark 4, for 30 minutes. Makes 4 servings.

Sformato di Spinaci

Cook 4 oz (120 g) frozen chopped spinach according to package directions. Drain well, and add to milk and crumbs in saucepan, omitting cauliflower and green beans. Season with grated nutmeg and grated lemon rind. Blend, following directions and other ingredients listed above. Makes 4 servings.

Sformato

As you can see from the two preceding recipes, these puddings are very versatile, for they can be made with any mixture of leftover vegetables. To make a lighter, airier company pudding—really a cross between a pudding and a soufflé—beat yolk and whites separately. Stir the lightly beaten yolks with the cheese, salt and pepper. Add green food colouring if desired; fold in egg whites. Transfer to a pudding basin (with lid) and set in baking tin. Pour water into the tin so it comes halfway to the top of the basin (at least 1 inch (2.5 cm) of water). Steam pudding in the oven at 375°F (190°C), Gas Mark 5, with lid on for 1 to 1¼ hours or until a straw inserted in centre comes out clean. Turn out on serving dish and garnish with roasted canned pimiento (rinsed, drained and cut into a heart or other shape). Makes 4 servings.

Ligurian Fish Stew (Ciuppin)

Ciuppin, the Italian fish stew, can be made of one kind of fish or of many. If just one variety is used, it might be crab or vongole (the tiny-neck clam). But just as often, you're likely to find in your ciuppin an interesting assortment of sea life.

8 teaspoons tomato purée
3 fl oz (90 ml) water
3 oz (90 g) diced carrots
2 oz (60 g) diced celery
1 garlic clove, crushed
¼ teaspoon rosemary
¼ teaspoon chives

1 tablespoon chopped fresh parsley
1 teaspoon beef stock powder
12 oz (360 g) skinned, boned fish, cut into bite-size pieces
1 teaspoon sherry flavouring or lemon juice

Combine purée, water, carrots, celery, garlic, rosemary, chives, parsley and stock powder in saucepan. Bring to the boil; cover and let simmer 20 minutes. Add the fish, cover pan, reduce heat and simmer 20 minutes longer or until fish flakes. Stir in wine flavouring or lemon juice and serve hot. Makes 2 servings.

Quick-Baked Fish with Oregano Sauce

9 oz (270 g) frozen fish fillets,
  thawed
Salt and pepper to taste
6 oz (180 g) frozen broccoli or 3 oz
  (90 g) spinach, defrosted

1 tablespoon margarine, melted
Paprika
Oregano Sauce (recipe follows)

Season fillets with salt and pepper. Make a bed of the vegetables in bottom of baking dish. Top with margarine and fish. Sprinkle top with paprika. Bake until fish is done. Serve with Oregano Sauce. Makes 3 servings.

Oregano Sauce

12 fl oz (360 ml) scalded skim milk
1½ slices white bread, made into
  crumbs

3 oz (90 g) grated Parmesan cheese
½ teaspoon oregano
¼ teaspoon pepper
1 teaspoon chicken stock powder

Combine all ingredients in saucepan; simmer 5 minutes stirring constantly. Serve hot with fish. Makes 3 servings.

Salmon and Green Bean Stew

12 fl oz (360 ml) water
4 oz (120 g) French style green
  beans, fresh or frozen
2 oz (60 g) diced celery and leaves
3 oz (90 g) diced potato
4 oz (120 g) drained, canned salmon

½ oz (15 g) nonfat dry milk,
  reconstituted with 2½ fl oz
  (75 ml) water
1 teaspoon dried onion flakes
1 teaspoon chopped fresh parsley
Pinch rosemary

Combine water, green beans, celery and potato in saucepan. Simmer until potato and green beans are tender. Stir in remaining ingredients and heat, but do not boil. Serve piping hot. Makes 1 serving.

Stuffed Sole Florentine (Sogliola alla Fiorentina)

1 oz (30 g) nonfat dry milk,
reconstituted with 5 fl oz (150 ml)
water
2 oz (60 g) cooked cauliflower
½ teaspoon lemon juice
½ teaspoon dried onion flakes
½ teaspoon salt

4 oz (120 g) coarsely chopped fresh
spinach leaves
4 tablespoons fresh parsley leaves
1½ oz (45 g) chopped, drained, canned
mushrooms
2 × 6 oz (180 g) fillets of sole

Blend milk, cauliflower, lemon juice, onion flakes and salt in blender
goblet, at medium speed until smooth. Gradually add 2 oz (60 g)
spinach and the parsley; blend at high speed after each addition, until
smooth. Combine remaining spinach and mushrooms with 2 tablespoons spinach sauce from blender; spoon evenly along centre of each
fillet. Fold ends of each fillet over filling; secure with wooden cocktail
sticks. Sprinkle with additional salt and lemon juice. Place fillets,
seam-side down, in shallow casserole. Evenly divide remaining sauce
over fillets. Bake at 350°F (180°C), Gas Mark 4, for 40 minutes. Makes
2 servings.

Tuna and Spinach Loaf (Polpettone di Tonno e Spinaci)

8 oz (240 g) drained, canned tuna,
flaked
12 oz (360 g) cooked frozen chopped
spinach, press out liquid through
strainer until well drained
4 oz (120 g) chopped onion
2 oz (60 g) chopped celery
1 tablespoon chopped capers

2 slices fresh white bread, made into
crumbs
4 eggs (2 uncooked, 2 hard-boiled, for
garnish)
1 tablespoon lemon juice
1 teaspoon Worcester sauce
4 slices of lemon, for garnish

Stock

2 tablespoons dried onion flakes
1 oz (30 g) coarsely diced celery and
leaves

4 sprigs parsley

Combine tuna, chopped spinach, onion, celery, capers, crumbs, 2 uncooked eggs, lemon juice and Worcester sauce in mixing bowl. Mix until thoroughly blended. Turn mixture onto a board holding 4 thicknesses of muslin about 14 × 15 inches (36 × 38 cm). Knead the tuna mixture until it forms a tight roll, about 2 inches (5 cm) in diameter. Wrap in muslin and tie at both ends. Put the roll into an oblong tin. Add ingredients for stock and cover with water. Bring to the boil, then reduce heat and simmer gently for 40 minutes. Remove roll from stock by lifting ends of muslin; let cool 10 minutes at room temperature, then remove the muslin. Refrigerate the roll and serve cold. Garnish each serving with 2 quarters of hard boiled egg and slice of lemon. Makes 4 servings.

Spaghetti Twists with Tuna

8 oz (240 g) drained, canned tuna, flaked
6 oz (180 g) green pepper, chopped
2 oz (60 g) chopped onion
1 garlic clove, crushed
4 tablespoons tomato purée

7 fl oz (210 ml) water
1 teaspoon salt
½ teaspoon oregano
¼ teaspoon chopped basil
¼ teaspoon pepper
4 oz (120 g) cooked spaghetti twists (cooked al dente)

Heat tuna, green pepper, onion and garlic in nonstick pan, turning to prevent scorching. Stir in tomato purée, water, salt, oregano, basil and pepper. Cook until thoroughly heated, about 5 to 10 minutes. Pour sauce over spaghetti. Makes 2 servings.

Aubergine Stuffed with Tuna*

2 × 8 oz (240 g) aubergines
8 oz (240 g) drained, canned tuna, flaked
2 slices white bread, soaked in water and squeezed dry
1 tablespoon chopped fresh parsley

⅛ teaspoon dry mustard
½ garlic clove, crushed
8 tablespoons tomato purée
6 fl oz (180 ml) water
Dash hot pepper sauce or cayenne pepper

Wash aubergines, cut into halves and scoop out, leaving 4 thick shells. Take thin slice from bottoms, if necessary, so shells 'sit' flat. Reserve pulp, and measure 14 oz (420 g). Thoroughly mix tuna, bread, parsley and mustard. Fill shells with mixture and set in baking tin. Brown garlic and diced aubergine pulp in nonstick pan. When brown, stir in tomato purée, water and hot pepper sauce. Bring to quick boil, pour over aubergine halves in tin. Bake at 375°F (190°C), Gas Mark 5, for 25 to 30 minutes or until aubergine shells are tender. Makes 4 servings.

Mussel Sauce

For linguine or Celery Spaghetti (see page 230).

8 fl oz (240 ml) Fish Stock (see page 11)	1 lb (480 g) finely chopped, drained, canned mussels
4 tablespoons tomato purée	1 tablespoon chopped fresh chives
½ teaspoon coarsely ground black pepper	1 tablespoon chopped fresh parsley
Salt to taste	¼ teaspoon oregano

Combine Fish Stock, tomato purée, pepper and salt in saucepan. Simmer 30 minutes. Add a little water if sauce is too thick. Stir in mussels, chives, parsley and oregano. Heat over low heat; mix well. Makes 4 servings. Serve over cooked pasta.

White Mussel Sauce

Use 4 oz (120 g) cooked celery, puréed in blender, in place of 4 tablespoons tomato purée in preceding recipe. Makes 4 servings.

Baked Mussels in Shells*

4 oz (120 g) onion, diced
1 garlic clove
8 oz (240 g) finely chopped, drained, canned mussels
2 tablespoons water

2 slices white bread, made into crumbs
$\frac{1}{2}$ teaspoon oregano
Salt and pepper to taste
2 teaspoons vegetable oil

Steam onions and garlic by covering with water in a shallow pan and cooking 5 to 8 minutes until water evaporates. Brown lightly. Press out juice of garlic with fork and discard garlic pulp. Stir in all remaining ingredients except oil and 4 teaspoons crumbs. Divide mixture evenly into 4 portions and spoon into mussel shells if available, or into 4 individual ovenproof dishes. Sprinkle with remaining crumbs. Spoon oil ($\frac{1}{2}$ teaspoon each serving) onto mussel stuffing. Bake in hot oven, 400°F (200°C), Gas Mark 6, for 10 minutes. Makes 4 servings.

Mussels Marinara

4 oz (120 g) diced onion
1 garlic clove, crushed
4 fl oz (120 ml) beef stock, made with $\frac{1}{4}$ stock cube
4 tablespoons tomato purée
3 fl oz (90 ml) water
2 fl oz (60 ml) Fish Stock (see page 11)
2 tablespoons wine vinegar

2 tablespoons chopped fresh parsley
$\frac{1}{4}$ teaspoon salt
$\frac{1}{8}$ teaspoon pepper
8 oz (240 g) cooked mussels (see note)
Grated lemon rind
2 slices white bread, toasted, each cut into 4 triangles

In saucepan, cook onions and garlic in stock for 20 minutes over low heat. Add tomato purée, water, Fish Stock, wine vinegar, parsley, salt and pepper. Bring to the boil, then let simmer for 10 minutes. Turn off heat. Stir in mussels and lemon rind. Divide mixture into 2 equal portions. Serve with 4 toast triangles each. Makes 2 servings.

Note: Scrub mussels under cold running water and remove long beards; scrape away excess material clinging to shells. Cover mussels with cool water and allow to stand 2 to 3 hours. Discard any mussels that float or that have shells that are not tightly closed. Place cleaned mussels in a saucepan with a small amount of water; cover and steam about 3 minutes, just until shells open. Discard any that do not open. Remove mussels from shells.

Scampi

12 oz (360 g) peeled large scampi	½ teaspoon sherry flavouring
3 tablespoons water	2 garlic cloves, crushed
2 tablespoons chopped fresh parsley	½ teaspoon salt
2 teaspoons lemon juice	Freshly ground pepper to taste

Cut scampi along the inside curve almost through to the outside curve, and gently open them so they lie flat. Combine water, parsley, lemon juice, flavouring, garlic, salt and pepper in large frying pan or chafing dish. Bring to the boil; add scampi and cook, stirring constantly, until scampi turn pink, 3 to 5 minutes. Serve scampi with sauce. Makes 2 servings.

Lobster fra Diavolo

12 oz (360 g) shelled lobster or crayfish	1 garlic clove
16 teaspoons tomato purée	2 tablespoons vinegar or lemon juice
4 fl oz (120 ml) water	1 tablespoon chopped fresh parsley
8 fl oz (240 ml) beef stock, made	½ teaspoon oregano
with ½ stock cube	Pinch of cayenne pepper and salt

Cut lobster meat into 1-inch (2.5 cm) pieces and set aside. Combine remaining ingredients, bring to the boil and cook rapidly until sauce is thick and bubbly, 15 minutes or so. Add lobster pieces, reduce heat to simmering temperature, and cook 5 to 8 minutes or until lobster is cooked. Makes 2 servings.

Barbecued Devilled Chicken (Pollo alla Diavola)

Use as much pepper as your palate dictates.

3 lbs (1 kg 440 g) chicken
  drumsticks and thighs, skinned*
Barbecue Sauce (recipe follows)

8 oz (240 g) cooked spaghetti or
  macaroni
Parsley or watercress sprigs

Barbecue Sauce

4 tablespoons tomato purée
3 fl oz (90 ml) water
$\frac{1}{2}$ teaspoon black pepper

$\frac{1}{2}$ teaspoon chilli powder
$\frac{1}{2}$ teaspoon basil
1 teaspoon beef stock powder

Grill chicken over red hot charcoal (or under grill) until done on all sides, turning as necessary. Bring ingredients for Barbecue Sauce to the boil. Keep hot on the grill. Serve well-done chicken pieces over cooked pasta; cover with Barbecue Sauce. Garnish with parsley sprigs. Makes 4 servings.

*A 3 lb (1 kg 440 g) chicken will yield about 1 lb (480 g) cooked meat.

Baked Chicken with Lemon (Pollo al Limone)

1 chicken, 3 lbs (1 kg 440 g), skinned
  and cut up*
Cut lemon
1 teaspoon salt
$\frac{1}{4}$ teaspoon paprika

$\frac{1}{8}$ teaspoon black pepper
2 fl oz (60 ml) chicken stock,
  made with $\frac{1}{4}$ stock cube
1 lemon, sliced

Rub chicken pieces on all sides with cut lemon. Sprinkle with salt, paprika and pepper. Bake in shallow tin at 350°F (180°C), Gas Mark 4, for 15 minutes. Pour in chicken stock and put lemon slices on top of chicken. Bake 45 minutes more, turning chicken several times. Serve hot. Makes 4 servings.

*A 3 lb (1 kg 440 g) chicken will yield about 1 lb (480 g) cooked meat.

Chicken with Peppers and Tomatoes

Follow preceding recipe. Fifteen minutes before chicken is done, add to tin 12 oz (360 g) roasted green or red peppers, which have been peeled, seeded and cut in thin strips; 6 oz (180 g) tomatoes, cut in half; and 1 crushed clove of garlic. Bake 15 minutes more. Makes 4 servings.

Chicken and Polenta—Venetian Style (Pollo con Polenta Veneziana)

Chicken

1 chicken, 3 lbs (1 kg 440 g), skinned
    and cut up*
Salt and pepper to taste
4 oz (120 g) finely chopped onion
1 garlic clove, crushed
12 tablespoons tomato purée
6 fl oz (180 ml) water

4 fl oz (120 ml) chicken stock
    made with ¼ stock cube
2 tablespoons chopped fresh parsley
¾ teaspoon salt
½ teaspoon sage
¼ teaspoon rosemary

Polenta

3 oz (90 g) dry yellow cornmeal
1 teaspoon salt

8 fl oz (240 ml) cold water
1 pint 4 fl oz (720 ml) boiling water

Sprinkle chicken with salt and pepper; arrange in grill pan, top with onion and garlic; brown nicely on all sides. Transfer chicken, onion and garlic to a large ovenproof casserole with lid. Combine tomato purée, water, stock, parsley, salt, sage and rosemary. Pour over chicken. Bake covered in preheated oven 350°F (180°C), Gas Mark 4, for 45 minutes, or until chicken is very tender. While chicken is baking, prepare polenta. Follow cooking directions on package or combine cornmeal, salt and cold water in a medium bowl. Gradually pour into boiling water, stirring constantly. Return to the boil, stirring constantly. Reduce heat, cover. Continue cooking over low heat, about 5 minutes, stirring frequently. Divide polenta equally into 4 large soup bowls. Divide chicken mixture over polenta. Makes 4 servings.

*See note on Baked Chicken with Lemon (Pollo al Limone) recipe.

Chicken Parmigiana

An easy-to-clean-up-after family lunch if you use shallow individual aluminium foil dishes. Serve with tomato purée mixed with water, if desired.

For each serving:

3 oz (90 g) skinned and boned chicken, preferably cut from breast
Salt and pepper to taste

4 fl oz (120 ml) chicken stock, made with ¼ stock cube
1 oz (30 g) mozzarella cheese

Season chicken with salt and pepper. Grill in shallow pan 4 inches (10 cm) from heat, basting frequently with stock; turn once. Don't overcook; chicken should be moist. Top chicken with a slice of mozzarella cheese and place in hot oven 400°F (200°C), Gas Mark 6, for 8 to 10 minutes, or until cheese melts. Makes 1 serving.

Chicken Cacciatore

A great Italian favourite frequently served with pickled sweet peppers.

1 chicken, 3 lbs (1 kg 440 g), skinned and cut up*
4 oz (120 g) sliced onion
2 garlic cloves
6 oz (180 g) tomatoes

4 tablespoons tomato purée
3 fl oz (90 ml) water
1 teaspoon salt
½ teaspoon crushed oregano
¼ teaspoon pepper

Brown chicken on all sides in large heated nonstick frying pan. Remove from pan and brown onion slices and garlic. Return browned chicken with remaining ingredients to pan; cover and simmer for 45 minutes (*do not boil*), until chicken is tender and sauce is thick. To reduce the sauce further, remove the chicken and cook liquid over high heat until it evaporates and thickens. Makes 4 servings.

*See note on Baked Chicken with Lemon (Pollo al Limone) recipe (see page 205).

Chicken Napolitano

12 oz (360 g) boned and skinned
chicken breasts
¼ teaspoon garlic powder
¼ teaspoon paprika
¼ teaspoon dried rosemary leaves,
crumbled

Salt and ground black pepper to
taste
3 oz (90 g) drained, canned
mushrooms
2 fl oz (60 ml) red wine vinegar
2 tablespoons dried parsley flakes

Season chicken with a combination of garlic powder, paprika, rosemary, salt and black pepper. Grill until brown; remove from grill and place in casserole. Cover with mushrooms, vinegar and parsley. Bake covered at 350°F (180°C), Gas Mark 4, for about 15 minutes or until chicken is tender. Makes 2 servings.

Turkey Tetrazzini

A sensational Italian opera singer who sang in America inspired the original version of this dish. It is probably more American than Italian. You may omit the toast triangles and serve it, more traditionally, over 2 oz (60 g) cooked rice.

1 teaspoon chicken stock powder or
1 stock cube
8 fl oz (240 ml) boiling water
2 teaspoons cornflour, dissolved in 2
tablespoons water
4 oz (120 g) skinned and boned cooked
turkey, diced
1 oz (30 g) cooked or drained canned
sliced mushrooms

1½ oz (45 g) green pepper, blanched
and diced
1 teaspoon diced pimiento
½ oz (15 g) nonfat dry milk,
reconstituted with 3 fl oz (90 ml)
water
1 teaspoon chopped fresh parsley
1 slice white bread, toasted and
quartered

Dissolve stock powder in boiling water in a saucepan. Place over low heat; add cornflour; heat until thick. Add turkey, mushrooms, green pepper and pimiento. Simmer 5 minutes. Add milk; reheat (*do not boil*). Place in shallow serving dish, sprinkle with parsley and serve with triangles of toast. Makes 1 serving.

Veal Chops Sorrento

1 lb (480 g) lean shoulder veal
  chops
3 oz (90 g) small mushrooms
8 fl oz (240 ml) tomato juice
6 oz (180 g) tomatoes, chopped
3 oz (90 g) green pepper, cut into
  strips

2 oz (60 g) onion, diced
½ garlic clove, crushed
½ bay leaf
1 tablespoon lemon juice
⅛ teaspoon sage
Salt and pepper to taste

Grill chops on rack 4 inches (10 cm) from source of heat for 4 to 5 minutes on each side. Put in small baking tin; add mushrooms, tomato juice, tomatoes, pepper, onion, garlic, bay leaf, lemon juice and sage. Season to taste. Bake at 400°F (200°C), Gas Mark 6, covered, for 20 minutes or until tender. Remove bay leaf. Makes 2 servings.

Veal and Vegetables in Orange Sauce

To use up meat left from the veal roast.

4 fl oz (120 ml) orange juice
4 oz (120 g) sliced, cooked veal
½ teaspoon sherry flavouring
½ teaspoon grated orange rind

2 oz (60 g) cooked small onions
Salt, pepper and garlic powder to
  taste

Heat orange juice in small saucepan. Add remaining ingredients and simmer gently just long enough to heat. Makes 1 serving.

Minced Veal in Aubergine Sauce

8 teaspoons tomato purée
2 fl oz (60 ml) water
3 oz (90 g) green pepper, cut into
  slivers about ⅛-inch (3 mm) wide
2 oz (60 g) diced celery
½ teaspoon onion powder
½ teaspoon Italian seasoning

¼ teaspoon salt
1 teaspoon chicken stock powder
1 bay leaf
3 oz (90 g) peeled and diced
  aubergine
6 oz (180 g) minced veal
2 oz (60 g) cooked rice (optional)

Combine tomato purée, water, pepper, celery, onion powder, Italian seasoning, salt, ½ teaspoon stock powder and bay leaf in a saucepan. Bring to the boil; cover and reduce heat. Add aubergine and continue cooking for about 15 minutes. Meanwhile, mix remaining stock powder with the veal and shape into a patty. Place in a nonstick tin and cook until well done. Remove from tin. Drain on a paper towel. Crumble veal, add to aubergine mixture and stir. Heat and serve over 2 oz (60 g) cooked rice if desired. Makes 1 serving.

Braised Shin of Veal (Osso Buco)

A piquant mixture of shin of veal and a succulent sauce made with garlic, parsley, lemon juice and tomato. Osso Buco is usually served over risotto.

1 × 8 oz (240 g) piece shin of veal, about 2½-inches (6 cm) thick
1½ oz (45 g) carrot, diced
2 oz (60 g) chopped celery
½ garlic clove, crushed
3 oz (90 g) tomato, peeled and chopped
4 fl oz (120 ml) tomato juice

12 fl oz (360 ml) chicken stock, made with ¾ stock cube
2 teaspoons dried onion flakes
¼ teaspoon rosemary
Salt and pepper to taste
1 tablespoon chopped fresh parsley
1 slice lemon or ½ teaspoon grated rind

Brown veal under grill 4 inches (10 cm) from source of heat for about 10 minutes, turning frequently; set aside. Lightly brown carrot and celery in nonstick saucepan; add garlic, tomato, tomato juice, stock, onion flakes and rosemary. Season to taste. Add veal, bring to a slow boil and simmer, covered, about 2 hours or until meat is tender. Just before serving, stir in parsley. Serve with lemon. Makes 1 serving.

Veal Piccata Milanese

12 oz (360 g) thinly cut veal (cut for escalopes)
2 tablespoons lemon juice
3 oz (90 g) diced mushrooms
8 fl oz (240 ml) chicken stock, made with ½ stock cube

1 tablespoon chopped fresh parsley
¾ teaspoon herbs (basil, rosemary, oregano)
½ teaspoon salt
Pinch pepper

Place veal slices between 2 sheets of greaseproof paper and pound on both sides with cleaver or heavy plate. Veal should be no more than ¼-inch (5 mm) thick. Cut in 1-inch (2.5 cm) squares. Brown on both sides in heated nonstick frying pan. Remove veal from pan, squeeze lemon juice over veal squares and keep hot. Wipe out pan. Brown mushrooms in pan; add chicken stock, chopped parsley, herbs, salt and pepper. Bring to the boil; let cook at high heat for 5 minutes, stirring often until liquid is reduced. Make a bed of the sauce on serving dish. Cover with veal. Makes 2 servings.

Veal Scallopini Calabrese

12 oz (360 g) boneless veal roast (rump), cut in 1½-inch (4 cm) cubes
6 oz (180 g) green pepper
6 oz (180 g) red pepper

3 oz (90 g) sliced mushrooms
4 tablespoons tomato purée
3 fl oz (90 ml) water
½ teaspoon oregano
Salt and pepper to taste

Grill veal and peppers on rack in grill pan until veal is brown on all sides and peppers are charred, turning as necessary. Transfer veal to shallow flameproof serving casserole. Cover veal with all remaining ingredients except peppers; put lid on casserole and let cook over moderate heat 20 minutes. Peel charred skin from peppers and remove seeds. Cut grilled peppers into strips and add to meat. Cook 10 minutes more. Serve hot. Makes 2 servings.

Meat-Stuffed Mushrooms Florentine

1½ oz (45 g) cooked spinach, finely
  chopped
2 oz (60 g) cooked minced meat
  (veal or chicken)
1 slice white bread, made into
  crumbs
2 fl oz (60 ml) skim milk
1 tablespoon chopped fresh parsley
2 teaspoons Worcester sauce

1 teaspoon dried onion flakes,
  reconstituted in 1 tablespoon
  water
¼ teaspoon garlic powder
Salt and pepper to taste
3 oz (90 g) large mushrooms caps
1 oz (30 g) sharp Cheddar cheese,
  grated

Combine spinach, meat and breadcrumbs in mixing bowl. Add milk, parsley, Worcester sauce, onion flakes and garlic powder. Mix thoroughly until all liquid is absorbed. Season with salt and pepper. Fill mushroom caps with mixture and top with grated cheese. Bake on nonstick tin at 375°F (190°C), Gas Mark 5 for approximately 25 minutes or until cheese is bubbly. Makes 1 serving.

Beefsteak Florentine (Bistecca alla Fiorentina)

The great steaks of Florence are prepared this way.

6 oz (180 g) boneless well-trimmed
  steak (use a tender cut such as
  fillet, porterhouse, T-bone, rib
  etc.)

1 wedge lemon
Salt and freshly ground pepper

Grill steak over charcoal on rack in grill pan set close to heat, turning once, 8 to 10 minutes, or until done to taste. This famous steak is always served rare in Florence, with a wedge of lemon. Add salt and pepper at the table. Makes 1 serving.

Hamburger alla Pizzaiola

2 × 6 oz (180 g) patties of minced
  beef
2 garlic cloves
4 tablespoons tomato purée

3 fl oz (90 ml) water
2 teaspoons fresh oregano or ¼
  teaspoon dried
¼ teaspoon salt

Grill patties on rack, about 4 inches (10 cm) from source of heat; turn once. Meanwhile, brown garlic lightly in a nonstick frying pan; add tomato purée, water, oregano and salt. Cook at high heat for 3 minutes. Add hamburgers to pan and heat for 1 minute longer, turning once. Serve with sauce. Makes 2 servings.

Meatballs with Spaghetti

1 lb 8 oz (720 g) minced beef
½ teaspoon onion salt
1 garlic clove, crushed
¼ teaspoon pepper
11 tablespoons tomato purée
8 fl oz (240 ml) water

1 tablespoon chopped fresh parsley
2 teaspoons dried onion flakes
½ teaspoon basil
¼ teaspoon fennel seeds (optional)
8 oz (240 g) cooked spaghetti

Combine minced beef, onion salt, garlic and pepper. Mix well. Shape into 12 equal meatballs. Grill on rack about 4 inches (10 cm) from source of heat for 5 minutes. Turn and grill 3 minutes more or until cooked throughout. Combine tomato purée, parsley, onion flakes, basil and fennel seeds, if desired, in a saucepan. Simmer 10 minutes. Add meatballs and simmer 5 minutes or until meatballs are heated throughout. Place 2 oz (60 g) spaghetti in centre of a plate. Divide sauce evenly. Pour one portion of sauce over spaghetti. Top spaghetti with 3 meatballs. Repeat 3 times with remaining meatballs, sauce and spaghetti. Makes 4 servings.

Meatballs in Spicy Sauce

1 lb 8 oz (720 g) minced pork
1 tablespoon chopped fresh parsley
$\frac{1}{2}$ teaspoon each ground fennel seed,
  onion powder and salt
$\frac{1}{2}$ teaspoon each grated lemon peel and
  Worcester sauce
$1\frac{1}{4}$ teaspoons minced fresh garlic
Pinch ground pepper
1 lb (480 g) canned crushed tomatoes
8 teaspoons tomato purée

2 oz (60 g) finely chopped onion
1 tablespoon chopped fresh basil or
  1 teaspoon dried basil leaves
$\frac{1}{2}$ teaspoon oregano leaves
$\frac{1}{4}$ teaspoon each celery seed and
  crushed red papper
1 bay leaf
6 oz (180 g) sliced mushrooms
8 oz (240 g) cooked macaroni

In a medium bowl combine pork, parsley, fennel, onion powder, salt, grated lemon peel, Worcester sauce, $\frac{1}{4}$ teaspoon garlic and pepper. Shape into 24 meatballs, each about 2 inches (5 cm) in diameter. Grill on a rack in grilling pan, about 4 inches (10 cm) from heat source, for 8 minutes or until cooked throughout. Turn once during cooking. In a medium saucepan combine browned meatballs, crushed tomatoes, tomato purée, onion, 1 teaspoon garlic, basil, oregano, celery seed, red pepper and bay leaf. Bring to the boil and lower heat. Cover and simmer, stirring occasionally, about 35 minutes. Add mushrooms and cook 15 minutes longer. Remove bay leaf. Serve over macaroni. Makes 4 servings.

Baby Lamb Steaks with Artichokes (Abbacchio con Carciofi)

2 leg of lamb steaks, 8 oz (240 g)
  each
Salt and pepper to taste
1 garlic clove, split
8 teaspoons tomato purée
2 fl oz (60 ml) water
3 oz (90 g) tomato, peeled and
  chopped

1 teaspoon dried onion flakes
¼ teaspoon marjoram leaves, finely
  chopped
Salt to taste
Gravy browning
4 oz (120 g) drained, canned
  artichoke hearts

Season lamb steaks; rub with garlic. Grill or barbecue on a rack 4 inches (10 cm) from source of heat, 5 minutes each side, or until well browned. Combine tomato purée, water, tomato, onion flakes and marjoram in saucepan; cook until sauce thickens; season; colour as desired with gravy browning. Divide sauce and artichokes evenly into two portions and serve with steaks. Makes 2 servings.

Melon and Ham

½ small cantaloupe melon, peeled
  and seeded

1½ oz (45 g) sliced cooked ham, 4
  thin slices
Batavian endive leaves

Cut cantaloupe half into 4 wedges. Wrap a folded piece of ham round the middle of each wedge. Secure with cocktail sticks. Serve on a bed of Batavian endive greens. Makes 1 serving.

Pork Perugia Style

4 lbs (1 kg 920 g) well-trimmed
  centre cut pork loin roast
3 garlic cloves, cut into slivers
1 teaspoon fennel seeds or rosemary

4 cloves
Salt
Pepper

For ease in carving, have butcher loosen the chine (back) bone by sawing across the rib bones. With the tip of a sharp pointed knife, cut small incisions in the meat and stick garlic slivers and fennel seeds into them. Insert the cloves along the top of the roast. Insert meat thermometer so bulb is in thickest part of roast, not touching bone. Place pork on a rack in a roasting tin. Pour water into tin. Roast pork at 325°F (160°C), Gas Mark 3 for 2 hours or until meat thermometer reaches 170°F (75°C). Baste with more water every half hour. Remove roast from oven and let stand 15 minutes so juices gather. Cut into thin slices and weigh 4 oz (120 g) portions. Serve salt and pepper at the table. Makes about 6 servings.

Risotto with Chicken Gizzards (Risotto alla Fiorentina)

Italian short grain rice is usual in authentic risottos because it absorbs a great deal of liquid but, as it is not widely available outside Italy, the uncooked long grain rice is substituted with no great harm to the dish. Cook rice following package directions, but substitute chicken stock (made with stock cube according to package directions) for the water. Measure 2 oz (60 g) cooked rice for each serving, then continue with the following recipe:

12 oz (360 g) green peppers, seeded and diced
6 oz (180 g) sliced mushrooms
2 teaspoons dried onion flakes
16 fl oz (480 ml) chicken stock, made with 1 stock cube, or tomato juice
Pinch of saffron or turmeric

½ teaspoon each basil and marjoram
1 lb (480 g) finely diced cooked gizzards or skinned chicken (see note)
12 oz (360 g) cooked rice (prepared in chicken stock)
Salt and freshly ground pepper to taste

Brown green peppers, mushrooms and onion flakes in nonstick pan. When lightly browned on all sides, add chicken stock, saffron, basil and marjoram. Cook for 10 minutes. Add diced gizzards (or chicken) and rice. Stir well. Serve as main dish. Season to taste with salt and pepper. Makes 4 servings.

Note: Remove all fat from gizzards and rinse in cool water. Place in saucepan and add enough cold water to cover. Cover pan and simmer until tender, 1 to 2 hours; add additional water during cooking if needed. Drain gizzards, reserve and chill liquid. It may then be skimmed of all fat and used as stock in recipes calling for chicken stock.

Chicken Liver Spaghetti

12 oz (360 g) chicken livers, cut in halves
2 garlic cloves, crushed
2 oz (60 g) onion, chopped
2 oz (60 g) chopped celery
¾ teaspoon oregano
¼ teaspoon basil
16 teaspoons tomato purée

3 oz (90 g) drained canned mushrooms, chopped
8 fl oz (240 ml) water
2 tablespoons chopped parsley leaves
½ teaspoon salt
Pinch pepper
4 oz (120 g) cooked spaghetti

Brown chicken livers on all sides in a large nonstick frying pan over moderate heat. Remove liver; dice and reserve. In same pan, cook garlic, onion, celery, oregano and basil until onion is tender. Add purée, mushrooms, water, parsley, salt and pepper; cover and cook 15 minutes. Add reserved chopped chicken livers; heat. Divide evenly over equal amounts of cooked spaghetti. Makes 2 servings.

Liver Pudding (Sformato di Fegato)

4 oz (120 g) onion, sliced
1 garlic clove, crushed
12 oz (360 g) beef liver, sliced ¼-inch (5 mm) thick
4 oz (120 g) cooked rice

1 oz (30 g) nonfat dry milk, reconstituted with 5 fl oz (150 ml) water
2 teaspoons vegetable oil
Freshly ground pepper to taste
2 teaspoons chicken stock powder
2 slices lemon

In nonstick frying pan cook onions and garlic by covering them with small amount of water and cooking over medium heat until soft. Allow water to evaporate and onions to brown. Remove from pan and set aside. Pour boiling water over liver. Drain and transfer to frying pan. Cook liver over medium-high heat 4 to 5 minutes, turning constantly, until all sides are browned. Do not overcook. Let cool. Transfer liver and onions to a blender goblet or food mill. Add rice, milk, oil, pepper and stock powder. Purée mixture. Transfer to a $7\frac{1}{2} \times 3\frac{1}{2} \times 2$-inch (19 × 9 × 5 cm) loaf tin; cover with foil and bake at 350°F (180°C), Gas Mark 4 for 25 minutes. Remove cover and continue to bake 10 to 15 minutes or until pudding is browned. Garnish with lemon slices. Makes 2 servings.

Sweet and Sour Chicken Livers Venetian Style

1 oz (30 g) diced onion
12 oz (360 g) chicken livers, cut into
  halves
6 oz (180 g) seedless green grapes
$\frac{1}{2}$ chicken stock cube, dissolved in
  1 tablespoon boiling water
1 tablespoon chopped fresh parsley

2 teaspoons red wine vinegar, or to
  taste
1 teaspoon salt
1 teaspoon wine flavouring
$\frac{1}{4}$ teaspoon dried sage leaves
Pinch pepper

In a medium nonstick frying pan cook onion over medium heat until translucent. Add livers and brown on all sides. Stir in remaining ingredients; cover and cook until livers are done and grapes are heated, about 5 minutes. Makes 2 servings.

Calf's Liver Trieste Style (Fegato di Vitello alla Triestina)

6 oz (180 g) peeled potatoes, diced
4 oz (120 g) onion, thinly sliced
3 oz (90 g) sliced tender celery
4 oz (120 g) carrots, cut in
  matchstick pieces

1 teaspoon chopped fresh parsley
1 clove, crushed to release fragrance
16 fl oz (480 ml) chicken stock,
  made with 1 stock cube
12 oz (360 g) calf's liver, sliced into
  bite-sized pieces

Combine potatoes, onions, celery, carrots, parsley, clove and chicken in saucepan. Bring to the boil; add liver, cover and simmer 30 minutes or until vegetables and liver are tender. Divide evenly in bowls. Makes 2 servings.

Brown Rice Piedmont Style (Risotto alla Piemontese)

2 fl oz (60 ml) beef stock, made with ¼ stock cube
8 oz (240 g) cooked brown rice (prepared in beef stock, made with stock cube according to package directions)
1 tablespoon dried onion flakes, reconstituted in 2 tablespoons

beef stock made with stock cube according to package directions
1 small white truffle, diced (optional)
2 teaspoons sherry flavouring
4 teaspoons margarine

Heat stock in saucepan. Add brown rice and onion flakes and warm over moderate heat. Stir in truffle if desired and sherry flavouring. Remove from heat. Add margarine, mix well and serve immediately. Makes 4 servings.

Lentils with Rice

8 fl oz (240 ml) chicken stock, made with ½ stock cube
3 oz (90 g) sliced celery
1½ oz (45 g) sliced carrot
6 oz (180 g) cooked dried lentils

2 oz (60 g) cooked rice
1 teaspoon chopped chives
1 teaspoon low fat spread
Pinch each of salt, pepper and sage or 1 teaspoon chopped fresh sage

Combine chicken stock, celery and carrot in saucepan, and cook until vegetables are soft, 15 to 20 minutes. Remove from heat, stir in remaining ingredients, mix well, and serve hot as main dish. Makes 1 serving.

Rice and Pea Salad

An interesting variation on the risi e bisi theme.

1 tablespoon mayonnaise	1 oz (30 g) cooked peas
½ teaspoon tarragon vinegar	2 tablespoons chopped celery
¼ teaspoon onion salt	1 tablespoon chopped pimiento
Salt and pepper to taste	10 capers
2 oz (60 g) cooked rice	Watercress

Combine mayonnaise, vinegar, onion salt, salt and pepper in medium bowl. Add rice, peas, celery, pimiento and capers. Toss. Chill. Serve with sprigs of watercress. Makes 1 serving.

Cooking Pasta

Follow package directions using rapidly boiling water. Don't skimp on the water . . . use the amount recommended on the package. Stir the pasta to keep it moving as it reaches the water, so it doesn't stick or cook unevenly.

Pasta is made in literally hundreds of shapes and it is usually possible to substitute one shape for another in a recipe. Most pasta products double in volume after cooking; egg noodles remain about the same.

In general, 8 oz (240 g) pasta should be boiled in 4 pints 16 fl oz (2 litres 880 ml) salted water (use 1 tablespoon salt).

Cooking time varies, depending on the size and type of pasta. Average cooking time for *al dente* pasta is 8 to 10 minutes. Pasta cooked *al dente* is chewy to the bite, which is the Italian way. Drain the pasta as soon as it is cooked but don't rinse under cold water unless it is to be served cold.

When measuring pasta after it is cooked, do not exceed your portion: 2 oz (60 g) cooked macaroni, spaghetti or noodles.

Pasta can be easily reheated. Put it in a colander or strainer and pour boiling water over it. Drain and serve.

Fettucini Carbonara

For a more professional touch, cheese may be tossed with fettucini at a side table. Serve with a mixed green salad for a fine lunch.

3 oz (90 g) sliced mushrooms
4 fl oz (120 ml) chicken stock,
  made with ¼ stock cube
½ oz (15 g) nonfat dry milk,
  reconstituted wth 2½ fl oz (75 ml)
  water

4 oz (120 g) cooked fettucini,
  drained
2 eggs, slightly beaten
2 teaspoons chopped fresh parsley
2 oz (60 g) freshly grated Parmesan
  cheese

Cook mushrooms in nonstick saucepan until they begin to brown. Add chicken stock, milk and cooked fettucini; reduce heat slightly. Slowly stir in eggs and parsley; stir constantly and continue cooking for about 2 to 3 minutes or until eggs are cooked. Remove from pan; toss with cheese. Makes 2 servings.

Fettucini and Celery Spaghetti

Follow preceding recipe but add a handful or more of the cooked Celery Spaghetti (see page 230) to the cooked macaroni before tossing as directed above. Makes 2 servings.

Rigatoni with Ricotta Sauce

2 oz (60 g) chopped onion
½ teaspoon crushed fresh garlic
1 lb (480 g) canned crushed tomatoes
8 teaspoons tomato purée
1 tablespoon chopped fresh basil
¼ teaspoon salt

8 oz (240 g) ricotta cheese
1 tablespoon chopped fresh parsley
Pinch freshly ground black pepper
4 oz (120 g) cooked rigatoni or
  other tube macaroni

In a medium nonstick saucepan cook onion and garlic, stirring occasionally, until soft. Add crushed tomatoes, tomato purée, basil and salt. Bring to the boil; lower heat and simmer for 20 minutes. In a small bowl combine ricotta cheese, parsley and pepper. Add cooked rigatoni and 4 fl oz (120 ml) of tomato sauce. Stir to combine well. Transfer rigatoni mixture to a medium shallow baking dish. Top with remaining sauce and bake at 375°F (190°C) Gas Mark 5 for 30 minutes or until mixture is bubbly. Makes 4 servings.

Macaroni with all-Vegetable Sauce, Sicilian Style

6 oz (180 g) diced aubergine
12 oz (360 g) green peppers, seeded and diced
2 oz (60 g) diced celery
1½ oz (45 g) sliced fresh mushrooms
2 tablespoons dried onion flakes
3 garlic cloves, crushed
5 oz (150 g) fresh or frozen cauliflower or broccoli florets
12 tablespoons tomato purée
6 fl oz (180 ml) water

2 fl oz (60 ml) beef stock, made with ¼ stock cube
1 tablespoon chopped fresh parsley
1 teaspoon basil
½ teaspoon oregano
½ teaspoon salt
¼ teaspoon rosemary
¼ teaspoon thyme
½ teaspoon burgundy or sherry flavouring
8 oz (240 g) cooked macaroni

Brown aubergine, green peppers, celery, mushrooms, onion flakes and garlic in a large nonstick frying pan, stirring constantly until vegetables are browned. Transfer mixture to a large saucepan; add cauliflower, tomato purée, water, stock, parsley, basil, oregano, salt, rosemary and thyme. Bring to the boil, reduce heat, cover saucepan and simmer for at least 30 minutes, or until sauce is thick and all vegetables are tender. Stir occasionally, bringing up the vegetables on the bottom. Add more stock, if necessary, to prevent scorching. Remove from heat. Put entire mixture through a food mill or strainer to purée, if desired. Stir in flavouring and mix well. Divide evenly into 4 portions. Serve each portion over 2 oz (60 g) macaroni. This sauce freezes well; divide into portions and label before freezing. Makes 4 servings.

Cannellini Tuscan Style (Cannellini alla Toscana)

3 oz (90 g) canned or peeled fresh
  tomato, chopped into small pieces
1 garlic clove, crushed
¼ teaspoon sage or 2 leaves fresh

Salt and pepper to taste
2 tablespoons hot water
6 oz (180 g) cooked dried
  cannellini (small white beans)

Combine tomato, garlic, sage, salt, pepper and hot water in a small pan. Simmer for 5 minutes. Add drained beans and continue to simmer for 5 more minutes to let beans absorb flavour of sauce. Makes 1 serving.

Macaroni with Cheese (Pasta al Formaggio)

8 teaspoons tomato purée
2 fl oz (60 ml) water
4 fl oz (120 ml) chicken stock,
  made with ¼ stock cube
1 tablespoon dried onion flakes
Pinch garlic powder

½ teaspoon Italian seasoning
Salt and pepper to taste
2 oz (60 g) cooked macaroni
2 oz (60 g) fresh grated cheese
  (mozzarella, Emmentaler, fontina,
  stach:no or Parmesan)

Place tomato purée, water, stock, onion flakes and garlic powder in saucepan. Add Italian seasoning. Simmer over low heat until thickened. Season with salt and pepper. Fold macaroni and cheese into sauce. Makes 1 serving.

Macaroni and Courgettes or Broccoli

Follow recipe above but fold 5 oz (150 g) cooked, sliced courgettes or 4 oz (120 g) broccoli florets into the sauce with macaroni and cheese. Makes 1 serving.

Pasta and Lentils

6 oz (180 g) cooked dried lentils
8 fl oz (240 ml) water
2½ oz (75 g) chopped carrots
2½ oz (75 g) finely chopped celery
2 oz (60 g) chopped onion
3 oz (90 g) tomato, peeled and chopped

1 teaspoon beef stock powder
1 small bay leaf
1 garlic clove, crushed
½ teaspoon salt
⅛ teaspoon pepper
2 oz (60 g) cooked macaroni
1 tablespoon margarine

Combine all ingredients except macaroni and margarine in medium saucepan. Bring to the boil; reduce heat; cover and cook 30 minutes. Remove bay leaf. Stir in macaroni; heat. Remove from heat; stir in margarine. Makes 1 serving.

Lasagne Naples Style (Lasagne alla Napolitana)

A luscious combination of tomato sauce, vegetables and cheeses. The sauce may be made ahead and refrigerated for a day, or frozen for weeks; defrost before use.

6 oz (180 g) peeled diced aubergine
12 oz (360 g) green or yellow peppers, seeded and diced
½ garlic clove, crushed
8 tablespoons tomato purée
6 fl oz (180 ml) water

1 teaspoon chopped fresh parsley
½ teaspoon salt
8 oz (240 g) cooked lasagne sheets, well drained
4 oz (120 g) grated Parmesan cheese
4 oz (120 g) sliced mozzarella cheese

Lightly brown aubergine, green pepper and garlic in a medium-size saucepan, stirring to brown all sides, 5 to 8 minutes. Add tomato purée and water and cook, uncovered, until sauce is very thick, about 30 minutes or until aubergine is tender. Watch and stir as necessary so sauce does not brown. Stir in parsley and salt. Mix well. Spread a thin layer of the sauce in the bottom of a rectangular baking dish. Put half the strips of lasagne on top and half of each of the two cheeses. Repeat with sauce, remaining strips of lasagne and remaining cheese. End with a layer of sauce. Bake at 350°F (180°C), Gas Mark 4, for 40 minutes. Let stand for 5 minutes before serving to make cutting easier. Makes 4 servings.

Herb Fingers

2 teaspoons low fat spread $\frac{1}{8}$ teaspoon oregano
$\frac{1}{8}$ teaspoon marjoram   1 slice white bread, toasted

Combine first 3 ingredients. Spread on hot toast. Cut in quarters, lengthwise. Keep hot in oven. Makes 1 serving.

Salty Sticks

1 slice white bread   stock powder and 1 tablespoon
1 tablespoon concentrated chicken   boiling water)
  stock ($\frac{1}{4}$ teaspoon chicken $\frac{1}{4}$ teaspoon coarse salt

Brush bread with stock, sprinkle salt on bread; bake at 375°F (190°C), Gas Mark 5, (moderate oven) 15 minutes or until bread is lightly browned. Cut into 4 equal strips. Makes 1 serving.

Garlic Bread

1 slice white bread, toasted   1 teaspoon vegetable oil
1 cut garlic clove   Salt and pepper to taste

While toast is hot, rub each side with cut clove of garlic and spread with oil. Cut into 1-inch (2.5 cm) strips. Sprinkle with salt and pepper and serve hot. Makes 1 serving.

Little Shells with Mushrooms and Peas (Maruzzine con Piselli)

3 oz (90 g) mushrooms
½ garlic clove
2 oz (60 g) frozen peas
1 tablespoon water
1 teaspoon parsley

Salt and pepper to taste
2 oz (60 g) cooked macaroni shells
  (maruzzine)
2 oz (60 g) grated Parmesan cheese

Brown mushrooms and garlic in nonstick pan until mushrooms release their liquid. Add peas, water, parsley, salt and pepper. Cook until peas are tender. Pour over heated macaroni shells. Stir in Parmesan cheese and serve. Makes 1 serving.

Pickled Artichokes

Artichoke with parsley, garlic and oil.

8 oz (240 g) frozen artichoke hearts
2 tablespoons vegetable oil
4 teaspoons vinegar
2 teaspoons chopped fresh parsley
¼ teaspoon salt

¼ teaspoon oregano
¼ teaspoon prepared mustard
⅛ teaspoon pepper
1 garlic clove, crushed

Cook artichoke hearts according to package directions; drain. Combine oil with remaining ingredients in bowl. Stir in artichoke hearts. Cover tightly and refrigerate until thoroughly chilled, 1 hour or longer, turning artichoke hearts occasionally in marinade. Makes 6 antipasto servings.

Artichokes Neapolitan*

4 oz (120 g) cooked artichoke hearts
(or combination of cooked
artichokes and peas)
1 oz (30 g) hard cheese, grated
1 teaspoon vegetable oil
1 teaspoon dried onion flakes,
reconstituted in 1 tablespoon water

1 teaspoon chopped fresh parsley
¼ teaspoon salt
¼ garlic clove, chopped
½ slice white bread, made into
crumbs

Make a bed of artichokes and other vegetables in small baking dish. Combine remaining ingredients and sprinkle on top. Bake at 400°F (200°C), Gas Mark 6 until hot and brown. Serve at once. (If the dish has been frozen, defrost, bake with aluminium foil cover.) Makes 1 serving.

Broccoli alla Romana

2 lbs (960 g) fresh broccoli
4 fl oz (120 ml) boiling water
1 teaspoon salt
⅛ teaspoon pepper

1 garlic clove, crushed
4 teaspoons vegetable oil
¼ teaspoon sherry flavouring or
lemon juice

Wash broccoli. Split ends of large stalks lengthwise into halves or quarters, depending on size. Place in large saucepan. Sprinkle with water, salt and pepper. Cover tightly; cook over moderate heat 15 to 20 minutes, or until stalks are just tender, but florets still crisp and bright green. Divide broccoli into 4 serving bowls. Mix garlic with oil and sherry flavouring. Stir mixture evenly into each bowl of broccoli. Makes 4 servings.

Broccoli Milanese

Asparagus spears can be prepared this way too.

4 oz (120 g) cooked broccoli florets
1 egg, beaten

1 slice white bread, made into
crumbs
1 oz (30 g) hard cheese, grated

Place broccoli in small baking dish and cover with egg; add crumbs and cheese. Bake at 375°F (190°C), Gas Mark 5 for 25 to 30 minutes, or until egg is set and crumbs are brown. Makes 1 serving.

Asparagus and Cheese Pizza

Pizza—pie—can be spicy and crusty in the familiar Sicilian style or soft and eggy as in this Northern version.

3 eggs	4 oz (120 g) cooked mushrooms,
6 oz (180 g) hot cooked rice	sliced
3 oz (90 g) grated sharp Cheddar	1½ tablespoons tomato purée
cheese	1½ tablespoons water
1 teaspoon salt	⅛ teaspoon pepper
7½ oz (225 g) chopped asparagus	

Slightly beat 1 egg, stir in rice, half the cheese and half the salt in small bowl. Mix well. Press firmly in even layer on bottom of a 9-inch (23 cm) pie plate. Cook asparagus in a minimum amount of water. Drain well in strainer. Beat remaining eggs slightly. Stir in mushrooms, tomato purée, water, pepper and remaining salt. Add asparagus. Mix well. Spoon over crust in pie plate. Bake in a preheated oven at 375°F (190°C), Gas Mark 5 for 20 minutes. Remove from oven. Sprinkle remaining cheese evenly over the top of vegetable mixture in pie plate. Return to oven. Bake 10 minutes more. Let cool 10 to 15 minutes and serve warm. Makes 3 servings.

'Creamy' Pesto Sauce*

Make this only when you have fresh basil, a herb you can grow in a sunny window box. Serve it over freshly cooked pasta or Celery Spaghetti (see page 230).

6 tender sprigs basil
6 sprigs parsley
4 teaspoons vegetable oil
4 oz (120 g) grated Parmesan cheese

$\frac{1}{2}$ oz (15 g) nonfat dry milk,
   reconstituted with 2$\frac{1}{2}$ fl oz
   (75 ml) water
1 teaspoon salt
$\frac{1}{4}$ teaspoon pepper
1 garlic clove

Combine in blender goblet and blend at medium speed until smooth.
Makes 4 servings.

Brussels Sprouts with Basil

1 lb (480 g) Brussels sprouts
2 fl oz (60 ml) chicken stock,
   made with $\frac{1}{4}$ stock cube

4 teaspoons margarine
1 tablespoon chopped fresh basil or
   $\frac{1}{2}$ teaspoon dried
Pinch tarragon

Wash Brussels sprouts in cold salted water, remove wilted leaves if
necessary. Cut a cross in stem ends. Place in saucepan and cover with
boiling water, add salt and bring to the boil. Simmer uncovered for 10
to 12 minutes or until just tender. Drain. Combine hot stock,
margarine, basil and tarragon and pour over Brussels sprouts. Makes 4
servings.

Cooked Endive Piquante

8 oz (240 g) endive
8 oz (240 g) Batavian endive
4 fl oz (120 ml) water
1 teaspoon beef stock powder

3 garlic cloves, crushed
2 tablespoons chopped fresh parsley
Salt to taste
Dash hot pepper sauce

Trim endives, removing tough, wilted or discoloured leaves. Wash
thoroughly in cold water to remove sand; drain. Break leaves into
1-inch (2.5 cm) pieces. Combine remaining ingredients in large saucepan; add endives. Cover tightly and cook 20 minutes or until Batavian
endive is tender. Serve hot. Makes 2 servings.

Celery Spaghetti

3 oz (90 g) celery sticks   Boiling water
                                   Salt

Cut the celery sticks into long thin strands about the size of thick spaghetti. Lay the strands in a large saucepan, pour on plenty of boiling water; stir in salt and cook until celery is limp, about 10 minutes, or to taste. Drain, serve with any of our pasta sauces. Makes 2 servings.

Celery Vinaigrette

Cover Celery Spaghetti with Vinaigrette Dressing (see page 138–139 and prepare 2 servings), chill for several hours. Use a shallow oval serving dish, garnish with cross made of red pimiento strips. Sprinkle with parsley or chopped capers for added colour. Makes 2 servings.

Caponata

14 oz (420 g) unpeeled aubergine,   1½ tablespoons capers, rinsed
   cut in 1-inch (2.5 cm) cubes   1 tablespoon chopped fresh chives
1½ teaspoons salt   1 teaspoon basil, crushed
4 oz (120 g) sliced celery   ¼ teaspoon pepper
6 oz (180 g) tomatoes, chopped   2 garlic cloves, crushed
4 tablespoons tomato purée   4 teaspoons vegetable oil
3 tablespoons lemon juice or vinegar

Sprinkle aubergine with 1 teaspoon salt and let stand for 15 minutes. Drain and dry. Brown in heated nonstick frying pan with celery. Add tomatoes and let cook for 10 minutes. Combine all remaining ingredients, except oil. Add to pan. Cook until vegetables are very soft, stirring occasionally, about 30 minutes; add a few tablespoons water if necessary to prevent sticking. Remove to a bowl; for fullest flavour cover and chill in refrigerator a day or two before serving. Stir in 1 teaspoon oil for each portion just before serving. Serve as antipasto, salad, vegetable or relish. Makes 4 servings.

Stuffed Mushrooms Venice Style (Funghi alla Veneziana)*

6 oz (180 g) mushroom caps
(select large uniform size)
2 oz (60 g) freshly grated Parmesan
or Romano cheese
1½ tablespoons chopped fresh chives
1 tablespoon chopped fresh parsley

2 teaspoons low fat spread
1 teaspoon sherry flavouring
1 teaspoon prepared spicy mustard
½ teaspoon tarragon
Salt and pepper to taste

Peel the mushroom caps if they are discoloured, otherwise wipe clean with damp towel. Combine remaining ingredients. Mash well. Fill mushroom caps with the stuffing. Makes 2 servings.

Baked Aubergine Parmigiana

2 oz (60 g) chopped onion
4 tablespoons tomato purée
5 fl oz (150 ml) water
¾ teaspoon salt
½ teaspoon oregano leaves

Pinch pepper
7 oz (210 g) peeled and thinly sliced
aubergine
4 oz (120 g) grated sharp Cheddar
cheese

Brown chopped onion in a nonstick frying pan. Add tomato purée, water, salt, oregano and pepper. Bring to the boil and simmer for 15 minutes. In medium baking dish alternate layers of sliced aubergine, tomato sauce and half the grated cheese; repeat layer of aubergine and layer of tomato sauce. Bake in moderate oven (350°F (180°C), Gas Mark 4) for 1 hour. A few minutes before the end of cooking time sprinkle remaining grated cheese over top and continue heating until cheese melts. Makes 2 servings.

Courgettes Parmesan*

4 oz (120 g) coarsely chopped onion
1 garlic clove, crushed
1 tablespoon chopped fresh parsley
1 teaspoon salt
¼ teaspoon pepper
¼ teaspoon rosemary

⅛ teaspoon oregano
1 lb 4 oz (600 g) thinly sliced courgettes
6 oz (180 g) tomatoes, peeled and chopped
4 oz (120 g) grated Parmesan cheese

Cook onion, garlic, parsley, salt, pepper, rosemary and oregano in a large nonstick frying pan, about 3 minutes or until onion is soft, stirring occasionally. Add courgettes and tomatoes, and cook 15 to 20 minutes, or until courgettes are tender. Turn mixture into a serving dish; sprinkle with Parmesan cheese. Makes 4 servings.

Courgette Pizza

1 lb 14 oz (900 g) peeled courgettes, cut into ¼-inch (5 mm) slices
1 tablespoon salt
2 slices white bread, made into crumbs
1 oz (30 g) grated Parmesan cheese
1 garlic clove, crushed

16 teaspoons tomato purée
4 fl oz (120 ml) water
2 fl oz (60 ml) chicken stock, made with ¼ stock cube
7 oz (210 g) mozzarella cheese, thinly sliced

Sprinkle salt over courgettes in a large bowl, and toss lightly. Let stand 20 to 30 minutes. Drain and discard liquid. Pat slices dry with paper towel. Combine bread crumbs, grated cheese and garlic in a medium mixing bowl. Combine tomato purée, water and stock in jug with a spout, such as a measuring jug. Transfer half the slices to a medium casserole. Sprinkle with half breadcrumb mixture, pour on half tomato purée mixture and cover with half of the mozzarella cheese. Repeat layers. Bake for 30 minutes or until courgettes are tender and cheese is melted. Remove from oven and allow to stand 5 to 10 minutes before serving. Divide evenly into 4 portions. Serve hot. Makes 4 servings.

Italian Relish

7 oz (210 g) unpeeled aubergine, cut
  in 1-inch (2.5 cm) cubes
6 oz (180 g) tomatoes, chopped
6 oz (180 g) green pepper, cut in
  1-inch (2.5 cm) pieces
4 oz (120 g) chopped onion

3 oz (90 g) seedless grapes
4 fl oz (120 ml) vinegar
4 fl oz (120 ml) water
½ teaspoon hot pepper sauce
¼ teaspoon bitters

Combine all ingredients in saucepan. Bring to the boil; cover pan,
reduce heat and simmer for 40 minutes, stirring frequently. Serve warm
or chill. Makes 4 servings.

Whole Green Bean Salad

1 lb (480 g) whole fresh French
  beans (see note)
2 fl oz (60 ml) beef stock, made
  with ¼ stock cube
2 tablespoons vinegar

4 teaspoons vegetable oil
1 tablespoon chopped fresh parsley
½ teaspoon salt
¼ teaspoon dried onion flakes
⅛ teaspoon pepper

Cook and drain beans. While they are still hot, add stock, vinegar,
oil, parsley, salt, onion and pepper. Toss well. Chill. Makes 4 servings.
Note: Remove tips at both ends. Cook beans in a large saucepan
containing plenty of boiling salted water. Best way is to drop them into
a strainer about 2 oz (60 g) at a time, then immerse strainer in water,
and keep there until beans are done. Beans should be tender but
cooked al dente, and with bright colour. Refresh beans quickly under
cold water. Drain and use immediately as above.

Salad of Endive, Sorrel and Strawberries

8 oz (240 g) Batavian endive
1 oz (30 g) sorrel leaves
2½ oz (75 g) very ripe strawberries

1 tablespoon vegetable oil
1 teaspoon lemon juice

Use only the white inside leaves of the endive (save the outside leaves for soup). Wash endive and sorrel leaves to remove all sand. Drain well and shake dry. Wrap in towels and refrigerate until ready to use. Arrange endive leaves in salad bowl; cut sorrel leaves into thin strips with scissors and sprinkle over endive. Add strawberries. Combine oil and lemon juice. Pour over salad and toss. Makes 1 serving.

Spinach Salad with Mustard Dressing

If the garlic taste lingers too long, chew a coffee bean.

4 oz (120 g) bite-size spinach
  leaves, thoroughly washed and
  dried (discard tough stems)
1½ oz (45 g) sliced mushrooms

1 tablespoon vegetable oil
2 teaspoons wine vinegar
1 teaspoon prepared mustard
1 garlic clove, crushed

Place spinach leaves and mushrooms in medium bowl. Combine oil, vinegar, mustard and garlic; toss with vegetables. Makes 1 serving.

Mixed Salad Rustica

The kind of everyday salad you're likely to find everywhere in Italy.

3 oz (90 g) small mushrooms,
  thinly sliced
8 oz (240 g) iceberg lettuce, chopped
8 oz (240 g) cos lettuce, chopped
4 oz (120 g) watercress, chopped

3 oz (90 g) tomatoes, sliced
3 oz (90 g) radishes, sliced
Mustard Dressing (see above)
  multiply amounts if necessary

Place all ingredients in a large bowl, toss, and divide into 4 equal portions. Serve with Mustard Dressing. Makes 4 servings.

Hearts of Palm and Watercress Vinaigrette

Make a bed of Batavian endive or cos lettuce leaves on a round serving dish. Prepare 1 lb (480 g) drained canned hearts of palm. Cut into spears lengthwise and then cut them in half. Arrange like spokes in a wheel on bed of lettuce. Place very crisp fresh watercress in centre of spokes. Between spokes add pieces of red pimiento. Spoon Lemony Vinaigrette Dressing (see page 189) over salad. Let stand 15 minutes before serving. Makes 4 servings.

Courgette Fingers in Lemony Vinaigrette

1 lb (480 g) peeled courgettes, cut in matchstick strips
Salt

Boiling water
Lemony Vinaigrette Dressing (see page 189)

Put courgettes in a medium saucepan with salted water to cover. Bring to the boil and continue cooking until vegetable is just done and becomes translucent, about 5 minutes. Transfer to colander, pour cold water over courgettes, drain, dry with paper towels. Cover with Lemony Vinaigrette Dressing and chill until ready to use. Makes 4 servings.

Courgette Fingers with Garlic

Prepare courgettes as directed above, bringing to the boil in saucepan and cooking until vegetable is done to taste. Drain. Divide between four salad plates. Combine 4 teaspoons vegetable oil, 1 garlic clove, crushed, 1 tablespoon each chopped fresh parsley and chives and salt and freshly ground pepper to taste. Spread one quarter of mixture over the vegetables on each of the salad plates, mix well, and serve hot. Makes 4 servings.

Tomato and Onion Salad

Lettuce leaves
3 oz (90 g) tomato, sliced
2 oz (60 g) onion, thinly sliced
1½ teaspoons chopped fresh parsley
1 teaspoon vegetable oil

½ teaspoon Dijon-style mustard
¼ teaspoon dried basil, oregano or
  thyme
¼ teaspoon salt
Freshly ground pepper to taste

Arrange alternating rings of tomato and onion slices on lettuce leaves. Combine remaining ingredients and pour over tomato and onion. Let stand a few minutes before serving. Makes 1 serving.

Chef's Salad (with egg and cheese)

2 oz (60 g) shredded lettuce
1½ oz (45 g) sliced mushrooms
1½ oz (45 g) green pepper, diced
1 oz (30 g) onion, sliced
1 pimiento, cut into strips
1 hard boiled egg, chopped
1 oz (30 g) mozzarella cheese, cubed

2 teaspoons nonfat dry milk,
  reconstituted with 2 tablespoons
  water
1 tablespoon mayonnaise
2 teaspoons lemon juice
1 teaspoon chopped capers
Salt and pepper to taste

Combine lettuce, mushrooms, green pepper, onion and pimiento in a large individual salad bowl. Toss in egg and cheese. Combine remaining ingredients in a small mixing bowl. Pour over salad and mix to combine. Makes 1 serving.

Fresh Fruit Cup (Macedonia di Frutta Fresca)

1 medium orange, peeled and diced
  (reserve juice)
¼ ripe small pineapple, cut in
  wedges

1 medium apple, diced (peeled if
  desired)
3 oz (90 g) seedless grapes
4 fresh flowers, washed and
  refrigerated

Dice fruits into pieces of uniform size. Mix together. Serve in stemmed dessert glasses. Garnish with rinsed fresh flowers . . . violets, sweet peas, tiny rhododendron centres, etc. Chill during dinner. Makes 4 servings.

Rum-Cherry Pudding*

4 eggs, separated
Artificial sweetener to equal 5
  teaspoons sugar, or to taste
1 lemon
1 teaspoon rum flavouring
$\frac{1}{4}$ teaspoon cherry flavouring

8 fl oz (240 ml) skim milk
4 slices white bread, made into
  crumbs
1 lb (480 g) canned stoned cherries,
  no sugar added

Use a small deep pudding basin or baking dish. Beat egg yolks in medium bowl, add sweetener, juice of lemon, rum and cherry flavourings and milk. Stir in breadcrumbs and the cherries. Whip egg whites until stiff. Fold into cherry mixture; transfer to pudding basin. Set the basin in a large pan and pour 1 inch (2.5 cm) hot water round basin. Bake pudding at 375°F (190°C), Gas Mark 5, for 1 hour or until set and firm in centre. Makes 4 servings.

Strawberry-Ricotta Pancake

1 slice white bread, made into
  crumbs
1 egg
2 fl oz (60 ml) skim milk

5 oz (150 g) strawberries (hull and
  slice)
2 oz (60 g) ricotta
  cheese
2 to 3 drops lemon juice

Beat breadcrumbs, egg and milk in mixing bowl until smooth. Pour into a heated 8-inch (20 cm) nonstick pan. Cook over low heat until top of pancake is full of broken bubbles and underside is brown. Turn with spatula and brown the other side. Turn onto a plate. Mix strawberries, cheese and lemon juice. Place in centre of pancake; fold over and serve. Makes 1 serving.

Coffee Ice (Granita di Caffè)

16 fl oz (480 ml) double-strength
coffee
1 teaspoon lemon juice

Whipped Topping (see
page 12)
4 pieces of lemon rind, curled
(optional)

Mix coffee and lemon juice. Pour into a shallow pan or metal ice cube tray (see note). Freeze, stirring occasionally to break up ice during freezing. Garnish with Whipped Topping, and lemon rind if desired. Makes 4 servings.

Note: If your metal ice cube tray has a stale smell, rinse it in a solution of warm water and bicarbonate of soda.

Strawberry Ice (Granita di Fragola)

1 lb 4 oz (600 g) ripe
strawberries
8 fl oz (240 ml) orange juice
Juice of ½ lemon

Artificial sweetener to equal 3
tablespoons sugar, or to taste
4 fl oz (120 ml) water

Wash and hull the berries just before use; blend until smooth; remove to bowl and add orange juice and lemon juice. Simmer sweetener and water in a saucepan for 5 minutes. Let cool and add it to the strawberry mixture. Pour the mixture into a refrigerator tray or 8 × 8-inch (20 × 20 cm) dish; let it freeze until firm, stirring well from time to time to prevent ice crystals from forming. Makes 6 servings.

Coffee Frappé

12 fl oz (360 ml) boiling water
1 tablespoon instant coffee
1 small cinnamon stick
Artificial sweetener to equal 2
teaspoons sugar, or to taste

2 teaspoons nonfat dry milk
Crushed ice
Grated orange rind

Combine water, coffee, cinnamon and artificial sweetener. Stir in nonfat dry milk. Cool. Remove cinnamon stick and pour coffee over crushed ice in two glasses. Sprinkle with orange rind. Makes 2 servings.

Coffee Rum Strata

14 fl oz (420 ml) water
1 tablespoon unflavoured gelatine
2 tablespoons instant coffee

Artificial sweetener to equal 8
teaspoons sugar, or to taste
⅛ teaspoon salt
⅛ teaspoon rum flavouring

Place 2 fl oz (60 ml) water in a small saucepan. Sprinkle gelatine over water and place over low heat for 2 to 3 minutes, stirring constantly until gelatine dissolves. Remove from heat. Stir in coffee, sweetener and salt. Add remaining water and stir to combine. Reserving 4 fl oz (120 ml) of the mixture, divide the remainder evenly into 4 dessert glasses and chill until almost firm. Meanwhile, stir rum flavouring into the reserved liquid and chill until slightly thicker than unbeaten egg whites. Beat reserved gelatine mixture on the high speed of an electric mixer until mixture doubles in volume. Divide evenly and spoon over first layer. Chill until firm, at least 1 hour. This can be made a day ahead of time. Topping will firm slightly, but remain fluffy. Makes 4 servings.

Ricotta Cheese Pie (Torta di Formaggio)

A liaison of cheese, eggs and flavourings. Omit the crust if you've used up your daily bread quota.

Pie Crust (recipe follows)
4 oz (120 g) ricotta cheese
½ teaspoon vanilla flavouring
Articial sweetener to equal 5
teaspoons sugar, or to taste

¼ teaspoon cinnamon
¼ teaspoon grated lemon rind
¼ teaspoon grated orange rind
2 eggs, separated

Prepare pie crust. Put ricotta cheese through a sieve or beat cheese with electric mixer until light and airy. Add vanilla flavouring, sweetener, cinnamon, lemon and orange rinds. Mix well. Beat in egg yolks, one at a time. Beat egg whites until stiff. Fold into cheese mixture and gently transfer to pie crust. Bake at 350°F (180°C), Gas Mark 4, for 50 to 60 minutes or until top is set and golden brown. Serve immediately or chill. Makes 2 servings.

Pie Crust

2 slices toasted currant bread, made   ¼ teaspoon vanilla flavouring
   into crumbs   3 tablespoons water

Preheat oven to 350°F (180°C), Gas Mark 4. Place breadcrumbs in mixing bowl. Add flavouring and water. Mix to a smooth paste. Press into a 7 or 8-inch (18 or 20 cm) pie plate using the back of a teaspoon. If it is difficult to mould, wet the back of the spoon with a little water. Bake for 10 minutes. Makes 2 servings.

'Sherry' Frost

4 fl oz (120 ml) cold water   Artificial sweetener to equal ½
1 oz (30 g) nonfat dry milk   teaspoon sugar, or to taste
1 teaspoon sherry flavouring   2 ice cubes
⅛ teaspoon vanilla flavouring

Place all ingredients except ice cubes in blender goblet; cover and blend at low speed to combine. Add ice cubes, one at a time, blending at high speed. Makes 1 serving.

Watermelon Ice

This granular sorbet is served either mushy or frozen. A few drops of red food colouring may be added if you wish.

1 lb 4 oz (600 g) seeded, cubed
watermelon
2 tablespoons fresh lemon juice

Artificial sweetener to equal 2
teaspoons sugar, or to taste

Place all ingredients in blender goblet and blend to purée. Pour into ice
cube tray with divider and freeze for 1 to 2 hours or until cubes are
crystallized. Return cubes to blender; blend to purée. Scrape down
with spatula if necessary. Divide evenly into sorbet glasses. Makes 4
servings.

Caffè Cappuccino

6 fl oz (180 ml) boiling water
1 tablespoon instant coffee
6 fl oz (180 ml) skim milk, scalded

Ground cinnamon or nutmeg
2 cinnamon sticks (optional)

Pour boiling water into blender goblet. Add instant coffee, then hot
milk. Blend on high speed until frothy. Pour into cups and dust with
cinnamon or nutmeg. May be served with cinnamon stick. Makes 2
servings.

JAPAN

*

The Japanese people, who are masters of technology, are equally skilled at the aesthetics of arranging flowers, designing perfect gardens, and preparing and serving food. A small people—though they are getting bigger as their menu pattern becomes more Westernized—they handle details with elegance and sophistication. In fact, they are artful at achieving 'naturalness', and cunning at keeping things looking simple. Everything they do has meaning and tradition; even the tiny vegetable garnishing the soup is part of a design plan in which perfection is the goal. Perhaps it would be more accurate to say that the goal is 'near perfection', because inherent in Japanese philosophy is the belief that perfection can never be achieved. To symbolize this inability to reach the ultimate, a Japanese craftsman will deliberately leave a thumbprint on his work, or drop a leaf on a meticulously groomed sand garden.

Although it has not achieved the universal popularity of that of its Far East neighbour, China, you'll like our taste of Japanese cooking.

Clear Soup (Suimono)

1 pint 12 fl oz (960 ml) chicken
  stock, made with 2 stock cubes
1 teaspoon Japanese shoyu (soy
  sauce)

Pinch of salt
Radish roses

Combine first 3 ingredients and bring to the boil. Place a radish rose in each of 4 bowls. Pour hot soup over and serve. (Japanese drink this from the bowl and do not use spoons.) Makes 4 servings.

Variation: *Add 2 oz (60 g) cooked slivered chicken or pork to each bowl.

Rice Chowder

2 pints (1 litre 200 ml) chicken
  stock, made with 2½ stock
  cubes
8oz (240 g) cooked chicken, diced
2 tablespoons Japanese shoyu (soy
  sauce)

1 teaspoon freshly grated ginger root
1 teaspoon sherry flavouring
Salt and pepper to taste
4 oz (120 g) cooked rice
2 oz (60 g) chopped spring onions

Combine chicken stock, chicken, shoyu, ginger, sherry flavouring, salt and pepper in a large saucepan. Bring to the boil. Divide chicken mixture evenly into 2 soup bowls. Add 2 oz (60 g) rice to each bowl. Pour liquid over each portion. Sprinkle each with 1 oz (30 g) spring onions. Makes 2 servings.

Variation: Serve piping hot soup in 4 covered casseroles. Carefully break an egg over rice chowder and cover. Eggs will poach in 3 to 4 minutes. Soup must be hot. Makes 4 servings.

Pickled Shrimps

8 oz (240 g) cooked, cleaned
  shrimps
4 oz (120 g) onion, chopped
8 tablespoons chopped fresh parsley
2½ fl oz (75 ml) wine vinegar
2 tablespoons vegetable oil

1 garlic clove
1 teaspoon salt
Pinch pepper
Lettuce leaves
Chinese Mustard (recipe follows)

Combine shrimps, onion and parsley in a bowl. Place all remaining ingredients except lettuce and mustard in blender goblet and blend. Pour over shrimps. Chill at least 1 hour, or overnight if possible, before serving. Line a serving bowl with lettuce leaves. Arrange shrimp mixture on leaves. Serve shrimps with Chinese Mustard. Makes 2 servings.

Chinese Mustard

5 tablespoons dry mustard
2 tablespoons water

$^{1}/_{2}$ teaspoon salt

Combine all ingredients to make a dip. Serve with Pickled Shrimps.
Makes 2 servings.

Sukiyaki

12 oz (360 g) boned sirloin steak
2 oz (60 g) onion, thinly sliced
3 oz (90 g) fresh mushrooms, sliced
4 oz (120 g) diagonally sliced celery
3 oz (90 g) green pepper, cut in
   $^{1}/_{4}$-inch (5 mm) wide strips
5 fl oz (150 ml) beef stock, made
   with $^{1}/_{4}$ stock cube

3 oz (90 g) bean sprouts
1 oz (30 g) bamboo shoots
2 tablespoons Japanese shoyu (soy
   sauce)
1 teaspoon salt
$^{1}/_{4}$ teaspoon pepper
4 oz (120 g) cooked rice

Grill steak on rack in grill pan until medium-rare. Remove from grill;
cool; thinly slice; set aside. Cook onion, mushrooms, celery and green
pepper in a large nonstick frying pan, stirring, for about 5 minutes.
Add all remaining ingredients except rice; add steak; heat. Serve,
divided evenly, over equal portions of rice. Makes 2 servings.

Steamed Egg Pudding (Chawan Mushi)

1 pint 4 fl oz (720 ml) chicken
   stock, made with $1^{1}/_{2}$ stock
   cubes
4 eggs, beaten

4 oz (120 g) diced cooked chicken
4 oz (120 g) cooked baby shrimps
2 oz (60 g) spinach leaves,
   chopped

Combine stock and eggs in a large bowl. Divide evenly into four
small individual casseroles. Add 1 oz (30 g) chicken and 1 oz (30 g)
shrimps to each casserole. Cover and place in steamer or on a rack in a
large pan with boiling water halfway up the sides of casserole. Cover
steamer and cook 20 minutes or until a knife inserted in the egg-

stock mixture comes out clean. Remove cover from casseroles and add one quarter of the spinach to each. Replace cover and steam for 5 minutes more or until spinach is soft and wilted. Makes 4 servings.

Variation: Combine 1 oz (30 g) bamboo shoots cut in matchstick pieces, 1 oz (30 g) sliced spring onions and 1 oz (30 g) green peas. Divide evenly into the 4 individual casseroles before steaming. Makes 4 servings.

Chicken Sukiyaki

1 lb 8 oz (720 g) skinned and boned chicken breasts
7½ oz (225 g) takenoko (bamboo shoots), sliced lengthwise ⅛-inch (3 mm) thick
4 oz (120 g) sliced celery
3 oz (90 g) sliced mushrooms, ¼-inch (5 mm) thick

2 oz (60 g) spinach, washed and stemmed
12 oz (360 g) cooked thin noodles
4 fl oz (120 ml) Japanese shoyu (soy sauce)
4 fl oz (120 ml) water
1 teaspoon sherry flavouring
4 oz (120 g) spring onions, cut in 2-inch (5 cm) lengths

Chill chicken breasts to almost freezing and slice thinly. This dish is ideally prepared in an electric nonstick frying pan, but any nonstick pan will do. Heat pan. Place sliced chicken in heated pan and allow to brown, turning occasionally until all pieces are a uniform colour. Add takenoko, celery, mushrooms and spinach. Mix to combine. Stir in noodles. Cook 1 to 2 minutes. In a small bowl combine shoyu, water and flavouring. Pour mixture over chicken and vegetables. Add spring onions. Bring to the boil and cook 4 to 5 minutes. Serve. Makes 4 servings.

Chicken Liver Teriyaki

1 lb 2 oz (540 g) chicken livers
Equal parts Japanese shoyu (soy sauce) and water

5 to 6 yoji (long bamboo toothpicks)
4½ oz (135 g) small tomatoes
Mustard Dip (recipe follows)

Marinate livers in shoyu and water for at least 1 hour. Remove livers from marinade, reserving liquid. Preheat hibachi or grill. Divide livers into 3 equal portions. Thread on yoji. Thread tomatoes on separate yoji. Grill liver on hibachi or on a rack in the grill for about 10 minutes on one side and 3 to 4 minutes on second side. Baste occasionally with reserved marinade. Place skewered tomatoes on hibachi or on rack in grill for last five minutes. Serve with shoyu and Mustard Dip. Makes 3 servings (1 liver yoji each and one third of the small tomatoes).

Mustard Dip

½ teaspoon dry mustard   ½ teaspoon or more water

Combine mustard and water and mix with a spoon until a heavy paste is formed. If softer paste is desired, add more water, a drop at a time, mixing after each addition. Serve with Chicken Liver Teriyaki.

Motsu-Gizzards

1 lb 8 oz (720 g) gizzards, split and   teaspoons sugar, or to taste
    washed   2 garlic cloves, crushed
16 fl oz (480 ml) water   2 teaspoons finely chopped fresh
8 fl oz (240 ml) Japanese shoyu (soy   fresh ginger root
    sauce)   8 oz (240 g) cooked rice
Artificial sweetener to equal 6

Combine all ingredients except rice in a large saucepan. Place over medium heat and cook 1½ to 2 hours or until gizzards are tender. Drain and discard liquid. Divide evenly into 4 portions. Serve each portion over 2 oz (60 g) rice. Makes 4 servings.

Tenderloin of Pork

12 oz (360 g) pork fillet   Freshly ground black pepper to taste
Japanese shoyu (soy sauce)

Insert meat thermometer into thickest portion of meat. Place fillet on a rack in the oven at 350°F (180°C), Gas Mark 4, and roast until meat thermometer registers 170°F (75°C). Remove from oven and sprinkle with shoyu and pepper. Slice across the grain into ¼-inch (5 mm) slices and serve with shoyu mixed with pepper as a dip. Makes 2 servings.

Pork Cucumber Salad

8 oz (240 g) sliced cooked pork
12 oz (360 g) cucumber, sliced

3 tablespoons vinegar
1 teaspoon dry mustard
1 tablespoon water

Place pork strips and cucumber in a large bowl. Combine vinegar, mustard and water. Pour over pork and cucumber. Turn carefully once or twice and serve. Makes 2 servings.

Salted Cucumber

1 lb 2 oz (540 g) cucumbers,
  unpeeled and sliced into ½-inch
  (1 cm) slices

Salt to taste
Japanese shoyu (soy sauce)
Dash wine vinegar (optional)

Combine sliced cucumbers and salt in bowl. Place weighted dish on top. After about 1 hour drain and serve with dash shoyu over them or as a dip. Add a dash of vinegar if you like. Makes 3 servings.

Squashed Radishes

3 oz (90 g) red radishes
2 leaves iceberg lettuce
1 tablespoon lemon juice or wine
  vinegar

1 teaspoon Japanese shoyu (soy
  sauce)
½ teaspoon sesame oil or vegetable
  oil

Wash radishes and trim away ends. Lay radishes on their sides and squash with flat side of cleaver or bottom of a flat frying pan or saucepan to produce colourful irregular shapes. Serve on lettuce leaves as a salad with dressing, made by combining remaining ingredients, poured over it. Makes 1 serving.

Soy with Radish (Shoyu No Daikon)

2 to 3 large daikon (radishes),*
about 2 lbs (960 g)

1 tablespoon Japanese shoyu (soy sauce)

Peel daikon and slice crosswise in about ¼-inch (5 mm) slices. Place in earthenware crock; pour shoyu over and turn a few times. Cover and store in cool place or refrigerator for at least 24 hours. Will keep a few days, but be sure to turn them daily. Serve as a side dish with meat or fish. Makes 8 servings.
*These large, tapered radishes, about 8 to 10 inches (20 to 25 cm) long, are very important in Japanese cuisine. They are sometimes known as Chinese radish and are available from speciality greengrocers and Asian stores.

Boiled Turnips

9 oz (270 g) peeled and diced small
turnips

12 fl oz (360 ml) stock, made
with 1 stock cube
Japanese shoyu (soy sauce)

Boil turnips in stock until tender, 8 to 10 minutes. Serve and sprinkle shoyu over them. Makes 4 servings.

Sunomono Dressing (For Japanese Vegetables)

I

3 tablespoons vegetable oil (or half
vegetable and half sesame oil)
2 tablespoons wine vinegar
2 tablespoons lemon juice

1 tablespoon Japanese shoyu (soy
sauce)
2 teaspoons sherry flavouring

Combine all ingredients in a jar with a lid. Shake well and pour over vegetables, fish or meat. If prepared prior to serving, shake again just before serving. Makes 3 servings.

II

6 tablespoons wine vinegar
Artificial sweetener to equal 1
   tablespoon sugar, or to taste

1 teaspoon Japanese shoyu (soy sauce)

Combine all ingredients in a small bowl. Pour over vegetables, fish or meat. Makes 3 servings.

Sukiyaki Orange Slices

2 medium oranges
4 fl oz (120 ml) orange juice
2 tablespoons Japanese shoyu (soy sauce)

1 tablespoon lemon juice
2 oz (60 g) sliced onion

Peel oranges; slice each orange into four slices. In a large pan, heat orange juice, shoyu, lemon juice and onion to boiling. Reduce heat. Add orange slices; heat. Divide portions equally. Makes 2 servings.

LATIN AMERICAN

*

No handful of dishes can do more than suggest the wonderful foods of Latin America. From country to country, different influences have been at work. In Mexico alone, where the background is not only Spanish but also Indian (from the primitive Soris to the civilized Mayas and Aztecs), there is a tremendous variety of taste-tempting dishes. In Argentina and Paraguay, the cuisines show strong Italian accents; in Colombia and Venezuela, certainly in wealthier homes, French foods are popular, as they are in Brazil, where the cuisine and life-styles mostly reflect the Portuguese colonization.

But Latin America also has some common denominators, not only in the Spanish language (except in Brazil) but also in its food tastes. Recipes which include garlic, onion, peppers and tomatoes, plus spices derived from hot red peppers, all recall their Iberian origins, as do the pucheros (stews), arroz con pollo (chicken with rice) and bean and cornmeal dishes.

So here, then, is a gourmet's tour for those who want to watch their weight while they enjoy the cuisines of Mexico, Central and South America.

'Cream' of Artichoke Soup

This soup may be served hot or chilled.

10 oz (300 g) frozen artichoke hearts
2 oz (60 g) chopped spring onions (white part) or onion
1 pint 4 fl oz (720 ml) chicken stock, made with 1½ stock cubes

Garlic powder to taste (optional)
Salt and pepper to taste
1 oz (30 g) nonfat dry milk, reconstituted with 5 fl oz (150 ml) water
3 thin slices lemon

Cook artichoke hearts following package directions. Add spring onions and continue cooking until tender. Add more water, if necessary. Reserve 2 artichoke hearts. Purée remaining artichoke-spring onion mixture in blender goblet, using the liquid from the cooking. Return puréed vegetables to saucepan. Add stock, garlic powder, salt and pepper. Simmer 10 to 15 minutes. Pour in milk; stir well and heat without boiling. Serve in bowls with dice of remaining 2 artichoke hearts. Top each serving with lemon slice. Makes 3 servings.

'Cream' of Vegetable Soup, Ranch Style (Sopa Ranchera)

2½ oz (75 g) diced carrots
4 oz (120 g) marrow, diced
4 oz (120 g) diced celery
1 tablespoon dried onion flakes
8 fl oz (240 ml) skim milk plus
  8 fl oz (240 ml) vegetable liquid
  or water

Pinch of nutmeg
Salt and pepper to taste
Garnish: watercress or chopped fresh
  parsley

Cook together diced carrots, marrow, celery and onion flakes in saucepan in 12 fl oz (360 ml) water until tender. Drain off liquid, measure and add to milk. Return to saucepan with vegetables. Sprinkle with nutmeg, salt and pepper. Heat without boiling. If watercress is available, chop 4 tablespoons and add to soup just before removing from heat. Parsley may be used instead. Makes 2 servings.

Asparagus Guacamole

Cut off the scales which hold sand and break the asparagus spears to remove the tough ends. (These ends can be peeled and cooked to make soup.) Cover spears with boiling salted water and cook 8 to 10 minutes or until tender. Drain. Purée in food mill or blender.

10 oz (300 g) cooked asparagus,
　puréed
2 oz (60 g) grated onion
1 tablespoon lemon juice

1 garlic clove, crushed
12 drops hot pepper sauce
$\frac{1}{2}$ teaspoon salt
$\frac{1}{4}$ teaspoon chilli powder
Freshly ground pepper to taste

Combine ingredients in bowl. Mix well. Serve in a bowl just as you would Guacamole. Makes 2 servings.

Cheese and Chilli Dip (Chile con Queso)

4 oz (120 g) processed hard cheese
2 oz (60 g) Cheddar cheese
1 oz (30 g) nonfat dry milk,
　reconstituted with 5 fl oz (150 ml)
　water
3 oz (90 g) tomato, finely chopped
1 fresh mild green chilli pepper,

cooked, seeded and chopped
3 oz (90 g) spring onions, finely
　chopped
$\frac{1}{8}$ teaspoon garlic powder or small
　piece of garlic
Pinch cayenne pepper (optional)

Dice cheeses and melt in double boiler or in saucepan, over low heat. When cheese melts, stir in milk; continue stirring until it is thoroughly mixed. Add tomato, chilli pepper, spring onions, garlic powder and cayenne. Heat thoroughly, stirring for about 15 minutes. Serve in fondue pot or in small covered dishes. Reheat if necessary. Use as dip for raw vegetables. Makes 3 servings.

Tomato Omelette

3 oz (90 g) tomato, peeled and diced
2 eggs, lightly beaten
$\frac{1}{4}$ teaspoon salt

Pinch of pepper
1 teaspoon chopped fresh chives

Cook tomato in small heated nonstick frying pan until it loses most of its moisture, stirring constantly. Add eggs and allow to set. Sprinkle with salt and pepper. Cook over moderately high heat. As mixture sets, lift up edges with fork, tilting the pan so that uncooked portions flow evenly to bottom. Serve soft set or turn with spatula to brown other side. Fold over and serve at once, sprinkled with chives. Makes 1 serving.

Baked Whiting with Tomato Sauce

6 oz (180 g) onion, finely chopped
9 oz (270 g) green peppers, diced
1 tablespoon chicken stock powder
9 oz (270 g) canned tomatoes, crushed
8 tablespoons tomato purée
6 fl oz (180 ml) water

$\frac{1}{2}$ small bay leaf
$\frac{1}{2}$ teaspoon thyme
$\frac{1}{4}$ teaspoon garlic powder
Pinch cayenne pepper
Pinch salt
2 lbs 4 oz (1 kg 80 g) boned whiting

Preheat oven to 350°F (180°C), Gas Mark 4. Cook onions until translucent in a nonstick frying pan. Add green peppers and sprinkle on stock powder; cook for 3 minutes. Stir in all remaining ingredients except fish; simmer for 20 minutes. Place fish in baking dish; top with sauce. Bake 25 to 30 minutes or until fish flakes with a fork. Makes 6 servings.

Chicken with Swiss Chard

2 × 6 oz (180 g) skinned and boned chicken breasts
12 fl oz (360 ml) water
2 oz (60 g) onion, chopped

1$\frac{1}{2}$ oz (45 g) diced carrot
6 oz (180 g) Swiss chard or spinach
Salt and pepper to taste

Brown chicken on both sides in nonstick frying pan, then transfer to saucepan and add water, onion and carrot. Cover and cook 20 minutes. Put stemmed Swiss chard on top of chicken, cover tightly and cook until chard is tender, 5 to 6 minutes; do not overcook chard as it gets bitter. Serve as stew. Makes 2 servings.

Baked Orange Chicken with Mushroom Stuffing

1 chicken 3 lbs (1 kg 440 g)
  skinned and cut in half*
Mushroom Stuffing (recipe follows),
  optional

½ teaspoon salt
¼ teaspoon cinnamon
4 fl oz (120 ml) orange juice
1 medium orange, unpeeled, sliced

Grill the chicken on all sides, turning to brown. Meanwhile prepare Mushroom Stuffing. Put stuffing in 12- × 8-inch (30 × 20 cm) baking dish. Add grilled chicken. Mix salt and cinnamon with orange juice, and pour over chicken. Top with orange slices. Bake in moderately hot oven (375°F (190°C), Gas Mark 5) 20 to 25 minutes until chicken is tender. Serve chicken with stuffing. Makes 4 servings.

Note: If too much browning occurs, cover with foil for last part of baking time.

*A 3 lb (1 kg 440 g) chicken will yield about 1 lb (480 g) cooked meat.

Mushroom Stuffing

1 tablespoon dried onion flakes,
  reconstituted
1 tablespoon chopped fresh parsley

1 garlic clove, crushed
12 oz (360 g) mushrooms,
  finely chopped

Combine onion, parsley and garlic. Mix with mushrooms and place in casserole. Bake as above. Makes 4 servings.

Chicken Nicaraguense

2 × 6 oz (180 g) skinned and boned
  chicken breasts
6 oz (180 g) green pepper, chopped
2½ oz (75 g) diced celery
2 oz (60 g) onion, chopped
2 oz (60 g) diced carrots
1 garlic clove, crushed

8 fl oz (240 ml) tomato juice
10 oz (300 g) sliced marrow
1 teaspoon cumin
Salt and freshly ground black pepper
  to taste
2 oz (60 g) fresh or frozen peas

Preheat oven to 350°F (180°C), Gas Mark 4. Brown chicken on both sides in nonstick frying pan, then transfer to a casserole. Add green pepper, celery, onion, carrot and garlic to the pan in which the chicken cooked. Cook briefly, stirring, until vegetables are cooked but crisp. Spoon the vegetables over the chicken and add the tomato juice, marrow, cumin, salt and pepper. Cover the casserole and bake for 20 minutes or until the chicken is tender when pierced with a fork. Add the peas, and return the casserole to oven, covered for 5 to 8 minutes. Makes 2 servings.

Chicken with Rice (Arroz con Pollo)

6 oz (180 g) boned chicken breast
2 oz (60 g) onion, finely chopped
1 oz (30 g) sliced mushrooms
1½ oz (45 g) tomato, peeled and
  chopped
1 oz (30 g) cooked peas

2 oz (60 g) cooked rice
1 tablespoon chopped pimiento
4 fl oz (120 ml) tomato juice
4 fl oz (120 ml) chicken stock,
  made with ¼ stock cube
Salt and pepper to taste

Place chicken under grill 4 inches (10 cm) from the heat. Cook for 8 to 10 minutes until brown, turning frequently. Remove skin and set chicken aside. Lightly brown onion and mushrooms in nonstick pan. Transfer to a small casserole; add tomato, peas, rice and pimiento. Cut chicken into small pieces and add to rice mixture. Add tomato juice and stock; remove lid and season to taste. Bake, covered, at 375°F (190°C), Gas Mark 5, for 15 minutes, until liquid is absorbed. Makes 1 serving.

Tripe with Tomatoes

2 lbs 4 oz (1 kg 80 g) precooked tripe
Salted water
½ lemon
10 fl oz (300 ml) chicken stock,
  made with 1 stock cube
6 oz (180 g) sliced onions
6 oz (180 g) green pepper, chopped
1½ hot green chilli peppers, finely
  chopped

2 garlic cloves, crushed
15 oz (450 g) canned tomatoes
2 tablespoons Worcester sauce
2 tablespoons chopped capers
1 tablespoon chopped fresh coriander
1 teaspoon oregano
Salt and pepper to taste
16 teaspoons tomato purée

Cover tripe with salted water in a large stainless steel saucepan. Squeeze in juice from lemon and include whole rind. Simmer until tender, about 2 hours. Drain and discard lemon rind. Cut tripe into 1-inch (2.5 cm) squares. Return to pan; set aside. In a nonstick pan, place 2 fl oz (60 ml) stock with onion, green pepper, chilli pepper and garlic. Cook, stirring occasionally, until onion becomes translucent. Add to pan with tripe. Add tomatoes, Worcester sauce, capers, coriander, oregano, salt and pepper and remaining stock. Simmer 15 minutes. Add tomato purée and stir to combine. Cover. Simmer 30 to 45 minutes or until tripe is very tender. Divide evenly and serve. Makes 6 servings.

Carbonado Bolivia

Usually served with rice.

1 lb (480 g) freshly grilled beef,	**4 oz (120 g) celery, sliced**
cut in cubes	**3 oz (90 g) tomato, diced**
1 pint 4 fl oz (720 ml) water	**2 oz (60 g) peeled and cubed carrot**
1 teaspoon cider vinegar	**1 oz (30 g) onion, chopped**
½ teaspoon salt	**½ teaspoon oregano**
1 bay leaf	**6 medium apricots, cut into halves**
½ teaspoon ground cumin	**and stoned (optional)**
6 peppercorns	**4 medium plums or 2 medium**
1 garlic clove, crushed	**peaches, quartered and stoned**

Place meat in saucepan with water, vinegar, salt, bay leaf, cumin, peppercorns and garlic. Cover and simmer slowly for about 1 hour. Add celery, tomato, carrot, onion and oregano. Stir to combine. Cook until vegetables are tender – crisp, about 20 minutes. Add fruit. Cover and cook 5 minutes longer. Makes 4 servings.

'Tacos'

Our version of Tacos.

4 oz (120 g) cooked minced veal
1 teaspoon chilli powder
1 teaspoon dried onion flakes,
  reconstituted in 1 tablespoon water
¼ teaspoon salt
¼ teaspoon onion powder
¼ teaspoon paprika

Dash hot pepper sauce
1 slice white bread
Wooden cocktail sticks
1 oz (30 g) shredded lettuce
'Creamy' Pimiento Dressing (see
  page 258)

Place veal in nonstick pan. Add seasonings and cook 5 minutes. Toast bread lightly. Spread meat mixture over half the toast; fold and hold in place with cocktail sticks. Combine lettuce and 1 tablespoon 'Creamy' Pimiento Dressing; cover taco. Makes 1 serving.

Homemade Chorizo*

12 oz (360 g) roasted pork
1 garlic clove
2 tablespoons vinegar or lemon juice
1 tablespoon chilli powder

1 teaspoon salt
Pinch of grated nutmeg, marjoram
  or cumin (optional)

Put roasted pork and garlic through the food mincer. Transfer to a medium mixing bowl. Add remaining ingredients, mix well and pack into a 16 fl oz (480 ml) crockery pot or glass jar, pressing it down with the back of a spoon. Cover tightly and refrigerate. Makes 4 servings.

Aubergine with 'Creamy' Pimiento Dressing

6 oz (180 g) diced aubergine
½ garlic clove, crushed
1 tablespoon lemon juice
1 teaspoon salt
2 oz (60 g) onion, chopped

1 oz (30 g) chopped celery
Cos lettuce
'Creamy' Pimiento Dressing (recipe
  follows)

Cover aubergine with water and bring to the boil. Add garlic, lemon juice and salt and simmer about 5 minutes until just tender. Drain and cool. Mix with onion and celery. Serve on lettuce with 'Creamy' Pimiento Dressing (recipe follows). Makes 1 serving.

'Creamy' Pimiento Dressing

3 oz (90 g) jar pimientos, drained
1 tablespoon white vinegar

1 teaspoon prepared mustard
$2\frac{1}{2}$ fl oz (75 ml) buttermilk

Place all ingredients in blender goblet. Blend until smooth. Makes 1 serving.

Aubergine Casserole (Berenjenas en Cacerola)

12 oz (360 g) aubergine, cut
  into $\frac{1}{2}$-inch (1 cm) slices
8 tablespoons tomato purée
6 fl oz (180 ml) water
2 tablespoons diced pimiento

2 mild green chilli peppers,
  cooked, seeded and chopped
1 tablespoon dried onion flakes
$\frac{1}{2}$ teaspoon ground cumin
$\frac{1}{2}$ teaspoon garlic salt
8 oz (240 g) grated Cheddar cheese

Place unpeeled aubergine in a single layer on a nonstick baking sheet; bake uncovered in hot oven (450°F (230°C), Gas Mark 8) until soft, about 20 minutes. Combine next 6 ingredients in a saucepan; bring to the boil. Lower heat and simmer, uncovered, for 10 minutes. Line bottom of a shallow medium casserole with a single layer of aubergine, spoon on half the sauce and sprinkle with half the cheese; repeat, ending with cheese on top. Bake, uncovered, until hot and bubbly, about 10 to 15 minutes. Makes 4 servings.

Aubergine with Cheese (Berenjenas con Queso)

6 oz (180 g) peeled and cubed
  aubergine
Salt
2 oz (60 g) Cheddar cheese, grated
$\frac{1}{2}$ medium apple, peeled and
  chopped

1 slice white bread, made into
  crumbs
4 tablespoons chopped fresh parsley
1 teaspoon vegetable oil

Sprinkle aubergine with salt in medium bowl; let stand 30 minutes; rinse well. Parboil aubergine in boiling water for 5 minutes; drain. Combine the aubergine, half the cheese and apple in a medium casserole. Mix the breadcrumbs, remaining cheese, parsley, ¼ teaspoon salt and oil; sprinkle over aubergine mixture. Bake at 350°F (180°C), Gas Mark 4, for 30 to 35 minutes. Makes 1 serving.

Chilli Con Carne

This may also be made using beef instead of pork.

12 oz (360 g) cooked dried red kidney or pinto beans, drained (save liquid)
½ beef stock cube
8 oz (240 g) roasted pork, cut into thin pieces
12 oz (360 g) canned tomatoes, chopped

6 oz (180 g) green pepper, diced
4 tablespoons tomato purée
3 fl oz (90 ml) water
1 tablespoon dried onion flakes
1 teaspoon chilli powder
½ teaspoon oregano
⅛ teaspoon ground cumin
2 garlic cloves, crushed

Make the liquid from beans up to 8 fl oz (240 ml) with water. Dissolve ½ stock cube in it. Combine all ingredients in a saucepan. Simmer about 40 minutes or until thick. Makes 4 servings.

Fresh Chilli Relish (Salsa)

3 oz (90 g) tomato
4 oz (120 g) onion
½ garlic clove

4 oz (120 g) can of chopped green chilli peppers or jalapeños

Chop tomato, onion, garlic and chilli peppers very finely. Store for up to one week (refrigerated in closed container). Makes 4 servings. Use as sauce for roasted meat or poached fish.

Chilli Sauce

2 pints 8 fl oz (1 litre 440 ml) mixed
  vegetable juice
4 fl oz (120 ml) wine vinegar
3 oz (90 g) celery, diced
3 tablespoons dried onion flakes
Grated fresh horseradish to taste
1 tablespoon steak sauce
1¾ teaspoons chilli powder

½ garlic clove, crushed to extract
  juices
1 teaspoon gravy browning
3 to 4 drops hot pepper sauce
Artificial sweetener to equal 1
  tablespoon sugar, or to taste
Salt and pepper to taste
1 chilli pepper, diced
1 bay leaf

Combine all ingredients in large saucepan; bring to the boil. Cover and simmer, stirring occasionally, until reduced by half. Remove bay leaf. Makes 24 servings, about 2 tablespoons each.

Black Bean and Rice Stew (Feijoada)

Black beans are a staple of the Brazilian diet but soybeans are catching on too—and are now a huge crop in this country.

6 oz (180 g) green pepper, diced
1 small garlic clove, crushed
½ teaspoon oregano
¼ teaspoon cumin
2 fl oz (60 ml) beef stock, made
  with ¼ stock cube

6 oz (180 g) cooked dried black
  beans
2 oz (60 g) cooked brown rice
1 oz (30 g) slice red onion

Combine green pepper, garlic, oregano and cumin in saucepan with 2 fl oz (60 ml) beef stock. Simmer 10 minutes; stir in black beans and rice and more stock if desired. Serve in bowl with slice of raw onion. Makes 1 serving.

Sweet Pepper and Mushroom Salad

12 oz (360 g) green peppers
12 oz (360 g) red peppers
6 oz (180 g) mushrooms

2 tablespoons lemon juice
2 garlic cloves, crushed
2 fl oz (60 ml) vegetable oil

Place peppers on rack under hot grill, turning frequently until skins are blackened, or hold peppers over gas flame, twisting to blacken skin on all sides. Pop them into a paper bag and let stand 10 minutes, then peel off skins under cold running water and remove seeds. Cut peppers into 1-inch (2.5 cm) strips. Cut mushrooms into thin slices from cap through stem. Sprinkle them with 1 tablespoon of the lemon juice to preserve colour. Combine with pepper strips. Combine garlic, oil and remaining 1 tablespoon lemon juice and let stand. Just before serving, pour salad dressing over mushrooms and peppers and serve at once. Makes 4 servings.

Shredded Beef and Orange Salad (Ensalada de Carne y Naranjas)

Cooked green beans or tender raw florets of cauliflower are good with this combination too.

4 oz (120 g) cooked shredded beef
1 oz (30 g) thinly sliced onion
1 medium orange, peeled and diced
1 tablespoon vegetable oil

1 teaspoon wine vinegar
$\frac{1}{4}$ teaspoon salt
Pinch pepper
Lettuce leaves

Combine meat, onion and orange in bowl; toss lightly until well mixed. Combine vegetable oil, vinegar, salt and pepper; shake well. Pour over meat-orange mixture; toss lightly until well mixed. Refrigerate covered at least 2 hours. Before serving, toss lightly again until well mixed. Serve on lettuce leaves. Makes 1 serving.

Mexican Rice (Arroz Mexicano)

3 oz (90 g) tomato, diced
1½ oz (45 g) diced carrot
2 oz (60 g) peas
1 oz (30 g) diced mushrooms
1½ oz (45 g) diced celery
2 teaspoons dried onion flakes
1 small garlic clove, crushed
1 teaspoon chopped fresh chives

1 teaspoon chopped fresh parsley
¾ teaspoon marjoram
⅛ teaspoon crushed red pepper or pinch of cayenne pepper or dash hot pepper sauce
4 fl oz (120 ml) chicken stock, made with ¼ stock cube
4 oz (120 g) cooked rice

Cook tomato, carrot, peas, mushrooms, celery, onion flakes, garlic, chives, parsley, marjoram and pepper in stock until celery is tender. Combine with rice. Cook until most of the liquid is evaporated or bake uncovered in moderate oven (350°F (180°C), Gas Mark 4) until liquid evaporates. Makes 2 servings.

Saffron Rice (Arroz Amarillo)

8 oz (240 g) cooked rice
4 fl oz (120 ml) chicken stock, made with ¼ stock cube
½ teaspoon dried onion flakes

Pinch saffron or turmeric
1 tablespoon finely diced pimiento, rinsed

Combine all ingredients, except pimiento, in saucepan. Cook over low heat until all liquid is absorbed. Add pimiento and mix well. Makes 4 servings.

Cumin Rice

Omit saffron from preceding recipe and substitute ½ teaspoon cumin. Makes 4 servings.

Chick Pea Cake (Torta de Garbanzos)

1 oz (30 g) nonfat dry milk,
reconstituted with 5 fl oz (150 ml)
water
12 oz (360 g) cooked dried chick
peas
4 eggs, separated

Artificial sweetener to equal 2
tablespoons sugar, or to taste
1 teaspoon brandy or wine
flavouring
1 teaspoon cinnamon

Pour milk into blender goblet; add chick peas and blend. Beat egg yolks until light in colour in a separate bowl. Add sweetener, flavouring and cinnamon; add chick peas and mix well. Beat egg whites until stiff but not dry. Fold into chick pea mixture. Pour into an 8 × 8 × 3-inch (20 × 20 × 8 cm) nonstick baking tin. Bake in moderate oven (350°F (180°C), Gas Mark 4) until centre is done, about 1 hour. Chill and serve cold. Makes 4 servings.

Pineapple 'Cheesecake'

6 oz (180 g) ricotta cheese
3 eggs, separated
1 tablespoon lemon juice
$\frac{1}{2}$ teaspoon vanilla flavouring
Artificial sweetener to equal 2
teaspoons sugar, or to taste

$\frac{1}{4}$ teaspoon salt
12 oz (360 g) canned crushed pineapple,
no sugar added, drained, reserve
juice
2 tablespoons unflavoured gelatine

Place ricotta cheese in a medium-size mixing bowl and beat with an electric mixer on high speed until smooth and fluffy, 3 to 4 minutes. Beat in egg yolks, one at a time, blending well after each addition. Add lemon juice, vanilla flavouring, sweetener and salt. Beat well. Stir pineapple into cheese-egg mixture. Pour pineapple juice into a small saucepan and sprinkle gelatine over. Heat to dissolve gelatine. Allow to cool. Beat egg whites until stiff but not dry. Pour pineapple juice-gelatine mixture into cheese-egg mixture. Mix well with a spatula. Fold in egg whites. Transfer to a 9-inch (23 cm) nonstick cake tin. Place tin in a water bath, with water coming up the sides of cake tin as high as batter mixture. Bake for 1 hour at 350°F (180°C), Gas Mark 4 or until cake is brown and dry on top. Cool. Refrigerate when cake reaches room temperature. Serve cold. Makes 6 servings.

Spiced Grapes

8 fl oz (240 ml) red wine vinegar
Artificial sweetener to equal 12
  tablespoons sugar, or to taste
3 sticks cinnamon

3 cloves
1 tablespoon dried onion flakes
$\frac{1}{2}$ teaspoon wine flavouring
9 oz (270 g) seedless grapes

Combine vinegar, sweetener, cinnamon, cloves, onion flakes and flavouring in a saucepan. Bring to the boil; lower heat and simmer 10 minutes. Pour over grapes. Cover and let stand until cool, then chill. Drain and discard liquid, cloves and cinnamon. Makes 6 servings.

Mexican Carrot Cake (Torta de Zanahoria)*

1 lb (480 g) finely grated carrots
4 teaspoons lemon rind, grated
4 teaspoons lemon juice
$\frac{1}{2}$ teaspoon vanilla flavouring
Artificial sweetener to equal 3
  tablespoons sugar, or to taste

4 tablespoons margarine, melted, or
  vegetable oil
4 eggs, beaten
2 slices white bread, made into
  crumbs

Combine carrots, lemon rind, lemon juice and vanilla flavouring; set aside. Combine sweetener with margarine; stir in eggs. Add crumb and carrot mixture. Bake in 9-inch (23 cm) cake tin with removable base in moderate oven (350°F (180°C), Gas Mark 4) for 1 hour or until top is browned and eggs set. Makes 4 servings.

Papaya with Lime Juice

1 medium papaya, cut into $\frac{1}{2}$-inch
  (1 cm) cubes

2 tablespoons fresh lime juice or
  lemon juice

Sprinkle lime juice over cubes in medium bowl and chill for at least 30 minutes before serving. Makes 2 servings.

Honduras Milk Shake

This frosty milk shake needs no added sweetener if you use a very ripe banana.

1 very ripe medium banana $\frac{1}{2}$ teaspoon vanilla flavouring
4 fl oz (120 ml) water   4 ice cubes
1 oz (30 g) nonfat dry milk

Use a banana with brown mottled skin. Put in plastic bag and freeze. Before use, slightly defrost banana, peel, cut into slices and put in blender goblet with water, milk, vanilla flavouring and an ice cube. Blend at low speed, adding one cube at a time. Serve in tall glasses. A deliciously sweet and frothy Summer milk shake. Makes 2 servings.

MIDDLE EAST

*

If Scheherazade had been entertaining a gourmet sultan, regaling him with fabulous recipes rather than Arabian fables, she could have spent a thousand and one nights just telling tales about aubergine, so exceedingly popular is that vegetable in Arabic countries. We, too, have culinary stories to recite, not only of aubergine but also of marvellous mint-scented soups and stews, of pilavs rich with cinnamon, of chunks of meat skewered and succulently roasted, of vegetables so deliciously stuffed that even a ruling sovereign will find them irresistible. And now, we hope you are as curious as the sultan was, and are prepared to listen to our Arabian tales.

Sweet Yogurt Soup

Iranians use an enormous amount of yogurt, especially in soup, and there are almost as many recipes for yogurt soup as there are cooks, with every cook adding his own personal touch. Here's one authentic soup that will provide a new taste sensation for most of us.

15 fl oz (450 ml) natural
  unsweetened yogurt
8 fl oz (240 ml) water
1 oz (30 g) prunes, stoned and
  quartered

6 oz (180 g) cucumber, peeled and
  cut in pieces
Salt and pepper to taste
1 tablespoon chopped fresh chives
  and/or dill
Parsley to garnish

Combine first five ingredients in blender goblet; blend until smooth. Stir in chives or dill. Chill and garnish with parsley before serving. Serve in bowls. Divide evenly into 4 servings.

Minted Consommé

3 tablespoons boiling water
2 tablespoons chopped fresh mint
  leaves

6 fl oz (180 ml) hot chicken
  stock, made with ½ stock cube

Pour boiling water over mint leaves and let stand 25 minutes. Combine
with hot chicken stock and serve at once. A pick-me-up that doesn't
put you down at weigh-in time. Makes 1 serving.

Lentil and Spinach Soup*

12 oz (360 g) freshly cooked dried
  lentils (reserve liquid)
Lentil liquid plus water to equal 1
  pint 4 fl oz (720 ml) liquid
9 oz (270 g) frozen chopped spinach,

thawed and well drained
1 tablespoon beef stock powder
3 oz (90 g) sliced onion
1 tablespoon lemon juice
Freshly ground pepper to taste

Combine lentils, liquid, spinach, stock powder and onion in a large
saucepan. Cover and simmer 20 minutes. Stir in lemon juice and serve
hot with sprinkling of pepper. Makes 3 servings.

Poached Egg with Garlic

5 fl oz (150 ml) buttermilk
1 teaspoon wine vinegar
1 garlic clove, crushed
Pinch each salt, paprika and pepper

Hot pepper sauce to taste
2 eggs, poached
Parsley to garnish

Combine buttermilk, vinegar, garlic, salt, paprika, pepper and hot
pepper sauce in a small saucepan. Beat together. Heat and divide into 2
small bowls. Slide 1 poached egg (careful not to break it) into each
bowl. Garnish with parsley and serve at once. Makes 2 servings.

Eggs and Cheese

4 oz (120 g) grated hard cheese   Salt and pepper to taste
4 eggs

Use 4 small ovenproof dishes. Into each dish sprinkle ½ oz (15 g) layer of cheese; break an egg over each cheese layer; cover with another ½ oz (15 g) of grated cheese. Sprinkle with salt and pepper and bake in preheated hot oven (400°F (200°C), Gas Mark 6) until eggs are done, about 6 minutes. Serve piping hot. Makes 4 servings.

Sweet and Sour Baked Fish

1 lb 8 oz (720 g) whiting fillet or striped
  bass fillet, cut into serving pieces
8 oz (240 g) onions, peeled and
  sliced
1 garlic clove
2 fl oz (60 ml) chicken stock,
  made with ¼ stock cube
1 teaspoon curry powder
¼ teaspoon cumin
Salt and pepper to taste
Pinch turmeric
6 oz (180 g) tomatoes, sliced into
  ¼-inch (5 mm) slices
2 fl oz (60 ml) lemon juice
Artificial sweetener to equal 2
  tablespoons sugar, or to taste

Wash fish in cold water and dry with paper towels. Place in nonstick baking dish. Steam onions and garlic in 2 fl oz (60 ml) chicken stock until soft, 5 to 6 minutes. Add curry, cumin, salt, pepper and turmeric and cook 2 minutes more. Spread over fish. Put tomato slices on top. Sprinkle with lemon juice and salt. Cover dish with aluminium foil and bake in moderate oven (350°F (180°C), Gas Mark 4) for 25 minutes. Remove from oven. Spoon off some liquid from pan and mix it with artificial sweetener. Put sweetened liquid back in pan, basting fish with it. Makes 4 servings.

Meat Patties with Aubergine

'Delicious' was the test-kitchen report when this was prepared.

12 oz (360 g) peeled aubergine,
   sliced ¼-inch (5 mm) thick
12 oz (360 g) minced beef
1 tablespoon dried onion flakes
1 tablespoon chopped fresh parsley

1 small garlic clove, crushed
1 teaspoon salt
Pepper to taste
4 tablespoons tomato purée, mixed
   with 3 fl oz (90 ml) water

Soak aubergine in cold water to cover for 10 minutes. Drain and dry. Set aside. Meanwhile combine beef, onion flakes, parsley, garlic, salt and pepper. Mix well, shape into 2 large even patties and grill on preheated rack, turning once. In baking dish make a layer of aubergine slices, add the grilled beef patties and top with remaining aubergine. Pour in tomato purée; cover and bake in moderate oven, (350°F (180°C), Gas Mark 4) for ½ hour. Serve hot. Makes 2 servings.

Sweet and Sour Beef with Beetroot

12 oz (360 g) lean steak, minced
12 tablespoons chopped fresh parsley
2 fl oz (60 ml) lemon juice
Pinch each pepper and paprika

6 oz (180 g) drained canned beetroot,
   reserve liquid
Artificial sweetener to equal 4
   teaspoons sugar, or to taste
Pinch salt

Combine beef, parsley, 2 tablespoons lemon juice, pepper and paprika. Mix well. Shape into 4 even patties and grill 4 inches (10 cm) from heat, on rack, turning once. Combine beetroot with reserved liquid and water to equal 12 fl oz (360 ml), remaining lemon juice, artificial sweetener and salt in saucepan. Bring to the boil; add beef and let simmer for 15 to 20 minutes. Serve hot. Makes 2 servings.

Lamb and Vegetable stew (Türlü Givech)

12 oz (360 g) trimmed boneless lamb
2 oz (60 g) onion, diced
6 oz (180 g) green pepper, cut in
   squares
3 oz (90 g) tomato, sliced
4 oz (120 g) green beans, sliced
3 oz (90 g) peeled aubergine, cut in

1½-inch (4 cm) cubes
5 oz (150 g) courgettes, cut in
   1½-inch (4 cm) cubes
3 oz (90 g) okra, sliced
Salt and pepper to taste
Paprika
8 fl oz (240 ml) water

Grill meat on rack under the grill, turning to brown all sides, about 15 minutes. Transfer to medium shallow casserole. Combine all remaining ingredients except water, mix well, and pour over lamb in casserole. Add water. Cover casserole and bake in moderate oven (350°F (180°C), Gas Mark 4) for 45 minutes to 1 hour, or until meat and vegetables are tender. Makes 2 servings.

Loola Kebab

1 lb (480 g) lean boneless lamb, cut
    from leg
8 oz (240 g) beef topside
4 tablespoons chopped fresh parsley
1 tablespoon chopped fresh chives
½ teaspoon black pepper
½ teaspoon allspice

Salt to taste
Cayenne pepper to taste (optional)
4 wooden sticks or skewers,
    12-inches (30 cm) long
4 oz (120 g) diced red onion
8 oz (240 g) cooked rice

Mince lamb and beef together. Add 2 tablespoons of the parsley, chives, black pepper, allspice, salt and cayenne pepper. Mix with hands until ingredients are well blended. Roll into 8 rolls each about 3-inches (8 cm) long (like sausages). Place 2 'sausages' on each skewer. Place on rack and grill over hot charcoal or indoors on a rack under the grill about 4 inches (10 cm) from source of heat and grill until done on all sides, turning to brown evenly. With side of knife, gently push rolls off skewers onto serving plates and serve hot over rice. Diced onions and the remaining parsley are the accompaniments. Makes 4 servings.

Liver Pilaf (Tockov Pilav)

1 lb (480 g) chicken livers
4 fl oz (120 ml) boiling salted water
4 oz (120 g) cooked rice
4 tablespoons tomato purée

2 fl oz (60 ml) water
1 tablespoon dried onion flakes
Parsley sprigs for garnish

Cook liver in 4 fl oz (120 ml) boiling, salted water until done; do not overcook; liver should stay soft and moist. Drain; if liquid is bitter discard and substitute chicken stock, otherwise reserve liquid.

Mince one quarter of the cooled liver using coarse blade of mincer. Return to pan with 2 fl oz (60 ml) reserved liquid or stock. Add rice, tomato purée, water and onion flakes. Stir to combine. Add whole livers and simmer gently for 15 minutes. Serve in bowls with parsley to garnish. Makes 2 servings.

Stuffed Tomato

6 oz (180 g) tomatoes
2 oz (60 g) onion, chopped
8 oz (240 g) cooked minced lamb,
   crumbled

4 oz (120 g) cooked rice
$\frac{1}{2}$ teaspoon chopped fresh mint
$\frac{1}{2}$ teaspoon chopped fresh dill
Salt and pepper to taste

Slice tops off tomatoes and remove and reserve pulp and seeds. Cook onion in nonstick pan; add lamb and heat through. Add tomato pulp, rice, mint, dill, salt and pepper. Fill tomato shells with mixture and replace tops. Place in casserole with 2 fl oz (60 ml) water and any filling that does not fit in tomatoes. Cover and bake at 325°F (160°C), Gas Mark 3, for 30 minutes. Serve hot. Makes 2 servings.

Aubergine Purée

Aubergine grilled over an open gas fire has a delicious smoked taste. Put it under cold running water and you can easily peel off charred skin.

1 large aubergine about 1 lb 8 oz
   (720 g)
4 oz (120 g) onion, finely diced
2 to 4 oz (60 to 120 g) finely diced
   celery (inside stalks)
1 garlic clove

1 tablespoon chopped fresh parsley
1 tablespoon lemon juice
Salt and pepper to taste
Lettuce leaves
4 teaspoons sesame or vegetable oil

Bake aubergine whole or grill on rack over open flame until it is very soft and collapsed on all sides. Peel off skin and remove any large seeds. Mash aubergine. Stir in onion, celery, garlic, parsley, lemon juice, salt and pepper. Serve on lettuce leaves. Make a well in each serving and, at the table, stir 1 teaspoon oil into each well. Mix. Makes 4 servings.

Minted Peas and Carrots

1 tablespoon margarine	$\frac{1}{8}$ teaspoon white pepper
1 teaspoon chopped fresh mint leaves	4 oz (120 g) cooked peas
$\frac{1}{8}$ teaspoon salt	4 oz (120 g) cooked sliced carrots

Heat margarine, mint leaves, salt and pepper in top of double boiler over boiling water until margarine melts. Mix in peas and carrots; heat. Makes 2 servings.

'Creamy' Garlic Spinach

4 oz (120 g) spinach	1 small garlic clove, crushed
Boiling water	1 teaspoon low fat spread (optional)
2 fl oz (60 ml) skim milk	

Place spinach in colander. Blanch by pouring boiling water over it. Drain and squeeze out moisture. Chop spinach and combine in a small saucepan with milk and garlic. Simmer until milk evaporates. Remove from heat. Remove garlic. If desired, stir in low fat spread until it melts. Serve immediately. Makes 1 serving.

'Creamy' Aubergine

4 oz (120 g) peeled and cubed aubergine	2 fl oz (60 ml) skim milk
	$\frac{1}{4}$ teaspoon salt
$1\frac{1}{2}$ fl oz (45 ml) water	Pinch freshly ground black pepper

In a small saucepan combine aubergine and water. Cover and cook, stirring often, until aubergine is soft. Add milk, salt and pepper and whip until it is the consistency of fluffy potatoes. Serve as meat accompaniment. Makes 2 servings.

Pickled Turnips

1 lb (480 g) sliced small white
turnips
2 oz (60 g) beetroot, sliced
Water to cover

Wine vinegar to cover
1 teaspoon salt
3 garlic cloves, crushed

Soak turnips and beetroot in water overnight. Drain and rinse. Place in jar or jars with all other ingredients for at least 3 days. These pickled rose-coloured turnips are very popular as meze (appetizer). Makes 4 servings.

Tooth of Love String Beans*

4 oz (120 g) sliced onion
9 oz (270 g) green peppers, diced
8 fl oz (240 ml) beef stock, made
with ½ stock cube
4½ oz (135 g) tomatoes, sliced
5 oz (150 g) diced celery

12 oz (360 g) frozen cut green beans
6 tablespoons chopped fresh parsley
¾ teaspoon salt
¼ teaspoon pepper
4 eggs

Cook onion and green peppers in stock until soft in wide shallow flameproof casserole. Add tomatoes, celery, beans, parsley, salt and pepper. Cover and simmer gently about 15 minutes or until tender. Just before serving, break each of the 4 eggs into a cup, then slide onto the vegetable mixture. Set the casserole in a hot oven (400°F (200°C), Gas Mark 6) and cook uncovered until the eggs are firm. Makes 4 servings.

Lebanese Salad

1 garlic clove
½ teaspoon salt
1 teaspoon mint or 1 tablespoon
  chopped fresh mint leaves

10 fl oz (300 ml) buttermilk
12 oz (360 g) cucumber, peeled and
  sliced
5 oz (150 g) cooked green beans

Mash garlic with salt and mint to a paste. Stir into buttermilk. Add cucumber slices and green beans. Chill. Makes 4 servings.

Rice 'Cream'

2 fl oz (60 ml) cold water
1½ teaspoons unflavoured gelatine
2 fl oz (60 ml) skim milk
Rind of ½ lemon, grated
Artificial sweetener to equal 2

tablespoons sugar, or to taste
Pinch salt
2 oz (60 g) cooked rice
4 oz (120 g) canned crushed
  pineapple, no sugar added

Pour water into blender goblet. Sprinkle gelatine over water to soften. Combine milk, lemon rind, sweetener and salt in a small saucepan, and bring to the boil. Add rice and simmer for 15 to 20 minutes or until no more of the liquid is visible. Transfer rice mixture to blender with softened gelatine. Reserve 2 tablespoons pineapple. Add remaining pineapple to mixture in blender and blend until smooth. Pour into a medium mixing bowl and add remaining pineapple, stirring to combine. Pour into small mould and refrigerate until set. Makes 1 serving.

Yogurt and Prune Pie*

This dessert treat comes from Yugoslavia, famous for its prunes, yogurt and the 'sweet tooth' of its people.

2 eggs, separated
10 fl oz (300 ml) natural
  unsweetened yogurt
Artificial sweetener to equal 1

tablespoon sugar, or to taste
½ teaspoon cinnamon
½ teaspoon nutmeg
2 oz (60 g) prunes, stoned and diced

Beat egg yolks. Add yogurt, sweetener and spices. Fold in prunes and stiffly beaten egg white. Turn into 8-inch (20 cm) pie plate. Bake at 450°F (230°C), Gas Mark 8 for 10 minutes; lower to 300°F (150°C), Gas Mark 2 and bake 15 to 20 minutes longer, or until browned. Makes 2 servings.

Yogurt Froth

10 fl oz (300 ml) natural
   unsweetened yogurt
¼ teaspoon salt

4 fl oz (120 ml) ice water
Fresh mint leaves

Beat yogurt until frothy, about 5 minutes. Add salt and ice water and beat another 2 minutes. Serve in tall glasses garnished with mint sprigs. Makes 2 servings.

Turkish Watermelon Drink

1 lb 4 oz (600 g) seeded, cubed
   watermelon
Artificial sweetener to equal 2

teaspoons sugar, or to taste
5 fl oz (150 ml) buttermilk

Combine all ingredients in blender goblet. Blend until smooth. Chill. Makes 4 servings.

POLAND AND RUSSIA

*

These two Slavic countries share not only a border but also a predilection for using dill and a taste for that great soup: borscht. It's a one-pot dinner meal for hearty eaters when prepared with chunky pieces of beef, or it can be served for lunch with a hard-boiled egg, a snowy peak of creamy cheese and an invigorating dash of lemon juice. You'll find a number of other less-familiar dishes from this part of the world, and we are sure you'll enjoy them, too.

Hearty Ukrainian Borscht

1 lb 8 oz (720 g) lean stewing beef,
   cut in ³/₄-inch (2 cm) cubes
8 oz (240 g) cooked beetroot
   cut in slivers, (reserve liquid)
1 pint 12 fl oz (960 ml) beef
   stock, made with 2 stock cubes
   (more if necessary)
1 bay leaf
4 × 3 oz (90 g) peeled potatoes

10 oz (300 g) shredded green
   cabbage
4 oz (120 g) sliced carrots
4 oz (120 g) diced onion
4 tablespoons tomato purée
3 fl oz (90 ml) water
4 tablespoons chopped fresh parsley
2 fl oz (60 ml) wine vinegar
Freshly ground black pepper

Grill beef on a rack until done. Transfer to large saucepan. Add beetroot and beetroot liquid, beef stock and bay leaf. Bring to the boil; let cook for 10 minutes. Add potatoes, cabbage, carrots, onion, tomato purée, water, parsley and vinegar. Cover saucepan and simmer very slowly for 1½ to 2 hours. Serve with a sprinkling of freshly ground black pepper. Makes 4 servings.

Quick and Easy Russian Borscht

6 oz (180 g) drained canned whole
   beetroot, finely grated (reserve
   liquid)
16 fl oz (480 ml) water
1 oz (30 g) celery, chopped
2 oz (60 g) onion, chopped

2 teaspoons beef stock powder or
   1 beef stock cube
Salt to taste
1 tablespoon lemon juice
Artificial sweetener to equal 1
   teaspoon sugar, or to taste

Measure 12 fl oz (360 ml) liquid from beetroot into a saucepan and add grated beetroot. Place water, celery, onion and stock powder in blender goblet; blend until smooth. Add to beetroot. Bring to the boil; lightly season. Simmer 15 minutes. Add lemon juice and sweetener. Makes 2 servings.

Polish Beetroot Soup (Barszcz)

Barszcz is made in dozens of different ways but always with beetroot and lemon juice, which gives this soup its typical slightly acid flavour.

6 oz (180 g) drained canned beetroot,
   finely chopped (reserve 8 fl oz
   (240 ml) liquid)
1 oz (30 g) chopped spring onions
6 oz (180 g) cucumber, peeled and
   finely diced
5 oz (150 g) pickled cucumber,
   finely diced

5 oz (150 g) cottage cheese
6 radishes, thinly sliced
2 teaspoons lemon juice
1 tablespoon chopped fresh dill
2 hard-boiled eggs, finely
   chopped
$\frac{1}{2}$ teaspoon grated fresh horseradish

Combine beetroot, spring onions, cucumber and pickled cucumber. Remove a cupful and set aside. Place remaining beetroot mixture in blender goblet; add beetroot juice and cottage cheese; blend until smooth. Place in bowl and add remaining ingredients. Mix thoroughly. Makes 2 servings.

'Cream' of Mushroom Soup

Almost as popular as borscht is a soup made from the famous Russian mushroom. We have given it the highly seasoned flavour, including dill, which the soup is supposed to have.

1 pint 4 fl oz (720 ml) water
4 teaspoons chicken stock powder
6 oz (180 g) mushrooms, finely
   chopped
1 tablespoon dried onion flakes
$\frac{1}{4}$ teaspoon chopped fresh dill

2 oz (60 g) nonfat dry milk,
   reconstituted with 8 fl oz (240 ml)
   water
1 teaspoon Worcester sauce, or to
   taste
Salt and white pepper to taste

Combine water, stock powder, $4\frac{1}{2}$ oz (135 g) of the mushrooms, the onion flakes and dill in a saucepan. Simmer for 10 minutes. Transfer to blender goblet; blend until smooth. Return to saucepan; add remaining ingredients. Heat thoroughly. Do not boil. Makes 4 servings.

'Creamy' Green Turnip-Top Soup

In farmhouses around the world, the first meal of the day is often a hearty soup. This one is favoured by Lithuanians.

$2\frac{1}{2}$ oz (75 g) turnip tops, finely
   chopped
12 fl oz (360 ml) chicken stock,
   made with 1 stock cube
1 oz (30 g) uncooked old-fashioned
   porridge oats

$\frac{1}{2}$ oz (15 g) nonfat dry milk,
   reconstituted with $2\frac{1}{2}$ fl oz
   (75 ml) water
Salt and pepper to taste

Pour boiling water over greens in strainer, then rinse several times in cold water and drain. Place greens in medium saucepan. Cover with stock and cook until almost tender; add oats and continue cooking until oatmeal is done and liquid almost evaporated. Cool slightly. Stir in milk, salt and pepper and simmer gently just long enough to heat; do not boil. Makes 1 serving.

Mushroom-Filled Pancakes with 'Sour Cream' Sauce

Pancakes

2 eggs
2 tablespoons water
2 slices white bread, cubed

Salt and pepper to taste
1 tablespoon chopped fresh parsley

Filling

4 fl oz (120 ml) chicken stock,
    made with ¼ stock cube
5 oz (150 g) drained and finely
    chopped canned mushrooms

2 oz (60 g) chopped spring onions
1 tablespoon chopped fresh dill
Salt and pepper to taste

Topping

5 oz (150 g) cottage cheese
2 tablespoons water

½ teaspoon lemon juice

Blend eggs, water, bread, salt and pepper in blender goblet until smooth; add parsley. Divide into 2 equal portions. Pour 1 portion, all at once, into a 9-inch (23 cm) nonstick frying pan. Tip pan quickly to spread batter evenly. Cook until underside is done and bubbles form on top. Turn over with a spatula and cook on the other side. Repeat with remaining batter. Set pancakes aside. Combine chicken stock, mushrooms and spring onions in a small saucepan. Cook until spring onions are tender. Remove from heat and drain. Add dill and season to taste with salt and pepper. Set aside. Place cottage cheese, water and lemon juice in blender goblet. Blend until smooth. Remove from blender. Place half the mushroom filling lengthwise along each pancake; roll up. Serve at once with topping. Makes 2 servings, 1 pancake each.

Aubergine Caviare Russian Style

One roasted seeded green pepper may be chopped and added with 2 teaspoons of vegetable oil.

1 × 1 lb (480 g) aubergine
2 oz (60 g) onion, finely chopped
3 garlic cloves, crushed
3 oz (90 g) tomato, peeled and
  chopped

1½ teaspoons wine vinegar
½ teaspoon salt
Dash hot pepper sauce

Pierce aubergine with fork in several places. Bake in moderate oven (350°F (180°C), Gas Mark 4) for 30 minutes, or until tender. Remove from oven and cool. Peel aubergine; chop. Combine 8 oz (240 g) chopped aubergine with remaining ingredients in a medium bowl. Chill. Makes 2 servings.

Beef 'Stroganoff' and Noodles

6 oz (180 g) boneless steak
4 oz (120 g) onion, diced
1½ oz (45 g) sliced mushrooms
8 fl oz (240 ml) tomato juice
1 tablespoon white wine vinegar
1 teaspoon beef stock powder

½ oz (15 g) nonfat dry milk,
  reconstituted with 2½ fl oz
  (75 ml) water
Salt and pepper to taste
2 oz (60 g) cooked noodles
½ teaspoon chopped chives

Grill steak on a rack until rare. Cut it in 2-inch (5 cm) strips; set aside. Lightly brown onion in nonstick frying pan. Add mushrooms, tomato juice and vinegar; add stock powder. Cook over moderate heat until mixture thickens, about 10 minutes. Add steak; pour in milk and season with salt and pepper. Heat thoroughly. *Do not boil.* Serve over noodles; sprinkle with chives. Makes 1 serving.

Hunter's Stew (Bigos)

Sweet dishes are favoured in Poland—apple thickens and sweetens this stew.

7 oz (210 g) reconstituted dried
  mushrooms, sliced
8 oz (240 g) onions, sliced
12 oz (360 g) tomatoes, chopped
2 medium apples, cored, peeled and
  sliced
1 tablespoon chicken stock powder
1 teaspoon gravy browning
½ teaspoon garlic powder

16 fl oz (480 ml) water
1 lb (480 g) sauerkraut, rinsed
½ bay leaf
Salt and pepper to taste
1 lb 8 oz (720 g) grilled and skinned
  chicken pieces
4 × 3 oz (90 g) boiled potatoes
  (optional)

Combine mushrooms, onions, tomatoes, apples, stock powder, gravy
browning and garlic powder in a large saucepan. Cook until onions are
translucent. Add water, sauerkraut, bay leaf, salt and pepper; mix
thoroughly. Place chicken pieces on top and cover. Simmer for 1 hour.
Serve with boiled potatoes, if desired. Makes 4 servings.

Vegetable Polonaise*

2 tablespoons low fat spread, melted
1 teaspoon lemon juice
Pinch garlic powder
1 slice white bread, made into
  crumbs

2 hard-boiled eggs, finely
  chopped
1 tablespoon chopped fresh parsley
Salt and white pepper to taste
8 oz (240 g) cooked broccoli or
  cauliflower

Combine low fat spread, juice and garlic powder and add to remaining
ingredients, except vegetables. Toss lightly. Place vegetables in a small
baking dish and cover with crumb mixture. Bake at 375°F (190°C),
Gas Mark 5, for about 15 minutes or until thoroughly heated. Makes 2
servings.

Baked Apple and Strawberry Compote

1 lb 4 oz (600 g) strawberries, sliced
1½ teaspoons sherry flavouring
Artificial sweetener to equal 4
  teaspoons sugar, or to taste

½ teaspoon cinnamon
4 medium apples, cored, peeled and
  sliced

Place 5 oz (150 g) strawberries in blender goblet. Add flavouring, sweetener and cinnamon; blend until smooth. Combine remaining berries and apples in a medium-size baking dish. Cover with puréed strawberries and toss lightly. Bake at 375°F (190°C), Gas Mark 5 for about 30 minutes or until apples are tender. Makes 4 servings.

PORTUGAL

*

Portuguese cookery, rich and varied though it is, is not well publicised, perhaps because it has been overshadowed by the Spanish. Both the Portuguese and Spanish are fond of garlic, onions, tomatoes, green peppers and parsley. But Portuguese cooking is more highly seasoned, since the Portuguese were explorers who introduced Indian, South African and South American spices, tastes and ancestry to their country centuries ago, as a natural result of their travels round the world and back.

Geography plays the major role, of course, in developing kitchen customs. Along the seacoast, which is the biggest border in Portugal, fish, especially cod (dried and sold as bacalhau) is a staple. In the mountains, partiality is shown to thick, hearty soups made of inexpensive ingredients. Eggs are popular throughout Portugal and are used in many different ways: poached in tomato sauce, over meat and in dessert puddings (though the favourite Portuguese dessert is just a peeled orange).

We've given you a sprinkling of everything so you can eat native Portuguese style wherever you are.

Bean and Pumpkin Soup, Beira Style

6 oz (180 g) cooked dried blackeyed
  peas
2 teaspoons dried onion flakes or
  1 oz (30 g) diced onion

2 oz (60 g) diced pumpkin
1 oz (30 g) finely diced celery
12 fl oz (360 ml) chicken stock,
  made with 1 stock cube

Combine all ingredients in saucepan. Simmer 40 minutes or until vegetables are tender and soup is thick. Makes 1 serving.

Potato and Kale Soup (Caldo Verde)

Most Portuguese cooks have their own way of making this soup.
Typically, the greens are cut into fine grasslike pieces with a special
shredding gadget sold for this purpose. A teaspoon of dried onion
flakes could be added for flavour, if desired. The potatoes are often
cooked in chicken stock rather than water. Because chicken stock is
quite salty, we do not add salt to our ingredients.

3 oz (90 g) dark green kale or 8 oz   1 pint 12 fl oz (960 ml) chicken
    (240 g) cabbage   stock, made with 2 stock cubes
12 oz (360 g) cooked potatoes, diced $\frac{1}{4}$ teaspoon black pepper

Wash the greens thoroughly, discard tough stems and discoloured
leaves. Stack greens (or roll cabbage leaves) and cut into strips. Add to
potatoes with stock; bring to the boil, and fast-simmer for about 10
minutes; do not overcook greens. Stir in pepper and serve at once.
Makes 4 servings.

Egg, Potato and Cheese Azores

$2\frac{1}{2}$ oz (75 g) cottage cheese   Salt and freshly ground pepper to
2 teaspoons vegetable oil   taste
$\frac{1}{2}$ teaspoon wine vinegar   1 hard-boiled egg, finely
$\frac{1}{2}$ garlic clove, crushed   chopped
$\frac{1}{4}$ teaspoon prepared mustard   3 oz (90 g) boiled potato, sliced
$\frac{1}{4}$ teaspoon chopped fresh parsley   Lettuce leaves
$\frac{1}{8}$ teaspoon dried coriander leaves   Parsley sprigs
    or pinch of crushed coriander
    seed

Combine cottage cheese with 1 teaspoon oil, vinegar, garlic, mustard,
parsley, coriander, salt and pepper. Combine egg with remaining oil.
Arrange potatoes on a bed of lettuce. Spread cottage cheese mixture
over potatoes. Top with egg mixture. Garnish with parsley sprigs.
Makes 1 serving.

Flounder Fillets with Mushrooms and Bread Stuffing

4 slices white bread
1 garlic clove, cut
4 × 6 oz (180 g) sole or flounder
  fillets
Salt and freshly ground pepper to
  taste

6 fl oz (180 ml) Fish Stock (see
  page 11)
3 oz (90 g) canned tomato, chopped
6 oz (180 g) mushrooms, sliced
2 tablespoons chopped fresh parsley
1 tablespoon dried onion flakes

Rub garlic over bread slices on both sides. Soak bread in hot water. Squeeze out excess liquid. Wash fillets and wipe them dry with paper towels. Top with bread. Roll from the short end; secure with wooden cocktail sticks. Sprinkle lightly with salt and pepper. Place in a baking dish. Add Fish Stock, tomato, mushrooms, parsley and onion flakes. Cover baking dish tightly. Bake in moderately hot oven (375°F (190°C), Gas Mark 5) until fish is done, or flakes easily with fork, about 30 minutes. If sauce is thin, drain it off into small saucepan and simmer until it is reduced. Season the sauce with salt and pepper if desired. Pour over the fish. Makes 4 servings.

Marinated Fish (Escabeche)

8 oz (240 g) cooked fish
2 oz (60 g) sliced onion
4 fl oz (120 ml) white vinegar
4 fl oz (120 ml) water
3 oz (90 g) green pepper, coarsely
  chopped
2 oz (60 g) cooked sliced carrot

1 oz (30 g) coarsely chopped celery
$\frac{1}{2}$ teaspoon pickling spice
$\frac{1}{4}$ teaspoon crushed dried hot pepper
$\frac{1}{2}$ garlic clove, crushed
Pinch salt and pepper
1 tablespoon chopped fresh parsley

Arrange fish in a shallow casserole. Lightly brown onion in nonstick frying pan. Add vinegar, water, pepper, carrot, celery, spice, crushed hot pepper and garlic. Simmer 2 to 3 minutes; add salt and pepper. Pour liquid over fish, let cool. Sprinkle with parsley, refrigerate overnight. Makes 2 servings.

Portuguese Cod with Cornmeal

1 lb 8 oz (720 g) cod or hake fillets,
  fresh or frozen
4 oz (120 g) chopped onion
2 garlic cloves, crushed
4 tablespoons tomato purée
3 fl oz (90 ml) water
1 clove

1 tablespoon chopped fresh parsley
1 teaspoon salt
⅛ teaspoon paprika
Pinch pepper
Pinch cumin
3 oz (90 g) dry cornmeal, cooked
  according to package directions

Thaw frozen fish. Cut into 1½-inch (4 cm) slices. Cook onion and garlic in nonstick pan until softened. Add tomato purée, water, clove, parsley, salt, paprika, pepper and cumin. Add fish; cover and cook until fish flakes easily when tested with a fork, about 10 minutes. Do not add extra water as the fish produces its own juices. Serve over cornmeal. Makes 4 servings.

Curried Fish Minho Style

The Portuguese were great navigators as well as imaginative cooks, and when they found the sea route to India more than 500 years ago, they lost no time in importing the spicy curry powder mixture popular in that exotic country.

4 fl oz (120 ml) chicken stock,
  made with ¼ stock cube
½ medium apple, peeled and diced
1 tablespoon dried onion flakes

½ teaspoon curry powder
Salt and pepper to taste
4 oz (120 g) cooked flaked fish

Combine stock, apple, onion flakes, curry, salt and pepper in medium saucepan. Heat for 1 minute. Stir in fish. Serve hot. Makes 1 serving.

Portuguese Shrimps

4 oz (120 g) shelled shrimps
1 teaspoon sherry flavouring
¼ teaspoon chopped fresh ginger
   root
¼ teaspoon salt
Pinch pepper
8 teaspoons tomato purée
2 fl oz (60 ml) water

1 teaspoon Worcester sauce
3 oz (90 g) green pepper, diced
3 oz (90 g) red pepper, diced
1 oz (30 g) spring onions, sliced
1 tablespoon dried onion flakes
1 teaspoon fennel leaves, chopped (if
   available) or pinch fennel seeds,
   or to taste

Season shrimps with sherry flavouring, ginger, salt and pepper. Let stand 20 minutes. Put into a saucepan with tomato purée, water, Worcester sauce, green and red pepper, spring onions, onion flakes and fennel leaves. Cover and simmer until shrimps are done, about 10 minutes. Do not overcook or they get tough. Shrimps are done when they turn pink. Makes 1 serving.

Beira Chicken

3 oz (90 g) skinned and boned
   chicken breast
1 teaspoon margarine

2½ oz (75 g) cottage cheese
Salt and freshly ground pepper to
   taste

Pound chicken breast until thin. Spread with margarine and put cottage cheese in centre. Roll; secure with wooden cocktail sticks. Place in individual ovenproof serving dish and bake in moderate oven (350°F (180°C), Gas Mark 4) until chicken is done, about 30 minutes. Sprinkle with salt and pepper and serve hot. Makes 1 serving.

Chicken Breasts Portuguese Style

2 × 6 oz (180 g) skinned and boned
chicken breasts
¼ teaspoon freshly grated or ground
nutmeg
Salt and freshly ground pepper to
taste

2 oz (60 g) nonfat dry milk,
reconstituted with 10 fl oz
(300 ml) water
1 teaspoon sherry flavouring
6 oz (180 g) sliced mushrooms

Place the chicken breasts between pieces of greaseproof paper and
pound lightly with a wooden mallet or the bottom of a frying pan on
both sides to flatten. Combine nutmeg, salt and pepper; rub on chicken
and pound on both sides; brown in nonstick frying pan on both sides;
remove from the pan and add milk, stirring. Heat, but do not boil;
simmer 2 minutes. Add sherry flavouring to milk and return the
chicken pieces to the pan. Cover and simmer about 10 minutes; turn
chicken, simmer another 10 minutes. Meanwhile in another pan, cook
the mushrooms, stirring, until they are softened. Pour over the chicken
and season with salt and pepper, if desired. Cover again and simmer a
few minutes longer. Serve hot. Makes 2 servings.

Portuguese Baked Chicken in Casserole
(Frango na Pucara)

1 roasting chicken, 3 lbs (1 kg 440 g),
skinned and cut in serving
pieces*
½ garlic clove, crushed
Salt, paprika and pepper to taste
8 fl oz (240 ml) orange juice
8 teaspoons tomato purée

2 fl oz (60 ml) water
6 oz (180 g) green pepper, diced
2 tablespoons soy sauce
2 to 3 teaspoons prepared mustard
2 medium oranges, peeled and
sectioned

Rub garlic over chicken and sprinkle all over with salt, paprika and
pepper. Put in earthenware casserole. Combine all remaining ingredients
except oranges; pour over chicken. Bake, covered, at 350°F (180°C),
Gas Mark 4, for 50 minutes. Add oranges; bake 5 to 10 minutes longer.
Makes 4 servings.
   Variation: Omit orange juice, oranges and soy sauce. Add 3 oz (90 g)

ISRAEL: Gefilte Fish with Horseradish (page 181); Fluffy Lemon Pie (page 185)

ITALY:
Antipasto (As Main Dish) (page 188);
Herb Fingers (page 225);
Garlic Bread (page 225);
Garlic Dressing (page 189);
Red Vinegar Dressing (page 189);
Mayonnaise (page 189)

JAPAN: Chicken Liver Teriyaki (page 245); Pickled Shrimp (page 243); Chinese Mustard (page 244); Clear Soup (page 242)

LATIN AMERICA: Chilli Con Carne (page 259); Mexican
Carrot Cake (page 264); Spiced Grapes (page 264)

MIDDLE EAST: 'Creamy' Aubergine (page 272); Loola
Kebab on a Bed of Rice (page 270)

POLAND AND RUSSIA: Hearty Ukrainian Borscht (page 276)

PORTUGAL: Sponge Cake Roll and Strawberry Filling (page 292); Whipped Topping (page 12); Portuguese Baked Chicken (page 288)

SCANDINAVIA: Swedish Meat Patties (Beef à la Lindstrom) with Yogurt (page 298); Danish Cucumber Salad (page 299); Cardamon Cookies (page 300)

THE SOUTH PACIFIC:
Skewered Bananas
with Dipping Sauce (page 308);
Philippine Chicken
and Veal Stew
(Adobo) (page 304)

SWITZERLAND: Stuffed Tomatoes (page 333); Dill Boiled
Potatoes (page 332)

THE UNITED STATES: New England Boiled Dinner (page 357); Black Bottom Cheesecake (page 375)

tomatoes, chopped, 8 oz (240 g) diced onion and ½ teaspoon sherry or brandy flavouring. Combine with remaining ingredients before baking as directed above.

*A 3 lb (1 kg 440 g) chicken will yield about 1 lb (480 g) cooked meat.

Portuguese Veal Roasted on a Spit (Vitela Assada no Espeto)

2 lbs 4 oz (1 kg 80 g) boned well-
   trimmed veal roast (from leg)
1 to 2 garlic cloves, crushed
½ bay leaf, crushed
1 small piece hot chilli pepper,
   crushed

1 teaspoon salt
1 teaspoon chopped fresh parsley
2 teaspoons wine vinegar
3 tablespoons stock, made from
   stock cube according to package
   directions

Wipe veal. Make a paste of remaining ingredients and rub on veal roast. Let stand 1 hour or longer. Roast in slow oven (300°F (150°C), Gas Mark 2) or secure on spit and cook on rotisserie until done, allowing 1½ to 2 hours. Makes 6 servings.

Portuguese Tomato Stew (Guisado de Tomate)

This is served as a border for scrambled eggs, over rice, with fish etc. Crushed garlic may be added.

5 oz (150 g) cooked diced green
   vegetables (asparagus tips, green
   beans, broccoli, courgette)
5 oz (150 g) cooked diced carrots,
   cauliflower or turnips
4 oz (120 g) cooked peas or diced
   artichoke hearts

2½ oz (75 g) cooked sliced
   mushrooms
4 oz (120 g) cooked onion, puréed
16 teaspoons tomato purée
4 fl oz (120 ml) water
Salt and pepper to taste

Select 3 or 4 vegetables from the list. Mix tomato purée and water in a saucepan and bring to quick boil. Add cooked vegetables and heat, stirring. Serve at once as a border for scrambled eggs. Makes 4 servings.

Beira Green Bean Stew

12 oz (360 g) potatoes, cut in pieces
1 pint 4 fl oz (720 ml) chicken
  stock, made with 1½ stock
  cubes
4 oz (120 g) onion, sliced

6 oz (180 g) tomatoes, peeled,
  seeded and sliced
1 lb (480 g) runner or green beans,
  cut French style (thin diagonal
  slices)

Cover potatoes with chicken stock; add onion and tomatoes. Cook
until potatoes are soft. Place vegetable mixture in blender goblet.
Blend until smooth. Return to saucepan and bring to the boil; add
beans. Lower heat and simmer until beans are tender and sauce is
reduced to desired consistency. Makes 4 servings.

Rice with Aubergine

6 oz (180 g) aubergine, peeled and
  cut into 1-inch (2.5 cm) cubes
1 teaspoon salt
4 fl oz (120 ml) chicken stock,

made with ¼ stock cube
4 oz (120 g) onion, chopped
4 oz (120 g) cooked rice

Sprinkle aubergine with salt in a medium bowl and let stand for 1 hour.
Drain off liquid. Cook onion in 2 fl oz (60 ml) stock in a covered pan
until tender, stirring occasionally. Add aubergine and continue to cook
until aubergine is done. Add rice and remaining stock. Heat. Makes
2 servings.

Soft Onion Purée (Cebolada)

To serve as a side dish for roast meat or chicken, usually with a 3 oz
(90 g) boiled potato for each serving.
  Slice 1 lb (480 g) peeled onions. Combine sliced onions with 8
fluid oz (240 ml) chicken stock, made with ½ stock cube, in a
medium casserole; cover casserole and cook at 300°F (150°C), Gas
Mark 2, 1 to 2 hours. Place in blender goblet and blend until smooth.
Stir in ½ teaspoon sherry flavouring if desired. Serve hot. Makes 4
servings.

Orange and Onion Salad

1 medium orange, peeled and thinly
sliced
2 oz (60 g) red onion, thinly sliced

2 fl oz (60 ml) orange juice
½ teaspoon brandy flavouring
1 slice lime or lemon

Arrange orange slices in centre of salad plate in overlapping rings.
Leave space for dip in middle. Make a border of onion slices separated
into rings. Combine orange juice and brandy flavouring in a small
bowl; add a slice of lime and place bowl in centre of salad plate. Makes
1 serving.

Kidney Bean Salad*

The Portuguese are as fond of beans as the Italians of pasta, and
they've devised almost as many ways of serving them. The plentiful use
of garlic is typical of Iberian cooking.

½ garlic clove
2 oz (60 g) assorted lettuce leaves,
cut
4 oz (120 g) cooked dried red kidney
beans
2 oz (60 g) chopped red onion

1 tablespoon chopped fresh parsley
2 teaspoons vegetable oil
2 teaspoons vinegar or lemon juice
⅛ teaspoon ground cumin
Salt and pepper to taste
Pinch cayenne pepper

Rub individual salad bowl with cut clove of garlic. Arrange lettuce in
bowl. Add a layer of beans, and a layer of onions. Sprinkle with
parsley. Repeat layers. Combine remaining ingredients and stir gently
into bean mixture in salad bowl. Makes 1 serving.

Banana Soufflé Pudding (Pudim de Banana)*

Very ripe bananas have their own natural sweetness, but if you wish,
you may add artificial sweetener to the egg yolk-banana mixture.

4 eggs, separated
1 oz (30 g) nonfat dry milk,
  reconstituted with 4 fl oz (120 ml)
  water
2 teaspoons vanilla flavouring
Artificial sweetener to equal 2

teaspoons sugar, or to taste
  (optional)
Few drops yellow food colouring
2 very ripe medium bananas sliced
¼ teaspoon cream of tartar
Pinch of salt

Preheat oven to 350°F (180°C), Gas Mark 4. Combine yolks, milk, 1 teaspoon vanilla, artificial sweetener and food colouring in the top of a double boiler. Cook over boiling water, stirring constantly, until thick. Fold in bananas and pour into 8-inch (20 cm) round baking tin. Beat egg whites with cream of tartar and salt, until stiff but still shiny. Fold in remaining vanilla. Top banana-egg mixture with egg whites. Bake 15 to 20 minutes or until meringue is golden brown. Serve chilled. Makes 4 servings.

Sponge Cake Roll (Brazo de Gitano)*

4 eggs, separated
Artificial sweetener to equal 4
  teaspoons sugar, or to taste
½ teaspoon cream of tartar
½ teaspoon vanilla or almond
  flavouring

1 oz (30 g) nonfat dry milk
2 slices white bread, made into
  crumbs
Filling (recipe follows)
Whipped Topping (see page 12)

Preheat oven to 350°F (180°C), Gas Mark 4. Beat egg yolks with an electric mixer until lemony in colour, about 5 minutes. Add artificial sweetener to equal 2 teaspoons sugar. Beat to mix about 30 seconds. Set aside. Wash beaters clean and dry well. Beat whites until foamy; combine cream of tartar with egg whites and beat until stiff but not dry. Fold in flavouring, nonfat dry milk and remaining sweetener. Fold yolks into whites until well blended. Fold in breadcrumbs, a little at a time, until well blended. Pour mixture into a 10 × 15 × 1-inch (25 × 38 × 2.5 cm) nonstick baking tin† and bake for 15 minutes or until a skewer inserted in the centre comes out dry. Use a long plastic spatula to help

†If a nonstick tin is not available, line any 10 × 15 × 1-inch (25 × 38 × 2.5 cm) baking sheet with aluminium foil or greaseproof paper. After baking, freeze until hard and then remove cake from tin. Peel off paper immediately. Let thaw completely before filling.

remove cake from tin. Loosen the bottom by forcing the spatula under the cake. Turn cake out onto a moist towel. Evenly trim away crisp edges. Place crisp edges in blender goblet and blend to form crumbs. Combine crumbs with filling. Spread on cake, reserving 4 fl oz (120 ml) for decorating top, and roll cake from short end. Wrap in aluminium foil and refrigerate. Before serving, decorate with reserved filling. Serve with Whipped Topping. Makes 4 servings.

Filling for Sponge Cake Roll

1 tablespoon unflavoured gelatine
2 fl oz (60 ml) cold water
10 oz (300 g) strawberries

Artificial sweetener to equal 2 teaspoons sugar, or to taste

Sprinkle gelatine over water in a small saucepan. Place over low heat and stir until gelatine dissolves. Crush strawberries with fork in a medium mixing bowl; add gelatine mixture and sweetener. Mix with electric mixer until well blended. Chill until almost set. Remove from refrigerator and remix with electric mixer to form a thick jam-like consistency. Spread on cake roll.

SCANDINAVIA

*

Scandinavians—the people of Denmark, Finland, Iceland, Norway and Sweden—share with the rest of us a taste for fine food and plenty of it. We all enjoy Danish pastries with coffee. The traditional Danish pastry is baked with butter, flour and yeast, frequently enriched with nuts and many other fattening ingredients. Our version is delicious, and you'll probably enjoy it more because you can have your portion as part of our Food Programme. Fruit soups from Finland and Norway are less well known than Danish pastry, but we think you'll like them, especially as a Summertime treat. You'll also find vegetables and salads for your *smorgasbord* buffet—a word and a method of entertaining that we borrowed from Sweden. Iceland should not be omitted from the roll call of Scandinavian countries. It is noted for its codfish, and our recipe for using it is as distinctive as it is authentic.

Bilberry Soup

A popular Norwegian soup. Our version is a luncheon main course. The berries could be served in buttermilk or yogurt as an alternative to the 'sour cream'.

16 fl oz (480 ml) water
10 oz (300 g) bilberries
½ teaspoon grated lemon rind
Pinch salt

10 oz (300 g) cottage cheese
1 teaspoon lemon juice
2 fl oz (60 ml) water

Combine water, berries, lemon rind and salt in a saucepan. Cook until berries are very soft. Serve cold in bowls with 'sour cream' topping. To make 'sour cream', combine remaining ingredients in blender goblet and blend until smooth. Makes 2 servings.

Vegetable Soup with Milk (Kesäkeitto)

A substantial everyday soup in Finland.

8 fl oz (240 ml) water
2 oz (60 g) cauliflower florets, diced
1 oz (30 g) shredded spinach, kale or
  cabbage
2 oz (60 g) diced celery
1 oz (30 g) diced carrot

1 oz (30 g) green peas
½ teaspoon salt
½ oz (15 g) nonfat dry milk,
  reconstituted with 2½ fl oz
  (75 ml) water
1 teaspoon chopped fresh parsley

Combine water, cauliflower, spinach, celery, carrot, peas and salt in a saucepan. Bring to the boil. Cover and simmer until vegetables are tender, 10 to 15 minutes. Remove from heat. Stir in milk and parsley and serve hot. Makes 1 serving.

Danish Style Breakfast Buns

2 slices wholemeal bread, made into
  crumbs
2 oz (60 g) nonfat dry milk
2 teaspoons baking powder
Artificial sweetener to equal 4

teaspoons sugar, or to taste
2 tablespoons low fat spread
2 eggs, lightly beaten
1 medium apple, peeled and finely
  chopped

Preheat oven to 375°F (190°C), Gas Mark 5. Place breadcrumbs, dry milk, baking powder and sweetener in a mixing bowl. Add low fat spread, mix well; fold in eggs and apple. Spoon into 6 nonstick patty tins and bake for 20 minutes. Makes 2 servings (3 buns each).

Scandinavian Fish Salad

Cod, flounder, halibut, herring, pike, sardines and whiting are some of the typical fish of this part of the world.

3 oz (90 g) peeled cooked potato, finely diced

1 oz (30 g) cooked beetroot, finely diced

2½ oz (75 g) pickled cucumber, finely diced

1 tart medium apple, finely diced

1½ oz (45 g) cooked carrot, finely diced

1 teaspoon chopped chives

2 tablespoons cider vinegar

Pinch salt and pepper

4 oz (120 g) cooked fillet of fish, flaked or diced

Parsley

Combine potato, beetroot, pickled cucumber, apple, carrot and chives. Stir in vinegar, salt and pepper. Add flaked fish and mix gently to avoid mashing the vegetables or fish. Pack into small wet mould (such as large coffee cup). Chill for several hours. Turn out onto dinner plate. Garnish with parsley. Makes 1 serving.

Poached Cod with Egg Sauce

4 fl oz (120 ml) Fish Stock (see page 11)

4 fl oz (120 ml) water

½ teaspoon butter flavouring

2 hard-boiled eggs, finely chopped

3 oz (90 g) tomato, peeled, seeded and chopped

2 tablespoons chopped fresh parsley

½ teaspoon salt

4 oz (120 g) poached cod or other fish

Combine Fish Stock, water and butter flavouring in a saucepan; cook over low heat for 2 minutes. Add eggs, tomato, parsley and salt. Continue cooking gently, stirring frequently, 5 minutes or until heated through. Place half the fish on each of 2 luncheon plates. Spoon half the egg mixture on each portion of fish. Makes 2 servings.

Poached Salmon Steaks with Creamed Mushrooms (Fiske med Champinjoner)

For a typical Scandinavian meal, serve poached salmon with 'Creamed' Mushrooms and spinach.

4 tablespoons salt
2 pints 8 fl oz (1 litre 440 ml) water
3 × 8 oz (240 g) salmon steaks

Lemon slices to garnish
Dill or parsley sprigs to garnish

Combine salt and water in roasting tin or fish kettle. Bring to the boil; reduce heat. Using a spatula, gently slide salmon steaks into water. Simmer fish 5 minutes or until fish flakes easily with fork. Remove fish with slotted spatula to paper towels; drain. Transfer to serving dish. Garnish with lemon slices and dill or parsley sprigs. Makes 3 servings.

'Creamed' Mushrooms

$4\frac{1}{2}$ oz (135 g) mushrooms, thinly
  sliced
4 fl oz (120 ml) water
1 bay leaf
3 tablespoons chopped fresh parsley
1 tablespoon dried onion flakes

2 peppercorns
$\frac{1}{2}$ teaspoon salt
1 oz (30 g) nonfat dry milk,
  reconstituted with 5 fl oz (150 ml)
  water

Combine mushrooms, water, bay leaf, parsley, dried onion flakes, peppercorns and salt in saucepan. Cover pan and cook until mushrooms are done, 8 to 10 minutes. Strain off liquid; remove bay leaf and peppercorns. Place liquid in blender goblet with half the mushrooms. Purée. Heat with milk and remaining mushrooms. Serve over poached salmon. Makes 3 servings.

Celery Salmon Loaf

4 oz (120 g) drained canned salmon,
  flaked
$1\frac{1}{2}$ oz (45 g) finely chopped celery
1 oz (30 g) onion diced
$1\frac{1}{2}$ oz (45 g) green pepper, diced
1 teaspoon chopped pimiento
1 tablespoon mayonnaise

1 teaspoon chopped fresh parsley
1 teaspoon wine vinegar
$\frac{1}{2}$ teaspoon chicken stock powder
2 teaspoons unflavoured gelatine
6 fl oz (180 ml) water
Lettuce

Combine salmon, celery, onion, green pepper and pimiento in a mixing bowl. Add mayonnaise, parsley and vinegar. Sprinkle in stock powder and mix well. Sprinkle gelatine over water to soften in a saucepan. Place over low heat, stirring until gelatine is dissolved. Add to salmon mixture. Turn mixture into a mould and chill in refrigerator until firm. Turn out on lettuce. Makes 1 serving.

Swedish Meat Patties (Biff à la Lindström)

If you mince your own beef at home, you can put the capers and onion flakes into the mincer too.

2 tablespoons dried onion flakes
6 fl oz (180 ml) water
1 lb 2 oz (540 g) finely minced beef
2 tablespoons capers, rinsed and
   chopped

Salt and pepper to taste
3 oz (90 g) cooked beetroot,
   shredded

Reconstitute onion in water. Combine in mixing bowl with beef and capers. Mix well; season to taste. Shape into six patties and grill on rack or open grill 5 to 6 minutes each side, or until deep brown in colour. Top with beetroot and serve. Makes 3 servings.

Beetroot in Aspic

Make this in pretty individual moulds which could go on a smorgasbord table.

3 oz (90 g) canned beetroot, cut
   into thin strips (reserve 4 fl oz
   (120 ml) liquid)
1 oz (30 g) diced celery
Artificial sweetener to equal ½
   teaspoon sugar, or to taste
4 teaspoons lemon juice

2½ fl oz (75 ml) chicken stock
   made with ¼ stock cube
¼ teaspoon dried onion flakes
1½ teaspoons grated fresh horseradish
Pinch celery salt
1 tablespoon unflavoured gelatine
3 tablespoons water
White pepper to taste

Place beetroot (with liquid), celery, sweetener, lemon juice, stock and onion in a small mould. Add horseradish and celery salt. Sprinkle gelatine over cold water in small saucepan to soften. Dissolve over low heat; stir into beetroot with a wooden spoon, mixing thoroughly. Season to taste with white pepper. Set in refrigerator, chill for several hours, or until gelatine sets. Makes 1 serving.

Dilled Tuna Salad

Dill, a herb of biblical days, is a characteristic seasoning in Sweden.

1 tablespoon mayonnaise
1 teaspoon lemon juice
$\frac{1}{4}$ teaspoon dried dill
$\frac{1}{8}$ teaspoon celery seed

Pinch paprika
4 oz (120 g) drained, canned tuna, flaked
1 white roll, 1 oz (30 g)

Combine all ingredients, except tuna and roll, in a small bowl. Add tuna; mix and chill. Serve on roll. Makes 1 serving.

Danish Cucumber Salad

This is served as a first course or in little saucers as a relish for meat, chicken and fish. For a refreshing luncheon salad, yogurt could be served with the cucumber.

12 oz (360 g) cucumber
$1\frac{1}{2}$ teaspoons salt
2 tablespoons water
2 tablespoons lemon juice

1 tablespoon chopped fresh parsley or dill
Freshly ground pepper to taste

Peel and score cucumber and cut into thin slices. Sprinkle with salt and let stand 2 hours. Drain and rinse thoroughly. Combine remaining ingredients in jar, shake well and pour over cucumber. Let stand at least 30 minutes. Makes 2 to 4 servings.

Pineapple Breakfast

6 fl oz (180 ml) water
Pinch salt
1 oz (30 g) uncooked quick-cooking
  porridge oats

2 oz (60 g) canned crushed
  pineapple, no sugar added
$\frac{1}{4}$ teaspoon cinnamon
4 fl oz (120 ml) skim milk

Bring water and salt to the boil in small saucepan. Sprinkle in cereal, stirring. Cook and stir over moderate heat 30 seconds. Remove from heat, cover and let stand for 30 seconds. Stir pineapple and cinnamon into cooked cereal. Serve with skim milk. Makes 1 serving.

Norwegian Cardamom Cookies*

Follow recipe for Almond Cookies (see page 100–101) but add $\frac{1}{2}$ teaspoon ground or powdered cardamom to egg-milk-breadcrumb mixture before beating. Makes 2 servings.

THE SOUTH PACIFIC

*

Dreaming of an unspoiled South Sea island where enchanting natives wearing colourful sarongs dance a lively hula? Does Malaysia sound as remote and romantic as Paradise? Chances are good that the island of your dreams has an airport, modern hotels and a few hundred thousand tourists visiting each year. But don't let that stop you from enjoying an exciting part of the world, where the Stone Age meets the twentieth century. Along with the natives, you'll find Americans on Samoa, British on Fiji and Cook's Island, French in Tahiti, and the Japanese in Guam. On the Philippines are the Malay, Chinese, Spanish and Americans, too. Indonesia is Hindu-Buddhist as well as Colonial Dutch. So in our South Pacific chapter, a little sample of the dazzling variety of palate-tingling foods which you can find in this picturesque part of the world, awaits you—prepared in our easy-on-the waistline style.

Indonesian Thick 'Creamy' Vegetable Soup (Sajur Lodeh)

Seasoning options include 1 chopped garlic clove and a pinch of ground coriander.

1 pint 4 fl oz (720 ml) chicken stock, made with 1½ stock cubes
1 tablespoon dried pepper flakes
1 tablespoon dried onion flakes
1 bay leaf
8 oz (240 g) combined shredded cabbage, green beans and

cauliflower (or bean sprouts)
4 oz (120 g) grated carrots
6 oz (180 g) cooked fresh broad beans or 8 oz (240 g) cooked thin noodles
2 oz (60 g) nonfat dry milk, reconstituted with 8 fl oz (240 ml) water

Bring stock, pepper flakes, onion flakes and bay leaf to the boil in a saucepan. Add shredded cabbage, green beans, cauliflower and carrots, and simmer for 30 minutes. Stir in broad beans or noodles. Cook for 3 minutes. Add milk and heat gently for 2 minutes more; do not boil. Remove bay leaf. Serve hot. Makes 4 servings.

Filipino Fish Soup

6 oz (180 g) tomatoes, sliced ½-inch
  (1 cm) thick
12 oz (360 g) green peppers, cut into
  rings ¼-inch (5 mm) wide
4 oz (120 g) onion, cut in thin slices

1½ teaspoons salt
1 pint 4 fl oz (720 ml) water
1 lb 8 oz (720 g) fish, cut into
  1½-inch (4 cm) slices
5 tablespoons chopped watercress

Combine tomatoes, green peppers, onion, salt and water in saucepan, and bring to the boil. Add fish and cook 5 to 8 minutes, or until fish is tender. Add watercress, heat 1 minute and serve at once. Makes 4 servings.

Javanese Egg and Potato in Red Pepper Sauce*
(Sambal Goreng Telor)

3 oz (90 g) cooked potato, cut in
  thin pieces
1 oz (30 g) chopped onion
1 small garlic clove, crushed
¼ teaspoon crushed red pepper
¼ bay leaf

1 oz (30 g) tomato, diced
2 fl oz (60 ml) beef stock, made
  with ¼ stock cube
2 fl oz (60 ml) skim milk
1 hard-boiled egg, cut in half

Brown potato, onion and garlic in nonstick frying pan, turning on all sides. Add pepper, bay leaf, tomato and beef stock. Bring to the boil, stirring often. Add skim milk and egg, and continue simmering, stirring gently, for 3 minutes. Makes 1 serving.

Mullet in 'Coconut Milk' Tahiti

1 lb 2 oz (540 g) mullet or whiting
   fillets, sliced
8 fl oz (240 ml) skim milk

1 teaspoon coconut flavouring
½ teaspoon salt
Watercress for garnish

Place fish slices in pan with milk. Simmer until fish flakes, turning once very carefully. Stir in coconut flavouring and salt. Garnish with watercress. Serve hot. Makes 3 servings.

Filipino Dip for Lobster

Float pieces of garlic in a small bowl of wine vinegar and serve as a dipping sauce for boiled lobster or other shellfish.

Shrimp Salad

2½ oz (75 g) cottage cheese
1 teaspoon water
¼ teaspoon lemon juice
2 oz (60 g) cleaned cooked shrimps,
   thinly sliced

¼ medium apple, peeled and finely
   diced
1 tablespoon mayonnaise
¼ teaspoon curry powder
Lettuce leaves

Place cottage cheese, water and lemon juice in blender goblet. Blend until smooth. Combine all remaining ingredients except lettuce in a mixing bowl; add cheese mixture. Toss lightly. Chill thoroughly. Serve on a bed of lettuce. Makes 1 serving.

Filipino Beans, Shrimps and Spinach

1 pint (600 ml) water
3 oz (90 g) tomato, sliced
4 oz (120 g) onion, finely diced
1 small garlic clove, crushed
Salt and pepper or soy sauce to
    taste

12 oz (360 g) cleaned shrimps
4 oz (120 g) cooked fresh broad
    beans
2 oz (60 g) cleaned spinach

Combine water, tomato, onion, garlic, salt and pepper in saucepan.
Bring to the boil. Lower heat and simmer for 15 minutes. Add shrimps,
beans and the spinach and return to simmer for 5 to 8 minutes more or
until shrimps are pink and firm. Makes 2 servings.

Philippine Chicken and Veal Stew (Adobo)

A typical stew which blends Oriental and Western cuisines. It is said
that a Philippine dish requires garlic and bay leaf from Spain, pepper
from Malay, soy sauce from China, and vinegar to prove it's a native of
the Philippines.

6 oz (180 g) skinned and boned
    chicken breasts, cut into 1-inch
    (2.5 cm) pieces
6 oz (180 g) boned veal, cut into 1-inch
    (2.5 cm) pieces
3 tablespoons cider vinegar
2 tablespoons soy sauce

1½ garlic cloves, crushed
½ small bay leaf
4 crushed peppercorns
16 fl oz (480 ml) water
Pimiento to garnish
4 oz (120 g) cooked rice, sprinkled
    with chopped fresh parsley

Grill chicken and veal on rack close to source of heat. Turn once to
brown on all sides. Transfer to flameproof serving casserole with cider
vinegar, soy sauce, garlic, bay leaf and peppercorns. Let stand at least 1
hour, turning meat pieces several times. Add water to cover meat.
Cover casserole and let simmer very slowly for 1 to 1½ hours. At the
end of the cooking process there should be very little sauce left in pan.
If necessary, remove lid and let simmer until liquid reduces. Remove
bay leaf. Garnish with pimiento. Serve each portion over 2 oz (60 g)
rice. Makes 2 servings.

Indonesian Curried Rice with Chicken (Nasi Goreng)

Indonesia, that great chain of islands between Malaysia and Australia, is a blend of many religions and peoples—Buddhists, Hindus, Malays, Arabs, Chinese and Dutch—and its famous national dish salutes this diversity.

4 oz (120 g) cooked chicken, cut into thin strips
4 oz (120 g) cleaned cooked shrimps, cut into pieces
6 fl oz (180 ml) chicken stock, made with ½ stock cube or Homemade Chicken Stock (see page 10)
2 garlic cloves, crushed
2½ teaspoons curry powder

Salt to taste
Pinch cayenne pepper
8 oz (240 g) cooked rice
4 oz (120 g) chopped spring onions
Shredded Egg Pancakes (recipe follows)
6 oz (180 g) cucumber or pickled cucumber, chilled, peeled and cut into strips

Marinate chicken and shrimps in separate bowls, each containing 2 fl oz (60 ml) chicken stock, 1 garlic clove, ¼ teaspoon curry powder, salt and cayenne, for at last 1 hour. Drain. Discard marinade. Pour remaining stock into a large heated nonstick frying pan or wok. Add chicken, shrimps, rice, 3 oz (90 g) spring onions, remaining curry powder, salt and cayenne; stir frequently until all ingredients are thoroughly heated through. Pour Nasi Goreng into warmed individual dishes. Sprinkle ½ oz (15 g) spring onions on each serving; add 1 serving of pancakes to each serving. Serve with cucumber or pickled cucumber strips. Makes 4 servings.

Shredded Egg Pancakes

4 eggs
1 tablespoon soy sauce

Freshly ground pepper to taste

Combine eggs, soy sauce and pepper, and beat well to make a thin batter; pour through a strainer to make the batter an even consistency. Pour one eighth of the batter into heated nonstick frying pan, swirling to coat pan. Cook until set on one side, turn and cook briefly on other side. Continue in this way until all batter is used (makes 8 pancakes). For each serving slice two pancakes into thin shreds. Serve with Nasi Goreng. Makes 4 servings.

Beef and Peppers, Manila Style

Serve over a bed of fluffy rice. For Nasi Kuning (yellow rice) cook the rice with a bay leaf and ½ teaspoon turmeric.

1 lb 8 oz (720 g) lean beef topside,
   cut ½-inch (1 cm) thick
1 tablespoon paprika
2 garlic cloves, crushed
12 fl oz (360 ml) beef stock, made
   with 1 stock cube

4 oz (120 g) sliced spring onions,
   including tops
12 oz (360 g) green peppers, cut in
   strips
2 fl oz (60 ml) soy sauce
6 oz (180 g) tomatoes, cut in thin
   wedges

Pound steak to ¼-inch (5 mm) thickness. Cut into ¼-inch (5 mm) wide strips. Sprinkle meat with paprika and set aside while preparing other ingredients. Brown beef on rack under grill, turning once. Combine meat in saucepan with garlic and stock. Cover and simmer 30 minutes. Stir in spring onions and green peppers. Cover and cook 5 minutes more. Stir in soy sauce. Cook about 2 minutes. Add tomatoes and stir gently. Makes 4 servings.

Sweet and Sour Pork Philippine Island

6 oz (180 g) lean boneless pork loin
4 fl oz (120 ml) chicken stock,
   made with ¼ stock cube
1½ oz (45 g) green pepper, diced
Pinch garlic powder
4 oz (120 g) canned crushed
   pineapple, no sugar added
Artificial sweetener to equal ½

teaspoon sugar, or to taste
1 tablespoon cider vinegar
2 oz (60 g) cooked rice
3 oz (90 g) tomato, cut into 6
   wedges
Salt to taste
½ teaspoon chopped fresh parsley

Grill pork 4 inches (10 cm) from source of heat 5 minutes on each side. Remove; cool; cut into 1-inch (2.5 cm) cubes. Place in a nonstick frying pan with stock, pepper and garlic. Simmer, stirring, until liquid has reduced to half its volume. Add pineapple, sweetener and vinegar. Fold in rice and tomato. Season to taste. Heat thoroughly over low heat, stirring gently, until liquid is absorbed. Sprinkle with parsley. Makes 1 serving.

Chicken Liver Samoa

12 oz (360 g) chicken livers
6 oz (180 g) green pepper, diced
4 oz (120 g) canned crushed
  pineapple, no sugar added

2½ fl oz (75 ml) soy sauce
1 tablespoon dried onion flakes
1 tablespoon prepared mustard

Cook chicken livers and green pepper in large nonstick frying pan; divide evenly into two small casseroles. Combine pineapple, soy sauce, onion flakes and mustard. Pour evenly over chicken livers. Bake at 350°F (180°C), Gas Mark 4 for 20 minutes. Makes 2 servings.

Bean Sprout, Celery and Apple Salad

8 oz (240 g) bean sprouts (see note)
4 oz (120 g) chopped celery
1 medium red apple, diced
1 tablespoon chopped chives
1 tablespoon chopped fresh parsley
2 lettuce leaves
1 tablespoon soy sauce

2 teaspoons lemon juice
Pinch dry mustard
¼ teaspoon chopped fresh ginger
  root
Artificial sweetener to equal 1
  teaspoon sugar, or to taste
Salt and pepper to taste

Combine bean sprouts, celery, apples, chives and parsley. Divide onto two lettuce leaves. Mix remaining ingredients and serve over salad. Makes 2 servings.

   Note: If you use canned bean sprouts, rinse in colander under cold water and drain well; if fresh bean sprouts, parboil first by covering with boiling water and cooking for 2 to 3 minutes. Drain well.

Peppery Hot Vegetable Dish

2 oz (60 g) onion, chopped
6 oz (180 g) peeled potatoes, cut in
1-inch (2.5 cm) dice
6 oz (180 g) peeled aubergine, cut in
1-inch (2.5 cm) dice
$\frac{1}{2}$ teaspoon salt
$\frac{1}{2}$ teaspoon dry mustard

$\frac{1}{8}$ teaspoon turmeric
$\frac{1}{8}$ teaspoon ginger
$\frac{1}{2}$ dried red chilli pepper, seeds
removed or $\frac{1}{2}$ teaspoon cayenne
pepper or to taste
10 fl oz (300 ml) water

Brown onions in nonstick pan. Add potatoes, aubergine, salt, mustard, turmeric, ginger and chilli pepper or cayenne. Lightly brown on all sides in hot frying pan, turning constantly. Add water, cover pan and cook until vegetables are tender and no liquid is left. Makes 2 servings.

Vegetable Salad-Stew Fiji Islands

You can drink it or eat it with a spoon. It's a warm-climate soupy salad, not unlike Spanish gazpacho, but this one shows the strong Hindu influence in Fiji, where more than 50 percent of the population originally came from India.

6 oz (180 g) tomatoes, peeled and
diced
4 oz (120 g) onion, chopped
4 tablespoons fresh coriander leaves
or parsley
1 teaspoon freshly chopped hot green

chilli pepper
$\frac{1}{4}$ teaspoon dry mustard
$\frac{1}{4}$ teaspoon ground cumin
Salt to taste
6 fl oz (180 ml) buttermilk

Place first seven ingredients in a large mixing bowl. Pour buttermilk over and stir to combine. Serve cold. Makes 2 servings.

Skewered Bananas with Dipping Sauce

At your next barbecue, skewer peeled medium bananas on bamboo skewers and barbecue (or grill) on all sides, turning as necessary. Allow $\frac{1}{2}$ banana per serving. Good with Dipping Sauce (recipe follows).

Dipping Sauce

2 small fresh hot red peppers, finely chopped or $\frac{1}{2}$ dried hot red chilli pepper (seeds removed) or $\frac{1}{2}$ teaspoon cayenne pepper or to taste

2 fl oz (60 ml) cider vinegar or lemon juice
1 teaspoon dried pepper flakes

Chop peppers and mix with vinegar or lemon juice and pepper flakes. Serve as a dip with bananas, pineapples or other fruits.

Balinese Fruit Salad

1 medium apple, peeled and grated
1 small pear, grated
6 oz (180 g) cucumber, peeled, seeded and grated
2 oz (60 g) grated carrot

1 tablespoon cider vinegar
1 teaspoon salt
1 teaspoon crushed red pepper
Dash coconut flavouring

Combine apple, pear, cucumber and carrot in bowl. Mix remaining ingredients and pour over fruits and vegetables. Refrigerate for at least 2 hours. Serve cold. Makes 4 servings.

Tahitian Pineapple-Coconut Mousse

2 tablespoons unflavoured gelatine
12 fl oz (360 ml) water
3 oz (90 g) nonfat dry milk, reconstituted with 12 fl oz (360 ml) water
$\frac{1}{2}$ teaspoon rum flavouring

$\frac{1}{2}$ teaspoon coconut flavouring
$\frac{1}{4}$ teaspoon vanilla flavouring
Artificial sweetener to equal 2 teaspoons sugar, or to taste
12 oz (360 g) canned crushed pineapple, no sugar added

Sprinkle gelatine over 8 fl oz (240 ml) water in a medium saucepan; heat, stirring until gelatine is dissolved. Pour gelatine mixture into blender goblet; add remaining water, milk, flavourings and sweetener. Blend at low speed until smooth. Add pineapple; blend at medium speed until smooth. Pour into a medium mould. Chill. Turn out. Makes 6 servings.

Coffee Jelly

1 tablespoon unflavoured gelatine
16 fl oz (480 ml) cooled coffee

Artificial sweetener to equal 2
teaspoons sugar, or to taste

Sprinkle gelatine over 4 fl oz (120 ml) coffee in small saucepan; stir over low heat until gelatine dissolves. Add remaining coffee and artificial sweetener. Pour into medium bowl; cover. Chill until firm. Makes 4 servings.

SPAIN

Sol y sombra—sunlight and shadow, simplicity and complexity—these are the elusive elements of Spanish culture. In the Gothic cathedrals and shaded Moorish mosques, the arched silent courtyards surrounding bubbling fountains, the romantic tracery of black iron against whitewashed stucco walls, lies the enchantment of Spain, a country where different forces of history, the European and the Arabic, met and fused in the eighth century.

Our Spanish chapter has recipes from some of the fifty provinces encompassed in the country. Each recipe has a typical and traditional Spanish flavour but has been modified to fit our Food Programme. Once you've sampled these dishes, you'll see why everyone is an *aficionado* of tempting Spanish cuisine.

Garlic Soup

3 pints (1 litre 750 ml) boiling water
16 garlic cloves, crushed
2 cloves
¼ teaspoon sage
¼ teaspoon thyme

Pinch cayenne pepper
Salt and pepper to taste
6 slices stale white bread, toasted and cubed
1 tablespoon chopped fresh parsley

Place water, garlic, cloves, sage, thyme, cayenne, salt and pepper in large saucepan. Bring mixture to the boil, lower heat, cover and simmer for 1 hour. Carefully add bread cubes, allowing them to become saturated, but remaining whole. Remove cloves before serving. Divide evenly into 6 soup bowls. Garnish each portion with ½ teaspoon parsley. Makes 6 servings.

Variation: After simmering for 1 hour, add 6 beaten eggs, pouring slowly and stirring constantly. Continue simmering until eggs are just set. Makes 6 servings.

Malaga Gazpacho

9 oz (270 g) ripe tomatoes, peeled and coarsely chopped

12 oz (360 g) cucumbers, peeled and coarsely chopped

6 oz (180 g) green pepper, seeded and coarsely chopped

4 fl oz (120 ml) water

2 fl oz (60 ml) wine vinegar, or to taste

3 tablespoons vegetable oil

1 garlic clove, crushed

Salt to taste

3 slices white bread, cubed

Chopped fresh parsley or chives

Combine first 8 ingredients in blender goblet. Blend at medium speed until smooth. Increase speed to high and add bread, a few cubes at a time, blending after each addition. Stir down with rubber spatula if necessary. Chill soup thoroughly. Garnish with parsley or chives before serving. Makes 6 servings.

Seville Gazpacho*

Omit bread from preceding recipe. Instead, add 1 diced hard-boiled egg to each bowl before serving. Makes 6 servings.

Hearty Bean and Vegetable Soup (Caldo Gallego)

16 fl oz (480 ml) beef stock, made with 1 stock cube

12 oz (360 g) cooked dried white beans

4 oz (120 g) boneless cooked beef, cut in strips

3 oz (90 g) boneless cooked ham, cut in strips

4 oz (120 g) peeled and cubed turnips

3 oz (90 g) tomato, peeled, seeded and quartered

6 oz (180 g) cabbage, shredded

2 tablespoons dried onion flakes

1 garlic clove, peeled and crushed

Salt and freshly ground pepper to taste

Combine all ingredients in a medium saucepan and bring to the boil. Cover and simmer gently until turnips are tender, 15 to 20 minutes. Divide evenly and serve. Makes 4 servings.

Cod Stewed with Aubergine (Merluza con Berenjenas)

6 oz (180 g) aubergine, cut into
  cubes
6 oz (180 g) green pepper, cut into
  small pieces
2 oz (60 g) onion, cut into small
  pieces
4 × 6 oz (180 g) cod steaks

8 fl oz (240 ml) water
2 oz (60 g) sliced celery
1½ teaspoons wine vinegar
½ garlic clove
Salt, pepper and paprika to taste
1 tablespoon chopped capers, rinsed

Place aubergine, green pepper and onion in a heated nonstick frying pan, turning often until the water from the aubergine evaporates. Put in cod steaks. Add water, celery, vinegar, garlic, salt, pepper and paprika. Simmer until fish is done. Sprinkle with capers. Serve hot. Makes 4 servings.

Baked Red Snapper with Potatoes

6 oz (180 g) red snapper fillets
Pinch each salt, cayenne pepper and
  paprika
3 oz (90 g) cooked potato, sliced
1 oz (30 g) chopped celery

3 oz (90 g) tomato, chopped
2 oz (60 g) onion, chopped
4 fl oz (120 ml) chicken stock,
  made with ¼ stock cube
½ teaspoon chopped fresh parsley

Season fish with salt, cayenne and paprika. Make a layer of potato slices and celery in a shallow casserole. Add fish. Top with tomato and onion. Pour in stock. Cover with aluminium foil. Bake in hot oven (400°F (200°C), Gas Mark 6) for 30 minutes. Garnish with parsley. Makes 1 serving.

Eggs with Tomato Topping (Tortilla de Tomate)

4 oz (120 g) chopped onion
6 oz (180 g) green pepper, chopped
Beef stock, prepared according to
    package directions
4 tablespoons tomato purée
7 fl oz (210 ml) water

1 teaspoon salt
1 teaspoon chilli powder
8 eggs
4 fl oz (120 ml) skim milk
Pinch pepper

To prepare topping, cook onion and green pepper in stock to cover, until they are soft. Stir in tomato purée, water, ½ teaspoon salt and chilli powder. Bring to the boil; then simmer, uncovered, about 10 to 15 minutes, stirring occasionally. Meanwhile, prepare omelette. Beat eggs, milk, remaining ½ teaspoon salt and pepper. Pour into heated large, nonstick frying pan and cook over low heat. As bottom of eggs set, loosen and lift edge with spatula, tilting pan to let uncooked portion run underneath. Continue lifting and tilting procedure until omelette is almost dry on top. Loosen omelette with spatula; fold or roll and tilt out onto warm serving plate. Serve immediately with hot topping. Makes 4 servings.

Octopus Stew (Cazuela de Pulpo)

⅛ teaspoon saffron or turmeric
4 fl oz (120 ml) boiling water
4 oz (120 g) onion, thinly sliced
6 oz (180 g) green pepper, chopped
12 oz (360 g) cleaned baby octopus
    cut into bite-size pieces
6 oz (180 g) tomatoes, sliced
1 tablespoon white wine vinegar
4 tablespoons chopped fresh parsley

1 garlic clove, crushed
½ bay leaf
½ teaspoon paprika
¼ teaspoon thyme
Salt and freshly ground pepper to
    taste
12 oz (360 g) cleaned shrimps
8 oz (240 g) cooked rice

Place saffron in a small bowl and add water. Let stand for at least 1 hour. If using turmeric, add with octopus, tomatoes, etc. Cook onion and green pepper in a large nonstick saucepan, stirring frequently until onion starts to brown. Add octopus, tomatoes, vinegar, parsley, garlic, bay leaf, paprika, thyme, salt and pepper. Cook uncovered 10 minutes. Cover and cook 10 minutes longer. Add shrimps. Cook uncovered 5 minutes longer or until shrimps are cooked. Do not overcook. Divide evenly into 4 portions. Serve each over 2 oz (60 g) rice. Makes 4 servings.

Perch Fillets Bay of Biscay

12 oz (360 g) perch fillets
Salt and freshly ground pepper to
 taste
2 oz (60 g) onion, finely chopped
4 tablespoons chopped fresh parsley
1 garlic clove, crushed
$\frac{1}{2}$ teaspoon thyme

3 oz (90 g) tomato, peeled and
 chopped
1 bay leaf
4 fl oz (120 ml) Fish Stock (see
 page 11)
4 fl oz (120 ml) water
2 tablespoons tomato purée
3 lemon slices

Sprinkle fish with salt and pepper and place in a shallow nonstick baking dish. Combine onion, parsley, garlic and thyme in a large nonstick frying pan. Cook, stirring occasionally, until onion becomes tender. Add tomato and bay leaf; continue to cook and stir until well blended. Mix in Fish Stock, water and tomato purée and simmer for 5 minutes. Remove from heat and pour over fish. Garnish with lemon slices and bake in moderate oven (350°F (180°C), Gas Mark 4) for 30 minutes, basting occasionally. Makes 2 servings.

Baked Fish with Mushrooms, Galicia (Pescado con Champiñones)

2 oz (60 g) thinly sliced onion
1 tablespoon chopped pimiento
4 fl oz (120 ml) onion stock, made
 with $\frac{1}{4}$ stock cube
12 oz (360 g) bass fillets, cut in 1-inch
 (2.5 cm) strips
$\frac{1}{2}$ teaspoon salt

Pinch pepper
Dash hot pepper sauce
Pinch nutmeg
3 oz (90 g) tomato, peeled and sliced
$1\frac{1}{2}$ teaspoons chopped chives
3 oz (90 g) thinly sliced mushrooms
2 tablespoons white vinegar

Layer onion slices evenly in baking dish. Sprinkle chopped pimiento over onion. Pour stock over onion and pimiento. Add fish strips.

Combine salt, pepper, hot pepper sauce and nutmeg; sprinkle on fish. Add tomatoes; sprinkle with chives and top with mushrooms. Pour vinegar over mushrooms. Cover dish tightly. Marinate 1 hour. Bake in hot oven (450°F (230°C), Gas Mark 8) 20 minutes or until fish flakes easily with fork. Makes 2 servings.

Fish Vinaigrette (Pescado a la Vinagreta)

1 lb (480 g) cooked fish fillets
(haddock or flounder), cut in
cubes
6 oz (180 g) cucumber, seeded and
sliced into cubes
2 tablespoons chopped fresh parsley
1 tablespoon dried onion flakes,
reconstituted

1 tablespoon chopped capers
1 garlic clove, crushed
2 tablespoons vegetable oil
2 tablespoons wine vinegar
Salt and pepper to taste
6 oz (180 g) tomatoes, peeled,
seeded and diced

Arrange fish in large bowl; add cucumber, parsley, onion flakes, capers and garlic. Sprinkle with oil and vinegar; season with salt and pepper. Toss gently to avoid breaking fish. Cover bowl and marinate in refrigerator about 2 hours. Add diced tomatoes and toss gently. Serve cold. Makes 4 servings.

Shrimps with Saffron

1 lb 8 oz (720 g) large cleaned shrimps
6 tablespoons lemon juice
$\frac{1}{4}$ teaspoon saffron or turmeric
3 parsley sprigs, finely chopped
1 garlic clove, crushed
1 teaspoon finely chopped fresh

thyme or $\frac{1}{2}$ teaspoon dried
$\frac{1}{2}$ bay leaf, crumbled
Salt and freshly ground pepper to
taste
4 teaspoons margarine

Dry shrimps and place in a bowl. Add lemon juice and saffron. Combine chopped parsley, garlic, thyme, bay leaf, salt and pepper. Add to shrimps and stir until they are well coated with the mixture. Remove shrimps from marinade, reserving liquid. Place on a baking sheet and grill about 4 inches (10 cm) from heat 4 to 5 minutes; turn once, continue grilling 1 to 2 minutes or until shrimps are cooked through. Do not overcook, as they will toughen. Heat marinade. Remove from heat and stir in margarine until it melts. Divide shrimps evenly into 4 portions. Pour one quarter of the sauce over each portion. Makes 4 servings.

Paella

15 oz (450 g) canned or fresh
   tomatoes, chopped
6 oz (180 g) onion, diced
6 oz (180 g) green pepper, diced
3 oz (90 g) frozen artichoke hearts,
   slightly thawed
1 tablespoon chopped capers, rinsed
1 garlic clove, crushed
$\frac{1}{4}$ teaspoon paprika
$\frac{1}{4}$ teaspoon thyme
$\frac{1}{8}$ teaspoon cinnamon
$\frac{1}{8}$ teaspoon saffron or turmeric

Salt and freshly ground pepper to
   taste
1 lb 2 oz (540 g) skinned and boned
   chicken breasts, cut into bite-size
   pieces
1 lb 2 oz (540 g) cleaned
   shrimps
12 oz (360 g) cooked rice, prepared
   in chicken stock
2 pimientos, chopped
Dash hot pepper sauce
3 oz (90 g) frozen peas

Combine tomatoes, onion, green pepper, artichoke hearts, capers, garlic, paprika, thyme, cinnamon, saffron, salt and pepper in paella pan or large shallow flameproof pan with lid. Cover and simmer for 15 minutes or until vegetables are tender. Remove lid and add chicken. Simmer 10 minutes, add shrimps; cook 3 minutes longer. Stir in rice, pimientos and hot pepper sauce. Top with peas and cook just long enough to heat peas. Makes 6 servings.

Chicken Valencia Style (Arroz con Pollo a la Valenciana)

6 oz (180 g) diced, skinned and boned chicken breast

8 fl oz (240 ml) chicken stock, made with ½ stock cube or 8 fl oz (240 ml) Homemade Chicken Stock (see page 10)

3 oz (90 g) canned or fresh tomato, cut in pieces

2 teaspoons dried onion flakes

¼ teaspoon garlic powder or ½ garlic clove, crushed

¼ teaspoon chilli powder or cayenne pepper to taste

2 threads saffron or pinch of turmeric

2 oz (60 g) peas

3 oz (90 g) cooked rice

Combine first 7 ingredients in a saucepan and simmer, uncovered, approximately 20 minutes or until mixture is reduced by about half. Stir in peas and cook 5 minutes. Add rice. Heat well but do not boil. Makes 1 serving.

Chicken Flamenco

4 × 6 oz (180 g) skinned and boned chicken breasts

Salt and pepper to taste

4 oz (120 g) onion, chopped

2 oz (60 g) celery, diced

6 oz (180 g) green pepper, seeded and diced

1 garlic clove, crushed

12 fl oz (360 ml) chicken stock, made with 1 stock cube

6 oz (180 g) mushrooms, sliced

1 tablespoon pimiento, cut in pieces

Season chicken with salt and pepper and brown in nonstick frying pan. Transfer to medium casserole. Add onion, celery, green pepper and garlic to pan and cook, stirring, for about 5 minutes or until tender-crisp. Spoon over chicken. Bring stock to the boil in a small saucepan and pour over chicken and vegetables. Cover casserole and bake in moderately slow oven (325°F (160°C), Gas Mark 3) 30 to 45 minutes or until chicken is tender. Meanwhile cook mushrooms in a hot nonstick frying pan for about 5 minutes. Shortly before chicken is done add mushrooms and pimiento to casserole. Return casserole to oven to finish baking. Makes 4 servings.

Saffron Beef

Roast top rump of beef on a rack in moderate oven (325°F (160°C), Gas Mark 3) until done. Cut as directed (see ingredients below), reserving natural juices extracted from meat during cutting.

1 lb (480 g) onions, thinly sliced
1 garlic clove, crushed
1 lb (480 g) cooked top rump of
   beef, cut into 1½-inch (4 cm)
   cubes
16 teaspoons tomato purée
4 fl oz (120 ml) water
Beef juices (see above)

10½ oz (315 g) tomatoes, peeled and
   diced
3 oz (90 g) green pepper, cut into
   1-inch (2.5 cm) squares
1 tablespoon loosely packed saffron
   or 2 teaspoons turmeric
½ teaspoon chopped fresh thyme or
   ¼ teaspoon dried
Salt and pepper to taste

Cook onions and garlic in a large flameproof casserole at moderately high heat, stirring constantly, until onions are wilted, about 5 minutes. Add remaining ingredients. Bring to the boil, stirring to combine. Cover and bake in moderately slow oven (325°F (160°C), Gas Mark 3) for 2 hours or until meat is tender. Makes 4 servings.

Spanish Meatballs (Albóndigas)

1 lb 8 oz (720 g) minced beef
1 tablespoon chopped fresh parsley
½ teaspoon salt
¼ teaspoon white pepper
⅛ teaspoon nutmeg
4 oz (120 g) chopped onion

12 fl oz (360 ml) beef stock, made
   with 1 stock cube
12 oz (360 g) tiny peas
6 oz (180 g) tomatoes, chopped
4 pimientos, diced
1 teaspoon brandy flavouring
½ teaspoon garlic powder

Combine minced beef, parsley, salt, white pepper and nutmeg; mix well; shape into meatballs about 1½ inches (4 cm) in diameter. Bake on rack in pan at 350°F (180°C), Gas Mark 4 for 15 minutes or until cooked right through. Turn once during baking. Cook onion in 4 fl oz (120 ml) of stock in saucepan over low heat for 5 minutes or until onions are just tender. Add peas, tomatoes, pimientos, flavouring, remaining stock, garlic powder and baked meatballs. Stir to combine. Simmer 5 to 7 minutes or until peas are done. Makes 4 servings.

Spanish Shredded Beef

1 lb 8 oz (720 g) cooked flank
  steak
4 oz (120 g) cubed, peeled turnip
4 oz (120 g) scraped carrot, sliced
3 oz (90 g) leeks, washed well and
  chopped
Water
6 oz (180 g) onion, chopped
6 oz (180 g) green pepper, seeded
  and chopped
$\frac{1}{2}$ fresh hot chilli pepper, seeded and
  chopped, or to taste

1 garlic clove, crushed
6 oz (180 g) tomatoes, peeled and
  chopped
1 bay leaf
$\frac{1}{8}$ teaspoon cinnamon
$\frac{1}{8}$ teaspoon ground cloves
Salt and freshly ground pepper to
  taste
2 pimientos, chopped
1 tablespoon chopped capers
  (optional)

Bring beef, turnips, carrots and leeks to the boil in a large saucepan in water to cover. Lower heat, cover pan and simmer gently until tender, about 1$\frac{1}{2}$ hours. Allow to cool sufficiently to handle. Remove meat from liquid; reserve liquid. Shred meat with fingers. Return meat to liquid, reserving 2 fl oz (60 ml) for later use. Cook onions, green pepper, chilli pepper and garlic in 2 fl oz (60 ml) reserved liquid in a covered saucepan until tender. Remove lid, add tomatoes, bay leaf, cinnamon, cloves, salt and pepper. Cook, stirring occasionally, until sauce is thickened and flavours are well blended. Remove bay leaf. Combine with remaining liquid and meat. Add pimientos and simmer 5 minutes longer. Add capers, if desired, and stir to blend. Makes 6 servings.

Spanish Stew (Cocido Madrileño)

12 oz (360 g) boneless stewing beef, cut
in cubes
1 pint 4 fl oz (720 ml) water
6 oz (180 g) green pepper, diced
4 oz (120 g) diced, peeled turnips
6 oz (180 g) cored cabbage, cut in
2 wedges
4 oz (120 g) onion, diced

$1\frac{1}{2}$ oz (45 g) sliced mushrooms
1 oz (30 g) diced celery
2 teaspoons beef stock powder
$\frac{1}{2}$ garlic clove, crushed
4 oz (120 g) cooked fresh broad
beans
Salt and pepper to taste

Cover beef with water, bring to the boil and cook until beef is tender, about 1 hour. Remove beef and refrigerate stock and beef separately. When fat congeals on stock, skim to remove and discard fat. Transfer 12 fl oz (360 ml) fat-free stock to saucepan. Add green pepper, turnips, cabbage, onion, mushrooms and celery. Add stock powder and garlic and simmer over low heat until vegetables are tender, about 40 minutes. Add beef and broad beans and season to taste. Reheat for 15 minutes. Makes 2 servings.

Lamb Kebabs la Mancha

The Moors invaded Spain from the South more than a thousand years ago. Arabic culinary traditions have strong roots here, including kebab cookery.

2 tablespoons lemon juice
1 teaspoon orange flavouring
$\frac{1}{2}$ teaspoon salt
$\frac{1}{4}$ teaspoon cumin
Pinch oregano

12 oz (360 g) boneless, lean lamb
cubes
3 oz (90 g) mushrooms
3 oz (90 g) green pepper, sliced
$1\frac{1}{2}$ oz (45 g) tomato, sliced

Combine lemon juice, orange flavouring, salt, cumin and oregano. Pour over lamb in bowl; toss lightly until well mixed. Let stand at room temperature 1 hour. On each of 2 skewers spear half the lamb, mushrooms, pepper and tomato in that order. Grill on a rack about 4 inches (10 cm) from source of heat for 10 minutes or until lamb is grilled to taste. Turn once during cooking. Makes 2 servings.

'Marinated' Pork with Pimiento

In Spain the midday siesta, which precedes the long and late dinner, provides plenty of time for 'marinating' the pork.

2 large or 3 small garlic cloves, crushed
1 teaspoon salt, preferably coarse
$\frac{1}{2}$ teaspoon freshly ground black pepper
1 lb (480 g) cooked boneless pork loin, cut in $\frac{1}{4}$-inch (5 mm) thick slices

12 oz (360 g) canned pimientos or 1 lb 8 oz (720 g) red peppers, seeded and cut into $\frac{1}{2}$-inch (1 cm) strips
12 fl oz (360 ml) chicken stock, made with 1 stock cube
1 lemon, cut into 6 wedges

With a mortar and pestle or back of a large spoon, mash garlic, salt and pepper together to form a smooth paste. Lightly spread pork slices with the paste, place them in a bowl, cover tightly and let stand for several hours or overnight in refrigerator. Brown pork slices, a few at a time, in a large nonstick frying pan and transfer to a plate. Add the pimientos to pan, stirring frequently; cook for 5 minutes or until most of the moisture is evaporated. Transfer pork to pan; add stock; cover tightly; reduce heat to low and simmer for 45 minutes or until pork is tender and shows no resistance when pierced with a fork. Remove pork and pimientos from pan, reserving liquid. Divide onto 4 individual plates. Liquid can be poured over each serving, if desired. Garnish with lemon wedges. Makes 4 servings.

Pork Español

1 lb (480 g) cooked pork, cut in strips $\frac{1}{2}$-inch (1 cm) wide
2 tablespoons cider vinegar
1 garlic clove, crushed
1 tablespoon dried onion flakes
$\frac{1}{2}$ teaspoon freshly ground pepper

$\frac{1}{2}$ bay leaf
Salt to taste
6 oz (180 g) canned tomatoes, chopped
8 oz (240 g) cooked rice

Combine pork, vinegar, garlic, onion flakes, pepper, bay leaf and salt in a large mixing bowl. Mix well to coat pork. Let stand 1 hour or longer. Combine meat and marinade with tomato and rice. Spoon into a medium casserole. Bake covered in moderate oven (350°F (180°C), Gas Mark 4) until heated through, about 30 minutes. Remove bay leaf. Makes 4 servings.

Garlic-Marinated Carrots

2 tablespoons wine or cider vinegar
1 tablespoon vegetable oil
1 garlic clove, crushed
Freshly ground pepper to taste

Oregano to taste
10 oz (300 g) thinly sliced boiled
  carrots

Combine first 5 ingredients to form a marinade. Add carrots; stir to coat with mixture. Let stand in refrigerator at least one day. Makes 2 servings.

Broad Beans with Cheese

2 oz (60 g) chopped onion
6 oz (180 g) green pepper, chopped
4 fl oz (120 ml) beef stock, made
  with $\frac{1}{4}$ stock cube
8 teaspoons tomato purée
2 fl oz (60 ml) water

$\frac{1}{2}$ teaspoon Worcester sauce
$\frac{1}{4}$ teaspoon salt
$\frac{1}{8}$ teaspoon cayenne pepper
6 oz (180 g) cooked broad beans
4 oz (120 g) grated Cheddar cheese

Cook onion and green pepper in stock over low heat 5 minutes or until onion is just tender. Add tomato purée and water; simmer 5 minutes. Stir in Worcester sauce, salt and cayenne pepper. Spoon half the cooked beans in an even layer in baking dish. Spoon half the grated cheese in an even layer over beans. Spoon half the vegetable-tomato purée mixture over cheese. Repeat layers with remaining beans, cheese and tomato purée mixture. Bake at 350°F (180°C), Gas Mark 4 for 15 minutes. Makes 2 servings.

Cucumbers with Orange Sauce (Cohombros con Salsa de Naranja)

1 lb 8 oz (720 g) cucumbers	¼ teaspoon salt
2 tablespoons concentrated frozen orange juice	⅛ teaspoon freshly ground pepper
1 tablespoon grated orange rind	4 teaspoons margarine

Peel cucumbers. Cut a thin slice off both ends. Score lengthwise with a fork on all sides and cut cucumbers in ½-inch (1 cm) slices. Cover slices with water and cook covered for 15 minutes. Drain cucumbers and set aside. Combine concentrated orange juice and rind, salt and pepper; heat, and add to cooked cucumber slices. Stir in margarine. Serve as a vegetable. Makes 4 servings.

Potatoes with String Beans (Patatas con Judías Verdes)

1 oz (30 g) onion, finely chopped	3 oz (90 g) peeled cooked potatoes, thinly sliced
8 fl oz (240 ml) chicken stock, made with ½ stock cube	5 oz (150 g) cooked string beans
¼ bay leaf	Salt and pepper to taste
¼ garlic clove	Garnish: 2 strips pimiento and parsley sprigs
Pinch ground cloves	

Lightly brown onion in nonstick frying pan. Add chicken stock, bay leaf, garlic and cloves. Simmer 10 minutes. Discard bay leaf and garlic. Layer potatoes over beans in pan with stock and simmer covered until well heated. Season to taste. Garnish with pimiento and parsley. Makes 1 serving.

Peppery Mushrooms (Champiñones Picante)

The seasoned mushrooms may be baked in the oven until they are crisp and crackly, if you prefer.

1 lb (480 g) mushrooms
3 small dried chilli peppers, chopped,
   or ½ teaspoon ground red pepper

2½ fl oz (75 ml) chicken stock,
   made with ¼ stock cube
Salt to taste

Wipe mushrooms clean. Slice them through stems and caps and brown in nonstick frying pan over moderate heat; add chopped chilli peppers and cook with mushrooms, stirring often. Pour in chicken stock and salt to taste. Simmer uncovered, 3 to 4 minutes, and serve hot. Makes 8 appetizer servings.

Valencian Rice (Arroz con Legumbres)

6 oz (180 g) tomatoes, peeled and
   cubed
5 oz (150 g) courgette, cut in small
   cubes
8 oz (240 g) cooked rice, prepared
   in onion stock

Salt and freshly ground pepper to
   taste
4 oz (120 g) cooked peas
2 tablespoons chopped pimiento
Dash hot pepper sauce

Cook tomatoes and courgette in nonstick pan on top of the stove, stirring, until most of the liquid evaporates. Transfer mixture to a medium casserole. Combine with rice and season with salt and pepper. Cover casserole and bake at 350°F (180°C), Gas Mark 4, for about 20 minutes or until heated through. Remove from oven, add peas, pimiento and hot pepper sauce, tossing to mix thoroughly. Makes 4 servings.

Variation: Omit tomatoes; combine rice with 16 fl oz (480 ml) tomato juice in casserole.

Widow's Rice (Arroz Viuda)

It's a dish that lives without meat, hence alone or widowed.

2 oz (60 g) onion, chopped
2 fl oz (60 ml) onion stock, made
  with ¼ stock cube
4 oz (120 g) cooked rice
10 teaspoons tomato purée
2½ fl oz (75 ml) water

1½ teaspoons chopped pimiento
1 teaspoon dried pepper flakes
½ teaspoon Worcester sauce
½ teaspoon seasoned salt
Pinch each pepper and garlic powder

Cook onion in stock over low heat in frying pan, 4 minutes or until just tender. Add rice, purée, water, pimiento, dried pepper flakes, Worcester sauce, salt, pepper and garlic powder; mix well. Cook over low heat 5 minutes or until heated through. Makes 2 servings.

Rice Salad (Ensalada de Arroz a la Valenciana)

8 oz (240 g) cooked rice, steaming
  hot
½ teaspoon sherry flavouring
12 oz (360 g) green peppers, seeded
  and cut in quarters
1 tablespoon dry mustard

1 teaspoon water
2 fl oz (60 ml) vegetable oil
2 fl oz (60 ml) wine vinegar
¼ teaspoon pepper
Salt to taste

Combine rice and sherry flavouring and let rice cool. Prepare peppers as directed in Ensalada a la Andaluza (see page 327). Moisten mustard with water to make a paste, in a large bowl; add oil, vinegar, pepper and salt. Mix to combine for a dressing. Stir in diced peppers and cooled rice. Marinate, refrigerated, at least 30 minutes. Makes 4 servings.

Tuna Fish and Bean Salad Basque Style

4 oz (120 g) drained, canned tuna
2 oz (60 g) cooked green beans
2 oz (60 g) canned wax beans
1 oz (30 g) celery, diced
2 tablespoons cider vinegar

1 tablespoon vegetable oil
½ garlic clove, crushed
Pinch each cumin, cloves, salt and
  pepper

Combine all ingredients in salad bowl and chill before serving. Makes 1 serving.

Black Bean Salad

4 oz (120 g) diced onion
1 lb 8 oz (720 g) green peppers, seeded and chopped
2 garlic cloves, crushed
1 lb 8 oz (720 g) cooked dried black beans
8 fl oz (240 ml) beef stock, made with ½ stock cube

Pinch oregano
Dash brandy flavouring
2 fl oz (60 ml) vegetable oil
2 fl oz (60 ml) wine vinegar
¾ teaspoon prepared mustard
Salt and freshly ground pepper to taste

Lightly brown onion, green pepper and garlic in heated nonstick saucepan. Add the beans, stock, oregano and brandy flavouring. Simmer for 45 minutes. Let cool. Combine oil, wine vinegar, mustard, salt and pepper. Pour over beans. Chill until ready to serve. Makes 4 servings.

Mixed Vegetable Salad (Ensalada a la Andaluza)

2 fl oz (60 ml) vegetable oil
2 fl oz (60 ml) wine vinegar
¼ teaspoon pepper
12 oz (360 g) cucumber, peeled, seeded and diced
Salt to taste
2 lbs 4 oz (1 kg 80 g) green peppers,

seeded and cut in quarters
6 oz (180 g) tomatoes, peeled, seeded and diced
½ garlic clove (optional)
1 tablespoon dried onion flakes, reconstituted

Mix oil, vinegar and pepper for a dressing; set aside. Place diced cucumber in bowl; sprinkle with salt and let stand 20 minutes. Liquid will accumulate. Drain and dry on paper towels. Remove to small bowl and toss with half the dressing. Grill peppers 4 inches (10 cm) from source of heat until skin browns and puckers, about 15 minutes. Watch carefully. Skin will look burnt when peppers are ready. Peel skin and dice peppers. Place in small bowl; sprinkle with salt and let stand 15 minutes. Place tomatoes in separate bowl, sprinkle with salt and let stand for 15 minutes also. Drain peppers and toss with remaining dressing. Drain tomatoes. Rub salad bowl with garlic if desired. Add cucumbers to green peppers and their dressing. Add tomatoes and onion flakes; toss lightly and chill. Makes 8 servings.

Banana Custard (Flan de Plátano)*

1 fully ripe medium banana, peeled,
  diced
Pinch cinnamon

Artificial sweetener to taste
2 eggs, beaten
8 fl oz (240 ml) skim milk

Spoon banana into two small ovenproof basins or a small baking dish. Sprinkle each with cinnamon. Combine sweetener and eggs in a mixing bowl. Heat milk in a saucepan (*do not boil*). Pour a little into eggs and mix well. Add egg mixture to remaining milk in saucepan, stirring constantly. Dividing evenly, pour over banana. Place basins or baking dish in a pan of hot water and bake in moderately hot oven (375°F (190°C), Gas Mark 5) 20 to 25 minutes or until set. Refrigerate. Serve cold. Makes 2 servings.

Almond-Flavoured Fruit Mould

$\frac{1}{2}$ medium pear
$\frac{1}{2}$ medium apple
2 canned pineapple slices, with 2
  tablespoons juice, no sugar added
1 tablespoon unflavoured gelatine

3 fl oz (90 ml) water
8 fl oz (240 ml) orange juice
Artificial sweetener to equal 1
  teaspoon sugar, or to taste
$\frac{1}{4}$ teaspoon almond flavouring

Core, peel and cut fruit into small cubes and place in a mould. Soften gelatine in water, juices and sweetener in a small saucepan. Heat to dissolve gelatine; remove from stove and add almond flavouring. Mix well. Pour liquid over fruit in mould and refrigerate. Makes 4 servings.

Citrus 'Rum' Drink

4 fl oz (120 ml) chilled orange juice
6 fl oz (180 ml) chilled low-calorie
  carbonated lemonade

$\frac{1}{2}$ teaspoon rum flavouring
Lemon or lime slice (to garnish)

Combine orange juice, lemonade and rum flavouring in glass. Garnish with lemon or lime slice. Makes 1 serving.

SWITZERLAND

*

Swiss cuisine is a hybrid, a blend of varied cultures that makes one delightful and unified whole. In three cantons—French, German and Italian—foods appropriate to their separate origins are served. Of course, in this health-conscious country the dairy products and green vegetables are very popular, and most Swiss restaurants feature salads and vegetables, raw as well as cooked. So do we.

The Swiss love desserts. So do we. We've satisfied everybody's craving for an authentic dessert to end the Swiss meal by including recipes for plum tart and a Rhubarb Meringue Pie. Or why not serve a tray of Gruyère or Emmenthal cheese and ripe fresh fruits, just as they do in Switzerland?

Bean Soup Basel Style

3 oz (90 g) cooked fresh broad beans, reserve cooking liquid
16 fl oz (480 ml) chicken stock, made with 1 stock cube
2 oz (60 g) finely chopped carrot
1 oz (30 g) chopped celery
1½ oz (45 g) green pepper, finely chopped
1 oz (30 g) chopped onion
Pinch basil
Pinch thyme
½ oz (15 g) nonfat dry milk reconstituted with 2½ fl oz (75 ml) water
Salt and pepper to taste

Place beans (with liquid) and stock in blender goblet. Blend until smooth. Pour into saucepan; add carrot, celery, pepper, onion and herbs. Simmer 20 minutes or until vegetables are tender. Add milk; reheat (do not boil). Season to taste and serve. Makes 1 serving.

Cheese Soufflé Lucerne

For mittagessen (lunch) try a cheese soufflé like this, with a dish of raw vegetables.

4 fl oz (120 ml) skim milk	1 slice white bread, made into
1 egg, separated	crumbs
1 oz (30 g) Emmenthal or Gruyère	$\frac{1}{8}$ teaspoon salt
cheese, grated	Pinch each paprika and nutmeg

Combine milk, egg yolk, cheese and breadcrumbs in a saucepan. Season with salt, paprika and nutmeg. Place over low heat. Cook and stir until mixture is slightly thickened. Set aside. Cool. Beat egg white with rotary beater until peaks form; fold into mixture. Pour into small ovenproof dish. Bake in moderately hot oven (375°F (190°C), Gas Mark 5) for 25 to 30 minutes. Makes 1 serving.

Caraway Bread Sticks

2 tablespoons margarine	1 teaspoon coarse salt
4 slices wholemeal bread	$\frac{1}{2}$ teaspoon caraway seeds

Spread $1\frac{1}{2}$ teaspoons margarine on one side of each bread slice. Sprinkle with seasonings. Place on nonstick baking sheet margarine-side up. Bake in hot oven (400°F (200°C), Gas Mark 6) for 10 minutes or until toasted. Cut toast slices in thirds. Makes 4 servings.

Veal and Cabbage Bake Zurich

2 oz (60 g) cabbage leaves	$\frac{1}{4}$ teaspoon salt
6 fl oz (180 ml) tomato juice	4 oz (120 g) cooked minced veal,
$\frac{1}{2}$ teaspoon nutmeg	crumbled
$\frac{1}{2}$ teaspoon dry mustard	

Cover cabbage leaves with water and bring to the boil. Cook until leaves become limp, but do not shred. Combine tomato juice, nutmeg, dry mustard and salt in a small bowl. Set aside. In an individual oven-proof casserole or serving dish, layer half the cabbage leaves, veal and tomato juice mixture. Repeat layers. Bake in moderate oven (350°F (180°C), Gas Mark 4) 15 minutes or until completely heated through. Makes 1 serving.

Swiss Steak Lugano

You'll find this kind of meat dish in the Italian canton, served with cooked pasta.

6 oz (180 g) boneless shoulder steak, ½-inch (1 cm) thick	1 oz (30 g) diced celery
8 fl oz (240 ml) tomato juice	2 oz (60 g) onion, sliced
8 fl oz (240 ml) beef stock, made with ½ stock cube	½ bay leaf
3 oz (90 g) tomato, sliced	Pinch garlic powder
	Salt and pepper to taste

Preheat grill. Place steak on rack under grill 4 inches (10 cm) from heat. Cook 3 to 4 minutes on each side until brown. Transfer to small saucepan. Add remaining ingredients; season to taste. Simmer over low heat for 30 minutes or until vegetables are cooked and sauce thickens. Makes 1 serving.

Pan-Brown Potatoes

2½ fl oz (75 ml) water	⅛ teaspoon tarragon
1 teaspoon onion stock powder	⅛ teaspoon salt
¼ teaspoon dried onion flakes	Pinch paprika
¼ teaspoon caraway seeds	6 oz (180 g) peeled cooked potato, sliced

Heat water to boiling in nonstick pan; add all remaining ingredients except potatoes; cover and cook 2 minutes. Add potatoes, cook over medium heat until liquid has evaporated. Makes 2 servings.

Dill Boiled Potatoes

2 lbs 4 oz (1 kg 80 g) new potatoes   1 tablespoon chopped fresh dill
1 teaspoon salt

Place unpeeled potatoes, water to cover and salt in a large saucepan; cover and boil slowly for about 30 minutes or until tender. Drain and peel. Sprinkle with dill. Serve hot. Makes 12 servings.

Spring Salad Bowl with Buttermilk Dressing

1 lb (480 g) iceberg lettuce, shredded   12 parsley sprigs or watercress
4 oz (120 g) watercress   6 Batavianendive leaves
8 radishes, thinly sliced   Buttermilk Dressing (recipe follows)
3 oz (90 g) celery, diced

Toss all the ingredients, except the endive, together in a large salad bowl. Arrange the endive leaves round the mixture. Serve with Buttermilk Dressing. Makes 6 servings.

Buttermilk Dressing

6 fl oz (180 ml) buttermilk   ¼ teaspoon dill seed
3 tablespoons mayonnaise   1 teaspoon chopped fresh parsley
1 teaspoon lemon juice   Salt and pepper to taste
½ teaspoon dried onion flakes

Combine all ingredients except salt and pepper in a mixing bowl. Mix well with hand whisk or fork until smooth. Season to taste. Divide into 6 portions and serve with Spring Salad Bowl. Makes 6 servings.

Stuffed Tomatoes

6 tomatoes, 3 oz (90 g) each
3 tart medium apples, peeled and
    grated
12 oz (360 g) diced celery
2 fl oz (60 ml) lemon juice

$\frac{1}{2}$ teaspoon salt
3 tablespoons vegetable oil
1 tablespoon chives or watercress,
    chopped

Cut a thin slice off top of each tomato; peel and remove seeds and pulp
(reserve pulp) leaving a thick shell. Turn tomatoes upside down to
drain. Combine apples, celery, lemon juice and salt with tomato pulp.
Let stand 20 to 30 minutes. Add oil; mix well. Use filling for tomatoes.
Top with chives or watercress. Makes 6 servings.

Rhubarb Meringue Pie*

9 oz (270 g) rhubarb, sliced
2 egg yolks, beaten
2 slices white bread, made into
    crumbs

Artificial sweetener to equal 4
    tablespoons sugar, or to taste
$\frac{1}{2}$ teaspoon grated lemon rind
Meringue (recipe follows)

Mix rhubarb, egg yolks, breadcrumbs, sweetener and lemon rind in a
bowl. Pour into 8 or 9-inch (20 or 23 cm) pie tin. Bake in preheated
moderately slow oven (325°F (160°C), Gas Mark 3) for 40 minutes or
until rhubarb is very tender. Remove from oven and top with
meringue. Bake an additional 15 to 20 minutes or until meringue
browns. Cool. Makes 2 servings.

Meringue

2 egg whites
Artificial sweetener to equal 2
    tablespoons sugar, or to taste

$\frac{1}{4}$ teaspoon vanilla flavouring
Pinch salt

Beat egg whites until stiff but not dry. Add remaining ingredients. Beat
to combine. Use with Rhubarb Meringue Pie. Makes 2 servings.

Plum Crumb Tart (Pflaumentorte)

¾ oz (20 g) uncooked quick-cooking
  porridge oats, prepared according
  to package directions
Artificial sweetener to equal 1
  tablespoon sugar, or to taste

2 medium plums, peeled, stoned and
  sliced
½ teaspoon lemon juice
1 tablespoon low fat spread

Combine porridge oats and sweetener; stir. Layer plum slices in bottom of a small casserole. Sprinkle with lemon juice. Spoon cooked oat mixture evenly over plum slices. Dot with low fat spread. Bake in moderately hot oven (375°F (190°C), Gas Mark 5) for 30 to 40 minutes or until plums are tender. Makes 1 serving.

Note: Serve with 5 fl oz (150 ml) skim milk.

THE UNITED STATES

*

America has been described as a 'melting pot' of races and cultures, and this mixed ancestry is reflected in a regional cuisine enriched by recipes handed down by immigrant families over the years. We've added dishes based on local specialities, too, which tended to stay more 'local' and build up a reputation before modern travel facilities made them available to everybody.

In this coast-to-coast coverage we've come up with dishes as varied as Californian Caesar Salad, Philadelphia Pepper Pot and Oyster Jambalaya. We've not forgotten American dessert specialities such as Chocolate Layer Cake and Apricot Brown Betty, and you can still enjoy delicious Black Bottom Cheesecake while following the Programme!

Broad Bean and Vegetable Soup

3 oz (90 g) cooked fresh broad beans
16 fl oz (480 ml) chicken stock,
    made with 1 stock cube
3 oz (90 g) diced carrots
2 oz (60 g) diced celery
½ teaspoon dried onion flakes
1½ oz (45 g) green pepper, diced
Pinch basil
Pinch thyme
½ oz (15 g) nonfat dry milk,
    reconstituted with 2½ fl oz
    (75 ml) water
Salt and pepper to taste

Place half the broad beans and stock in blender goblet; blend until mixture is liquified. Pour into a saucepan; add carrots, celery, onion flakes, green pepper and remaining stock. Bring to the boil: add basil and thyme. Simmer for 20 minutes or until carrots are tender. Add milk and remaining broad beans; reheat. Season to taste. Makes 1 serving.

Chicken Okra Soup with Rice

To spike up the flavour, add ½ teaspoon finely chopped fresh hot chilli pepper or hot pepper sauce to taste.

8 oz (240 g) okra
8 oz (240 g) cooked rice
6 oz (180 g) tomatoes, peeled,
    seeded and chopped

1 pint 12 fl oz (960 ml) chicken
    stock, made with 2 stock cubes
¼ teaspoon allspice
Salt and pepper to taste

Wash okra well with a brush to remove surface fuzz, slice and cook in boiling water until just tender. Rinse in colander. Combine cooked okra, rice, tomatoes, stock, allspice, salt and pepper in a saucepan. Simmer, covered, 10 to 15 minutes; stir well and serve hot. Makes 4 servings.

Philadelphia Pepper Pot

1 lb (480 g) precooked
    honeycomb tripe, cut into ¼-inch
    (5 mm) pieces
2 tablespoons dried onion flakes
1 pint 4 fl oz (720 ml) chicken
    stock, made with 1½ stock
    cubes
8 oz (240 g) diced celery
6 oz (180 g) sliced carrots

3 tablespoons chopped fresh parsley
2 teaspoons mixed dried herbs:
    marjoram, basil, summer savory,
    thyme
Dash hot pepper sauce or pinch
    cayenne pepper
2 cloves
4 × 3 oz (90 g) cooked and peeled
    potatoes

Wash and scrub tripe thoroughly. Cover generously with cold salted water, using about 1 teaspoon salt. Bring to the boil and simmer until tripe is tender, about 1½ to 2 hours. Add more water if necessary as tripe must be immersed as it cooks. Drain tripe. Combine tripe with remaining ingredients in saucepan. Cover and cook for 45 minutes. Serve hot. Makes 4 servings.

Philadelphia Pepper Pot with Veal

Use only 8 oz (240 g) of the tripe. Cook as directed above. Add 8 oz (240 g) cooked diced veal left from a roast or inexpensive cut, to saucepan, and follow preceding recipe. Makes 4 servings.

Haricot Bean Soup

A hearty soup, a favourite in the United States Senate restaurant.

3 oz (90 g) cooked dried haricot
  beans, drained, reserving liquid
1 oz (30 g) diced celery
1½ oz (45 g) diced cooked carrot
1 oz (30 g) chopped onion

¼ teaspoon garlic powder
¼ small bay leaf
1½ oz (45 g) boneless cooked ham,
  finely diced
Salt, pepper and ground cloves to
  taste

Combine liquid from cooked beans and enough water to make 12 fl oz (360 ml) in a medium saucepan. Add celery, carrot, onion, garlic and bay leaf. Simmer 15 minutes or until vegetables are tender. Remove bay leaf. Add beans and ham. Heat through. Season with salt, pepper and cloves to taste. Makes 1 serving.

Manhattan Fish Chowder

Chowder is from the French chaudière, the pot in which fish soup is made.

12 oz (360 g) cod or haddock fillets
  (or combination), fresh or frozen
  and defrosted
1 pint 5 fl oz (750 ml) boiling water
6 oz (180 g) peeled potatoes, diced
1½ oz (45 g) diced carrot
2 oz (60 g) chopped celery
2 oz (60 g) chopped onion

6 oz (180 g) tomatoes
4 teaspoons tomato purée
2 teaspoons Worcester sauce
¾ teaspoon salt
¼ teaspoon pepper
¼ teaspoon thyme
Chopped fresh parsley for garnish

Cut fish into 1-inch (2.5 cm) pieces and refrigerate. Combine water, potatoes, carrot, celery, onion, tomatoes, tomato purée and seasonings, except parsley, in saucepan. Cover and simmer for 40 to 45 minutes or until vegetables are tender. Add fish. Cover and simmer about 10 minutes longer or until fish is done. Sprinkle with parsley. Serve hot. Makes 2 servings.

Red Snapper Chowder, Florida Style

1 red snapper, about 2 lbs (960 g), cut in 4 large pieces
4 oz (120 g) onion, sliced
12 tablespoons tomato purée
6 fl oz (180 ml) water

12 oz (360 g) green peppers, finely diced
4 oz (120 g) chopped celery
1 garlic clove, crushed
Few drops hot pepper sauce or small hot pepper pod

Cover fish with water; cook until it is tender. Remove and discard skin and bones and flake fish. Return 1 lb (480 g) of flaked fish to water in which it was boiled. Add everything but the hot pepper sauce. Cook until vegetables are tender. Stir in hot pepper sauce. Serve in bowls. Makes 4 servings.

Variation: Make chowder above, adding ½ teaspoon thyme and a bay leaf. Other fish could replace the red snapper. Makes 4 servings.

Gloucester Mussel Chowder

16 fl oz (480 ml) water
12 oz (360 g) peeled potatoes, cubed
16 fl oz (480 ml) Fish Stock (see page 11)
8 oz (240 g) diced celery
2 tablespoons dried onion flakes
1 garlic clove
1 bay leaf

1 teaspoon chopped fresh parsley
1 lb (480 g) drained canned mussels, minced
2 oz (60 g) nonfat dry milk, reconstituted with 10 fl oz (300 ml) water
Salt, freshly ground pepper and paprika to taste

Combine 16 fl oz (480 ml) water, potatoes, Fish Stock, celery, onion flakes, garlic, bay leaf and parsley in saucepan. Bring to the boil, then simmer until potatoes are tender. Remove bay leaf. Put through strainer (or purée in blender in two batches), making certain to press everything through. Put back into saucepan with mussels; add milk and heat well without boiling. Add salt, pepper and dusting of paprika. Makes 4 servings.

Quick Crab Cioppino Fisherman's Wharf

4 oz (120 g) onion, chopped
2 garlic cloves, crushed
8 tablespoons tomato purée
6 fl oz (180 ml) water
8 fl oz (240 ml) Fish Stock (see page 11)
12 oz (360 g) tomatoes, sliced
3 tablespoons chopped fresh parsley
2 tablespoons chopped fresh basil or 1 teaspoon dried

12 oz (360 g) cleaned shrimps
4 oz (120 g) drained canned crab meat, flaked
4 oz (120 g) drained canned mussels
Salt and freshly ground pepper to taste
1 tablespoon sherry flavouring
Chopped fresh parsley for garnish

Cook onion and garlic in a nonstick pan for a few minutes or until onion is tender-crisp, stirring occasionally to prevent sticking. Add tomato purée, water, Fish Stock, tomatoes, parsley and basil. Cover and simmer for 30 minutes. Add shrimps and cook 5 minutes or until they are pink. Add crabmeat, mussels, salt and freshly ground pepper. Heat but do not boil. Stir in sherry flavouring. Divide into 4 bowls, sprinkling each portion with parsley. Makes 4 servings.

Pennsylvania Dutch Pickled Eggs and Beetroot*

16 fl oz (480 ml) wine vinegar
Beetroot liquid and water to equal 4 fl oz (120 ml)
Artificial sweetener to equal 1 tablespoon sugar, or to taste
Small piece cinnamon stick

2 cloves
Pinch of allspice
2 hard-boiled eggs, shelled
4 oz (120 g) diced cooked beetroot (reserve liquid)
Lettuce

Combine vinegar, beetroot liquid and water, sweetener, cinnamon, cloves and allspice in saucepan. Bring to the boil, then simmer for 10 minutes. Pour into wide jar. Add eggs and beetroot. Refrigerate two days before use. Serve on bed of lettuce. Makes 2 servings.

Aubergine and Cornmeal Soufflé

8 fl oz (240 ml) skim milk
¾ oz (20 g) uncooked cornmeal
3 oz (90 g) cooked aubergine, puréed
4 teaspoons tomato purée
2 tablespoons water

½ teaspoon salt
¼ teaspoon oregano
¼ teaspoon basil
Pinch pepper or to taste
2 eggs, separated

Pour milk into saucepan; sprinkle in cornmeal, stirring with wooden spoon. Simmer 10 minutes or until mixture thickens. Remove from heat; add aubergine, tomato purée, water, salt, oregano, basil and pepper; cool. Add egg yolks and mix well. Beat egg whites until stiff peaks form; fold into mixture. Pour mixture into nonstick baking dish and bake at 400°F (200°C), Gas Mark 6 for 15 minutes, then lower temperature to 325°F (160°C), Gas Mark 3, and bake an additional 20 minutes or until top crust is golden brown. Serve immediately. Makes 1 serving.

Cheese Strata

1 slice white bread
1 oz (30 g) sliced Cheddar cheese
1 oz (30 g) nonfat dry milk,
   reconstituted with 5 fl oz (150 ml)
   water
1 egg

¼ teaspoon dried onion flakes
¼ teaspoon prepared mustard
¼ teaspoon salt
Dash Worcester sauce
Dash hot pepper sauce

Cut bread into two slices by slicing in half, horizontally. Place one slice of halved bread on the bottom of a 6 or 7-inch (15 or 18 cm) heatproof shallow baking dish; place cheese on bread; top with remaining bread slice. Beat together remaining ingredients; pour over layers of bread and cheese. Bake 40 to 50 minutes at 325°F (160°C), Gas Mark 3 or until puffy and golden brown. Makes 1 serving.

Corn Pones

Corn pones are often served to accompany fish dishes. Serve them piping hot from the oven, along with icy cold buttermilk straight from the fridge.

3 oz (90 g) uncooked cornmeal
¼ teaspoon salt
2 teaspoons baking powder

4 teaspoons margarine
4 fl oz (120 ml) boiling water

Combine cornmeal, salt and baking powder in medium bowl. Add margarine and boiling water. Stir until margarine melts. Cool just enough to handle. Divide mixture into four equal portions. Shape each portion into an oval by patting between your hands. Bake on nonstick baking sheet at 350°F (180°C), Gas Mark 4 for 1 hour. Makes 4 servings.

Indian Corn Pudding with 'Cream' Topping*

8 fl oz (240 ml) skim milk
¾ oz (20 g) uncooked cornmeal
Artificial sweetener to equal 1
   tablespoon sugar, or to taste
Pinch each cinnamon, nutmeg
   allspice, ginger and cloves
1 egg, well beaten

½ oz (15 g) nonfat dry milk,
   reconstituted with 2½ fl oz
   (75 ml) water, chilled
Artificial sweetener to taste
½ teaspoon grated lemon rind
   (optional)

Bring milk to the boil in a small saucepan; add cornmeal gradually, beating with wire whisk. When mixture starts to thicken, set aside to cool. When mixture is almost cool, stir in sweetener, spices and egg. Pour into a small nonstick baking dish and bake at 325°F (160°C), Gas Mark 3, for 1 hour. Make topping: combine milk, sweetener and lemon rind, if desired. Whip with rotary beater for 10 minutes or until foamy. Serve immediately on top of hot pudding. Makes 1 serving.

Lost Bread* Pain Perdu (French Toast, Creole Style)

Many New Orleanians prefer it this way—serve with a wedge of lemon to be squeezed onto the toast at table. One serving may be easily baked in a toaster-oven, or the recipe may be multiplied for family service. To make this a classically Creole breakfast, serve it with café au lait. For one serving combine 4 fl oz (120 ml) each of steaming hot coffee and scalded skim milk.

2 fl oz (60 ml) skim milk	1 slice white bread
⅛ teaspoon vanilla or brandy flavouring	1 egg, separated
	Pinch grated lemon rind

Combine milk and flavouring in a shallow plate or pie plate. Soak bread in mixture, turning once, until bread absorbs all the liquid. Beat egg yolk lightly with lemon rind in a small mixing bowl. Beat egg white until stiff in a separate mixing bowl. Fold into yolk mixture. Place soaked bread on a nonstick baking sheet. Cover bread with egg mixture. Bake at 350°F (180°C), Gas Mark 4 for 25 to 30 minutes or until egg becomes golden brown. Makes 1 serving.

Rock Salmon Poor Boy

4 × 6 oz (180 g) rock salmon fillets	½ teaspoon dried onion flakes
Salt and pepper to taste	2 dashes hot pepper sauce
8 teaspoons tomato purée	4 slices white bread, toasted
2 fl oz (60 ml) water	6 oz (180 g) pickled cucumber,
1 teaspoon prepared mustard	thinly sliced

Place fish fillets in grill pan; season with salt and pepper. Grill about 4 inches (10 cm) from heat until fish flakes easily with touch of fork; set aside. Combine tomato purée, water, mustard, onion flakes and hot pepper sauce in a saucepan; simmer for about 10 minutes until thickened. Spread over toast; cover each slice of toast with a fillet and top each with 1½ oz (45 g) sliced pickled cucumber. Makes 4 servings.

Baked Mackerel

1 × 8 oz (240 g) mackerel, cleaned
    and split
6 fl oz (180 ml) chicken stock,
    made with ½ stock cube
1 lemon slice

2 oz (60 g) onion, thinly sliced
Salt and pepper to taste
Paprika
Dash hot pepper sauce
1 tablespoon margarine

Place fish in small baking dish. Add stock and lemon. Place onion slices on top of fish, then sprinkle with salt, pepper, paprika and hot pepper sauce. Cover with aluminium foil. Bake in hot oven (400°F (200°C), Gas Mark 6) for about 15 minutes or until fish flakes easily with touch of fork. Remove fish and onion with slotted spatula; place onion on serving plate. Drain excess liquid from baking dish and return fish to dish. Pierce fish lightly; spread with margarine and return to oven for 30 seconds until margarine melts. Makes 1 serving.

Native Granola

3 oz (90 g) uncooked porridge oats
2 teaspoons poppy seeds
¼ teaspoon cinnamon
⅛ teaspoon allspice
⅛ teaspoon nutmeg
⅛ teaspoon salt
1 medium apple, peeled, cored,
    finely chopped

2 oz (60 g) nonfat dry milk
2 tablespoons unflavoured gelatine
4 fl oz (120 ml) boiling water
4 teaspoons margarine
¼ teaspoon vanilla flavouring
¼ teaspoon coconut flavouring

Combine oats, poppy seeds, cinnamon, allspice, nutmeg, salt and apple and spread evenly on a rectangular nonstick shallow baking tin. Bake at 250°F (120°C), Gas Mark ½, for 45 minutes. Remove from oven; grill 2 inches (5 cm) from heat source until golden brown. Remove from grill; mix in milk and gelatine. Combine water, margarine and flavouring in a measuring jug; stir until margarine melts. Pour over oatmeal mixture, stirring quickly with a fork to combine. Mixture will be lumpy. Cool. Makes 4 servings.

Note: May be served in cereal bowl with additional boiling water.

Key Lime Fish Medley (Dinner in a Dish)

1 lb 8 oz (720 g) skinless fish fillets,
fresh or frozen and thawed (use
flounder, mullet, sole, etc.)

Vegetable Bed

1 lb (480 g) cooked vegetables
(asparagus, bean sprouts, broccoli,
cauliflower, aubergine, kale,
mushrooms, well-drained spinach
or courgettes), see note
2 teaspoons dried onion flakes

2 teaspoons dried pepper flakes
1 teaspoon salt
Pinch pepper
2 fl oz (60 ml) fresh lime juice
12 oz (360 g) tomatoes, thickly
sliced

Topping

4 tablespoons margarine
1 tablespoon chopped fresh parsley
$\frac{1}{2}$ teaspoon salt

$\frac{1}{4}$ teaspoon pepper
8 oz (240 g) cooked rice

Use a large shallow baking dish, oven-to-table type. Make a bed of the vegetables (which should be cut into fairly uniform pieces. Sprinkle onion and pepper flakes on top. Cut fish into 2-inch (5 cm) squares and arrange on the vegetable bed. Season with salt, pepper and lime juice and refrigerate for at least 30 minutes. When ready to use, put slices of tomato on top of fish, mash together all ingredients for topping, except rice, and dot over the tomatoes and fish. Bake in moderately hot oven (375°F (190°C), Gas Mark 5) for about 20 minutes or until fish flakes and tomatoes are tender. Serve each portion of fish with pan juices over 2 oz (60 g) fluffed cooked rice. Makes 4 servings.

Note: Don't put the liquid left from cooking vegetables down the drain! Leftover liquid may be cooked down to about 4 fl oz (120 ml) and poured over fish before it is baked. Or use the liquid for reheating cold rice. Or combine leftover liquid with chicken stock for a first-course soup.

Fish Grilled in Foil with Vegetables

You can bake these bundles on a baking sheet in a hot oven, allowing same timing. Other vegetables could be substituted.

For each serving:

1 × 6 oz (180 g) fish fillet, fresh preferred (thawed if frozen)
1 × 14-inch (35 cm) square heavy duty aluminium foil
1 × 3 oz (90 g) peeled potato, partially cooked (about 10 minutes), sliced
2 oz (60 g) frozen small onions, defrosted

2 oz (60 g) celery, cut in thin strips and partly cooked (about 5 minutes)
1 × 3 oz (90 g) tomato, in 3 slices
Salt, pepper and paprika to taste
Optional seasoning: Ground ginger, garlic, Worcester sauce, lemon juice and hot pepper sauce

Cut fish into 1-inch (2.5 cm) chunks and place on aluminium foil sheet. Add potato, onion, celery and tomato slices. Sprinkle with salt, pepper and paprika and add optional seasonings to taste. Wrap packet with a double fold on top and at the ends, making the packet as flat as possible. Be sure coals are ash-grey, then put packet on grill and cook 20 to 25 minutes, turning at least once. Makes 1 serving.

Prepare Ahead Note: For serving a larger quantity, prepare the packets several hours ahead, refrigerate until ready to use.

Hexel

Hash in the Pennsylvania Dutch style.

4 oz (120 g) diced onion
1 small garlic clove, finely chopped
1 lb (480 g) cold cooked fish, in large flakes
12 oz (360 g) peeled cooked potatoes, diced

4 oz (120 g) diced cooked beetroot
2 fl oz (60 ml) vinegar
½ teaspoon salt
¼ teaspoon pepper or to taste
12 oz (360 g) pickled cucumbers

Brown onion and garlic in large nonstick pan. Add all remaining ingredients except pickled cucumbers. Mix well; cover and let cook slowly to heat thoroughly and blend flavours, stirring as needed. Serve hot and well browned with sliced pickled cucumbers. Makes 4 servings.

Baked Stuffed Red Snapper

2 × 6 oz (180 g) red snapper fillets   Salt and pepper to taste
1 teaspoon lemon juice   Stuffing (recipe follows)

Place one fillet on nonstick baking tin. Heap stuffing on fillet. Top with remaining fillet. Sprinkle fish with lemon juice, salt and pepper. Bake in preheated moderately hot oven (375°F (190°C), Gas Mark 5) for 25 to 30 minutes or until fish flakes. Makes 2 servings.

Stuffing

2 oz (60 g) finely chopped celery   ½ teaspoon rubbed sage
1 tablespoon dried onion flakes   ½ teaspoon butter flavouring
3 oz (90 g) mushrooms, chopped   2 slices fresh white bread, made into
4 fl oz (120 ml) chicken stock   crumbs
   made with ¼ stock cube   Salt and pepper to taste
1 tablespoon chopped fresh parsley

Cover celery and onion flakes with water in a saucepan, and cook until celery is tender. Drain and combine celery and onion flakes with remaining ingredients; season to taste and mix well. Fill red snapper fillets. Makes 2 servings.

Tuna and Potato Casserole

12 oz (360 g) cooked potatoes, sliced (see note)

1 lb (480 g) drained canned tuna, flaked

4 fl oz (120 ml) potato liquid

4 fl oz (120 ml) chicken stock, made with ¼ stock cube

8 teaspoons tomato purée

2 fl oz (60 ml) water

1 oz (30 g) nonfat dry milk, reconstituted with 5 fl oz (150 ml) water

2 teaspoons chopped fresh parsley

Place 3 oz (90 g) of potato slices in each of 4 individual ovenproof casseroles. Top each with 4 oz (120 g) tuna. Combine potato liquid and stock in a medium saucepan. Stir in tomato purée and water. Bring to the boil. Simmer for 15 minutes. Stir in milk. Beat the sauce smooth with a wire whisk, or pour into blender goblet and blend. Divide evenly and pour into casseroles. Sprinkle with parsley and bake at 400°F (200°C), Gas Mark 6 for 20 minutes. Makes 4 servings.

Note: To prepare potatoes, place them in a medium saucepan with 16 fl oz (480 ml) water, 2 teaspoons dried onion flakes, 1 teaspoon salt and 1 garlic clove, crushed; bring to the boil and cook until potatoes are tender. Remove potatoes from liquid and weigh portions for use in recipe. Reserve 4 fl oz (120 ml) potato liquid.

Sarasota Kedgeree

6 fl oz (180 ml) chicken stock, made with ½ stock cube

2 oz (60 g) cooked rice

1 hard-boiled egg, sliced

2 oz (60 g) cooked cold flaked fish

1 teaspoon margarine (optional)

Heat stock in small saucepan; add rice, egg slices and fish. Bring to the boil; transfer to serving bowl and stir in margarine, if desired. Makes 1 serving.

Shrimp de Jonghe

Developed by a Chicago-American restaurateur and still served in homes and restaurants throughout the United States.

2 fl oz (60 ml) vegetable oil
2 slices white bread, made into fine
  dry bread crumbs
3 tablespoons chopped fresh parsley
1 tablespoon crushed garlic
¾ teaspoon salt

¼ teaspoon paprika
Pinch cayenne pepper or few drops
  hot pepper sauce
1 teaspoon coconut flavouring
1 lb 8 oz (720 g) cleaned shrimps

Combine oil, breadcrumbs (reserve 2 tablespoons), chopped parsley, crushed garlic, salt, paprika, cayenne and coconut flavouring. Toss shrimps lightly in mixture until shrimps are well coated. Mix well. Turn into shallow pan. Sprinkle reserved breadcrumbs on top. Bake uncovered, in moderately hot oven (375°F (190°C), Gas Mark 5) until shrimps are tender, about 40 minutes. Makes 4 servings.

Oyster Jambalaya

1 oz (30 g) chopped celery
2 oz (60 g) finely chopped onion
3 oz (90 g) tomato, diced
4 fl oz (120 ml) Fish Stock (see
  page 11)
⅛ teaspoon salt
½ small garlic clove, crushed

Pinch cayenne or black pepper or
  dash hot pepper sauce
Pinch each thyme and ginger
Pinch each ground coriander and
  fennel
4 oz (120 g) drained canned oysters
2 oz (60 g) cooked rice

Cook celery and onion in nonstick pan. When softened, add tomato, Fish Stock, salt, garlic, cayenne and other seasonings. Cook for 20 minutes. Add oysters and rice. Let simmer gently, uncovered, until fairly dry. Mix well and serve hot. Makes 1 serving.

Bayou Shrimp-Stuffed Peppers

2 × 6 oz (180 g) green peppers
2 oz (60 g) cooked rice
4 oz (120 g) cleaned cooked tiny
  shrimps
4 teaspoons tomato purée
2 tablespoons water

1 teaspoon grated fresh horseradish
Dash hot pepper sauce
⅛ teaspoon lemon juice
Salt and pepper to taste

Remove stem end and seeds from green peppers. Dip in boiling water; let stand for a few minutes; drain. Combine rice, shrimps, tomato purée, water, horseradish, hot pepper sauce and lemon juice in a mixing bowl. Mix well; season to taste. Stuff peppers with the mixture and bake at 425°F (220°C), Gas Mark 7, for 25 minutes or until filling is thoroughly heated and peppers are tender. Makes 1 serving.

Shrimp Rémoulade (or Arnaud)

As served in New Orleans, Atlanta and many other cosmopolitan cities.

8 oz (240 g) cleaned cooked shrimps.

Rémoulade Sauce

2 tablespoons finely diced celery
1 tablespoon vegetable oil
1 tablespoon vinegar
$\frac{1}{4}$ teaspoon salt
$\frac{1}{4}$ teaspoon prepared spicy mustard
$\frac{1}{4}$ teaspoon prepared horseradish

$\frac{1}{4}$ teaspoon chopped chives
$\frac{1}{4}$ teaspoon washed capers
Pinch paprika and dash hot pepper
   sauce or pinch cayenne pepper
Pinch garlic powder
Pepper to taste

Marinate shrimps in serving bowl, in Rémoulade Sauce made by combining all remaining ingredients. Refrigerate for at least 30 minutes before use, turning shrimps frequently in the sauce. Serve with sauce. Makes 2 servings.

Seafood 'Newburg'

3 oz (90 g) cooked cauliflower
2 fl oz (60 ml) tomato juice
$\frac{1}{2}$ chicken stock cube
$\frac{1}{2}$ oz (15 g) nonfat dry milk,
 reconstituted with $2\frac{1}{2}$ fl oz
 (75 ml) water
$\frac{1}{2}$ teaspoon lemon juice

$\frac{1}{4}$ teaspoon sherry flavouring
$\frac{1}{4}$ teaspoon dried onion flakes
$\frac{1}{8}$ teaspoon paprika
4 oz (120 g) cooked crabmeat, cleaned
 shrimps or lobster meat
Pinch pepper
$\frac{1}{2}$ teaspoon chopped fresh parsley

Place cauliflower, tomato juice, stock cube, milk, lemon juice, flavouring, onion flakes and paprika in a blender goblet and blend until smooth. Pour into saucepan; add seafood. Heat thoroughly. Season with pepper; sprinkle with parsley. Makes 1 serving.

California Orange-Tuna Salad

8 oz (240 g) drained, canned tuna,
 flaked
1 medium navel orange, peeled and
 cut in bite-size pieces (reserve
 rind)

1 teaspoon freshly grated orange
 rind
2 oz (60 g) chopped celery
2 tablespoons diced pimiento
2 tablespoons mayonnaise
Lettuce

Combine tuna, orange pieces, rind, celery and pimiento; mix well. Stir in mayonnaise. Serve on lettuce. Makes 2 servings.

Chicken Salad Staten Island

4 fl oz (120 ml) tomato juice
$\frac{1}{2}$ teaspoon celery seeds
$\frac{1}{4}$ teaspoon lemon juice
$\frac{1}{4}$ teaspoon tarragon
Pinch onion powder
4 oz (120 g) skinned and boned cooked
 chicken, diced

3 oz (90 g) peeled boiled potato, cubed
2 oz (60 g) cooked artichoke hearts,
 quartered
2 oz (60 g) sliced celery
Shredded lettuce

Bring first 5 ingredients to the boil in a small saucepan; reduce heat. Cover and simmer 5 minutes. Combine all remaining ingredients except lettuce in medium bowl; stir in hot marinade. Cover and chill. Serve on shredded lettuce, using marinade as dressing. Makes 1 serving.

Barbecue Chicken Texas Style

The basting sauce adds the smoky sweet flavour.

8 fl oz (240 ml) low-calorie cola
4 tablespoons tomato purée
1 tablespoon dried onion flakes
1 teaspoon Worcester sauce
1 teaspoon lemon juice

1 teaspoon salt
1 garlic clove, crushed
1 lb 8 oz (720 g) chicken pieces,
   skinned*

Add cola to tomato purée in medium saucepan, stirring to combine. Add all remaining ingredients except chicken; heat to boiling. Reduce heat and simmer 5 minutes. Pour barbecue sauce over chicken in shallow casserole. Marinate at room temperature, 30 minutes, turning once. Remove chicken; return sauce to saucepan; keep warm. Grill chicken for 20 minutes 5 to 6 inches (13 to 15 cm) from charcoal which has turned ash-grey, brushing occasionally with sauce. Turn chicken; grill 15 to 20 minutes longer. Serve with remaining sauce. Makes 2 servings.

*1 lb 8 oz (720 g) chicken pieces will yield about 8 oz (240 g) cooked meat.

Picnic Chicken

$\frac{1}{2}$ teaspoon garlic powder
$\frac{1}{4}$ teaspoon paprika
$2\frac{1}{2}$ fl oz (75 ml) lemon juice
$2\frac{1}{2}$ fl oz (75 ml) wine vinegar
$2\frac{1}{2}$ fl oz (75 ml) water

$\frac{1}{4}$ teaspoon allspice
$\frac{1}{4}$ teaspoon salt
$\frac{1}{8}$ teaspoon dry mustard
1 lb 8 oz (720 g) chicken pieces,
   skinned*

Combine garlic powder and paprika in a small foil packet; reserve. Heat all remaining ingredients, except chicken, in a small saucepan.

Bring to the boil. Place chicken in a heatproof dish with a lid, which can be transported. Marinate chicken, uncovered, in refrigerator, at least 1 hour. Cover and transport. At picnic site, remove chicken from marinade; sprinkle with garlic powder and paprika. Grill, 4 inches (10 cm) from heat source, turning once, 40 minutes or until chicken is tender. Brush occasionally with marinade. Makes 2 servings.

*1 lb 8 oz (720 g) chicken pieces will yield about 8 oz (240 g) cooked meat.

Devilled Chicken Legs

1 garlic clove, cut	3 oz (90 g) tomato purée
3 lbs (1 kg 440 g) chicken legs, skinned*	3 fl oz (90 ml) water
1 teaspoon salt	12 tablespoons prepared mustard
¾ teaspoon pepper	

Rub garlic over chicken; sprinkle with salt and pepper. Place in shallow medium casserole with lid. Mix tomato purée, water and mustard. Pour over chicken in casserole. Bake covered, in moderate oven, 350°F (180°C), Gas Mark 4, 45 minutes or until chicken is done. Makes 4 servings.

*3 lbs (1 kg 440 g) chicken legs will yield about 1 lb (480 g) cooked meat.

Roast Turkey with Onion Sage Stuffing

To New Englanders, Thanksgiving without sage stuffing would be as unthinkable as celebrating the day minus turkey and pumpkin.

1 oven-ready turkey, 6 to 8 lbs	16 fl oz (480 ml) chicken stock,
(2 kg 880 g to 3 kg 840 g)	made with 1 stock cube
Salt	

Place turkey, breast side up, on rack in shallow pan. Season and roast at 325°F (160°C), Gas Mark 3, for 2 to 2½ hours. Baste every 20 minutes with stock until done. Weigh portions (4 ounces (120 g) per portion) and serve with stuffing. Makes about 6 to 8 servings.

Onion Sage Stuffing

8 oz (240 g) onion, chopped
1 oz (30 g) finely diced celery
1½ teaspoons sage
4 fl oz (120 ml) chicken stock,
  made with ¼ stock cube

2 slices white bread, cut into ½-inch
  (1 cm) cubes
8 teaspoons low fat spread
2 teaspoons chopped fresh parsley
Pinch salt

Lightly brown onion, celery and sage in large nonstick frying pan. Remove from heat; add stock and remaining ingredients. Transfer to a casserole and bake 30 minutes (same oven as turkey). Divide into 4 portions and serve with turkey. Makes 4 servings.

Roast Spring Chicken with Cherry Sauce

1 oven-ready spring chicken,
  1 lb 12 oz (840 g)*
8 fl oz (240 ml) chicken stock,
  made with ½ stock cube

2 tablespoons chopped celery
Salt and pepper to taste
4 oz (120 g) cooked rice
Cherry Sauce (recipe follows)

Place chicken on a rack in small baking tin. Combine stock, celery and seasonings. Place in blender goblet; blend until smooth. Bake at 400°F (200°C), Gas Mark 6, about 40 minutes, or until tender. Baste occasionally with stock mixture. Remove skin. Serve on bed of rice with Cherry Sauce. Makes 2 servings.

*A 1 lb 12 oz (840 g) spring chicken will yield about 6 to 8 oz (180 to240 g) cooked meat.

Cherry Sauce

8 oz (240 g) canned stoned sweet
  cherries, no sugar added

8 fl oz (240 ml) water
2 teaspoons lemon juice

Put all but 10 cherries in blender goblet with water and lemon juice. Blend until smooth. Pour into small saucepan and simmer for a few minutes until thick. Add remaining cherries and heat. If sauce becomes too thick, add a little more water. Makes 2 servings.

Green Pepper Stuffed with Veal and Soybeans

1 × 6 oz (180 g) green pepper,
seeded and cut in half
3 oz (90 g) cooked, dried soybeans
2 oz (60 g) boneless cooked veal,
diced
2 tablespoons chopped celery
1 oz (30 g) finely grated carrot
½ teaspoon dried onion flakes,

reconstituted in 1 tablespoon
water and drained
8 teaspoons tomato purée
2 fl oz (60 ml) water
Salt and freshly ground pepper to
taste
½ slice white bread, made into
crumbs

Boil green pepper in water to cover in a medium saucepan for 3 minutes.
Remove from water and drain. Combine soybeans, veal, celery, carrot
and onion flakes in a medium mixing bowl. Add tomato purée and
water and stir to combine. Season with salt and pepper. Fill pepper
halves with as much of the mixture as will fit. Spoon the rest over the
bottom of an individual ovenproof casserole. Arrange filled peppers
on soybean mixture. Sprinkle half the breadcrumbs over each green
pepper half. Bake for 5 to 7 minutes at 425°F (220°C), Gas Mark 7 until
breadcrumbs begin to brown. Lower heat to 375°F, (190°C), Gas Mark
5 and continue baking for 15 minutes or until pepper is tender. Serve
hot in casserole dish. Makes 1 serving.

New Orleans Hamburger 'Bordelaise'

1 teaspoon chopped chives
1 teaspoon vegetable oil
¼ teaspoon garlic salt
⅛ teaspoon wine flavouring or
bitters

Pepper to taste
4 oz (120 g) grilled boneless
steak or minced beef
patty

Combine first 5 ingredients and pour onto steak or patty just before
serving. Makes 1 serving.

Heart Stew

12 oz (360 g) cooked beef heart,
  cut into thin slices (see note)
12 fl oz (360 ml) water
4 oz (120 g) sliced celery

6 oz (180 g) onion, sliced
½ teaspoon chopped fresh parsley
1 garlic clove, crushed
Salt and pepper to taste

Combine heart, water, celery, onion, parsley, garlic, salt and pepper; bring to the boil; lower heat; cover and simmer 15 to 20 minutes or until meat is tender and vegetables are cooked. Makes 3 servings.

Note: Beef heart is best prepared by slow cooking. Wash well, remove fat, cut in half lengthwise to remove arteries, veins and blood. Place in deep saucepan, add salted water to cover (½ teaspoon salt for each pint (600 ml) of water). Cover and simmer until tender, about 3 to 4 hours.

Kidney Stew

2 oz (60 g) onion, finely chopped
1 garlic clove, crushed
6 oz (180 g) tomatoes, peeled and
  chopped
1 hot chilli pepper, seeded and
  chopped

1 tablespoon cider vinegar
Salt and freshly ground pepper to
  taste
8 oz (240 g) cooked lamb kidneys,
  thinly sliced

Cook onion and garlic in a nonstick frying pan, stirring constantly until onion is tender, but not browned. Add tomatoes, chilli pepper, vinegar, salt and pepper. Stir to combine and cook 5 minutes or until sauce is thickened and well blended. Add kidneys to sauce and heat through. Do not overcook as kidneys toughen very quickly. Divide into 2 portions. Makes 2 servings.

Maryland Spiced Ham

Often served with cooked kale.

12 oz (360 g) cooked boneless ham,
  cut into 4 equal slices
3 strips lemon rind, 2-inches (5 cm)
  long
4 fl oz (120 ml) water
Artificial sweetener to equal 4

tablespoons sugar, or to taste
2 tablespoons lemon juice
1 teaspoon grated lemon rind
$\frac{1}{4}$ teaspoon cloves
$\frac{1}{4}$ teaspoon mace or ginger

Bake ham on rack, in slow oven, 325°F (160°C), Gas Mark 3 for 30 minutes. Remove from oven and put lemon strips on top. Return to oven and continue baking for 30 minutes longer. Meanwhile, combine water, sweetener, lemon juice, lemon rind, cloves and mace or ginger; simmer 5 minutes. When ham has been baked for a total of 1 hour, increase oven temperature to 400°F (200°C), Gas Mark 6. Spoon sauce over ham every 10 minutes for 30 minutes. Serve hot or cold. Makes 4 servings.

Plantation Ham Loaf

2 tablespoons unflavoured gelatine
2 fl oz (60 ml) cold water
8 fl oz (240 ml) tomato juice
1 tablespoon lemon juice or cider
  vinegar
$\frac{3}{4}$ teaspoon paprika

$\frac{1}{4}$ teaspoon onion salt
4 tablespoons mayonnaise
12 oz (360 g) green peppers, seeded
  and chopped
12 oz (360 g) cooked boneless ham,
  finely diced

Sprinkle gelatine over cold water in top of double boiler. Add tomato juice, lemon juice, paprika and onion salt. Cook over boiling water until gelatine is dissolved. Set mixture aside to cool and thicken. Fold in mayonnaise, green pepper and ham. Transfer to medium mould and refrigerate until firm. Makes 4 servings.

New England Boiled Dinner

3 lbs (1 kg 440 g) boneless lean beef
   roast (any inexpensive cut)
1 garlic clove, crushed
1 tablespoon pickling spice
5 to 6 peppercorns
1 lb 8 oz (720 g) cabbage, cut into
   8 wedges

1 lb 8 oz (720 g) peeled small
   potatoes
8 oz (240 g) diced turnips
8 oz (240 g) small white onions,
   parboiled
1 lb (480 g) carrots
Parsley sprigs and chopped fresh
   parsley to garnish

Roast the beef on a rack in the oven at 375°F (190°C), Gas Mark 5 until done. Transfer to a large saucepan and cover with water. Bring rapidly to the boil. Add garlic, pickling spice and peppercorns. Cover and simmer for 3 hours or until beef is very tender. Remove meat from pan and keep hot. Add all remaining ingredients, except garnish, to pan. Cover and cook briskly until tender, about 25 to 30 minutes. Drain vegetables and arrange round weighed, sliced meat. Makes 8 servings.

Chicken Liver Turnovers

8 fl oz (240 ml) chicken stock, made
   with 1 stock cube
8 oz (240 g) sliced celery
3 oz (90 g) diced onion
12 oz (360 g) chicken livers, cut in
   quarters

1 teaspoon Dijon-style mustard
½ teaspoon curry powder
Pinch each salt and pepper
2 slices white bread, cut horizontally to
   make 4 thin slices

Preheat oven to 400°F (200°C), Gas Mark 6. Combine stock, celery and 1 oz (30 g) onion in a small saucepan. Simmer until celery is tender. Transfer mixture to blender goblet and blend until puréed; return to saucepan. In nonstick frying pan combine chicken livers, 2 oz (60 g) onion, mustard, curry powder, salt and pepper and cook until livers are done to taste. Transfer liver mixture to a small bowl and, using a fork, mash livers. Stir in 2 tablespoons of puréed celery sauce. Roll each slice of bread flat. Place ¼ of liver mixture on each. Moisten edge of bread with water; fold from corner to corner so edges form a triangle.

Place on a nonstick baking sheet and seal edges with a wet fork. Bake for 10 minutes until tops are lightly browned. Turn and bake 10 minutes longer. Heat remaining sauce and serve over turnovers. Makes 2 servings.

Sweet-Sour Pork Blade Steak

2 fl oz (60 ml) wine vinegar
2 fl oz (60 ml) water
1 tablespoon chopped chives
1 tablespoon diced pimiento
1 teaspoon dried onion flakes
$\frac{1}{2}$ teaspoon thyme

$\frac{1}{2}$ teaspoon salt
Artificial sweetener to equal 1
 tablespoon sugar, or to taste
2 pork blade steaks, 8 oz (240 g)
 each, cut $\frac{3}{4}$-inch (2 cm)
 thick

Combine all ingredients except pork steaks in a shallow dish; place pork steaks in marinade. Cover; marinate in refrigerator 3 hours, turning occasionally. Place pork steaks on rack in grill pan. Grill about 4 inches (10 cm) from heat source, basting with marinade; turn steaks; baste and grill until done. Pork must be served without any trace of pink either in the meat or in the juice. Makes 2 servings.

Orange Baked Pork Chops

2 trimmed centre-cut pork chops,
 4 oz (120 g) each
Salt and pepper to taste
2 oz (60 g) onion, sliced
2 fl oz (60 ml) tomato juice
$\frac{1}{2}$ teaspoon grated lemon rind

4 oz (120 g) canned orange sections,
 no sugar added, drained (reserve
 juice)
Pinch marjoram
1 teaspoon chopped fresh parsley

Season chops and grill on a rack 4 inches (10 cm) from source of heat, 4 to 5 minutes on each side until brown. Turn off grill and place chops in a small baking dish. Add onions, tomato juice and lemon rind to pork chops. Arrange orange sections on top; add juice. Sprinkle on marjoram. Bake covered at 400°F (200°C), Gas Mark 6, for 15 to 20 minutes, or until onion is tender. Place pork chops on serving dish and top with sauce. Garnish with parsley. Makes 1 serving.

Baked Lamb Patties with Green Apple Sauce

4 fl oz (120 ml) water
2 medium green apples, cored and
   sliced
¼ teaspoon cinnamon
⅛ teaspoon nutmeg

12 oz (360 g) minced lamb
1 teaspoon grated lemon rind
½ teaspoon pepper
1 teaspoon salt

Combine water, apples, cinnamon and nutmeg in nonstick pan. Cook over low heat, stirring frequently for 8 minutes or until apples are tender. Keep warm over boiling water or very low heat. Combine lamb, lemon rind, pepper and salt; mix well. Shape meat into an even number of patties, about 2½ × 1-inch (6 × 2.5 cm) each. Grill on rack about 4 inches (10 cm) from source of heat for 6 minutes, or until cooked throughout. Serve each portion of meat with half the apple mixture. Makes 2 servings.

Soybeans

This excellent bean is grown extensively in the U.S. An almost perfect food—unadulterated, highly nourishing, easy to digest, easy to grow and inexpensive—we added it to our Food Programme years ago. Soybeans are quite bland and take on the flavour of the other ingredients you serve with them.

In China, soybeans are known as the 'food of the ancients' but in America, it's the young people who are 'into' them. How about trying them for yourself?

Soybean Cutlets with Tomato Sauce

6 oz (180 g) cooked dried soybeans
1½ oz (45 g) cooked mushrooms,
  finely chopped
1 oz (30 g) finely chopped celery
½ teaspoon chicken stock powder
1 teaspoon dried onion flakes
¼ garlic clove, crushed

1 teaspoon Worcester sauce
1 teaspoon chopped fresh parsley
8 teaspoons tomato purée mixed with
  2 fl oz (60 ml) water
Salt and pepper to taste
¼ bay leaf

Purée beans in blender goblet, pushing down with rubber spatula as needed. Transfer to mixing bowl. Add mushrooms, celery, stock powder, onion flakes, garlic, Worcester sauce, parsley and sufficient tomato purée mixed with water to moisten. Season to taste. Shape into 2 patties. Bake at 375°F (190°C), Gas Mark 5, 20 minutes in nonstick baking tin. Place bay leaf and remaining tomato purée and water mixture in saucepan and simmer to blend flavours; season and serve over cutlets. Makes 1 serving.

Soy Spinach Loaf

6 oz (180 g) cooked, dried soybeans
2 fl oz (60 ml) water
1 teaspoon chicken stock powder
1 teaspoon dried onion flakes,
  reconstituted
Pinch garlic powder
Pinch thyme

Pinch basil
3 oz (90 g) cooked spinach, finely
  chopped
1 oz (30 g) cooked diced celery
1 slice wholemeal bread, made into
  crumbs
Salt and pepper to taste

Combine beans, water, chicken stock powder, onion flakes, garlic powder, thyme and basil in blender goblet. Blend until smooth. Transfer to mixing bowl. Fold in spinach, celery and breadcrumbs and season to taste. Turn into a small nonstick loaf tin and bake at 400°F (200°C), Gas Mark 6 for 35 minutes. Makes 1 serving.

Marrow-Cheese Soufflé

8 oz (240 g) mashed, cooked marrow
½ oz (15 g) nonfat dry milk,
   reconstituted with 2½ fl oz
   (75 ml) water

2 oz (60 g) grated Cheddar cheese
2 tablespoons margarine
Salt and pepper to taste
2 eggs, separated

Preheat oven to 350°F (180°C), Gas Mark 4. Combine marrow with milk, cheese, margarine, salt and pepper in a baking dish. Add the well-beaten egg yolks. Beat egg whites until stiff but not dry and fold into the marrow mixture. Set baking dish in tin of hot water in oven for 30 to 40 minutes. Makes 2 servings.

Cape Cod Luncheon Soufflé

6 oz (180 g) cooked and peeled
   potatoes
1 teaspoon dried onion flakes
4 fl oz (120 ml) water
4 oz (120 g) grated carrots

4 oz (120 g) boned cold cooked fish,
   flaked
Salt and pepper to taste
2 eggs, separated

Preheat oven to 350°F (180°C), Gas Mark 4. Blend potatoes, onion flakes and water in blender goblet until thick and smooth. Remove to bowl; stir in carrots, fish, salt and pepper. Fold in slightly beaten yolks. Beat egg whites until stiff. Fold egg whites into fish mixture. Place in baking dish and set dish in larger tin with 1 inch (2.5 cm) warm water. Bake for 30 to 40 minutes. Makes 2 servings.

New England Baked Broad Beans

1 lb 4 oz (600 g) cooked fresh broad
   beans
4 tablespoons tomato purée
3 fl oz (90 ml) water
Artificial sweetener to equal 2

tablespoons sugar, or to taste
1 tablespoon Worcester sauce
½ teaspoon ginger
½ teaspoon dry mustard

Combine all ingredients in baking dish or casserole. Bake in moderately hot oven, 375°F (190°C), Gas Mark 5, until lightly browned on top, about 1 hour. Makes 8 servings.

Baked Beans with Fruit

To above ingredients, add 2 sliced medium apples, 6 medium apricot halves and 4 oz (120 g) canned crushed pineapple, no sugar added. Arrange in layers, alternating with the seasonal beans. Bake as directed above. Makes 8 servings.

Lancaster County Cabbage*

Skim milk is sometimes substituted for the water.

10 oz (300 g) shredded cabbage
4 fl oz (120 ml) boiling salted water
5 oz (150 g) cottage cheese

$\frac{1}{4}$ teaspoon celery seed
Salt and pepper to taste

Combine cabbage and boiling salted water in saucepan. Cover and cook 5 minutes, until cabbage is barely tender. Do not drain. Stir in remaining ingredients and serve when cheese is melted. Makes 2 servings.

Rhode Island Apple-Carrot Casserole

2 medium apples, peeled, cored and
  sliced
4 fl oz (120 ml) cold water

9 oz (270 g) cooked sliced carrots
4 teaspoons margarine
$\frac{1}{8}$ teaspoon cinnamon

Combine apples and water in a small saucepan; cover and cook until apples are tender. Drain and combine with remaining ingredients in a medium casserole. Mix well. Bake at 350°F (180°C), Gas Mark 4 for about 15 minutes. Makes 4 servings.

Cauliflower-Orange Relish

To serve with roast chicken or beef.

2 tablespoons freshly squeezed lemon
  juice
14 oz (420 g) cauliflower, broken
  into small florets
8 oz (240 g) onion, sliced and
  separated into rings
6 oz (180 g) green pepper, seeded
  and cut into strips
8 fl oz (240 ml) white vinegar

6 fl oz (180 ml) water
$\frac{3}{4}$ teaspoon salt
8 peppercorns, crushed
$\frac{1}{2}$ teaspoon celery seeds
$\frac{1}{2}$ teaspoon tarragon leaves
2 teaspoons freshly grated orange
  rind
4 medium oranges

Pour boiling water and lemon juice over florets, onion rings and green pepper strips to cover; let stand while preparing vinegar mixture. Combine vinegar, water, salt and spices in saucepan. Grate rind from one of the 4 oranges to measure 2 teaspoons; add to vinegar mixture. Bring to the boil; reduce heat and simmer 5 minutes. Peel oranges and cut into bite-size pieces; set aside. Drain water from cauliflower; add orange pieces. Toss lightly. Pour hot vinegar mixture over cauliflower mixture. Cool; cover and chill several hours or overnight. Stir occasionally to allow flavours to blend. Makes 8 servings.

Curly Kale

You will need an enamel, stainless steel or ceramic pan. Do not use aluminium or iron for cooking kale as these metals darken the vegetable and make it bitter. Before measuring, separate stalks of kale, discard bruised tough leaves and heavy stems and ribs. Wash well.

5 oz (150 g) kale
$\frac{1}{2}$ garlic clove, crushed
Seasoning salt to taste

Freshly ground pepper to taste
2 teaspoons margarine

Cover leaves with boiling salted water in saucepan. Add garlic and cook until leaves are tender, 5 to 10 minutes. Drain; chop coarsely.

Season with seasoning salt and pepper and stir in margarine. Mix and serve hot. Makes 2 servings.

Long Island Peas and Potato Stew

12 oz (360 g) new potatoes, scrubbed clean
8 fl oz (240 ml) boiling water
2 teaspoons dried onion flakes

¾ teaspoon salt
¼ teaspoon pepper
8 oz (240 g) frozen or fresh peas
2 teaspoons chopped fresh parsley

Combine all ingredients except peas and parsley in saucepan. Bring to the boil, cover and simmer until potatoes are tender. Add peas and parsley; cook 5 minutes longer. Serve in soup bowls with pot 'liquor'. Makes 4 servings.

Yankee Pan-Scalloped Potatoes

6 fl oz (180 ml) water
Pinch garlic powder
2 oz (60 g) onion, chopped
2 teaspoons chicken stock powder
1 tablespoon chopped pimiento

2 teaspoons chopped fresh parsley
Salt and pepper to taste
3 oz (90 g) peeled boiled potato, thinly sliced

Heat water in a small pan, add garlic powder and onions and cook until onions are tender. Stir in all remaining ingredients except potatoes. Layer potatoes over onion mixture. Cover and simmer until potatoes are heated. Remove lid and continue cooking until liquid is reduced. Makes 1 serving.

Oven-Baked Potato Chips

12 oz (360 g) potatoes, with skin

Salt or barbecue salt, pepper, and paprika to taste

Scrub potatoes, but do not peel. Wipe dry. Cut potatoes into slices about ¼-inch (5 mm) thick and arrange one layer deep on shallow nonstick baking sheet. Sprinkle with salt, pepper and paprika (or other seasonings to taste). Bake in hot oven (400°F to 425°F (200 to 220°C), Gas Mark 6 to 7) until potatoes are browned, about 10 minutes each side. Makes 4 servings.

Maine Pumpkin Pudding

2 fl oz (60 ml) water
1 tablespoon unflavoured gelatine
2 fl oz (60 ml) boiling water
4 oz (120 g) cooked or canned
  pumpkin (see note)
2 oz (60 g) nonfat dry milk

¼ teaspoon apple pie spice or to
  taste
¼ teaspoon maple flavouring
Artificial sweetener to equal 1
  tablespoon sugar, or to taste
6 to 8 ice cubes

Pour water into blender goblet. Sprinkle gelatine over water to soften. Add boiling water. Blend about 30 seconds. Add all remaining ingredients except ice cubes and blend until smooth. Add ice cubes one at a time, blending after each addition, until all the cubes are used. Pour into dessert glasses. Serve immediately, or chill if desired. Makes 4 servings.

Note: To cook raw pumpkin, cut it in half, remove seeds and stringy parts, and cut off rind. Cut pumpkin into pieces and steam over low heat for 25 to 30 minutes. Pumpkin contains water, and in a heavy pan over a low flame, no added water should be required. (If necessary, add just enough water to keep it from burning.) Drain the cooked pumpkin well, then purée it in a food mill or blender. Cooked pumpkin may be frozen for future use. Weigh it in 3 oz (90 g) portions and defrost as needed.

Purée of Sorrel

To serve with fish.

8 oz (240 g) cleaned and stemmed
  sorrel
Chicken stock, made with stock
  cube according to package
  directions

4 teaspoons margarine
½ oz (15 g) nonfat dry milk,
  reconstituted with 2½ fl oz
  (75 ml) water

Steam sorrel in steamer basket placed in saucepan so sorrel does not touch water. When very tender, drain thoroughly and purée in food mill or blender until very smooth. Put into saucepan with just enough chicken stock to keep it from burning; heat through; remove from heat and stir in magarine and milk. Makes 4 servings.

Succotash

American Indian origin.

6 oz (180 g) cooked whole-kernel
  corn
6 oz (180 g) cooked fresh broad
  beans
2 tablespoons margarine
2 teaspoons dried onion flakes

½ teaspoon salt
⅛ teaspoon pepper
½ oz (15 g) nonfat dry milk,
  reconstituted with 2½ fl oz
  (75 ml) water
Chopped pimiento

Combine all ingredients except pimiento in a double boiler. Heat over boiling water. Garnish with pimiento. Makes 4 servings.

Tomato Scallop*

12 oz (360 g) tomatoes
12 oz (360 g) green peppers, cut into
  long strips, ½-inch (1 cm) wide
4 oz (120 g) sharp Cheddar cheese,
  grated

2 slices white bread, made into
  crumbs
Salt and paprika to taste
4 teaspoons low fat spread

Peel tomatoes and cut into thick slices (about 4 per tomato). In casserole arrange layers of half the tomatoes, pepper strips, cheese, breadcrumbs, salt and paprika. Dot evenly with margarine. Repeat layers. Bake at 425°F (220°C), Gas Mark 7 until crumbs are brown, about 30 minutes. Makes 4 servings.

Holiday Wild Rice Dressing

To serve as a side dish with roast chicken, turkey or wild game.

5 oz (150 g) uncooked wild rice
1 pint 8 fl oz (840 ml) Homemade
  Chicken Stock (see page 10)
4 oz (120 g) diced celery
3 oz (90 g) sliced mushrooms
4 oz (120 g) diced onion or shallots

8 oz (240 g) cooked brown or white
  rice
¼ teaspoon sage
2 teaspoons sherry flavouring
  (optional)

Rinse wild rice in water several times. Bring chicken stock to the boil. Add wild rice. Cover tightly and cook over low heat, about 30 minutes. Drain. Measure 12 oz (360 g) cooked wild rice, reserving liquid. (Remaining rice may be frozen.) Brown celery, mushrooms and onion in nonstick frying pan. Combine with wild rice and brown or white rice, sage and wine flavouring if desired. Mix well, adding reserved liquid to desired moistness. Bake in casserole in oven with roasting chicken or at 350°F (180°C), Gas Mark 4 for about 30 minutes. Makes 10 servings.

Courgettes with Parsley and Onion

1 lb 4 oz (600 g) sliced courgettes,
  cut in ½-inch (1 cm) slices
1 teaspoon salt
6 fl oz (180 ml) water
3 tablespoons chopped fresh parsley
1 tablespoon dried onion flakes

1 tablespoon freshly squeezed lemon
  juice
¼ teaspoon freshly grated lemon
  rind
4 teaspoons margarine

Cook courgettes with salt in water in a covered pan until just tender, 8 to 10 minutes. Drain. Add parsley, onion flakes, lemon juice and lemon rind. Heat quickly, turning courgette slices. Transfer to 4 individual vegetable plates and stir 1 teaspoon margarine into each serving of vegetable. Serve at once. Makes 4 servings.

California Caesar Salad

A popular West Coast salad, modified to the Food Programme requirements. The lettuce should be washed, dried, wrapped in towel and kept crisp in refrigerator. If watercress droops, crisp it in ice-cold water, dry thoroughly, wrap, and keep in refrigerator until ready to serve.

1 tablespoon vegetable oil
½ garlic clove, crushed
1 teaspoon Worcester sauce
1 teaspoon lemon juice
Pinch each salt, pepper and dry
    mustard
Assorted salad greens (round or cos

lettuce, Batavian endive, and
watercress)
1 oz (30 g) freshly grated Parmesan
cheese
1 slice white bread, toasted, cut into
cubes and dried in slow oven
1 egg, coddled for 1 minute

Combine oil, garlic, Worcester sauce, lemon juice, salt, pepper and mustard in jar with lid; shake well. Tear greens into individual salad or soup bowl. Sprinkle with Parmesan cheese, bread cubes and contents of jar. Add egg and toss lightly to mix well. Serve immediately. Makes 1 serving.

Lettuce Wedges with Russian Dressing

The salad served in restaurants all over America.

1 tablespoon mayonnaise
1 tablespoon tomato purée
1½ teaspoons hot pepper sauce
1 teaspoon chopped chives

1 teaspoon finely chopped pimiento
2 oz (60 g) lettuce, cut in wedges
    (remove wilted outer leaves)

Combine all ingredients except lettuce; mix well. Serve over lettuce.
Makes 2 servings.

Tossed Green Salad with Mohawk Dressing

Try colourful peppery watercress; curly endive with its tangy taste and
crunchy texture; firm flavourful cos; and, of course, round or cabbage
lettuce.

8 oz (240 g) round lettuce
8 oz (240 g) cos lettuce

6 oz (180 g) radishes, sliced
Mohawk Dressing (recipe follows)

Rinse lettuce, wrap loosely in a clean damp towel and chill. Just before
serving break lettuce into bite-size pieces. Add radish slices. Toss.
Place on a chilled salad plate and serve with Mohawk Dressing. Makes
4 servings.

Mohawk Dressing

2 fl oz (60 ml) wine vinegar
2 tablespoons tomato purée
2 tablespoons vegetable oil
1 garlic clove

1 teaspoon chopped chives
$\frac{1}{4}$ teaspoon paprika
Freshly ground pepper to taste

Combine all ingredients in blender goblet. Blend about 3 minutes.
Serve over Tossed Green Salad. Makes 4 servings.

Spiced Tomato Aspic

1 pint 4 fl oz (720 ml) tomato juice
2 tablespoons unflavoured gelatine
1 tablespoon lemon juice or cider
   vinegar
1 teaspoon grated fresh horseradish
1 teaspoon celery seeds

1 teaspoon Worcester sauce
$\frac{1}{2}$ teaspoon onion powder
Pinch cayenne pepper
Lettuce leaves
Parsley sprigs (optional)

Pour 8 fl oz (240 ml) tomato juice into medium saucepan; sprinkle with
gelatine; heat slowly until gelatine dissolves. Remove from heat; add

seasonings and remaining tomato juice. Pour into 6 individual moulds. Chill until set. Turn out on lettuce leaves. Garnish with parsley, if desired. Makes 6 servings.

Dried Apple Slices (Schnitz)

A Pennsylvania Dutch schnitzing party was as much a community event as the quilting bee. To reconstitute apple, cover with water and let stand several hours. Use the water in which the apple soaked.

8 medium apples, peeled and cored   2 tablespoons lemon juice
3 pints (1 litre 750 ml) water

Cut each apple into 8 thin wedges. As apples are sliced, dip them into a large bowl containing water and lemon juice. (This prevents dis-colouration.) Let stand 1 minute. Drain and dry slices immediately. Place apple slices on baking racks or sheets and place in oven set at 200°F (100°C), Gas Mark ¼. Let bake until fruit is dry, 4 to 5 hours. Cool and store in cool dry place, or pack in freezer paper (8 wedges = 1 apple) and seal tightly; store in tightly closed tin can. Makes 8 servings.

Apricot Brown Betty

24 canned apricot halves, no sugar
  added, or 12 ripe medium apricots,
  stoned and sliced
4 fl oz (120 ml) apricot liquid (or, if
  fresh apricots are used, use half
  lemon juice, half water)
2 slices white bread, cut into small
  cubes

4 teaspoons margarine, melted
Artificial sweetener to equal 2
  tablespoons sugar, or to taste
1 teaspoon cinnamon
¼ teaspoon allspice
¼ teaspoon salt
1 teaspoon grated lemon rind, or ½
  teaspoon vanilla flavouring

Combine all ingredients and mix well. Bake in covered pudding dish in moderate oven (350°F (180°C), Gas Mark 4) for 50 to 60 minutes. Makes 4 servings.

Plum Brown Betty

Substitute 8 medium plums for the apricot halves and use 3 tablespoons lemon juice and 3 tablespoons water. Follow preceding recipe. Makes 4 servings.

Apple Strawberry Chiffon

2 fl oz (60 ml) cold water
1 tablespoon unflavoured gelatine
2½ fl oz (75 ml) boiling water
2½ oz (75 g) whole strawberries,
   reserve 2 strawberries
¼ teaspoon strawberry flavouring

2 oz (60 g) nonfat dry milk
Artificial sweetener to equal 4
   teaspoons sugar, or to taste
8 to 10 ice cubes
½ medium apple, peeled and diced

Sprinkle gelatine over cold water in blender goblet to soften. Add boiling water; blend until gelatine dissolves. Add strawberries, flavouring, milk and sweetener. Blend until smooth. Add ice cubes, one at a time, blending after each addition. Pour into medium mixing bowl. Immediately fold apple into mixture and spoon into 2 dessert glasses. Top each with a whole strawberry and chill. Makes 2 servings.

Banana Peach Pudding*

1 slice white bread, diced
½ medium banana, peeled and diced
1 medium peach, peeled and diced
2 eggs
½ oz (15 g) nonfat dry milk,
   reconstituted with 2½ fl oz
   (75 ml) water

½ teaspoon vanilla flavouring
Artificial sweetener to equal 4
   teaspoons sugar, or to taste
8 fl oz (240 ml) skim milk

Place bread, banana and peach in a small overproof dish. Combine eggs, reconstituted milk, flavouring and sweetener in a mixing bowl and beat well. Heat skim milk over low heat, but *do not boil*, and gradually add to egg mixture. Pour over bread and fruit mixture. Set ovenproof dish in a pan of hot water and bake at 350°F (180°C), Gas Mark 4 for 25 minutes or until set. May be served hot or cold. Makes 2 servings.

Cranberry Sorbet Parfait

15 oz (450 g) cranberries
12 fl oz (360 ml) water
2 teaspoons unflavoured gelatine
2½ fl oz (75 ml) water

Artificial sweetener to equal 4
   tablespoons sugar, or to taste
Whipped Topping (see page 12)

Reserve 6 berries. Heat cranberries and water in medium saucepan just until cranberry skins pop open. Press cranberries through a seive into a shallow pan, discarding skins. Soften gelatine in the 2½ fl oz (75 ml) water. Stir into hot cranberry purée; add sweetener; cool 30 minutes. Place in freezer; freeze until firm. Put into a chilled bowl. Using an electric mixer, beat until thick and mushy. Spoon into parfait or dessert dishes alternating with Whipped Topping (end with Whipped Topping). Cover; return to freezer. Remove from freezer 10 to 15 minutes before serving. Garnish each parfait with a reserved berry. Makes 6 servings.

Pineapple on Pineapple Strawberry Compote

You can't improve on fresh pineapple picked truly ripe and sweet and served in its natural state, but if the pineapple you bought is immature, here's one way to conceal it.

5 oz (150 g) strawberries
2 tablespoons water
½ teaspoon vanilla flavouring

4 oz (120 g) canned crushed
   pineapple, no sugar added
1 small pineapple, cored, peeled and
   cubed

Blend strawberries, water and vanilla in blender goblet until smooth; combine with crushed pineapple in large bowl. Stir in fresh pineapple. Chill. Makes 6 servings.

Banana 'Nut' Brownies*

4 eggs, separated
1 oz (30 g) nonfat dry milk
2 tablespoons chocolate flavouring
2 teaspoons almond flavouring

Artificial sweetener to equal 4
  tablespoons sugar, or to taste
4 ripe medium bananas, quartered
4 slices white bread, made into
  crumbs

Place egg yolks, milk, flavourings and sweetener in blender goblet. Blend at medium speed to combine. Gradually add banana pieces and continue to blend until very smooth. Transfer mixture to large bowl. Fold in breadcrumbs until uniformly combined. Beat egg whites until stiff but not dry. Fold into batter. Pour into 8-inch (20 cm) square nonstick baking tin. Bake at 375°F (190°C), Gas Mark 5 for 1 hour and 15 minutes. Makes 4 servings.

Chocolate Layer Cake with Vanilla Filling*

4 eggs, separated
2 fl oz (60 ml) water
4 teaspoons chocolate flavouring
Artificial sweetener to equal 5
  teaspoons sugar, or to taste

4 slices white bread, made into fine
  crumbs
1 oz (30 g) nonfat dry milk
Vanilla Filling (recipe follows)

Place yolks in mixing bowl. Add water, flavouring and sweetener. Whip until frothy. Add breadcrumbs and milk; mix. Beat egg whites until stiff peaks form. Carefully fold egg whites into yolk mixture. Use a nonstick 8 × 8 × 2-inch (20 × 20 × 5 cm) baking tin. Pour batter into tin and bake at 350°F (180°C), Gas Mark 4 for 1 hour or until a skewer inserted in the centre comes out dry. Remove from tin and place on rack to cool. Slice in half horizontally. Spread one layer with Vanilla Filling. Replace top layer. Makes 4 servings.

Vanilla Filling

4 tablespoons unsalted margarine
1 oz (30 g) nonfat dry milk

Artificial sweetener to equal 1
  tablespoon sugar, or to taste
$\frac{1}{2}$ teaspoon vanilla flavouring

Cream margarine in a small bowl. Add milk and sweetener and beat until fluffy. Add flavouring slowly and continue beating to blend. Spread evenly between cake layers. Makes 4 servings.

Mocha Cheese Cake*

1 tablespoon unflavoured gelatine
6 fl oz (180 ml) water
5 oz (150 g) cottage cheese
1 oz (30 g) nonfat dry milk

1 teaspoon chocolate flavouring
$\frac{1}{2}$ teaspoon instant coffee
Artificial sweetener to equal 1
  tablespoon sugar, or to taste

Sprinkle gelatine over 2 fl oz (60 ml) cold water in blender goblet. Heat remaining water to boiling; add to softened gelatine; blend at low speed until gelatine dissolves. Add remaining ingredients; blend at medium speed and then high speed until smooth. Pour into 2 individual serving dishes; chill. Makes 2 servings.

Red Currant-Apple Cake

1 oz (30 g) nonfat dry milk
2 fl oz (60 ml) chilled orange juice
$\frac{1}{2}$ medium apple, cored and chopped
5 oz (150 g) red currants
2 teaspoons lemon juice
$\frac{1}{4}$ teaspoon cinnamon

$\frac{1}{8}$ teaspoon maple flavouring
$\frac{1}{8}$ teaspoon vanilla favouring
Artificial sweetener to equal 1
  tablespoon sugar, or to taste
2 slices white bread, toasted and
  grated

Combine milk and orange juice in a large bowl and whip until stiff, using a hand or electric mixer. Fold in remaining ingredients. Line a small loaf tin with greaseproof paper. Transfer all ingredients to tin and bake at 350°F (180°C), Gas Mark 4 for 1 hour. Remove and cool thoroughly. Makes 2 servings.

Black Bottom Cheesecake*

16 teaspoons unflavoured gelatine
8 fl oz (240 ml) cold water
16 fl oz (480 ml) boiling water
2 lbs (960 g) canned pineapple
 chunks, no sugar added
8 oz (240 g) nonfat dry milk
Artificial sweetener to equal 4
 tablespoons sugar, or to taste

1 tablespoon grated lemon rind
2 teaspoons vanilla flavouring
2 tablespoons unsweetened cocoa
 powder
Few drops brown food colouring
 (optional)
1 lb (480 g) ricotta cheese

Soften 8 teaspoons gelatine in 4 fl oz (120 ml) cold water in blender goblet. Add 8 fl oz (240 ml) boiling water; blend until gelatine dissolves. Add half the pineapple, milk, sweetener, lemon rind, vanilla and all the cocoa and food colouring. Blend until smooth. Transfer to a large mixing bowl; beat in half the cheese with a wire whisk or rotary mixer. Pour into 9 × 3-inch (23 × 8 cm) pan with removable base, reserving half a cup for decoration. Place pan in refrigerator until almost firm. Repeat above procedure with remaining ingredients but do not reserve any mixture. Pour over chocolate layer; refrigerate until slightly firm. Place reserved chocolate mixture in a piping bag with a plain tip. Draw 3 circles, one inside the other. With the tip of a knife, from the outside to the centre, drag the knife through the circles to make pointed designs. Refrigerate until firm. Makes 8 servings.

Country Sponge Cake*

4 eggs, separated
4 slices white bread, made into fine
 crumbs
2 oz (60 g) nonfat dry milk

Artificial sweetener to equal 3
 tablespoons sugar, or to taste
1 teaspoon vanilla flavouring
½ teaspoon lemon flavouring
½ teaspoon orange flavouring

Preheat oven to 350°F (180°C), Gas Mark 4. Beat egg whites in a small bowl until stiff but not dry. Beat egg yolks in medium bowl until thick and lemon coloured; stir in all remaining ingredients except whites. Fold egg whites into yolk mixture. Pour into a 10-inch (25 cm) nonstick oblong cake tin. Bake for 30 to 35 minutes. Makes 4 servings.

Cherry Yogurt Pops

10 fl oz (300 ml) natural
  unsweetened yogurt
8 oz (240 g) frozen stoned
  cherries

1 teaspoon fresh lemon juice
Artificial sweetener to equal 1
  tablespoon sugar, or to taste

Combine all ingredients in blender goblet and blend until smooth. Divide evenly into 4 plastic freezer containers. Freeze until crystals form. Insert wooden skewer in centre of each. Freeze until firm. Remove from containers. Makes 4 servings.

Cold Coffee Soufflé*

2 tablespoons unflavoured gelatine
4 fl oz (120 ml) water
1 pint (600 ml) skim milk
3 eggs, separated
Artificial sweetener to equal 4
  tablespoons sugar, or to taste

4 teaspoons instant coffee powder
1 teaspoon salt
1 teaspoon vanilla flavouring
¼ teaspoon cream of tartar

In top of double boiler, sprinkle gelatine over water to soften. Add milk, egg yolks, sweetener, coffee, salt and vanilla. Place over boiling water; cook, stirring constantly, until mixture thickens slightly. Chill until the consistency of unbeaten egg white. Beat egg whites until frothy; add cream of tartar. Continue beating until stiff peaks form. Fold egg whites into coffee mixture. Pour into a pretty soufflé dish. Chill until firm. Turn out. Makes 3 servings.

Chocolate Froth

8 fl oz (240 ml) water
2 teaspoons unsweetened cocoa
  powder
2 oz (60 g) nonfat dry milk,
  reconstituted with 5 fl oz (150 ml)
  water

Artificial sweetener to equal 4
  teaspoons sugar, or to taste
4 ice cubes

Bring water to the boil; stir in cocoa until dissolved. Place in blender goblet; add all remaining ingredients, except ice cubes; blend. Add ice cubes, one at a time, blending after each addition until crushed. Chill. Makes 2 servings.

Lemon Meringue Pudding*

1 egg, separated
8 fl oz (240 ml) low-calorie
  carbonated lemon lime drink

2 tablespoons lemon juice
1 tablespoon unflavoured gelatine
Artificial sweetener to equal 1
  teaspoon sugar, or to taste

Combine egg yolk, lemon lime drink, lemon juice and gelatine in small saucepan. Cook over low heat, stirring, until gelatine dissolves and lemon mixture thickens slightly (do not boil). Pour into an individual soufflé dish; cool. Beat egg white and artificial sweetener until stiff but not dry. Place mounds of egg white on lemon mixture; spread to edge of dish. With back of spoon, pull up points on meringue. Bake in preheated oven, at 425°F (220°C), Gas Mark 7, 3 to 4 minutes or until slightly browned. Makes 1 serving.

METRIC CONVERSION TABLE

Liquids

1 fl oz	30 ml
2 fl oz	60 ml
3 fl oz	90 ml
4 fl oz	120 ml
5 fl oz	150 ml
6 fl oz	180 ml
7 fl oz	210 ml
8 fl oz	240 ml
9 fl oz	270 ml
10 fl oz	300 ml
11 fl oz	330 ml
12 fl oz	360 ml
13 fl oz	390 ml
14 fl oz	420 ml
15 fl oz	450 ml
16 fl oz	480 ml
20 fl oz (1 pint)	600 ml
24 fl oz	720 ml
30 fl oz (1½ pints)	900 ml
32 fl oz	960 ml
35 fl oz	1 litre
40 fl oz (2 pints)	1 litre 200 ml
45 fl oz (2¼ pints)	1 litre 250 ml
50 fl oz (2½ pints)	1 litre 500 ml
60 fl oz (3 pints)	1 litre 750 ml
70 fl oz (3½ pints)	2 litres
80 fl oz (4 pints)	2 litres 250 ml

Solids

1 oz	30 g
2 oz	60 g
3 oz	90 g
4 oz	120 g
5 oz	150 ml
6 oz	180 g
7 oz	210 g
8 oz	240 g
9 oz	270 g
10 oz	300 g
11 oz	330 g
12 oz	360 g
13 oz	390 g
14 oz	420 g
15 oz	450 g
16 oz (1 lb)	480 g
17 oz	510 g
18 oz	540 g
19 oz	570 g
20 oz (1¼ lb)	600 g
24 oz (1½ lb)	720 g
28 oz (1¾ lb)	840 g
32 oz (2 lb)	960 g
36 oz (2¼ lb)	1 kg 80 g
40 oz (2½ lb)	1 kg 200 g
48 oz (3 lb)	1 kg 440 g
56 oz (3½ lb)	1 kg 680 g
64 oz (4 lb)	1 kg 920 g
68 oz (4¼ lb)	2 kg 40 g
72 oz (4½ lb)	2 kg 160 g
80 oz (5 lb)	2 kg 400 g

INDEX

*